printed with a grant

Figure Foundation

that the degree turn

Making the News Popular

THE HISTORY OF COMMUNICATION

Robert W. McChesney and John C. Nerone, editors

A list of books in the series appears at the end of this book.

Making the News Popular

Mobilizing U.S. News Audiences

ANTHONY M. NADLER

UNIVERSITY OF ILLINOIS PRESS
Urbana, Chicago, and Springfield

1 2 3 4 5 C P 5 4 3 2 1
∞ This book is printed on acid-free paper.

Library of Congress Cataloging-in-Publication Data
Names: Nadler, Anthony M., 1978– author.
Title: Making the news popular : mobilizing U.S. news audiences / Anthony M.
Nadler.
Description: Urbana : University of Illinois Press, 2016. | Series: History of communication | Includes bibliographical references and index.
Identifiers: LCCN 2015047525 | ISBN 9780252040146 (hardback) | ISBN 9780252081637 (paperback)
Subjects: LCSH: Journalism—United States—History—21st century. | News audiences—United States—History—21st century. | American newspapers—Marketing—Research. | Television broadcasting of news—United States. | BISAC: LANGUAGE ARTS & DISCIPLINES / Journalism. | HISTORY / United States / 20th Century.
Classification: LCC PN4867.2 .N33 2016 | DDC 071/.730905—dc23
LC record available at http://lccn.loc.gov/2015047525

Contents

Acknowledgments

As I imagine is the case with any book, the insights, ideas, and inspirations behind this one have come from so many people and places. I can pinpoint and acknowledge only a fraction of those who have contributed. I first started research into and writing about efforts to popularize commercial U.S. news while working on a Graduate Research Partnership Fellowship with Mary Vavrus at the University of Minnesota. Throughout graduate school and beyond, Mary has been an invaluable mentor and thinking partner who introduced me to so many questions and intellectual resources, all the while helping steer me toward living a grounded and meaningful life in academe. Kathy Roberts Forde introduced me to the richness and nuance of journalism history, provided me with a model of engaging and philosophical historical writing, and has offered endless encouragement, guidance, and wisdom. Mary and Kathy have both offered incisive feedback on versions of this manuscript. As a graduate student, I was very fortunate to be able to start developing the ideas and research in this book while studying in a city I love and learning from deeply thoughtful and generous faculty, including Ron Greene, Lisa Disch, Laurie Ouellette, Mark Pedelty, Gil Rodman, and Ed Schiappa.

I want to thank my colleagues and students at Ursinus College who have helped push my thinking and provided many opportunities that made it possible for me to continue this research. I have had several conversations with classes that have stimulated new ways of thinking and novel questions for me about the circulation and popularization of news. My colleagues in the Media and Communication Studies Department at Ursinus—Lynne Edwards, Jennifer Fleeger, Sheryl Goodman, Kirstie Hettinga, Jay Miller, and Louise Woodstock—have created an invigorating and supportive departmental home. I received material support that helped make this research possible, including a Mellon Special Travel Grant through Ursinus and a Doctoral Dissertation Fellowship at the University of Minnesota. In 2006 I served as a Graduate Research Fellow at the Free Press in Washington, D.C., and colleagues there helped me see possibilities for political organizing and advocacy for building a more robust and democratic media.

Conversations have always been my most important sources of inspiration for developing hypotheses and deeper empathy and understanding. Among the many people whose discussions I have greatly benefited from are Rebecca and Scott Blakely, Carla Brooks, Christina Ciesel, Matt Crain, Brian Creech, Bob Dardenne, Brian Dolber, Marty Foix, Melody Hoffmann, Richard Leppert, Bill Lindeke, Sarah Humpage Liuzzi, Jonathan Marks, Mark Martinez, Jesse McClelland, Robert Mejia, Matthew Meyer, John Nerone, Molly Niesen, Helen Morgan Parmett, Victor Pickard, Kate Ranachan, Scott Schway, Ben Scott, Joe Tompkins, Derek Turner, Kristine Weglarz, Emanuelle Wessels, and Julie Wilson. Many of these conversations started because of the Union for Democratic Communication. I want to thank all who have helped keep the UDC going as a haven for critical research and analysis. I want to also offer a special thanks to those who generously offered their time to speak with me about insights from their experiences in the world of news, especially Sid Bedingfield, Charles Bierbauer, Jeff Cohen, Jeremy Iggers, Jonathan Klein, Dan Sullivan, and Doug Underwood. While I turned to texts as the main anchors of my research, these discussions provided enlightenment and direction.

I have been grateful to be able to work with the wonderful editors and staff at the University of Illinois Press. I especially want to thank Danny Nasset for picking this project up as a proposal and helping me through revision and reviews. I would like to thank the two anonymous reviewers who offered sharp perceptions and probing questions. This book is much stronger because of their feedback, and I greatly appreciate all the time they have invested in this project. Annette Wenda provided careful copyediting and helpful suggestions for sharpening ideas and prose. Sheila Bodell created the index.

This book would certainly not have been possible without Alice Leppert. She read many drafts, offered a plethora of insights, and provided essential encouragement.

Last, I want to thank my mother and father, Kathy and Richard Nadler. This book is dedicated to both of them.

Making the News Popular

INTRODUCTION

The Problem of Making News Popular

In early 2009, as the newspaper industry appeared to be in a panic-inducing free fall, *The Daily Show* host Jon Stewart offered an unusual proposal for its rescue. Speaking with former CNN chair Walter Isaacson, Stewart floated his own idea for revitalizing the teetering newspaper industry, a plan quite different from the solutions that Isaacson was promoting. Stewart suggested, "You know how when you read newspapers and the newsprint comes off on your hands? What if we made that a highly addictive narcotic? So that if you read it, you'd be like, 'I gotta get my hands on another newspaper, man.'"[1]

The idea of narcotizing newspapers circulated quickly among the news production community through mentions in outlets like *Editor and Publisher* and NPR's *On the Media.* The joke must have struck a nerve with news workers, as Stewart's humor mixed with the journalistic fantasy of an audience rapturously addicted to news.

The exchange between Stewart and Isaacson raises some critical questions about news and its circulation as popular media: How can news be made appealing for broad audiences? How can an audience—or, to use a more civic-minded concept, a public—be mobilized by a news outlet?[2] These questions are as important to media companies seeking a profit as they are to activists and reformers aspiring to create journalism that can propel and sustain new forms of democratic community. Stewart's remark offers a metaphor, albeit a disturbing one, that highlights some of the complexities in the quest for news appeal. News media, like narcotics, appeal to consumers not only through conforming to preexisting tastes, but also by actively shaping audiences' tastes, desires, and habits. While addiction has its limits as a metaphor for understanding the interaction between news outlets and their publics, it does evoke the mutually constitutive nature of the relationship between media circulation, public engagement, and desire. It suggests something beyond the idea that the commercial press simply "gives the people what they want."[3]

This book explores different models for popularizing and democratizing news that have been influential in the United States over the past several decades. One of my major arguments is a historical one: since the 1970s, the U.S. news industry has undergone a philosophical paradigm shift, moving away from an ideal of professional autonomy and into a "postprofessional" period characterized by an affirmation that consumers' preferences should drive news production. To be clear, I do not mean to imply that individual journalists have given up on all of their professional commitments, or their ethical standards, in the postprofessional period. What has changed, rather, is on an institutional level. The professional model assumed that experienced journalists had a special capacity to judge what should be on the news agenda and how to present it. The turn toward postprofessional journalism signals a declining faith in the editorial discretion of professional journalists and an embrace of the market-driven principle of consumer choice. The turn away from an ideal of professional autonomy toward consumer demand has been an uneven one. The most prestigious national and metropolitan newspapers and the news divisions of the national broadcast networks were not especially at the forefront of these changes and at least partially resisted the retreat from professional ideology. This might explain why some journalism scholars, as well as high-profile critics, who are most attuned to prestige outlets have overlooked some of the profound market-oriented changes in U.S. news organizations since the 1970s.

This postprofessional paradigm, I argue, extends into the digital age. Many of the noteworthy innovations in online and mobile news media—from social news sites to news aggregators and applications designed to cull news based on users' friends and their associated preferences—represent a continuation of the desire to let users' preferences set the agenda of news organizations. Yet the story more often being told about digital journalism is that it represents a historical rupture. There are, unsurprisingly, both utopian and dystopian inflections of the rupture narrative. Many lament the decline of investigative reporting, global bureaus, and the kind of local beat reporting that usually depends on strong metropolitan newspapers.[4] Yet arguably the most influential story about this moment is one that suggests digital media have precipitated a shift away from a mass media age, when news media could be controlled by a professional elite, toward the dawning of a participatory and networked news culture.[5] Dan Gillmor, in his influential book *We the Media,* describes online networks as enabling citizens to switch from twentieth century–style news institutions that "treated the news as a lecture" to an interactive age in which "news reporting and production will be more of a conversation, or a seminar."[6] This echoes a sentiment expressed throughout recent debates about the future of news in the digital age. Yet the sentiment also predates online news, and a similar desire and promise to create forms of news more responsive to consumers surfaced in discussions about transforming U.S. news in the decades prior to widespread Internet access.

Mobile and digital technologies clearly offer exciting new possibilities for creating and circulating news. They afford opportunities for broadening the inclusiveness of public culture. Nonetheless, the discourse surrounding digital-age journalism conceals a historical continuity when today's journalistic experiments are distinguished only from the height of twentieth-century professionalism. Many of the underlying promises prominent in contemporary discussions about empowering news users online—toppling gatekeepers, prioritizing user feedback—have been invoked for decades by news managers and market researchers. Understanding trends in digital news solely as a break from journalistic traditions leads to an amnesia that makes new technologies seem all the more powerful and epoch shaking. Such amnesia lends itself to overlooking the ongoing problems with an idealized vision of a news media with an agenda that simply reflects the preferences and interests of media consumers and users.

Beyond the historical claim that the U.S. news industry has adopted a postprofessional orientation, this book also engages with democratic theory and critical theory to highlight contradictions and shortcomings in the postprofessional or demand-driven news paradigm. Given that very strong feelings (both negative and positive) about the professional paradigm still linger, I want to emphasize that my argument in no way implies a call to return to a news media dominated by professionalism or neutral expertise. Nor is the approach I take one that criticizes postprofessional journalism based on the journalistic norms and standards set by professionalism. Rather, my criticism largely falls under the terms of an "immanent critique," accepting the principal value animating postprofessional journalism—an aspiration for a press responsive to the democratic will of the public—while showing how postprofessional practices fall short of that lofty, but elusively complicated, goal.[7]

The defining motif of the postprofessional age is a call to reject a paternalistic news media. In the ideology of professional journalism, news organizations were supposed to serve as trustees, charged with looking after the public interest. Professional journalists were charged with weeding through the endless abyss of world events and using their professional discretion to sum up all the news fit to print or broadcast. For postprofessional journalism, popular preference has undermined the authority once claimed by professional judgment. The new defining ideal is that consumers should decide what counts as news, what news is most important, and how the stories of the day should be told. Perhaps no one stated this philosophy more succinctly than Reagan-era Federal Communications Commission (FCC) chair Mark Fowler, who famously declared, "The public's interest . . . defines the public interest."[8] Fowler was trying to undermine the notion that media regulators could identify a public interest independent of consumer demand. The advocates of postprofessional journalism have conjured the same type of suspicion for professional journalists claiming to be experts capable of telling the public what kinds of news we *should* value most highly.

This book examines several attempts made by key groups of news producers to shift control over the news agenda away from professional expertise and put it in the hands of ordinary news consumers: the market-centered newspaper movement epitomized by Gannett's *USA Today* (chapter 2), the creation of a distinct genre of news amid competition among the major U.S. cable news channels (chapter 3), and the growth of online social news sites tapping into collaborative filtering as a mechanism for democratizing the news agenda (chapter 4). Each of the cases represents models of news that have tried to implement different ways of gauging popular preferences and making news production responsive to those preferences. In the conclusion, I discuss how public conversations on the future of news remain stymied by a continued embrace of the demand-driven paradigm.

None of these approaches merely satisfies audiences' existing preferences. Instead, each has helped to mobilize audiences with particular interests and attachments to news. The following chapters explore how news organizations supposedly heeding consumer demand have made investments and devoted resources to bringing certain kinds of publics together. As democratic theorists stretching from John Dewey to Michael Warner have recognized, publics are not found but made.[9] Many forces can pull groups together to form publics, but media outlets clearly have a crucial role in this process in modern life. This is not to say that media organizations have absolute control over audiences or that they are all-powerful tastemakers. Nonetheless, public discussions about journalism in the postprofessional age too often ignore the role of news institutions in activating and stimulating popular interest, or a lack thereof, in current affairs, community, and democratic life.

Putting History into the Future of News

Today, major news organizations are radically rethinking their business models. New experiments in journalism proliferate daily on the Web. The "future of journalism" has become a topic of wide speculation and intense discussion among industry leaders, journalists, politicians, academics, and the public at large. This is clearly a moment of possibility, a chance to reimagine how to build a media infrastructure that engages diverse publics in democratic debate and decision making. Of course, there are many obstacles to turning this crisis into a situation that sparks genuine reflection on the political and social choices for building a media system conducive to democracy. One overarching challenge is that media structures have been depoliticized, meaning that constructing a functioning media system has not been subject to the same kind of public debate as putting into place systems for education, taxation, or even health care. As Robert McChesney argues, "The operating assumption in most discussion of the U.S. media system is that media are the natural province of the market."[10] Hence, too often today's crisis is understood solely in market terms, as the faltering of a particular business model. The mantra of many leading voices in public debates about the future of news—including Clay Shirky, Jeff Jarvis, and Yochai Benkler—is that "traditional" news organizations simply need to get out of the way or adapt to the changing needs of users in the digital media environment.

Tied to this deference to the market is a limited view of how ordinary citizens might want to engage in news. Much of the received wisdom about what news audiences want derives from particular representations that came to dominate the thinking of the mainstream news industry over the past several decades. Even among digital enthusiasts, who have been so eager to espouse the attractions of participatory news among a small slice of news junkies, there has been little challenge to the notion that a broad swath of the public simply does not find stories about public life to be engaging. Most of the digital news start-ups that have drawn the fascination of critics proclaiming a bright future for digital news have been aimed largely at audiences profiled as well-educated and heavy-news-consuming groups. This includes nonprofits like *MinnPost* and the *Voice of San Diego* as well as for-profit start-ups such as *Vox.com* and *Talking Points Memo.* As the following chapters explore, industry discourses have often framed popular audiences as drawn toward spectacle, patriotic self-congratulation, and consumer-oriented news. Industry representations of audiences have also suggested that, beyond a small group of elite, news consumers are driven away by complexity and perspectives that question a "commonsense" worldview.

These representations were chosen over others for particular reasons that suited the strategic needs of media companies at certain times. This is not to say these representations were driven primarily by an active interest in suppressing popular political engagement. Rather, the way news organizations understand their consumers reflects imperfect guesses mostly aimed toward enhancing short-term sales, ratings, or readership. Even thinking only in terms of enhancing audience size and profitability, there is no guarantee that the dominant strategies of targeting news audiences actually optimized these results.

Media companies may misinterpret their users' desires or try to cater to one aspect of these desires while neglecting others. Even leaders within the news industry have acknowledged such concerns. One example of this is the concern that traditional news organizations had for too long catered to users' momentary interests at the expense of building a long-lasting and loyal relationship. Market-driven newspapers, for example, tried to make news more like other forms of entertainment. In some cases, this may have boosted short-term sales while creating a long-term problem, as consumers were eventually offered more and more entertainment options and lost their attachment to news as something with a unique appeal. Dan Sullivan, a former chief research director at the *Minneapolis Star-Tribune,* argues that the news industry spent many decades thinking only about satisfying short-term, immediate interests based on a "manufacturing model" of selling products.[11] In fact, until 1997 when newspaper companies were reclassified under the information group, the U.S. Census Bureau classified newspaper companies as a manufacturing group, a subset of paper products. Sullivan says the manufacturing model was especially appealing to publicly owned companies, with investors intently focused on quarterly profits. However, he argues that model represents a way of thinking detrimental to newspapers' long-term survival and their need to establish a sense of unique value among readers. In short, the ways that news organizations imagine their audiences' interests do not simply reflect essential truths. Yet nor are the assumptions made by commercial media organizations *mere* imaginations. They are imaginations that have material consequences, as media organizations deploy considerable resources to mobilize viewers, readers, listeners, and users around such images.

The 1970s serve as a starting point for this inquiry into how news audiences have been imagined in the milieu of U.S. postprofessional journalism. Around this time, attracting more people to news fare took on a renewed urgency for major media companies. The foundations of the professional paradigm of journalism began to falter. As I examine in chapter 1, a number of factors contributed to this trend: an increasing pressure for newsroom profits; a crisis in the authority of journalism, as critics from the Left and Right grew suspicious of claims to journalistic objectivity; and an uprising among journalists calling for an aesthetic revolution and a more literary form of news storytelling under the name of "new journalism."[12]

In the words of Daniel Hallin, the 1970s brought about the "passing of high modernism" in U.S. journalism. For Hallin, high modernism represents "an era when American journalists felt they had overcome all the basic contradictions which historically have troubled the practice of journalism."[13] He argues that the high modernists' acceptance of the ideology of objectivity and professionalism developed in the historical context of what historians refer to as "the liberal consensus" that flourished among civic and business leaders. At the same time, most major news organizations enjoyed an unprecedented economic security. Many newspaper owners reveled in high profit margins afforded by their monopolistic control over local markets. Television broadcast networks all benefited from oligopoly. Broadcasters saw newscasts, in part, as a way to fulfill public service obligations. Television networks were willing, at least for a while, to put aside a quest to maximize profits during the news hour, often aiming for prestige over ratings. Then the social and political tumult of the late 1960s brought a rather abrupt end to the liberal consensus. Beginning around the same time, the economic security of news organizations started to decline in sometimes dramatic, though uneven, ways. These factors shook the confidence of the high-modern model of professional journalism, and a renewed emphasis on understanding audiences and their desires developed as a response to this crisis.

In such moments of intense competition for news audiences, the strategies news producers use to attract audiences have not been constant throughout time. One of my key arguments is that making news popular is *not* simply a matter of tapping into the logic of a timeless psychology: that audiences are always hungry for the scandalous, or the sensational, or the fantastic. Sometimes producers frame their views of audiences in this apparently eternal and transcendental way. Yet what is accepted as scandalous or sensational, or sensational in just the right way to pique interest, changes over time. When it comes to popularizing news, aesthetic principles, promotional tactics, and public relations strategies have emerged, receded, and undergone modification amid the shifting currents of culture and media institutions.

For just one example of changing trends, compare the popularization tactics associated with the "yellow journalism" of the 1880s and 1890s to those of *USA*

Today in its early years during the 1980s. One of yellow journalism's favored tactics for selling papers was the newspaper crusade. Reporters working for Joseph Pulitzer and William Hearst attempted to stir passions, even outrage. During some of their better moments, they targeted corrupt government or corporate practices, hoping to promote as a cause célèbre an ongoing story, rallying public demands for change. William Hearst, arguably the most successful and sensational publisher of this time, referred to his model as "a journalism of action." According to historian Joseph Campbell, Hearst's conception of the journalism of action entailed that newspapers should "inject themselves, conspicuously and vigorously, in righting the wrongs of public life, and in filling the void of government inaction and incompetence."[14]

Readers of *USA Today* would be hard-pressed to find this kind of advocacy or crusading journalism; certainly, this was not one of the paper's primary strategies for seeking popular appeal during its early years. Instead, *USA Today* envisioned its readers as busy consumers more inclined to wanting to know more about personal concerns or entertainment—health, travel, sports, and the like—than to be stirred by such calls for change. As I discuss in chapter 2, the format of *USA Today* and its imitators embodied these assumptions about their audiences, organizing their papers around capsules and colorful graphics to facilitate the consumer mentality assumed by marketers to be their readers' natural inclination. While both yellow journalism and the market-driven journalism epitomized by *USA Today* have been criticized for putting popularity before professional responsibility, they represent two very different approaches to the popularization of news.

A History of "Cultures of Production"

One approach to exploring how news organizations have revised their understandings of their audiences, and taken up new strategies for appealing to them, would be to look closely at how these changes have taken place in one news outlet or a small group of them. In this book, I draw examples from particular organizations, such as *USA Today* and Fox News, which helped initiate models for popularizing news that were widely imitated by their peers. Yet on another level, basic expectations about what defines the news and its genres are set not by individual news organizations; rather, news genres come to be defined by the loosely coordinated ways in which competing outlets continually reproduce similar products. While news outlets often seek to establish something of a unique identity for themselves, they also work together to maintain "news" as a consistent and recognizable category itself. Different news formats—such as daily newspapers, local television news broadcasts, and network television news—also maintain their own genre characteristics. This book focuses on how trade organizations, marketers, industry leaders, and Web entrepreneurs have attempted to change basic expectations for particular genres of news in response to perceived crises, not how single organizations have sought to distinguish themselves.

When groups of news outlets imitate one another and share a recognizable style and other identifiable characteristics, these news organizations tend to hold a common view of how to define "news" (at least within their genre), how the news agenda should be set, and the modes through which it should be presented. Such beliefs are encoded in news outlets' routines and procedures. Competing news outlets may band together to fend off competitors outside their genre or to tackle problems facing their entire industry. When the U.S. newspaper industry worried that readers were starting to abandon the habit of reading newspapers in the 1970s, hundreds of North American newspapers contributed funds to the Newspaper Readership Project (NRP) as part of a coordinated effort to solve the problem.[15] Many newspapers began embracing a marketing paradigm and turning to focus groups and readership surveys as procedures for discovering "truths" about their readers.

This book focuses on moments when competing news organizations together participated in efforts to revise journalistic tradition within their genres, as they adopted new understandings of their audiences' desires. When news outlets come to share similar ways of thinking about how to produce news and appeal to audiences, they share what I call a common "culture of production." I borrow this term from Paul du Gay, John Caldwell, and scholars associated with the cultural economy tradition.[16] Speaking most directly to entertainment-oriented film and television, Caldwell uses the notion of cultures of production to emphasize that "film and television . . . do not simply produce mass or popular culture (a much studied perspective for over seven decades), but rather film/TV production communities themselves are cultural expressions and entities involving all of the symbolic processes and collective practices that other cultures use: to gain and reinforce identity, to forge consensus and order, to perpetuate themselves and their interests, and to interpret the media *as* audience members."[17] Thinking of production processes as cultural helps to point to a range of factors influencing the logic of production. News production, from this view, can be examined as a set of practices informed by a host of historical legacies and cultural tendencies, from organizational routines to producers' conceptions about their audiences to news workers' stylistic preferences and assumptions about citizenship and political life. Accounting for the role of such factors shows that news producers are not simply driven by ahistorical or "noncultural" factors, such as economic imperatives of efficiency or profit maximization, technological capacities, or transcendental principles of journalism. The concept of "cultures of production" highlights the ways that the particular beliefs and values of the groups that produce commercial cultural products—including news outlets—influence the form (and content) of those products. The term conceptualizes an important location that Simon Cottle describes as "between the economic determinations of the marketplace and the cultural discourses within media representations," where there "lies a terrain that has yet to be fully explored and adequately theorized."[18]

Thinking of news producers as cultures of production can also help to explain the influence media organizations wield over cultural production without either obliterating or exaggerating that influence. On one end of this spectrum, classic liberal and neoclassical theories of economics suggest that producers have little influence over which cultural goods circulate in a capitalist society. These theories assume media producers merely respond to the external demands of the marketplace and frame consumer demand as the ultimate force determining media production.[19] At the other end of the spectrum, a certain strand of criticism casts media producers as agents motivated only by their own ideological interests. This perspective can frame the suppliers as all-powerful, and it suggests that their "rational" (though ethically suspect) self-interests determine the media they produce. The "culture of production" perspective suggests that news producers' beliefs and values shape news in ways that cannot be reduced just to what is cheapest to make, most profitable to sell, or most accords with their ideological interests. This does not mean that basic economic calculations or alignments between ruling elites and news producers should be overlooked. But in commercial news markets, producers are neither mere servants of demand nor overlords capable of dictating exactly what news content consumers must accept.

While the term *cultures of production* is something of a neologism, it only helps name a familiar, persistent phenomenon. Media researchers drawing on ethnographic techniques have long documented how news production is shaped by news outlets' internal values and organizational routines.[20] Sociologists have also demonstrated that cultural producers often imitate each other and that "fads" (among producers rather than consumers) can spread quickly throughout an industry.[21] The faddishness of the media business community is one example of how clusters of beliefs, values, and intuitions among a select group of producers can influence the circulation of culture more broadly.

What Is "Popular" News?

As a quick judgment, it can seem relatively easy to distinguish news that is made for popular audiences from news that is, say, directed toward political elites or very specialized communities (HealthCareITNews does not exactly come to mind when thinking about popular news). Nonetheless, the notion of popularity can yield a variety of different meanings. To name just a few: popular could be defined by how widely news circulates; by how broadly a form of news is enjoyed, trusted, or appreciated; or by how well it reflects the "authentic" interests of its public and speaks to their experiential understandings of the world. These differences do not necessarily reflect competing analyses of the same object, something called "the popular," which exists as a reality independent of its description. Competing ways of identifying the popular arise because there are disagreements (or simply different choices made) about what sorts of questions to ask and what aspects of cultural processes to foreground. Since this book examines efforts to popularize news, it is worth clarifying the approach I am taking to understand the popular.

"The popular" has been a productive, contentious, and somewhat elusive notion for scholars. Several decades ago, cultural studies scholars introduced fresh perspectives on the study of popular culture. One of the primary ways by which cultural studies scholars have sought to define the distinctiveness of their approach to the popular is by emphasizing that popular culture is not simply a form of culture that is imposed on its participants. One of the most important contributions of cultural studies scholarship has been its recognition and critique of intellectuals' long history of denigrating cultural forms associated with "mass" culture, especially forms associated with women and working-class audiences. Cultural studies scholars have constructed their own sense of identity partially on narratives that draw on a difference between cultural studies and "mass culture" theorists such as Theodor Adorno, Max Horkheimer, and Dwight McDonald. Whereas mass culture theorists are believed to have, in the words of Andrew Ross, portrayed popular audiences as "a populace of dopes, dupes, and robots mechanically delivered into passivity and conformity by the monolithic channels of the mass media and cultural industries," cultural studies scholars have taken pains to show a more complicated dynamic in struggles over hegemony within popular culture.[22] Thus, one of the key characteristics of most cultural studies approaches to the popular involves locating "the popular" as something that audiences have an active stake in, not just a fabrication of the owners of the means of industrial production.

Showing commercial popular culture to be more than an artificial, administrated culture leads to a number of challenges. First, cultural studies scholars typically want to avoid lapsing into what Andreas Huyssen calls "the naive notion that mass culture is identical with traditional forms of popular art, rising spontaneously from the masses."[23] A second challenge, in an era of postmodern suspicions of claims regarding "authenticity," has been to find something to contrast with the notion of imposed cultural standards. Far from wanting to obliterate the distinction between authentic and imposed cultural forms, much of cultural studies scholarship tends to reject an absolutism that would categorize a cultural form as either entirely authentic or entirely imposed. Yet because it remains essential to mark popular culture as "not entirely imposed," most cultural studies scholars invoke some notion of a partial authenticity, even if that term itself has rarely been embraced, that can be found in elements of popular culture. These are the elements that are not imposed from top-down production processes; rather, they reflect the organic, bottom-up cultural creativity of popular audiences.

I suggest that cultural studies scholars have primarily used three different methods for identifying the authentic elements in popular culture. One method has been to emphasize the activity of meaning making in reception and consumption, which helpfully frames popular culture as a set of practices rather than a collection of texts or objects. A second method has been to argue that for texts to become popular, they must speak to "legitimate" or real desires and liberatory yearnings held by popular audiences, even if these same texts offer unrealistic solutions for how these desires can be fulfilled without society needing to undergo structural changes. Finally, theorists such as Stuart Hall have illustrated hybrid origins of commercial popular culture in which commercial producers make use of materials (dialects, tropes, beliefs, attitudes, and the like) that arise at least partially from an organic context of the everyday culture of working people. For instance, Hall offers an analysis of the language in the *Daily Mirror* illustrating the hybrid origins of the elements of popular culture and pointing to connections between industrial and organic cultural production: "The language of the Daily Mirror is neither a pure construction of Fleet Street 'newspeak' nor is it the language in which its working-class readers actually speak. It is a highly complex species of linguistic ventriloquism in which the debased brutalism of popular journalism is skillfully combined and intricated [*sic*] with some elements of the directedness and vivid particularity of working-class language. It cannot get by without preserving some elements of its roots in a real vernacular." In this passage, Hall contrasts the artificiality of a "pure" commercial fabrication with the elements of the "real" (authentic) vernacular contained in the actual Fleet Street–contrived newspeak.

Taking the notion of the popular as connected to some form of authentic cultural expression, many scholars concerned with popular culture and journalism have directed their attention toward forms of journalism far from the center of its professional practices. From certain perspectives, the preferred elements of professional journalism—objectivity, inverted pyramids, "hard" news—appear to be imposed by an insular and elite group, a group championing modernism's privileged styles of abstract and detached discourse and concern for formal political institutions. Hence, many cultural studies scholars have turned largely to what John Langer calls "the other news," such as tabloids and stories along the lines of sensational crime, disaster, celebrity, and cute pets, in search of the popular. As Barbie Zelizer observes, cultural studies engagements with journalism "migrated to those dimensions of journalism that were most distant from its pronounced sense of self—the tabloid, the alternative newspaper, the online relay."[24]

Searching for popular elements of journalism only in its marginalized forms presents a number of limitations. First, such an approach may have a particular value in certain European media markets, particularly among print media, that does not carry over easily into the United States. In much of Europe, newspapers are targeted more rigidly by class. Tabloid papers aimed at a working-class readership often have circulation figures much higher than "quality" or "serious" papers aimed more toward upscale audiences. However, in most U.S. news markets, for newspapers as well as local and national television news programming, the lines of class stratification do not break down in the same way. For most U.S. news sources, it makes more sense to categorize the highest-circulating sources as "mainstream" rather than "tabloid." Since the early twentieth century until recently, the most widely circulated forms of news in the United States, such as major metropolitan daily papers and broadcast news programs, have enjoyed a broad, cross-class consumer base.

Given a concern with demonstrating that marginalized, tabloid news forms are not just for dupes or plied upon working-class audiences as weapons of mass distraction, many cultural studies scholars have offered what I call semiotic-affective approaches to popular news (and other genres of popular culture). These approaches take as their primary concerns the meanings, pleasures, and affects that are experienced and created by individuals and groups in their interactions with popular culture. In contrast, I offer what could be called a circulation approach to the popular, in which my concerns center not on the affects, meanings, or experiences of individual subjectivities as they engage the news, but rather on the popular as a structured space offering a platform for socially coordinated meaning making, affect, and action. From this vantage point, the popular is the mediated space in which "publics," using that term in the sense that John Dewey and Michael Warner use it, are formed. Popular news circulates broadly throughout a community and forms a shared point of connection among its members, a sense of synchronicity. Members of communities may themselves have preexisting connections and common self-conceptions—based on geography, ethnicity, religion, taste, profession, and so on—but popular media may itself end up playing a role in bringing the community together and defining or contesting its boundaries and identity.

The circulation approach to popular news starts by asking how certain forms of news achieved widespread exposure and visibility among a population. This is the lens through which I frame "popularization" in this study. Here, popularity means pervasiveness. The pervasiveness of certain news forms may certainly have to do with their connection to organic elements of popular culture or to widespread affective investments in the topics or styles of these forms of news reporting. But this is not always so, nor is a sense of cultural resonance—a likability connected to a reflection of one's everyday experiences—the sole reason that some forms of news spread widely while others do not. Consider how *USA Today* achieved its national circulation, for instance. Allen Neuharth and the founders of the newspaper thought they were making a product that fitted well with popular tastes and preferences in terms of how to prioritize what news to cover and how to present it. Yet they knew the popularity of their paper depended on much more than that. Gannett executives carefully orchestrated the paper's launch and a gargantuan promotional campaign that involved a star-studded first-issue event, discounts for hotels that would give copies of *USA Today* to guests, a massive telephone-outreach campaign to build subscribers, and the placement of thousands of newspaper stands throughout the country. Such promotional tactics are all elements of popularization. Focusing only on textual qualities of different news forms to explain their popularity misses much of the action. Without taking account of economic, institutional, and regulatory context, the contest among news sources vying for broad circulation might mistakenly be taken for a merit-based competition for who can produce the most appealing news narratives.

It is this meaning of popularity that is operationalized in readership and circulation figures, ratings, and payments for delivering targeted advertisements. In the sense that popular news is pervasive, popular news becomes a feature of the general landscape of everyday experience. Popular news is part of "the commons," and it is the news that serves as a basis for imagined communities and the cultural currency of social interaction. Pervasive news—on any scale from global to national to among smaller niche groups—serves as a social glue helping to hold communities together. People value popular news not just for the informational or entertainment value of the content in itself but also because it offers a sense of connection and synchronization with a community.

Part of the appeal of popular news is an experience of being part of an imagined community—a subjective perception of being part of a public connected through the circulation of news. Yet news also connects people in a more material sense. Popular news provides common points of reference that help enable all sorts of other social interactions and rituals to take place: online and offline discussions of news topics, jokes about current affairs, and coordinated gatherings such as elections, rallies, and sporting events.[25] This notion of popularization frames the challenge of understanding how certain forms of news have become so pervasive as not just a quest to discover why the pervasive forms have a resonance with audiences. Cultural resonance may be a necessary condition for achieving popularity, but it is not a sufficient condition. The critical task is to explain not only why it is that certain news forms appear to be liked and circulate widely but also why other forms that might also prove resonant do not enjoy the same limelight.

Mobilizing Audiences

A close analysis of the modern efforts to popularize news offers insights for contemporary discussions about the future of news and rebuilding a vibrant news media. This analysis challenges barriers in these discussions that have limited ways of thinking about future possibilities. First, it contests the idea that audience desires and tastes are somehow fixed. Too often the debates over the future of news are framed as if the dispute is over a factual claim—what kinds of journalism do audiences actually want? What new business models can satisfy those desires? By exploring the different strategies that news makers have pursued to popularize news, I suggest that making news popular is not only a matter of responding to an audience's preexisting interests; it is also a matter of *mobilizing* publics and creating new forms of feedback between news outlets and their publics. There is never a single answer to the question of "What do audiences want?" but rather a range of potentials and capacities for interest that can be activated by media, social movements, political parties, and other institutions and actors. Media producers must choose the part they are going to play and how they are going to try to stimulate interest and mobilize their audiences.

Second, seeing different paths for creating popular news might weaken or even eliminate an unfortunate binary that has, too often, kept a choke hold on creative thinking about the possibilities of news making. This is the binary between tabloid news and serious journalism. Too often business leaders, news critics, and media scholars paint a choice between serious news outlets practicing journalism in accord with their own professional values or news that panders to tastes for entertaining and sensational news.

James Carey's distinction between "models of" reality and "models for" reality helps illuminate reasons to historicize and diversify the ways we think about popular news audiences. Carey suggests that all models of reality (all representations claiming to depict what already exists in the world) also function as models for reality (as designs for constructing a shared social world). As Carey describes this process, "We first produce the world by symbolic work and then take up residence in the world we have produced."[26] Representations of news audiences and their interests lead to practices that create and constitute audiences that correspond to such representations. To use another of Carey's metaphors, representations of reality function as blueprints. Of course, some blueprints will never be built. Blueprints might fail because their architects have made flawed assumptions about the structural integrity of their designs or because their projects proved too arduous to build or attracted no commitments from people with the requisite capital. The same is true about how we understand news audiences. Not every model for engaging audiences will be compatible with a particular cultural and social environment. Even more so, not every model for a news audience will be backed by those with the necessary resources to test its viability.

The blueprints news outlets have for audiences are twofold: they include producers' *conceptions* of their audiences and their *strategies* for mobilizing them. By conceptions, I mean the beliefs or truths accepted by producers about what audiences want and how they "work" psychologically and socially. For instance, some news producers have conceived of their audiences as self-interested and lacking curiosity about foreign news. Others have posited their audiences as sophisticated cosmopolitans who want to follow international fashions and political trends. With a conception of a potential audience in mind, producers design strategies for creating the kind of fare that will appeal to their imagined audiences. For example, cable news producers have imagined their audiences to be strongly attached to distinctive on-air personalities; this has led to a strategy all the major cable news channels use: creating an anchor star system and promoting much of their programming on the basis of these personalities. For another example, adding opportunities for reader comments to online articles is a strategy, one oriented toward attracting readers who are presumed to have a desire for participatory exchange.

Producers' strategies for engaging their audiences are linked to their conceptions of audience motivations. When a newspaper builds on a strategy of expanding resources devoted to reviews of consumer products, this is justified based on a conception of audiences as consumer oriented. In the early 1990s, as newspapers were emphasizing more visually compelling formats, *Newsday* columnist Sydney Schanberg said, "The primary strategy has been to copy and adapt all those television techniques in which success is founded on a very short American attention span."[27] Schanberg's phrasing clearly highlights the relationship between what kind of strategies news organizations pursue for promoting the circulation of their products and assumptions made about the nature of audiences. When audiences are conceived as having short "American" attention spans, the strategies for luring them will be based on this presumption.

The chapters that follow turn to case studies of cultures of production that have created influential models for how to attract popular audiences to news: the rise of high-modern professionalism, the market-driven newspaper movement, the prime-time cable news model, and social news websites. Each of these groups of news producers has contributed visions for popularizing news fare. Each reacts against the professional model of journalism and attempts to offer a means for democratizing the news media by meeting consumer preferences.

In chapter 1, I explore how the ideal of professional autonomy came to prominence in U.S. journalism and why this ideal came up against enormous pressures by the late 1960s and 1970s. Many perceptive journalism scholars have sought to explain the origins of journalistic professionalism and the idealization of objectivity. This chapter offers a synthesis of this scholarship, paying close attention to the kinds of evidence scholars have used to show different factors—cultural, political, economic, and institutional—as prompting the adoption of the objectivity ideal and the related commitment to journalistic professionalism. I argue that sifting through this scholarship suggests that journalistic professionalism served as a strategic response on the part of media owners to new social conditions taking shape largely during the first half of the twentieth century, including changing consumer demands, journalists' desires for occupational prestige, fears of regulatory intervention into the news business, a shifting political culture, and increasingly monopolistic media markets. The ideals of professionalism never simply reflected popular preferences for a shared cultural worldview reflected in the form of professional journalism; still, professional journalism became a critical part of U.S. popular culture. It was able to win the trust of a broad audience base and become part of their media habits enough to ensure the dominance of the professional news model for some time. The pervasiveness of journalistic professionalism peaked during the time Hallin refers to as the period of high-modern U.S. journalism. The beginning of this period was marked by what Victor Pickard refers to as the "postwar settlement" when various media reform efforts were quelled by a promise of journalistic professionalism as a form of news industry self-regulation.[28] Yet by the late 1960s, the foundations of high modernism were in peril—social activism and political polarization were making claims to objectivity less tenable, feminists and other activists were exposing deeply ingrained biases and exclusions in dominant forms of journalistic professionalism, and the economic security major news organizations had enjoyed in the postwar period was starting to slip. I look at some of the alternatives to professionalism that began to emerge during this tumultuous time and explore why an editorial ideal based more on meeting consumer demand rather than professional discretion appealed to media owners and managers.

In chapter 2, I examine the "market-driven news" movement that began to spread throughout the newspaper industry in the late 1970s. By analyzing accounts of the movement from journalists and researchers and in trade journals such as *Presstime* and *Editor and Publisher,* I reconstruct how the market-driven newspaper movement took form as a culture of production that had a wide-ranging influence on U.S. news. This movement sprang out of a fear that newspapers were losing their connection with readers. Many of the predictions about the future of readership seemed quite dire. Industry leaders felt that newspapers had to undergo a fundamental shift in their editorial philosophy—that newspapers could no longer define and prioritize news solely based on the professional judgment of editors and journalists. Instead, they proposed that papers needed to reimagine their role as servants not to an abstract public interest but to their readers' professed interests and desires. Readers' preferences had to be taken into account systematically and fundamentally. Industry leaders turned to marketing researchers and specialists to help them rethink how newspapers could be more responsive to consumer demand. Even though marketing research produced complex and sometimes contradictory results about what readers and potential readers wanted, advocates of market-driven journalism tended to present a fairly consistent narrative about the interests of readers. The market-driven newspaper, with Gannett's *USA Today* as its most high-profile example, rendered a picture of news audiences as busy, self-focused, identified more as consumers and spectators than engaged citizens, and overall lacking a curiosity for nuance in public debates. Conceiving of audiences as naturally inclined spectators and consumers, news producers enhanced the visual spectacle of news presentation and emphasized the genre of "news you can use" items.

In chapter 3, I turn to cable news. For more than a decade, CNN spread to cable systems across the United States with no major competitors. Yet I argue that what is commonly thought of as "cable news" today—as a distinct genre or style of news storytelling—did not start to fully emerge until Fox News and MSNBC launched in 1996, beginning the "cable news wars." During its first decade and a half, CNN largely drew on the conventions of television and radio broadcast news, fashioning much of its programming as a kind of televisual wire service. CNN still brought innovation to news storytelling during this time; the channel refined methods for drawing out the excitement of witnessing breaking news events. CNN also started to introduce some new kinds of programming, such as *Larry King Live* and *Crossfire.* Yet I argue that most of the distinctive characteristics associated with cable news, wherein it started to break away from high-modern conventions, evolved only after 1996. The competition led to an atmosphere with each outlet fighting first for ratings, while CNN had initially put at least as much emphasis on fighting for its respectability as a news outlet. With the start of the rating wars, cable news producers positioned themselves as seeking to respond to audience desires, like the market-driven newspaper movement. However, cable producers have conceptualized their audiences and their relationship with their audience quite differently from the market-driven newspaper movement. For market-driven newspapers, readers are self-interested consumers determined to get the most value out of their time with the paper. Cable news producers tend to see their viewers more as "obsessive" rather than rational consumers, hooked on the thrill of breaking news, partisan clashes, and the opinionated fulmination of star hosts. While the market-driven newspapers saw surveys and focus groups as key to revealing their readers' desires, cable news has relied more on the instincts of programming gurus and star anchors. This has led to a more demagogical approach in which the talking heads of networks become stand-ins for popular audiences themselves.

Chapter 4 examines attempts to popularize and democratize news online through collaborative filtering. Collaborative filtering offers a means to replace the role of professional editors in setting the news agenda and deciding which stories deserve the most prominence. Instead of professional editors, collaborative filtering relies on algorithms to sort, rank, and prioritize the news based on the activity of large groups of Web users. Many different news sites have added some aspect of collaborative filtering, but I focus especially on social news sites (such as Reddit, Newsvine, and Slashdot) because they allow their users to make conscious voting choices about which stories should be most prominent.

These sites epitomize the defining characteristics of the social Web—interactivity, user-generated content, and collaborative creation—and apply them to news. For many promoters and commentators, social news sites represent the "democratization of news." They seem to operationalize the kind of collective intelligence and participatory democracy that Web enthusiasts believe the Internet can leverage to generate a more robust and democratic news system than mass media ever provided. However, I argue that the democratic promise of these sites is limited. Like market-driven journalism, they too rely on a libertarian approach to democratizing news that implies news institutions should merely respond to individual preferences. Social news sites shape and channel the preferences their users express. A serious effort to democratize news, I argue, should address the conditions under which users express and form their preferences.

Dilemma for Democracy: Journalism Serving Democracy vs. Journalism Operating Democratically

Since even before the French and American Revolutions, advocates of modern democracy have seen journalism as essential to democratic society.[29] Contemporary political theorists and communication scholars also embrace this connection. Political scientist Timothy Cook argues that the news media should be seen as governing institutions themselves. James Carey has gone so far as to suggest that democracy and journalism are "two names for the same thing."[30] Even without accepting Carey's position entirely, it is clear that news media are part of a civic infrastructure essential for democratic governance. As is the case with legislatures, judicial bodies, and elections, the structure of news media has a major influence on the kinds of political culture and activity that can flourish in a society. The organization of news media serves as a critical civic architecture for contemporary democracies. Given that such a weight hinges on the relationship between the press and other sectors of democratic society, it is not surprising that news workers, business leaders, and citizens have long lauded the goal of "democratizing news."

But what does it mean to democratize news? This phase can bring to mind different meanings, each tied to competing ideals for journalism and democracy. Nonetheless, parties proposing to democratize news—much like those promising to democratize culture, education, and so on—often speak as if "democratizing" something could have only one clear and uncontroversial meaning: decentralizing authority, curtailing the power of the elite, and empowering ordinary citizens.

Each time a group of news organizations, or a journalistic movement, has sought to expand the popular appeal of news fare, it has done so in the name of democratization. Few of the spokespeople who have seen market-driven newspapers, cable news, or user-curated online news as ways to democratize news have seen much need for engaging in questions about normative theories of democracy and the press. Yet all of these attempts at reform raise such questions. So it is useful to develop an analytic framework for understanding competing claims about democratizing news.

Two different types of conflict complicate any wish for an easy consensus around what it means to democratize news. The first, and most visible, conflict stems from clashing ideological and normative visions. People have different ideas about how news institutions should serve in democracy and, ultimately, different notions of democracy itself. What social responsibilities must media institutions fulfill in order for democracy to function? One path toward answering this question has arguably established itself as a dominant perspective in Western democracy. As James Curran argues, over the past century there has been a broad consensus, particularly in the United States and United Kingdom, that assumes that "the primary democratic tasks of media are to inform, scrutinize, debate, and represent."[31] This is the "Fourth Estate" vision of journalism, in which journalists are ennobled as watchdogs of the powerful, as pursuers of truth, and as disseminators of a wide range of political opinions and viewpoints.[32] Yet, as Curran acknowledges, there are important tensions both within this umbrella vision and outside of it. One of today's most heated controversies about the normative role of journalists concerns their function as arbiters of truth. Should journalists present "both sides" of a public dispute without intervention? Or would a democratic press better serve this goal if journalists try to leave behind what Jay Rosen calls the "lame formula of he said, she said journalism" and assert their own analysis and perspectives on what is truthful in the dispute? This debate is but one example of the kinds of tensions that arise from different visions for how the press should best serve democratic dialogue and opinion formation.

This type of conflict over the proper role of journalism in democratic governance obviously leads to important and difficult questions. Yet there is a second kind of ambiguity in the phrase "democratizing the news" that leads to another conflict, one that has generally not been acknowledged or clearly perceived. When advocates of market-based reform speak about democratizing the news, their aim, ostensibly, is to democratize control over the *production* of news. They see competition and market accountability as a way to shift power and control over the news agenda away from an elite group—professional journalists—to ordinary citizens. Critics of market-driven approaches, however, tend to speak about democratizing news in quite different terms. They see it in terms of democratizing the social *function* of news—how well news media serve the democratic public—rather than its production process. Proponents of the journalism reform movements explored in this book—from market-driven journalism to online social news—rarely even make claims about enhancing the ability of news institutions to fulfill a normative social function. Instead, their promise is to apply democratic principles to deciding how the news agenda is defined, selected, and presented. They want to democratize news by making news producers more accountable to the tastes and demands of ordinary consumers. This same demand has surfaced among certain left- and right-leaning critics of professional journalism.

The enthusiasm for democratizing news production stems, at least in part, from a reaction against the technocratic approach taken by the professional model of journalism. Professionalism assumed that trained experts could make unbiased choices, and there was no need for public debate or a participatory process to identify news values. Today, such a sanguine faith in the neutrality of professionalism no longer seems tenable.

The potential clash between democratizing the social function of news and its production process has created something of a conundrum. How is it possible for democratic ideals to pull news media in different directions? Let's say one ascribes to a theory of democracy that assumes the need for a media system that provides citizens with convenient access to crucial political information and a wide range of views on controversial topics. Such a theory takes it as a precondition of democratic governance that that kind of media system must be in place. It does not offer citizens the option of choosing a radically different media system. If citizens favor, say, a media system that reinforces only a narrow range of socially acceptable views, they cannot both satisfy their demand and still remain democratic citizens under such a theory of democracy. Similarly, most theories of democracy suggest it is impossible for a community to remain genuinely democratic if its citizens actively choose to enact a fascist political system. These hypothetical examples, of course, are caricatures. They do not reflect the nuance of realistic, contemporary scenarios. But hopefully they illuminate the crucial tension between those who propose democratizing news in the name of "giving people the news they want" and those who speak in terms of the democratic functions that journalism must serve as a social institution. It is certainly possible to hold both a normative vision that news media live up to particular ideals for serving democracy and a desire that news values and operative procedures should be decided by ordinary citizens. But to hold on to these two ideals at the same time entails hoping that all citizens come to accept your own basic vision of what the press should be, and there is always, of course, a chance that will not work out so smoothly. This is the tension between democratizing the production process of news and democratizing its social function.

There are many ways to imagine how news media might operate more democratically than the professional model. Market-based approaches to news represent only one alternative to professionalism. In the late 1960s and especially during the early 1970s, many different types of alternatives took root during a heyday of journalistic experimentation. These experiments included a new emphasis on investigative reporting (a model Hallin describes as "critical professionalism"),[33] the emergent style of "new journalism" that brought subjective experiences and a greater range of literary technique, an explosion of underground newspapers, and some attempts to expand the boundaries of professional journalism by creating opportunities for more women and journalists of color to join the professional ranks. Yet as I argue in chapter 1, this period of exploration did not last long. The postprofessional model—orienting journalists toward the satisfaction of market demand—established itself as the most dominant influence on well-funded news institutions by the end of the 1970s.

The postprofessional vision of journalism driven by consumer preferences has been at the heart of alternatives to professionalism from *USA Today* to cable news to social news sites. From this perspective, news values should be left to the "invisible hand" of the market as it reaches for a television remote, grabs a paper at a newsstand, or clicks on a news link. This approach suggests that the forms of journalism that sell best or attract the most users or readers should prevail as a matter of democratic principle, not the news preferred by a cabal of professional editors.

I hope the choice between journalism serving democracy and journalism operating democratically feels a bit dissatisfying. I present this distinction not to reify these positions but to describe a frequently unacknowledged, yet central, conflict in debates surrounding the integrity of the news. It is a conflict that has taken on new inflections in the digital age but still revolves around the same conceptual dilemmas as in previous decades. As news executives and managers embraced a market-driven philosophy about the news agenda, many critics, including working journalists, balked. From the 1970s to the early 2000s, critics frequently expressed their woes about the decline of professionalism through the narrative of the "commercialization of news." Commercialization represented an erosion of journalists' professional autonomy under waves of market pressure. In recent years, commercial pressures have intensified, as news organizations struggle to compete in a digital media landscape. In addition to commercialization, many journalists now complain about the "hamsterization" of their jobs—as they face pressures to increase traffic and hit counts through constantly churning out tweets, Facebook updates, blog posts, online video, and every other variety of online media. In this environment, instead of greedy owners, managers, and marketers being portrayed as the villains, it is the Internet itself that often takes the blame in laments about the withering of professional journalism.

Media scholars have had mixed reactions to complaints about the decline of professional journalism. Scholars writing from perspectives influenced by the traditions of political economy and critical theory usually sided with critics of the commercialization of news, seeing it as a sign of democratic disintegration and the diminishment of the public sphere.[34] Yet it is important to note that many from this tradition have never embraced the professional model as an ideal, either.[35] For many of these critics, commercialization represents only a further deterioration from an already compromised state of professional journalism. Other scholars have focused their critiques almost exclusively on professional journalism by identifying its strategic rituals and rhetorical ploys that serve to maintain its privileged cultural authority.[36]

Some scholars influenced by a cultural studies tradition have tended to focus on the shortcomings of the mainstream critique of the commercialization of journalism. Such scholars see this narrative of decline as itself saturated with class-based and masculine biases.[37] Undoubtedly, mixed in with some expressions of concerns about the shift from a professional to a commercially driven editorial philosophy are reactionary fears; these stem from the notion that a professional class, composed mostly of men, is losing its power to set the cultural parameters for what counts as legitimate news. Cultural studies scholars have tended to approach anxieties about the displacement of professional standards in journalism as fears about the "tabloidization" of news. Tabloidization has, of course, been reviled by many commenters, but some scholars have seen a more hopeful side to tabloidization. Tabloidization might also be understood as a process through which commercial pressures make news organizations more responsive and accountable to the diverse tastes and desires of popular audiences. Cultural studies scholars have demonstrated how tabloid styles frequently incorporate popular modes of expression and subject matter linked to the lifeworlds of subordinated groups. As Catharine Lumby has noted in an analysis of tabloidization across Western media, "The tabloid trend has put 'private' issues on the nightly televisual map, from domestic violence and child abuse, to relationships, addiction, eating disorders, parenting problems and sexuality. It blurs the boundaries between women's stuff and traditional public policy matters."[38] The professional model of journalism left relatively little opening for groups to challenge borders between the public and the private.

Having a robust conversation about the future of news requires addressing the conflict between these two desires: to have a news media that functions to serve the needs of the democratic public sphere and one that democratizes the production of journalism so that the definition of news, and the boundaries marking matters of public concern, can be contested. Yet in too many current debates, we are offered a choice between journalism that can be either "serious" or "entertaining." This framing pits an ascetic ideal of news that focuses on flat-toned reportage of government proceedings against delectable spectacles on the order of murder trials, sex scandals, and celebrity arrests. Clearly, there are many potential forms of journalism that do not fall so easily on either side of this dichotomy. Investigating how the commercial imagination has generated a set of fixed ideas about news audiences and exploring alternative concepts of audiences and strategies for creating publics can help us escape this forced choice.

Rethinking democratic journalism requires a paradigm for democracy beyond that of the liberal model of the market. Understanding media through classic economic conceptions of the marketplace fails to acknowledge the interdependent dynamics in media production, circulation, and interpretation. A key problem here is the classic economic assumption of "exogenous preferences." Basic liberal economic models assume that tastes and preferences for goods are properties of individual consumers.[39] In this view, consumers form their preferences for news fare as autonomous subjects, more or less independent of the influence of media marketing or the ways that an existing media landscape cultivates particular tastes. Postprofessional journalism holds up consumer choice as the supreme arbiter of a democratic news system based on this ideal. The chapters ahead will highlight the shortcomings and contradictions this model has encountered over the past several decades. They will also illustrate the powerful continuity of faith in exogenous preferences among champions of consumer-driven news online and offline. The inability of news organizations to ever simply "give people what they want" suggests that media preferences are endogenous; if the media we consume shape our habits, tastes, and our shared social world, then the demand for news is not independent of the supply. News producers do not simply satisfy the audience's demand for news. They also channel it, mold it, and even invent it.

Taking the endogenous nature of the relationship between news consumers' wants and producers' actions into account, we are forced to face more complex questions about what a democratically operating journalism might be. How is it that journalism can both give form to its public's demands for news and still operate democratically as a response to public will? What role does journalism have to play in constituting engaged citizens? These are the questions that need to be made more prominent in debates about the future of journalism. Such questions become more urgent once it becomes clear that democratizing news is not simply a question of knowing what it is that the public already wants; rather, the task is to think creatively, ethically, and inclusively about how democratic publics can be mobilized and maintained.

CHAPTER 1

A View from Somewhere

The Making and Unmaking of the Age of Professional Journalism

> Now how is this network news determined? A small group of men, numbering perhaps no more than a dozen anchormen, commentators, and executive producers, settle upon the 20 minutes or so of film and commentary that's to reach the public. . . . The American people would rightly not tolerate this concentration of power in Government. Is it not fair and relevant to question its concentration in the hands of a tiny, enclosed fraternity of privileged men elected by no one and enjoying a monopoly sanctioned and licensed by Government?
>
> The views of the majority of this fraternity do not—and I repeat, not—represent the views of America.
>
> —Spiro Agnew, November 13, 1969

A week after President Richard Nixon delivered a major address declaring a need for national unity in the midst of the Vietnam War, Vice President Spiro Agnew staged an event in Des Moines, Iowa, to call for "more responsible" journalism.[1] In Agnew's view, television news commentators' reactions to Nixon's speech had been laced with negativity, skepticism, and elite condescension directed against not only the president but, even more disturbingly, the people who had elected him. Such skewed coverage, as Agnew saw it, was quite typical of the unelected "privileged fraternity" of professional journalists despite their claims to professional objectivity. Agnew painted a portrait of the world of professional journalism, especially on the national television networks, as antidemocratic and mired in its own form of urbane provinciality. Agnew was certainly not the only critic of the dominant news institutions and their professional routines during the social and political upheavals of the late sixties. In fact, professional journalism claims to objectivity came under fire not only from a new wave of conservatives fomenting backlash against the era's social movements, but also from many leaders and participants in those left-leaning social movements. Many movement participants charged that the press largely represented established power and its values, and some saw it as stained by the biases of a workforce dominated by middle-class white men. Although it is hard not to sense in Agnew's critique a rhetorical maneuver favoring his own political agenda, many of the themes he sounded against news outlets in this speech continued to strike a chord over the following decades. Professional journalism, according to Agnew, fostered elitism, insularity, and alienation from everyday citizens and consumers, and it disguised its own biases' untenable claims to objectivity.

The following chapters will explore models for journalism that have been reacting against the professional journalism that reached its apex in the post–World War II period in the United States. This chapter explores how professional journalism came to take on a particular institutional, stylistic, and ideological form and the social, economic, and political forces that led to a crisis of that hegemonic form by the 1970s. The process of establishing journalism as a profession has been a contentious one. It has also been an object of fascination for many journalism historians, especially those who have heeded, in one way or another, James Carey's influential call for a cultural history that would approach journalism as "a highly particular type of consciousness, a particular organization of social experience."[2] At the forefront of historical accounts of the professionalization of journalism have been questions about the origins of the ideal of journalistic "objectivity," the defining value of twentieth-century professional journalism in the United States.[3] How did a voice claiming the status of a nonbiased observer come to dominate the news industry's organization of social experience? Objectivity was a key notion that enabled news organizations to claim an authority to tell the story of the world's goings-on from a position above the fray of politics and clashes among particular points of view. Objectivity promised to ground journalistic discourse as a way of knowing that could be distinguished from political advocacy and public relations.

Many historians have offered rich accounts of the rise of journalistic objectivity and professionalization, so this chapter proceeds differently from those that follow. My goal here is to offer what Kathy Roberts Forde calls a "synthetic history"—a weaving together of various historical accounts—of the rise of professionalism and objectivity and an overview of factors that led to a shaken confidence in professionalism by the 1970s. Journalism's professional ideals have particular histories; they are not commandments that were once handed down from the heavens or rules inscribed by founders of modern democracy. Yet even among working journalists, this historical memory can easily be lost. When journalistic standards appear eternal, they also seem immutable. Even when there is a willing attitude to reimagine how journalism should be practiced—as there is today among bloggers, entrepreneurs, and others—knowing something about the conditions in which professionalism arose can help assess contemporary alternatives to it.

Exactly how to explain the rise of objectivity has been an area of disagreement among researchers and historians. This is true even among the historians influenced by cultural and social historical approaches to understanding journalism that were inspired by fresh ideas offered by James Carey and Michael Schudson in the 1970s. Much of the disagreement regarding the origins of objectivity, I argue, has more to do with highlighting different points of emphasis rather than irreconcilable hypotheses. Nonetheless, these differences in emphasis are important. Some historians have asked how objectivity and professional norms resonated with cultural sensibilities of news audiences. Others have focused on the role journalists themselves played in transforming their craft into a profession.[4] Still others focus on political or economic structures that can account for the shift toward professionalization. Disputes over which of these factors to prioritize matter to the extent that the genealogy of professionalism and objectivity can help reveal some of its current social functions and the kinds of alternatives it displaces. These are also disputes over historical memory. Accounts of professionalization that emphasize the role it played in supporting dominant power might be criticized as expressions of a conspiratorial mindset; more positive accounts of the origins of objectivity might be criticized for expressing the biases of liberal pluralism and neglecting power and hegemony.

The historical literature on professionalism and objectivity supports a view that acknowledges many cultural, economic, and political preconditions that have made it possible for professional journalism to take shape. However, the approach I take here highlights how media managers and owners have had a decisive influence in favoring the kind of professionalism that became dominant. For news organizations, professionalism was a strategic response to social changes. Journalists themselves had some influence over this process, to be sure, but their interests were not as well organized as those who controlled the means of production. If working journalists themselves had more power as a group to formulate their own agenda, George Seldes's alternative vision of professional journalism might have been more widely adopted. Seldes, a Newspaper Guild radical and pioneering critic of the modern press, proposed that a professional code should bar newspaper owners from any control over the editors who made decisions about content. Seldes became an object of hatred among publishers; journalists may have legitimately feared for their jobs to indicate any support for his vision.[5] Most rank-and-file journalists seem to have accepted or acquiesced to a vision of professionalism that was preferred by their employers—one that clearly had some benefits for journalists as an occupational class, even if more tempered than what Seldes was proposing. Still, journalists' employers were not able to act without constraint. News organizations had a position of relative power, of course, but they had to respond to pressures from politicians, their advertisers, their workers, and their readers and listeners. The perspective I present here focuses on the story of how demands from these various groups took shape and how news organizations responded to them strategically through constructing a model of professional journalism. Professional journalism evolved as news organizations sought to secure the legitimacy, popularity, and profitability of their businesses while fending off threats of government intervention.

The first two sections of this chapter focus on two periods that have proved particularly important in the historiography of journalistic objectivity in the United States: the blossoming of early industrial journalism, especially the "penny press" of the 1830s and 1840s, and the years during and just following the Progressive Era, from about the 1890s to the early 1930s. During the first period, news organizations started making claims that they could separate facts clearly from opinions. The latter period represents the time in which journalism adopted its modern professional form and institutional structures such as journalism schools and professional associations emerged. The third section of the chapter outlines the solidification of professionalism during the post–World War II years when a compromise among commercial interests, the public, and journalists appeared to have been found through incorporating elements of "social responsibility" into commercial journalism. In the final section, I discuss several factors that contributed to a crisis of professionalism in the late 1960s and early 1970s, a crisis that prompted the news industry to search for new models and strategies for retaining both profitability and popular legitimacy.

Early Origins of Professionalism

Despite an ample historical record at their disposal, historians of the press have encountered many problems in tracing the genealogy of professional journalism. To start, there is the difficulty of defining key terms, especially *objectivity*.

Editors and reporters did not regularly employ the term *objectivity* in reference to reporting until the late 1920s.[6] Yet news values connected to objectivity—such as accuracy, fairness, factual reporting, and emotional detachment—became part of the journalistic imagination long before that time. Did these values reflect the essence of what would later be called "objectivity"? When and why did these values become part of a journalistic creed? Were the animating norms of professionalism cultivated before modern institutional structures began to support them?

In an influential essay published in 1974, James Carey named a stubborn pattern in U.S. journalism history, what he called "the Whig interpretation of journalism history," which "views journalism history as the slow, steady expansion of freedom and knowledge from the political press to the commercial press, the setbacks into sensationalism and yellow journalism, the forward thrust into muckraking and social responsibility."[7] Since the publication of Carey's essay, the oft-mentioned figure of Whig history became an important point of contrast for cultural and social historians, many of whom have reacted against stories about the rise of objectivity that had become cherished by the profession and journalism schools. Probably the most self-assuring and celebratory of these explanations had been that objectivity came about through a "natural history" of newspapers as they followed a teleological evolution. The natural history argument was most famously articulated by sociologist Robert Park, who suggested that the history of the newspaper needed to be approached as the history of a "surviving species," one evolving toward greater sophistication and complexity as old forms died off.[8] Another popular account of news history suggested an affinity between journalistic progress and technological progress, linking objectivity and nonpartisan news to the influence of the telegraph.[9]

Michael Schudson's *Discovering the News* (1978) offered a groundbreaking and nuanced exploration of many factors leading to the rise of journalistic objectivity that had been largely ignored by previous histories. In this book, Schudson argues that while modern objectivity did not come into full development until the 1920s, important predecessors to the values of modern objectivity took hold in the penny press that began to flourish first in New York and other eastern cities during the 1830s and 1840s. These penny papers set trends favoring fact-driven news over commentary, orienting sales toward a mass audience, initiating claims of political independence, and shifting toward greater independence from party control.[10] This nascent form of news, Schudson claims, reflected the values of a "democratic market culture" of the Jacksonian era, one made possible by new economic and political opportunities and the urbanization patterns that were breaking apart traditional societal bonds and social structures.

While Schudson's work has been broadly admired, many have voiced a similar set of criticisms. Schudson's narrative of the penny press foregrounds a middle-class consensus rather than social conflict. David Mindich, Daniel Schiller, and Richard Kaplan all suggest that Schudson is too optimistic about the egalitarianism of Jacksonian democracy.[11] Schiller's *Objectivity and the News* (1981) offers an extended argument supporting Schudson's notion that the penny press represented the beginning of what would become journalistic objectivity, but rendering a very different picture of the social relations from which it sprang. Whereas Schudson focuses on the consumer-oriented values of the rising middle class, Schiller suggests penny papers echoed a politically charged, antielite attitude that resonated with a public composed of different classes. In Schiller's account, the penny press appropriated some of the rhetorical appeal of an earlier labor press, but it incorporated this rhetoric into a worldview more palatable to the economically rising merchant class.

While Schudson and Schiller offer competing explanations for why penny papers embraced notions of fairness and impartiality, they both suggest successful penny papers mobilized popular longings and sensibilities in particular ways. In her sweeping study of nineteenth-century U.S. journalistic standards, Hazel Dicken-Garcia found, to her own surprise, that when it came to attitudes about the press's political role and partisan impartiality during the first half of the nineteenth century, "the 'inner circle' of journalists, closer to the press and its operations than were nonjournalists, simply represented more contracted views that nevertheless flowed from society's larger values."[12] Hence, histories of this period suggest public attitudes played a major role in the rise of proto-objective news values. Public attitudes might have been more central during this period than later ones because the fledgling mass newspaper industry had not yet had a chance to coalesce around a set of organized mobilization strategies of its own. It was also an era of relatively low barriers to entry into the market. Schiller explicitly argues that the penny press artfully manipulated popular rhetoric. An alternative press form might have marshaled similar values in a different direction. As Schiller documents, the labor press of the early 1800s (exemplified by papers such as the *Mechanics' Free Press* and the *Working Man's Advocate*) showed promise as a culturally viable and popular model for news among certain classes. But this critical press could not sustain the necessary capital base.[13] So even with the relatively open and nonconcentrated media market of the 1830s, not every form of news that could appeal to audiences proved economically viable.

The Professionalization of Journalism

It was not until the early twentieth century that all the major components of modern professional journalism came into place. During this period, an institutional foundation for professional journalism took shape. Professional associations became stronger, the first journalism schools were founded, and ethical codes for journalists were created. Values that had circulated among newspapers in haphazard ways—separating facts from opinions, claims to accuracy and fairness, a privileging of emotional detachment—came together under a new order that emphasized objectivity as a cardinal value and offered journalism a claim to specialized knowledge.

Professionalism became an aspirational ideal that many news organizations started to promise to their readers or listeners. The antics and sensationalism that had characterized the "yellow journalism," epitomized by Pulitzer's and Hearst's wildly successful New York tabloids, became less prominent. News organizations were turning away from the flamboyance and sensation that had flourished in the yellow journalism of the 1880s and 1890s. This movement was not uniform; tabloid-style journalism certainly did not disappear. On the whole, early-twentieth-century U.S. news outlets sought to win public attention and loyalty not only with attention-grabbing tactics but also with the promise of an objective rendering of what their professional editors deemed most important for audiences to know. The *New York Times* was a forerunner of this tendency; by the 1920s, it had established its reputation as the most influential and emulated news source in the country.[14] Like the *Times,* newspapers across the country began promising to readers they could select "All the News That's Fit to Print."

Press historians provide several accounts of the driving factors for the professionalization of journalism. Some histories emphasize factors internal to the business of news, such as a newfound occupational identity among journalists and big changes in patterns of newspaper ownership. Other explanations have to do with more external factors, in the sense that changes in news production reflected the effects of change occurring in other social institutions or changes in cultural beliefs.[15] The external explanations need to offer detail showing how broader changes bored their way into the field of journalism. In this section, I explore four groups of factors giving rise to U.S. journalism's professionalization from the late 1890s into the early 1930s: modernist attitudes toward knowledge, a realignment of political power structures, journalists' drive for occupational esteem, and the news industry's public relations efforts. Each of these factors had a role in giving rise to modern journalism. Nonetheless, I argue here that understanding how powerful newspaper owners and broadcasters operationalized professionalism as a public relations strategy is especially crucial. The strategic embrace of professionalism by industry leaders has been largely ignored by some of the most influential histories of this transition. My argument is not that the news industry's interests alone led to professionalization. Rather, I suggest the wide adoption of a particular vision of professionalism—championing a limited autonomy for journalists—represented the industry's strategic response to the broader social conditions it was confronting in the early twentieth century.

The Rise of Modernism as a Cultural Epistemology

One group of theories explains journalistic professionalism as an outgrowth of shifts in cultural attitudes and the rise of a modernist sensibility after World War I. From this view, journalistic objectivity spoke to a modernist outlook that was decidedly less optimistic on the inevitable moral and social progress of Western civilization. It also entailed a renewed questioning of basic assumptions about the competence of democratic citizens and an increasingly complex understanding of truth.[16] Schudson offers an especially probing account of how journalistic objectivity represented a reaction against the very epistemological assumption—that facts speak for themselves—that many critics have mistakenly associated with the animating principle of objectivity itself. He argues that journalistic objectivity in the 1920s signaled a significant departure from earlier claims to factuality and impartiality. Whereas earlier journalism's emphasis on factual accuracy and its realist qualities belonged to a nineteenth-century attitude of "naive empiricism," Schudson says, "It would be a mistake to read contemporary views of objectivity into the fact-mindedness of the 1890s. Objectivity is an ideology of the distrust of the self."[17] This sense of distrust of the self—and of democratic society more generally—was most acute among a rather small minority. Yet this minority included key groups—intellectual pundits and the most educated, upper-middle-class news consumers—with an outsized influence on news production. Among this group was Walter Lippmann, who Schudson claims was among the first writers to articulate an aspiration for an objective-style journalism based on a model of scientific procedure and rigor.

New models of human psychology circulating in the early twentieth century also questioned rationality as the essence of the human mind. This challenge came not only from Freud's notion of the unconscious but also from the behaviorism school in psychology, which suggested humans were conditioned through and through by their environments.[18] Vast technological changes, expansions in trade, and increasing interdependence among geographically dispersed people and specialized forms of knowledge led to the concern that modern life was becoming too complex for any single individual to fully understand. The booming post–World War I public relations industry also contributed to this doubt. According to Richard Streckfuss, one motivation for objectivity as a disciplined style of reporting came from the "realization that even if the humans were fact-gatherers and users, propagandists were manipulating facts and clouding issues, making the 'facts' delivered by the press a tainted commodity, thus tainting public opinion."[19] Yet Streckfuss also recognizes an optimistic side of professionalism, "a belief that the scientific method, applied to human affairs (including journalism) via the comparatively new social sciences (chiefly sociology, psychology, political science and economics) could open the door to human betterment."[20] The values associated with this kind of disciplined professionalism—its faith in technical rationality and bureaucratically sanctioned expertise—reflected the mores of middle-class Progressivism of the time.

Political Theory of Journalistic Objectivity

The political theory of objectivity looks to political culture and the institutional structures of U.S. political parties to explain the conditions that gave rise to professional journalism. The most compelling and well-documented account of this relationship is Richard Kaplan's *Politics and the American Press: The Rise of Objectivity, 1865–1920.*[21] Basing much of his argument on an in-depth study of Detroit's major daily newspapers, Kaplan shows that the press's distance from partisan affiliation was a crucial development opening the path for professionalization. As the strong party system of the nineteenth century loosened its hold on politics, the press touted claims of its own professional autonomy from the parties.

The affectively intense party attachments of readers throughout the nineteenth century made the pursuit of partisan niche audiences a crucial strategy for newspapers to enhance and secure their subscriber bases. This was the era of the mass party. The charged atmosphere of partisan politics sprang out of a distinct political culture that would undergo immense transformation in the early twentieth century. As Kaplan describes, "Far from accepting our contemporary notion of politics as [a] matter of private beliefs and individual interests, the nineteenth century saw communal public displays of political allegiances as central to the practice of citizenship." Party attachments were not necessarily grounded on ideology or policy preferences but tied to ritualistic performances, an indebtedness to political favors, and community bonds.[22]

Kaplan's research shows a rapid decrease in partisan bias in newspapers in the years following the presidential election of 1896. In this election, the controversial populist William Jennings Bryan won the Democratic presidential nomination, but many Democratic papers rejected Bryan because of his antagonism toward the wealthy. After suffering electoral losses that year, many Democrats joined Progressive activists in crusading against party machines. Electoral reforms, such as the introduction of the secret ballot and a move to replace caucuses with primaries, encouraged voters to become more independent from parties. These reforms, along with increasing public skepticism of parties, led to an enormous leap in split-ticket voting during the first years of the twentieth century.[23] As partisan loyalties became less important to average citizens and readers, Kaplan argues that publishers realized that "political advocacy would be a weak inducement for the reader to subscribe."[24]

Whereas the partisan press had sought authority for its competing depictions of reality through party leaders and partisan standards, the twentieth-century press turned instead to elected officials speaking qua elected officials, not as partisan spokespersons. To secure this new legitimacy, the press stayed within the ideological frameworks articulated by powerful officials. When there were disagreements among such voices, journalists juxtaposed different elite views against each other without inserting their own judgments. This is what Kaplan sees as the essence of the form of objectivity as operationalized by twentieth-century professionalism. Hence, journalism legitimized professionalism through "linking their fortunes to the elite" and privileging official voices. This, of course, compromised the press's independence from political power and made it especially difficult for any views to circulate that were not represented by prominent officials.

Objectivity and Occupational Solidarity and Esteem

Working journalists clearly had something to gain in terms of status and esteem from a transformation of their occupation into a profession. Becoming a profession, after all, comes with privileges. Hence, several scholars have looked to journalists themselves, and their desire for occupational stature, to explain the rise of twentieth-century professionalism. Once again, it is Michael Schudson who offers some of the most compelling analysis along these lines. He observes that objectivity holds a "moral force" among journalists—that it is not merely a notion accepted as standard practice but an ideal that has been passionately defended and exalted.[25] To explain journalists' deep emotional investment in objectivity, Schudson suggests that it plays a central role in journalists' core sense of identity and binds them together as an occupational culture. Professional objectivity also differentiated journalists from a competing occupational group that was growing rapidly at the start of the twentieth century—propagandists and public relations strategists.

Still, other evidence suggests limits in the role journalists themselves played in transforming the news industry toward an ideal of professionalism and shaping the contours of what that professionalism would entail. Journalists at the turn of the century were struggling for better standards of living and job security. Given their relative lack of success at securing better working conditions, it would be hard to account for major changes in press practices as an expression of journalists' own interests.[26] Schudson himself points to ways in which professionalization led to new types of managerial control over journalists, restricting their writing styles and opportunities for public commentary. Based on close readings of the trade press and press criticism at the beginning of the twentieth century, Douglas Birkhead argues, "The professionalization of the press, however, was only marginally an occupational development. . . . Professionalism became a standard and justification for *controlling* reporters in the news organization."[27] Suggesting further evidence for this thesis, the Newspaper Guild at various times opposed the classification of journalism as a profession by the National Labor Relations Board, while the American Newspaper Publishers Association (ANPA) supported it, because such a classification would mean less protection for journalists as workers.[28]

Objectivity and Professionalism as Industry Public Relations Strategy

Media owners and publishers played a decisive role in shaping the concept of professional journalism in the United States. The increasing consolidation of newspaper ownership in the early twentieth century plays a crucial role in the story behind the rise of objectivity as a hegemonic norm. Newspaper chains and group ownership started to spread in the late nineteenth century, with E. W. Scripps and William Randolph Hearst as notable pioneers. Consolidation and chain ownership exploded in the first decades of the 1900s, as market changes made taking over rival papers more lucrative and increased barriers of entries for new papers.[29] In 1900 chain newspapers accounted for about 10 percent of the national circulation; this figure was up to 43 percent by 1930.[30] News markets were transforming from highly competitive local marketplaces, with popular attention divided among many competing papers, to situations in which many local areas had only one or two papers wielding monopolistic or oligopolistic control of their markets.[31] These shifts appear to have been driven more by production-side factors—increasing reliance on advertising revenue, which gave a great advantage to larger-circulation papers, thus prompting consolidation—than responses to popular preferences. With less competition and increasing revenues coming from advertising, newspaper owners and publishers appeared very powerful. As monopoly and oligopoly power grew, Progressive reformers and activists grew increasingly suspicious of the growing class of media moguls.

The process of consolidation of U.S. newspapers, along with the deflating of popular partisan loyalties, pushed metropolitan newspapers to move toward a strategy of pursuing an undifferentiated mass audience rather than niche partisan audiences. As Kaplan notes, media owners at the turn of the century were also increasingly under the influence of what is now commonly called a "Fordist" vision of mass production tied to the assumption of a homogenous mass-market taste. News publishers saw their business as analogous to so many other industries going in this direction at the turn of the century. This way of understanding the audience was part of an emerging culture of production in the news industry, one that would continue to accelerate in the broadcast era of national news media. Yet the notion that the tastes of the vast majority of U.S. residents could converge around a single nonpartisan definition of news should not be taken for granted. In European news markets, for instance, much of popular journalism remained mobilized around partisan, ethnic, and class-based identities. Newspaper owners in the United States made heavy investments in mobilizing popular attachments to a vision of mass news, while market consolidation and rising barriers of entry made it difficult for outlets promoting alternative conceptions of news to become as widely available and convenient.

U.S. newspapers' turn-of-the-century press consolidation came under fire in magazines like the *Nation* and *Collier's* and trade publications such as the *Journalist,* as Marion Marzolf documents in her careful analysis of press criticism.[32] Much of this criticism was directed toward the entire commercial news system, not just individual reporters or papers. Critics argued that newspapers at the turn of the century were corrupted by the increasing influence of advertising, skewing stories or avoiding topics to protect the interests of advertisers. Some critics believed large newspaper owners simply had too much power in a democratic society. Out of this criticism grew several suggestions for reforming the press as a whole, including new legal tactics to strengthen libel law and proposals for creating nonprofit "endowed newspapers" that could be protected from commercial interests. As Marzolf surmises, "Professionalism was a less threatening and more credible means of press accountability for journalistic insiders than either the endowed press or legal restraints."[33] In support of the self-regulating professionalism route, major news publishers such as Joseph Pulitzer and Joseph Medill made hefty donations to endow journalism schools rather than fund competing nonprofit newspapers.

In this same time period, a wave of class-conscious social activism and criticism identified the mainstream press as an ideological agent of the moneyed classes. Upton Sinclair wrote in 1919, "Not hyperbolically and contemptuously, but literally with scientific precision, we define Journalism in America as the business and practice of presenting news of the day in the interest of economic privilege."[34] Schiller frames media moguls' support for professionalism as part of a broad movement toward a vision of what he calls, following Herbert Gans, "responsible capitalism." Objectivity and professionalism became a buffer, helping commercial newspaper companies stake a claim to their legitimacy as they monopolized local markets and as daily newspapers not owned by wealthy individuals or corporations began to disappear.

Robert McChesney offers evidence that professionalization became a conscious strategy supported by trade associations like the American Newspaper Publishers Association to deflect the widespread critique of concentration and probusiness bias in the news. According to McChesney, "By the 1890s, over 1,000 populist journals, organized into the National Reform Press Association, dedicated themselves to countering the hostility and deceit of the business-run commercial press and the ANPA."[35] Although much of the populist and socialist press was not able to survive long into the twentieth century because of their unwillingness to work with advertisers, the assault against the increasingly concentrated newspaper business continued to escalate. In the 1912 elections, all of the top presidential challengers to Taft, including Theodore Roosevelt and Woodrow Wilson, criticized the procapitalist bias of the press.[36] Newspaper owners started to see government regulation of the press as a serious threat. Part of this threat materialized in 1912 when Congress passed the Newspaper Publicity Act, which required all newspapers benefiting from postal subsidies to clearly mark the difference between editorial content and paid advertising.

McChesney argues that this immense pressure led major publishers and the ANPA to adopt a threefold strategy to fight for their survival—the same game plan that would be used by media industry leaders in every media policy debate since that time. The first two planks of this strategy were to include as little coverage of these debates in the news as possible and to use the First Amendment "as a bludgeon to prevent adoption of government policies that might interfere with their commercial prerogatives."[37] The last plank was to offer industry self-regulation—primarily the professionalization of journalists—as the appropriate response to its problems. Objectivity served as a promise that newspapers could still fairly represent the world and fulfill the democratic functions of the press even when its means of production were controlled by a concentrated group of large business owners.

Assessing the Four Hypotheses on Professionalization

All four of these explanations offer plausible and well-documented accounts of factors contributing to the institutional professionalization of journalism.

These explanations are not necessarily mutually exclusive. Factors external to the news industry—namely, emerging cultural attitudes and shifts in political culture—set conditions of possibility for different kinds of journalism to emerge. Internal factors within the news industry in large part determined which of the possible forms of journalism would be pursued and mobilized with the support of the news industry's resources.

Professionalism offered some discursive resources for practicing journalists while also enabling institutional forms of control. Journalists could draw on the ideals of professionalism to justify special rights and privileges, such as claims to a right to protect the confidentiality of sources. Yet professionalism also limited journalists' range of options for how to go about their work. Jay Rosen has described professionalism as an exchange that came out of a negotiated peace between journalists and media owners in which "journalists gain their independence and in exchange they give up their voice."[38] Journalists could invoke their professional autonomy only to the extent that they could make a case they were following the standard professional practices embraced by dominant media organizations. Journalists had to be vigilant not to express anything that powerful groups could construe as journalists' own opinions or biases, though professionalism also insulated journalists from critique from less powerful outside groups.

Journalism's High-Modern Period

While the seeds of modern professionalism were planted in the first decades of the twentieth century, it would not come into full bloom until midcentury. Only then did a particular vision of professionalism achieve hegemony across almost all major U.S. news outlets. It was only after World War II that U.S. journalism entered what Hallin describes as journalism's "high modernism" period. Hallin characterizes the high-modern phase as a time when:

> American journalism was dominated by a culture of professionalism, centered around the norm of "objective" reporting and rooted in the conviction that the primary function of the press was to serve society by providing citizens with accurate, "unbiased" information about public affairs. This culture of professionalism was what Siebert, Peterson and Schramm (1956) called the "social responsibility" model of the press, and it was widely seen by media scholars and practitioners alike, in this period when modernization theory dominated intellectual life, as the final result of the natural evolution of the news media as a social institution.[39]

By the end of the 1920s, many major schools of journalism had been founded; newspaper consolidation had left many towns, even cities, with only one daily newspaper; and "objectivity" had been enshrined in the code of ethics adopted by the American Society of Newspaper Editors (ASNE).[40] Nonetheless, from the 1920s until the end of World War II, the dominance of a particular vision of professional and objective journalism continued to be uneven, variable, and contested by multiple constituencies.

Throughout the Depression era, criticism of the press was rampant.[41] Much of it went hand in hand with the political fervor over the New Deal. Critics continued to charge newspapers with favoring the interests of big business; public distrust in the press rose during the 1930s and, outside of the war years, the 1940s as newspapers especially were widely perceived to have a probusiness and Republican bias.[42] Franklin D. Roosevelt himself repeatedly accused the press of such bias. Roosevelt even suggested to his radio audience that radio and film were more informative than newspapers because they provided direct channels of communication, while newspapers tried to tell people what to believe.[43] Though many newspaper editorial boards had initially supported Roosevelt when he was first elected in 1932, this trend turned against him as he threw his clout behind prolabor legislation such as the National Industrial Recovery Act, which proposed regulating wages, working conditions, and business responses to union organizing.

By the late 1930s, the Newspaper Guild, founded by journalists in 1933, had come to define itself clearly as a Congress of Industrial Organizations trade union rather than a professional society. The guild became one of the most politically engaged of the CIO unions.[44] The ANPA campaigned against prolabor initiatives proposed by Roosevelt and other Democrats, charging that they threatened the freedom of the press if applied to newspapers. Guild members fought back through lawsuits and public advocacy as proponents of a different conception of press freedom, one that entailed an alternative vision for journalistic professionalism. The publishers conceived of freedom of the press distinctly as a negative liberty—a right preventing government from any type of regulation (including labor regulations) that would restrict publishers' control over their news businesses. In contrast, guild members fought for a vision of freedom of the press that Ben Scott describes as a "majoritarian view" of the free press. This perspective suggests the First Amendment was meant to protect "the public's right to hear all points of view in a free, fair, and full sphere of deliberation."[45] On numerous fronts, guild members claimed that strengthening their bargaining power would better protect such a view of press freedom than granting unilateral control to publishers.

Meanwhile, other contests over the nature of journalistic professionalism accelerated in the 1930s. Newspapers and radio journalists were engaged in a battle with each other over legitimacy and journalistic authority as well as public trust.[46] Some journalists challenged the stylistic norms that had been developing with professionalism, advocating for a kind of "interpretative reporting" that differed from the standard notion of event-centered, objective journalism by emphasizing explanations of social context and ongoing concerns rather than a singular focus on news events.[47]

Press criticism quieted somewhat during World War II. However, the legitimacy crisis news organizations had been experiencing during the Depression burst into life again after the war. The war had illuminated the power of mass media, and both liberals and conservatives became concerned about the government's ability to shape wartime coverage.[48] Yet progressives and labor advocates continued to see commercial control as equally dangerous. As civil and labor activists were calling for legal reforms such as tightening antitrust laws and recognizing journalistic licenses, a group of prominent intellectuals assembled to analyze the contemporary problems of the press. With funding provided by Henry Luce, University of Chicago president Robert M. Hutchins chose thirteen renowned academics to work with him starting in 1943 to "begin an inclusive inquiry into the nature, functions, duties and responsibilities of the press in America," an inquiry that covered radio and documentary film as well as print.[49] This group, known as the Hutchins Commission, met for two and a half years and conducted more than 225 interviews.

The Hutchins Commission's most famous report, *A Free and Responsible Press* (*AFRP*), was a landmark statement about the mid-twentieth-century debates about journalism. Few of the solutions offered by the report were new or unusual; the commission itself prefaced its report by saying, "The most surprising thing about [the committee's recommendations] is that nothing more surprising could be proposed."[50] Yet the significance of this report was that it articulated a high-profile compromise on tensions between the commercial and public service functions of U.S. journalism that would become hegemonic for decades to come. Though the work of the Hutchins Commission was fraught with internal and external tension, the vision of a responsible commercial press articulated in *AFRP* set a paradigm that would be adopted by the news industry to fend off criticism over the following decades.[51] The model for the press advocated by the Hutchins Commission, later described as the "social responsibility" model, argued that the press had particular duties to a democratic society beyond its commercial interests.[52] Yet ultimately, *AFRP* suggested that these duties could be accomplished by a self-regulating commercial press, even in monopolistic conditions. It urged media organizations to voluntarily dedicate themselves to public service and to support greater professional education for journalists.

The final version of the Hutchins Commission reflected what Victor Pickard describes as a "postwar settlement" that coincided with the end of a powerful movement advocating structural media reform. This settlement was "marked by three assumptions: Media should remain self-regulated, practice nominal social responsibility, and be protected by a negative freedom of the press—negative in the sense that it conceived freedom of the press as privileging the rights of media owners over those of listeners, readers, and the broader public."[53] The postwar settlement brought security to the news industry as threats of meaningful regulations ceased. It also meant that most major news outlets had come to a consensus to keep up at least the appearance of supporting relatively unfettered professional journalism. Even outlets that had unabashedly promoted their owners' political views up until the early postwar period, such as the staunch-conservative *Chicago Tribune,* would move away from overt signs of partisanship outside of editorial pages and adopt a stance of professional objectivity.[54]

The postwar settlement marked the beginning of U.S. journalism's high-modern period. The reigning philosophy of journalistic professionalism—a promise to make decisions about news based on the autonomous discretion of journalists and editors—was the cornerstone of the commercial news media's vow to social responsibility. This style of professionalism, perhaps unsurprisingly, rarely challenged pervasive Cold War ideologies. The postwar press tended to act with deference to public officials, giving them much control over setting the news agenda and its priorities.[55] Independent investigations into claims made by official sources were not a routine part of high-modern journalism, and political controversies tended to be limited to situations in which conflicts existed among official sources. Even one of the most oft-cited memories of journalistic courage during the 1950s—journalists turning against Senator Joseph McCarthy—relied in part on coordination with high officials. The Eisenhower administration and Republican leaders in Congress who had turned against McCarthy began helping the press do the same.[56]

As Hallin shows, several cultural, economic, and political factors converged to support the stability of high-modern journalism from the late 1940s into the 1960s. Most major news organizations—both monopoly newspapers and broadcast news outlets—enjoyed an economic security that insulated them from the need for risky innovations. High modernism also took shape in the backdrop of what political historians have called the period of "liberal consensus." The two dominant political parties and leaders of major social institutions broadly agreed on several key ideas about postwar governance: support for the basic tenets of a limited liberal government, the belief that a consumer economy and limited welfare state had achieved a durable compromise between capital and labor, and support for anticommunism.[57] The liberal consensus also helped promote popular respect for authority, allowing for a more credulous press than might have been accepted in more suspicious times.

High Modernism's Crumbling Foundation

The fabric holding high modernism together began to fray in the late 1960s. Amid the social and political upheavals, the liberal consensus was falling apart. The civil rights movement was probably the first major force to start unraveling its seams, though for a while both civil rights activists and southern reactionaries could be kept at some distance from the centers of power in the northern states. Certain civil rights leaders, especially Martin Luther King Jr., deftly found ways to make use of high-modern journalistic conventions to reveal some of the traumas and cruelty of the Jim Crow South. Yet as the social movements grew throughout the decade, participants increasingly saw the mainstream press as an accomplice in supporting status quo ideology. One sign of distrust among sixties peace activists, feminists, anticapitalist revolutionaries, and the youthful counterculture was an explosive underground press. By 1969 at least five hundred underground papers were in operation, serving different constituencies, many of them publications coming directly out of social and political movements.[58] These publications ranged from *Ramparts,* which became a national haven for many well-known Left writers from Susan Sontag to Eldridge Cleaver to Noam Chomsky, to local papers such as the *Berkeley Barb,* Detroit's *Fifth Estate,* and Jackson, Mississippi's the *Kudzu.*

Conservatives started reacting against the press, too. As Spiro Agnew and other conservatives charged the national media with elitism and bias, Reed Irvine founded the right-wing watchdog group Accuracy in Media (AIM) in 1969. The group started flooding newspapers with critical letters to the editor, attacking a perceived liberal bias. If their letters were not published, they sometimes ran them as paid advertisements. By the mid-1970s, AIM members were purchasing stock in major newspapers so they could attend shareholder meetings and chastise the press for its failings and biases.[59] Another part of this conservative reaction against mainstream professional journalism—albeit one that seemed like a small part at the time—came in the form of Television News, Inc. Founded in 1973 largely by funds provided by the beer tycoon Joseph

Coors, TVN was a video news service providing preproduced stories for local broadcasters. Although the organization was clearly set up to deliver news from a right-wing perspective, it claimed nonpartisan neutrality. Roger Ailes, who would later become president of Fox News, gained his first experience managing a conservative news network with the short-lived TVN.[60]

Along with these political and cultural challenges, news companies also faced greater economic insecurity and mounting pressures for increased revenues. High modernism's peak occurred as high profit margins and stabilized markets meant news organizations could still please their owners while devoting resources to the social responsibility end of the postwar bargain. Such complacency would not last into the 1970s and 1980s. As the next chapter explores, even though profit margins generally remained high among newspapers during these decades, owners became increasingly anxious about declining readership and sought drastic measures to keep readers engaged. For metropolitan newspapers, their confidence began to shake in the 1960s, as they began to worry more about their competition with television news and noticed a trend in declining readership. Yet it would not be until the mid-1970s that the industry would rally together around the perception of a crisis in readership.[61] Along with fears about declining readership, several other factors pushed newspapers toward a greater concern with the bottom line throughout the 1970s and into the 1980s: a growing number of publicly held companies with an emphasis on quarterly profits, economic decline in the core urban areas where newspapers had thrived, general economic contractions affecting their advertisers, and an anticipation as early as the mid-1970s of computer-based technologies that could displace some of their classified and advertising revenues.[62]

The economics of television news were also changing. In their early decades, television networks had been able to portray their news services' programming as a public service that did not make a profit. Networks and stations proudly held up their news programs to rebuke charges that television represented a vast wasteland.[63] Since the Radio Act of 1927, commercial broadcasters had secured their exclusive rights to a particular slice of spectrum on the promise that they serve "public interest, convenience, and necessity." News programming became a popular way for broadcasters to justify their claim to be serving the public interest. Television executives promoted the idea that news programs were actually "loss leaders," requiring more in expenditures than they brought in revenuewise. However, new evidence suggests these claims have always been dubious; it appears that network news executives used strategic accounting practices, such as purchasing in-house services and equipment at inflated prices, to make it look like news divisions were not profitable when in fact they were generating greater revenue than expenses.[64] Nonetheless, news divisions still had the luxury of not having to squeeze as much profit out of their programming as possible.[65]

Yet television broadcasters also faced more pressure for greater news profits starting by the 1970s. Local news broadcasts were becoming the most profitable programming segments for many local stations. Unlike their syndicated entertainment programs, local stations did not have to share earnings from these time slots with national networks. Local news stations pioneered the use of "newsroom consultants," who brought in market-research techniques and transformed the presentation and substance of local news broadcasts.[66] The use of market research in local news was an early sign of a new logic of news selection that would increasingly compete with the ideal of professional autonomy.

On yet another front against high-modern professionalism, journalists themselves began to rebel against journalistic professionalism's ideological, stylistic, and institutional norms. Young journalists participating in anti–Vietnam War protests and other social movements were particularly wary of professionalism's tendency to defer to authority. They were influenced by the romantic and critical sensibilities of the era. These influences manifested themselves in the push for two new directions in journalism: the literary style of "new journalism" and a surge in investigative journalism. The "new journalism" of the 1960s was a style of literary or narrative journalism that emphasized a personal voice, a literary attention to revealing significance through detail, and often a fascination with life on the margins of society. Writers such as Joan Didion, Tom Wolfe, Norman Mailer, and Gay Talese became some of the best-known practitioners of this mode of journalism, but it was also incubated in alternative and start-up outlets such as *Rolling Stone* and *Crawdaddy*. The new journalism movement drew on a well-established narrative tradition of journalism, which had been subordinated to the inverted-pyramid and detached style characteristic of the high-modern journalism.[67]

Although investigative journalism never disappeared after the muckrakers of the Progressive Era, it experienced a lull in the postwar era and a resurgence in the 1960s and early 1970s. James Aucoin notes several factors that catalyzed this reemergence, including a major legal decision resulting in greater protection from libel suits and new technologies such as portable tape recorders and computers that aided investigative reporters in collecting and analyzing data.[68] Yet he argues that the move toward greater investigative journalism was driven primarily by "sociocultural developments" that came along with the social and political movements of the 1960s and 1970s. He suggests that the sociocultural conflicts of the era "caused journalists and media owners to be more accepting of adversarial, investigative reporting and editing," while it disposed audiences to "become more receptive of this kind of reporting."[69] However, Aucoin may be suggesting too consensual of a process insofar as he implies media owners proved to be willing fellow travelers in the sociocultural currents taking journalism in new directions.

Working journalists had to apply direct pressure, often risking their jobs, in trying to convince media owners and managers to open themselves to more critical reporting and more diverse workplaces. One force pushing for a more adversarial form of journalism was a "reporter-power" movement that sprang into being after the police crackdown at the 1968 Democratic National Convention in Chicago.[70] This movement embraced an ideal of workplace democracy among journalists working not for the underground press but for major dailies. For the mainstream press, James Boylan observes the reporter-power activist mounted a "new dissident movement, quite unlike anything seen before."[71] Movement participants founded several journalism reviews.

Although the label "journalism review" might have sounded tame and been chosen strategically for its resonance of respectability, these reviews became a home for radical press criticism coming from journalists willing to critique their own news outlets. For instance, the first year of the *Chicago Review* included "accounts of the suppression of stories about police brutality; censorship and unfair treatment of employees of the City News Bureau, owned and operated by the Chicago news-papers; kindly treatment of corporations in the business pages and elsewhere."[72] Similar reviews launched all over the country in places such as Providence, St. Louis, and the Twin Cities all ran on a voluntary basis by journalists who covered their local press critically. Writing for these reviews led to many firings, forced resignations, and demotions, a fate experienced by seven of the eight founders of the *Philadelphia Journalism Review* and four of the five of the *Houston Journalism Review.*[73] A. J. Liebling played a leading role in the reporter-power movement and used one of the reviews to organize counterconventions that took place concurrently with those of the American Newspaper Publishers Association. In 1972 more than three thousand journalists gathered at one of the counterconventions and passed a platform calling for greater freedom from management for journalists.[74]

Women journalists and journalists of color, as well as other social movement activists, also had to push hard against media organizations and the culture of a professional journalism dominated by white males. They struggled to improve media representations and create more opportunities for a diverse newsroom workforce. Journalists representing social groups excluded from the dominant ranks of high-modern journalism not only sought inclusion within its existing framework but also highlighted biases in professionalism underlying presuppositions and news values while pushing for significant changes.

High-modern journalism had been practiced by a relatively homosocial group of white male professionals. Women, nonetheless, made major contributions to early professional and high-modern journalism, though they often did so by creatively appropriating the space of the "women's pages," where they had more control and relatively greater freedom from male censorship.[75] By the 1970s, women journalists were actively organizing to change their working conditions. Throughout the decade, women journalists won a series of major class-action discrimination suits against news organizations such as the Associated Press, the *New York Times*, the *Washington Post*, *Newsweek*, and NBC.[76] It was not until a court ruling in 1971 that women were finally admitted to the National Press Club and no longer pushed to the balcony.

In the late 1960s, African American journalists started forming local groups advocating for better coverage of issues relating to Black life and better opportunities for African Americans in major news organizations.[77] This was occurring at the same time as African Americans were forming professional organizations in other fields, including psychology (1968), social work (1969), and the Congressional Black Caucus (1970).[78] In New York, African American journalists formed a group called Black Perspective and in Chicago the Black Media Group.[79] These groups not only promoted better coverage of black life and job opportunities, but also had to defend reporting styles that white employers often judged as contrary to the norms of professional journalism. According to Dawkins, "For many blacks, their attempts to cover black Americans with more depth and breadth than just riot or crime reporting were dismissed by whites as advocacy reporting."[80] There were several attempts to bring African American journalists together into a national group, and in 1975 the National Association of Black Journalists created an enduring institution. In the years and decades following, Hispanic journalists, Asian American journalists, Native American journalists, and lesbian and gay journalists would all form national associations.

Searching for Alternatives

As journalism's high-modern period has faded, the ideals of professional journalism have faced increasing skepticism, even disdain. For activists, professionalism and objectivity often seem like a ruse, a method for smuggling in a particular way of viewing the social order as if that view represented neutrality. For market populists, professionalism can seem stuffy and condescending. Do professionals really need to decide for audiences what news they should be consuming? Aren't the qualities associated with professional journalism—its impersonal style and detachment—the characteristics that have been turning people off from news? As proponents of tabloids, talk shows, blogs, and emerging formats make the case that they represent truly "popular" news, it can seem as if objectivity and other characteristics of professional journalism simply represent what has been *imposed* on audiences. Yet historical research complicates such claims and challenges stark divisions between elite professional norms and popular forms. Penny papers started inching toward objectivity as a way of courting a popular readership, proclaiming themselves to be promoting popular values and an egalitarian approach to knowledge. After World War I, professional norms responded to popular anxieties about relativism and monopolization of the press. In short, professionalism arose as news outlets sought to develop relationships with audiences in particular contexts. Such "relationships," however, have never represented consensus or agreements made with all parties on equal footing. News standards have never merely *reflected* popular consciousness. Rather, this chapter has examined research documenting that journalism's professional ideals and institutional structures have been the subject of a complicated negotiation among media owners, advertisers, journalists, political leaders, social movements, and popular audiences (as fractured and unorganized as such audiences tend to be).

In both the commercial market and the political sphere, the power to shape news production has never been equally distributed. High-modern professionalism largely came about as media owners and organized groups of publishers responded strategically to pressures from various groups. One way of looking at the special power media owners have had is through the distinction between "contract makers" and "contract takers." Contract makers, of course, have the privilege of drawing up an offer. They can put the other party in the position of accepting or rejecting it, with little room for modifying its terms. In neoclassical economic theory, competition is supposed to equalize the differentials between buyers or workers as contract takers and sellers or producers as contract makers. If one seller is not offering a deal that best satisfies the buyer's wants, this gives other sellers an opening. Yet this friction-free vision of preference maximization has never fitted well with the reality of media markets, certainly not throughout the twentieth century, as professionalism took its modern form. Audiences (and working journalists) found themselves in the position of contract takers in regards to most of their negotiations with news outlets and media owners because they lacked a meaningfully different array of convenient choices. The market did not provide a vigorous competition among news sources characterized by diverse journalistic philosophies. Of course, a consumer could always choose not to read the newspaper or tune in to any of the broadcasts, but given that news sources did have a lot to offer even if they were not perfect, this situation puts audience members in disadvantageous take-it-or-leave-it positions.

In the late 1960s and the first half of the 1970s, however, some of the contract takers in the world of news were starting to organize and make new demands. The unrest of the sixties led to a moment when, in the words of David Halberstam, "for a while there was a genuine struggle over who would define news, the people in the positions of power or the people in the streets."[81] As social movements were challenging news organizations' powers to define news, so too were groups of journalists themselves making new demands of media institutions. As I have described above, journalists were banding together to advocate for greater autonomy, more diverse workplaces, and more experimentation with the range of styles and perspectives offered in daily newspapers and television news.

In the face of the multiple challenges to the order of high-modern journalism, the news industry started to open itself, willingly or not, to alternative practices and models. The late 1960s and especially the early 1970s were a particularly uncertain moment for U.S. journalism. Not unlike the situation many see in today's crisis of journalism, in the early 1970s an established journalistic paradigm seemed to be fading before a new one had arrived to take its place. Scholars such as Daniel Hallin, Robert McChesney, and John Nichols, who have consistently been generally critical of the commercial press and any nostalgia for its past, have suggested the early seventies may have represented a particularly hopeful moment for U.S. journalism.

Interest in narrative journalism, particularly in its historical form as "new journalism," was probably near its peak in 1973 when Tom Wolfe published an anthology theorizing and initiating a canonization process for the form. More women and people of color were entering the workforce at major news outlets than ever before. Certainly, these journalists continued to face prejudices and institutional barriers. The swing toward greater equality in terms of numbers, especially for journalists of color, ended up muted. At the American Society of Newspaper Editors, the Minority Employment Committee was formed in 1971 and the Women's Rights Committee in 1972, though both faced numerous institutional barriers, as Gwyneth Mellinger notes in her careful history of struggles for newsroom diversity within ASNE.[82] But during the early seventies, sexism and racism in the newsroom at least started to be named and critiqued; for women journalists and journalists of color who had wedged their foot in the door of major news outlets, it may have been more possible than at any other time to believe that significant changes were possible. Investigative reporting, too, was finding increasing support and prestige in the newsroom. With the publication of the Pentagon Papers in 1971 and the Watergate investigation, adversarial and investigative journalism came to define journalistic prestige. Hallin suggests that a new model of "critical professionalism" ascended at this time. This critical turn entailed that "journalists who had previously deferred to party and group leaders or to state officials increasingly began to insert their independence to scrutinize elites and established institutions on behalf of their readers and of 'society' or 'the public.'"[83]

Yet the trajectory toward critical professionalism was losing momentum by the mid-1970s.[84] In Hallin's analysis, news organizations retained some of the skepticism toward authority associated with the critical turn of the 1960s and 1970s, but much of this critical force morphed into an increasingly cynical attitude. Journalists, on guard against seeming naive in the face of the public relations efforts of politicians, made political strategy and maneuvering the center of their political stories. Such a focus diverted attention from issues and policy arguments, giving journalists an opening for asserting their own expertise over matters of strategy rather than the more thorny issues of substantive politics. Although elements of more descriptive and narrative journalism became incorporated in the increased space allotted for feature writing, by the late 1970s new journalism had lost its luster.[85] It seemed to no longer spur enthusiasm by exciting journalists with a revolutionary way of imagining how the story of news could be told. Women and journalists of color continued to gain positions in major news organizations, but the pace of these gains often proved to be disappointing.[86] According to Sally Lehrman, Knight Ridder Chair of Journalism in the Public Interest at Santa Clara University, even by 2009, "more than 42 percent of print newsrooms across the country employ no black, Asian American, Latino, or American Indian journalists at all."[87]

Though certain directions of change in the news industry slowed as the 1970s wore on, leaders in the news industry did not just turn back to an older vision of professionalism. Instead, in the late 1970s and 1980s, a new movement began building steam in newspapers and television news studios across the United States. The leaders of this movement also spoke about promises of more democratic news. However, this movement was not led by "people in the street" or young journalists stirred by social movements or the romantic fires of new journalism. This time it was news executives and market researchers who charged forth demanding bold changes in the process of selecting news. Their message: give consumers what they want!

CHAPTER 2

Bringing Marketing into the Newsroom

U.S. Newspapers and the Market-Driven Journalism Movement

> The new marketing philosophy brings a newspaper's own interest into greater harmony with society's interests. . . . Essentially, the new marketing philosophy for newspapers is that we are a consumer-goods business, filling informational, entertainment and other needs of consumers. Our long-term goal, therefore, should be to adjust our newspaper to our readers' needs. That's newspaper marketing coming of age!
>
> —Rick Kaspar, "Marketing News," *Presstime* (December 1984)

Perhaps Dickens's phrase "It was the best of times, it was the worst of times" captures the mood most prevalent in the U.S. newspaper industry from the late 1970s up to the early 1990s. For newspapers, or at least their owners and shareholders, this was a time of both curses and triumphs. The industry experienced a significant blow to its confidence as business leaders became convinced that newspapers were losing the centrality they once had in public and cultural life in the United States. By the late 1970s, industry leaders came to believe that newspapers as a whole faced an ominous problem with dwindling readership.[1] While the U.S. population was growing, newspaper circulation remained stagnant. Young people, in particular, appeared to be losing interest in newspapers. These observations sent fears throughout the world of print journalism that the daily newspaper was an institution in decline. Many forecasters saw a bleak future for newspapers—a betrayal of readers and then advertisers—unless dramatic changes could be made. And made soon.

Yet these gloomy predictions came at the same time that much of the industry was flourishing financially as never before. For many papers, profits were soaring. By the end of the 1980s, many of the major newspaper companies, including the New York Times Company and the Washington Post Company, were making ten times the annual profits (in actual dollars) that they had been in 1975.[2] According to one brokerage firm's analysis, the value of publicly traded newspaper stocks leaped 587 percent during the 1980s, almost twice the increase of the Dow Jones Industrial Average.[3] Newspaper profit margins also averaged much higher than most other U.S. industries during this time.[4]

The curious situation of the newspaper industry during this period defies straightforward explanations of supply and demand. A tangle of issues complicates newspaper economics. The cost of newsprint, the ability of papers to leverage monopoly rates from local advertisers, the ratio of advertising to editorial content papers choose to run, and the labor costs of gathering different types of news are just some of the variable factors that all play a role in newspaper profits. Nonetheless, the long stretch of good economic times (for most papers) coupled with severe doubts about the industry points to a peculiar set of circumstances. Financial opportunities and anxieties afforded possibilities for change, and the newspaper industry began to restructure itself. This "restructuring" touched many different aspects of the business, including trends in ownership, management, and the very content of news itself.

This chapter explores one major force behind the changes that took place in the U.S. newspaper industry as it sought new methods to gain and retain readers while making large profits. Beginning in the 1970s, market researchers began to have more influence on newspapers than they ever had before.[5] Industry leaders relied on lessons taken from market research in attempts to "reinvent" the newspaper as a medium.[6] Newspapers across the country tried to popularize their products by listening to what marketers said the changing public was demanding. Gannett's *USA Today* became the national emblem of the move toward a market-driven philosophy of journalism, its shining star. The stunning rise of *USA Today* as the first national general-interest daily inspired many other papers to adopt some of the features most associated with *USA Today*—colorful graphics, short stories and capsulated summaries, and an emphasis on "happy news," along with weather, sports, and entertainment.[7] Newspapers owned by some of the largest chains appeared to latch on to these changes most quickly,[8] and dailies across the United States sought to enhance their popular appeal through adopting marketing techniques and creating a product designed to satisfy consumers' desires. This led to a "market-driven journalism" movement, as papers turned to marketing specialists to reconnect themselves with large audiences.

Many of the changes newspapers have made since the 1970s deserve praise, especially efforts to expand the definition of news beyond breaking events and the actions of public officials. Based on evidence from a large content-analysis study comparing what ten newspapers covered in 1964–65 to what they covered in 1998–99, Michael Schudson and Leonard Downie point to some valuable aspects of the move away from the high-modern style of journalism. It is worth quoting their analysis at length:

> Newspapers moved from a preoccupation with government, usually in response to specific events, to a much broader understanding of public life that included not just events, but also patterns and trends, and not just in politics, but also in science, medicine, business, sports, education, religion, culture, and entertainment.
>
> These developments were driven in part by the market. Editors sought to slow the loss of readers turning to broadcast or cable television, or to magazines that appealed to niche audiences. The changes also were driven by the social movements of the 1960s and 1970s. The civil rights movement taught journalists in what had been overwhelmingly white and male newsrooms about minority communities that they hadn't covered well or at all. The women's movement successfully asserted that "the personal is political" and ushered in such topics as sexuality, gender equity, birth control, abortion, childhood, and parenthood. Environmentalists helped to make scientific and medical questions part of everyday news reporting.[9]

Downie and Schudson suggest a degree of harmony between the goals of civil rights activists, feminists, and environmentalists and the market pressures newspapers faced. Indeed, consumers influenced by social movements undoubtedly exerted a degree of economic force on newspapers. However, market-driven journalism cannot claim responsibility for expanding the scope of the types of social and cultural questions on the radar of mainstream journalism. Marketers have not been the champions of social movements, nor have they been the only ones criticizing standard notions of professional journalism. The kind of journalism advocated by marketers, by and large, was not focused on illuminating connections between everyday lived experiences and civic struggles. If feminists politicized the personal, this chapter demonstrates how market researchers struck a different chord: "commercialize the personal" would have been a better tagline. The marketing mentality pushed papers toward an expansion of reporting on travel, food, personal electronics, and personal health in ways that addressed readers as self-interested consumers. It is worth keeping in mind that "markets" themselves affect industries not directly but through processes of mediation. The demands of the market always need to be interpreted. While market-driven journalism reiterated populist critiques of elitism, it also drove newspapers further away from engaging seriously with the groups of citizens not seen as desirable by advertisers.[10]

I argue here that the movement to make a marketing mentality central to news production was one of the most significant factors leading to a paradigm shift in U.S. journalism in the 1970s and 1980s. This shift has been noted by several leading media historians, though they have not emphasized the role of this new managerial philosophy.[11] Daniel Hallin, Kevin Barnhurst, and John Nerone see the 1970s as a time when a period of "high modernism in U.S. journalism" was coming to an end.[12] As described in the previous chapter, the high-modern period represented the height of a mode of news production ruled by the logic of professionalism and bureaucratic hierarchy. For Barnhurst and Nerone, this mode of journalism sought to present "knowledge to a citizenry composed of rational individuals," but in its very form it exercised a mode of power over readers that insisted on the omniscience of the paper's "'objective' master-voice."[13] High modernism suffered from a technocratic approach to news and the biases in taste and outlook associated with the social position of the mostly white male professionals who filled its ranks. High modernism also insulated news producers from criticism from and dialogue with most social groups. At the same time, high modernism had also insulated newsrooms from certain market pressures and secured a level of professional autonomy for journalists and editors.

Given the social and political climate of the late 1960s and early 1970s, it is not surprising that newspapers sought new ways to relate to their readers that would not rely on a posture of patriarchal authority that had become associated with professional authority. Newspapers needed to address calls for a more inclusive definition of news, and there were many possible alternatives to the high-modern style. Advocates of market-driven journalism pushed for one kind of alternative. They had an enormous influence on the direction that many U.S. newspapers took, as they left behind aspects of the high-modern ideology amid anxieties concerning declining readership. First and foremost, marketing advocates told the news industry that it needed to start treating readers as customers. These customers could be pleased only if newspapers understood their desires through marketing research, created content to suit those desires, and adjusted their management structures to make their organizations responsive to consumer needs. Marketing advocates tended to portray newspaper readers as a group who had grown frustrated with journalists' notions of what should count as news, believing that journalists favored a definition of news focusing too narrowly on electoral politics, political controversy, and social problems. Instead, marketing advocates suggested that readers were much more interested in entertainment and self-focused news. They also imagined readers as distracted and hurried by busy routines, wanting news that was easily scannable, graphically depicted when possible, and presented in bite-size bundles. It is important to note, as I will explore in further detail, that such views about readers' desires were not always consistent with actual research findings.[14] But with or without consistent empirical support, this vision of readers had a powerful sway in the industry and with marketing advocates, who began to suggest their journalistic colleagues were out of touch and elitist if they resisted it. This context gave rise to what Barnhurst and Nerone call the "late modern" period of U.S. journalism. They characterize this as a time when "news arrived at its nadir, thoroughly pessimistic in regard to its readers, who it conceived as lacking knowledge, paying little attention to public affairs, and requiring constant visual cajoling (by marketing techniques) to show any response."[15]

Why did many newspapers start making such assumptions about their readers? That is one of the questions I explore in this chapter. To be fair, most papers did not envision their readers only as civically uninterested imbeciles. Yet I argue there was indeed a major transformation in how newspaper managers understood their readers as they latched on to a new vision of market-oriented news. They adopted a different schema of the ideal relationship between news producer and consumer. This new schema was epitomized by the highly influential research report "The Changing Needs of Changing Readers," written by Ruth Clark. In this landmark report, Clark's major premise was that it was time for a "new social contract" between newspapers and their readers.[16] Clark posited that readers were fed up with the contract that had defined high-modern journalism's professionalism. Its terms had been set so that professional editors made all the decisions about the news agenda. Now, readers wanted their own input. Clark warned newspapers that readers were demanding more say in the news agenda and were going to use their purchasing power to make sure those demands were met.

Heeding the kinds of demands outlined in the Clark report, newspapers started to reorganize decision-making power in newsrooms. In his incisive *When MBAs Rule the Newsroom,* Doug Underwood documents the growing influence that business-minded news managers started to attain from the late 1970s through the 1990s. The book's title captures the disenchantment many professional journalists felt with these changes. A former journalist himself, Underwood describes the transformation as "newsrooms [became] micromanaged to meet the business agenda of top management and where the consequences of market research [became] everywhere in evidence."[17] The new class of management within newspapers became mediators who spoke on behalf of readers to tell journalists and editors what it was that readers wanted.

According to these new mediators, readers seemed to be saying that they had limited interest in playing an active role in public life. Readers were envisioned as time-pressed consumers, more interested in "news-you-can-use" type of items than stories that would open up debates within their communities or governments. As Clark told editors, "One of the dominant traits of modern society, particularly since Vietnam, is a general concern with one's self, a turning away, in a sense, from large, complex issues that seem beyond the reach of individual thought or action."[18]

Some researchers found readers wanting more local news; others found readers generally more interested in national and international stories. Some found readers wanted shorter stories, while others found readers wanted more explanation and context.[19] Some found that readers indeed wanted more "serious" news, but others pointed to conclusions in the opposite direction.[20] Other researchers suggested that content itself did not appear to matter much, at least not as a determining factor of how widely read a newspaper would be.[21] Yet the bare-bones findings of marketing research surveys, with their p-values[22] and margins of error, have not had the most impact on daily newspapers over the past few decades. Rather, it has been interpretations of this data and a set of master narratives about what ordinary news consumers want that have had such an influence on newspapers.

This chapter focuses on why market research became so central to the newspaper industry's efforts to avert its own collapse and how industry leaders extracted particular themes from marketing discourses to justify new management styles and changes in news content. I argue that the growing strength of corporate management and particular responses to the perceived problem of declining readership gave rise to a culture of production that pushed for a market-driven model of journalism. Market-driven newspapers targeted their investments toward recruiting readers who could be hailed as self-interested consumers. They promoted approaches to defining and presenting the news agenda in ways that emphasized decontextualized, scannable news and "news you can use." In no way did this mean that newspapers abandoned a substantial focus on so-called hard news. However, under the influence of an audience image provided by marketers, newspapers channeled most of their attempts to popularize news into efforts to speak to readers as consumers.[23] Stories about government investigations, political institutions, and divisive social issues did not disappear, but they were not promoted as the resources newspapers could use or revamp creatively to connect with audiences. My main argument in this chapter is that the market-driven journalism movement led to a culture of production that left newspapers with a restricted set of tools for popularizing news. By and large, newspapers used their promotional resources to woo audiences in accord with the image that had been provided by marketers—an image of an inwardly focused audience with little interest in participating in the public sphere. Advocates of this approach argued that it represented a more democratic approach to news making than professionalism, since their goal was to cater to the interests and tastes of ordinary readers. Yet market-driven news failed to live up to its populist idealism, never finding a mechanism that could simply gauge readers' independent desires for news without, in some ways, shaping those very desires. Ultimately, the market driven newspaper movement may have helped to undermine the distinctive place of newspapers in the broader media landscape. This movement might even share partial responsibility for the industry's current crisis. As newspapers lost their distinctiveness from other media (or failed to articulate it clearly), they might have also lost the loyalty of readers.

Constructing the "Readership Problem"

One of the major factors that has led to today's crisis of journalism is a long-term decline in readership that seems to have begun sometime around the middle of the twentieth century. Even in retrospect, it is difficult to identify a precise time when this decline started. A number of measures have been used to quantify the overall health of the newspaper industry—for example, total circulation, household penetration rate, total numbers of daily papers published, survey results of the number of people saying they read newspapers regularly—but each of these tells a somewhat different story about the history of readership patterns. Each measure requires interpretation. For instance, with a focus on household penetration rate, it appears that readership peaked during two periods, once in the late 1920s and then again in the late 1940s.[24] During both of these times, there were more than 1.3 newspapers in circulation per U.S. household. Since the early 1950s, the penetration rate has been moving downward without any major rebounds, and it was around 1970 that the rate dropped below the 1:1 ratio. However, not all of this decline can be blamed on people losing interest in the news or turning to other media to get it. Household sizes have been shrinking, as more people live alone or have fewer children. Also the penetration rate has been affected by the closure of papers competing against each other and the decline of afternoon editions. Leo Bogart estimates that from 1960 to 1987, a decline of more than 9 million daily editions can be attributed to paper closures or the cancellation of editions.[25] So looking at the decreasing household penetration rate alone cannot distinguish a decrease in demand for newspapers from a decrease in supply.

Though such complications make precision difficult, a trend toward waning readership over the past several decades seems clear in hindsight. Some see the loss of newspaper readership as something that was inevitable due to social, cultural, or technological factors beyond the control of the newspaper industry (for instance, increasing mobility and new media alternatives).[26] However, Thomas Leonard presents strong arguments that put this inevitability into question. He points to several demographic changes in U.S. society from the 1950s to the 1990s that should have helped newspapers grow.[27] College graduation rates, which correlate positively with newspaper readership, grew substantially. Many more people became stock shareholders and started following sports leagues, and newspapers have long been a favorite source of information about stocks and sports. More recent arguments declaring that digital technologies and the Internet "naturally" have a devastating effect on newspaper readership can be put into question by pointing to cross-cultural comparisons. In places such as Finland and Japan, print newspaper readership remains very high, even among younger audiences, despite plentiful access to digital technologies.[28] Print readership patterns may change soon, but the attachment to the kinds of journalism provided by newspapers still holds strong among youth in these countries.

From the vantage point of news workers in the early 1970s, it was not entirely clear that a downward trend in readership was being established. The numbers did not speak for themselves, and there was variation in circulation trends for different newspapers. Was readership really falling across the industry, or was the suffering localized? By the end of the decade, the decline of readership was largely considered to be an industry-wide problem and one that presented a substantial threat. Yet it is doubtful this would have become such a widely accepted belief if key leaders in the newspaper business had not worked hard to construct a narrative of decline, making sense of the data and assembling anecdotes in order to spur editors and publishers across the country into taking action.

The fact that the "readership problem" was framed as a threat to the newspaper industry as a whole and that news organizations acted together to offer a collective response should not be taken for granted. Probably, the most influential group framing this problem for newspaper owners and managers was the Newspaper Readership Project. This special project was set up by several industry associations, including National Association of Broadcasters and the American Newspaper Publishers Association, and more than 870 individual newspapers across the United States and Canada donated funds to support it. Leo Bogart offers the most thorough account of the NRP and how its original backers convinced news managers and executives across the United States (and many Canadians) that they needed to band together to tackle the readership problem. Bogart himself played a pivotal role in the integration of market research into newspapers, though as his memoirish account of the NRP makes clear, he urged a greater caution and rigor in applying marketing research to newspapers than he saw many newspapers using. The NRP played a major role in defining the problem and making the case throughout the industry that declining readership was a pressing problem for newspapers as a whole. This was not the first reaction for many newspaper owners, as Bogart wrote:

> Each newspaper hung on its own statistical track record and saw its fortunes as somehow independent of those great abstract trends that represented the industry. . . . The loss of readership took place so gradually that one of the Readership Project's major tasks was to alert newspaper managements to the reality and seriousness of the decline. This required a strong communications effort to sensitize newspapers to the problem and urge them to do something about it, individually and in concert.[29]

Bogart was a leading figure in the NRP, an effort that lasted from 1977 to 1983, as researchers involved in the project investigated declining readership and what strategies the industry could take to reverse it. The researchers working for the NRP began telling a story and presenting data that portrayed danger ahead if it did not take collective action. At the same time, however, NRP researchers needed to be careful that their findings would not be used by competing media formats to woo advertisers away from newspapers.

Established trade organizations, especially the American Newspaper Publishers Association, also played a prominent role in efforts to organize an industry-wide response to the readership problem. Since its founding in the late nineteenth century, the ANPA organized lobbying efforts on behalf of newspapers and helped formulate strategic responses to specific antagonists of the newspapers' business interests, such as organized labor, radio news producers, and television broadcasters.[30] The difference with the ANPA's role in tackling the readership problem, in part because it was so nebulous, was the industry focus on self-transformation. Once the readership problem was named, it became a justification for pushing for changes to both what kinds of news were produced and the organizational structure of newspaper companies.

The fear of losing readers, along with a taste for maintaining flattering profit margins and Wall Street appeal, led to a push for newspapers to make dramatic changes. Conversations about the need for transforming newspapers took place in many venues. They happened at convention gatherings, in the pages of trade journals, in forums hosted by training institutes such as the American Press Institute, in the pages of popular newspapers and magazines themselves, and undoubtedly in lunchrooms, bars, and myriad informal settings in which journalists, editors, and business leaders discussed the state of the industry. While some publishers and editors had gut instincts and clear convictions about what was to blame for the newspaper's loss of stature, others were stirred by a sense of mystery behind these changes in news habits. Michael O'Neil, one of the first cochairs of the Newspaper Readership Council, a group assembled by the American Society of Newspaper Editors to investigate the problem of readership, wrote: "The phenomenon of declining newspaper readership is an extraordinary mosaic of social and behavioral influences that still lie beyond the reach of definitive research.... [W]e know very little about the subtle forces that seem to be weakening the emotional ties of many readers.... [A]nalyzing the chemistry of individual relations is difficult enough; explaining group attitudes is even more challenging."[31]

To try to untangle some of these subtle forces, newspaper executives turned to market researchers who brought social scientific methods to bear on the problem. The NRP was the first major effort undertaken to uncover the causes and formulate an industry-wide response. By the end of its six-year stint, the NRP had produced a vast array of material, including dozens of research reports, from "The Daily Diet of News" to "Fifteen Case Histories in Circulation Management" to "Women in the Eighties"; training-session material for district managers, circulations' phone-room staff, and carriers; at least seven ad campaigns ranging from a niche campaign targeting groups such as "foxy fashionables" and "earthy plant lovers" to general campaigns such as "Don't You Hate Not Knowing?" (trying to invoke anxiety in those not keeping up with the news); support services and educational materials for "Newspaper in Education" programs that brought newspapers into school curricula; and four promotional films celebrating the achievements of the newspaper industry.[32]

As the NRP dissolved in 1983, it had yet to solve the readership problem, but it had established a pattern of institutional response that would be repeated over and over again throughout the following decades. That pattern was that industry leaders would turn to researchers to define the causes of declining readership and then, drawing lessons from this research, create training programs or resource guides. Several new institutions sprang up for producing and disseminating readership research. ASNE started producing *The Editors' Exchange*, a newsletter focusing on readership concerns and featuring results from original readership studies. The Newspaper Research Council was founded in 1977 with 75 news companies as members; by the late 1990s, the ranks of the NRC had swelled to more than 450 members. The *Newspaper Research Journal* was also founded in 1979, with an intent of focusing on practical issues regarding newspaper management.

Partnerships between news industry organizations, foundations, and academe supported much of the research. One of the largest projects involving these partners was the Readership Institute, which was founded in 1999 as part of the Media Management Center at Northwestern University. The founding mission of the Readership Institute was to explore "actionable research, field-testing of readership-building ideas and measurement of their success, and education and training for the newspaper industry on readership-building best practices."[33] Some of these issues were also addressed by the Gannett Center for Media Studies (later named the Freedom Forum Media Center), which was housed at Columbia University from 1985 to 1996. During its partnership with Columbia, the Freedom Forum Media Center tried to preserve academic freedom while creating a bridge between media industries and academic researchers.[34]

Reimagining the Romance between Readers and Editors

A number of diverging responses to the readership problem emerged during this period. Some researchers looked to deep sociological roots and saw the problem connected with the faltering economies of urban centers; many journalists thought newspapers simply needed to strengthen their commitments to professionalism to assure readers of high-quality coverage. I will discuss these alternatives later in the chapter, but the most influential response to the readership problem was the turn toward a market-driven approach to news. The basic premise of this approach was that to popularize news and increase readership, newspapers needed to bring the logic of marketing deeper into the production process. Proponents of this approach believed newspapers needed to turn toward a more market-oriented model for thinking about their relationship with readers, and they thought focus groups, surveys, and other forms of consumer research could be used to tell editors and publishers what audiences wanted from news.

Readership research was not entirely new in the 1970s, but new questions started to be posed then and its use greatly expanded. Much of the industry-funded research on newspaper readers carried out before the 1970s sought to document how widely read newspapers were, who was reading them, and the effectiveness of newspaper ads. This kind of research, of course, was undertaken to make newspapers more appealing to advertisers. In the 1970s, much more marketing research started focusing on efforts to appeal to subscribers, to understand their desires so as to produce a newspaper that would meet those desires. Such research reflected a changing attitude about news production. Rick Kaspar, a former Knight Ridder executive writing in the ANPA's journal *Presstime* in 1984, captured this shift by saying, "The battle cry at newspapers is no longer 'sell whatever we produce.' Now it's, 'Produce what the market needs.'"[35] With this mentality, newspaper executives and managers started to look to marketing specialists to understand just what it was that readers were demanding.

Although not all advocates of market-driven journalism promoted exactly the same tactics, they largely shared some general assumptions of what needed to change in newspaper production:

1. Newspapers needed to become more like other fields of production and seek to please their readers as consumers. These consumers had their own interests, desires, and needs, all of which might clash with the judgment of the small group of professional journalists.
2. Newspapers needed to incorporate the findings of market research into decisions about the content of news.
3. The newspaper consumer looked very different from the public citizen, whom professional journalists had sought to address. The consumer differed from the citizen both in his or her cognitive makeup and in his or her motivations for reading the news. Cognitively, the consumer had a shorter attention span, a poorer memory, and a greater propensity to have his or her attention stimulated by spectacle. In terms of motivation, the consumer was much more at home in the marketplace pursuit of self-interest rather than in a public sphere in which the citizen would pursue a common good.

Proponents of the market-driven approach offered at least two lines of reasoning for why the industry should move away from accepting professional judgment as the basis of news decisions in favor of a customer service orientation. The first reason was survival. By this logic, anyone who accepted that newspapers were valuable to society, even someone leery about marketing, should embrace the marketing approach because it offered the only hope for saving newspapers from a catastrophic decline in readers.[36] A second argument was that marketing was not only a necessary strategy but also a good in itself. By giving readers input in the production process, marketing would democratize news institutions and humble the inflated egos that had grown out of the profession's self-image. In a 1993 essay on reinventing the newspaper, Frank Denton, then editor of the *Wisconsin State Journal,* hit on both of these themes: "Ironically, salvation, or at least survival, may lie in a discipline that journalists long have distrusted and disparaged: marketing. Aside from all the potential friction between prosocial journalism and the profit demands of the marketplace, marketing in its purest form is providing ideas, goods, and services in exchanges that satisfy the consumer and the provider."[37]

Along with the promise that the marketing approach could democratize news, its advocates painted a picture of professional journalism as elitist and out of touch with popular audiences. A 1981 ASNE report titled "Editors and Readers" began with this seething portrait of editors' condescension toward readers: "From time immemorial, editors have been blithe spirits—largely untouchable, unteachable, and utterly independent. They listen to the dicta of few except their publishers. Vox populi be damned."[38] Yet the report predicted that such attitudes were, thankfully, starting to change as newspapers brought in marketers and economic circumstances began forcing editors to begin listening to their readers. Giving a Press-Enterprise lecture in 1989, James Batten, then chief executive officer of Knight Ridder, told journalists, "The days when we could do newspapering *our* way, and tell the world to go to hell if it didn't like the results, are gone forever."[39] This kind of populist critique of professionalism, however, was coming not directly from readers but from news executives and managers. Criticism directed against journalists' claims to professional autonomy reflected a broad cultural mobilization, as market competition and consumer sovereignty were being held up as a superior form of governance to institutions run according to professional expertise. It also advanced the case for managers to seize more control in the newsroom.

News executives and managers trained to think in marketing terms reaped certain benefits from the market-driven news movement. Executive salaries were going up faster than those of other employees. New institutes and programs sprang up to provide training and workshops for journalists and editors wanting to become leaders in their organizations by bringing in marketing ideas.[40] Editors and executives started earning bonuses and other financial rewards tied to reaching profit goals.

Changing News of Changing News Organizations

When Ruth Clark died in 1997, the *New York Times* ran an obituary titled "Ruth Clark, 80, Pollster Who Changed an Industry."[41] The *American Journalism Review* also ran a reflection on Clark's remarkable influence, "Ruth Clark Changed the World of News." Clark's own life story represents an intriguing slice of twentieth-century drama. Clark defected with her family from the United States to the Soviet Union in 1950. Just three years later, they returned after being quickly disillusioned with Soviet life. Later, Clark's daughter, Judith, became a member of the Weather Underground and was convicted for her involvement in a robbery in which three people had been killed. Yet what Clark was most remembered for by the *New York Times* and the *American Journalism Review* was not her adventurous life, but her role as the author of an extremely influential piece of marketing research: her 1979 report, "The Changing Needs of Changing Readers: A Qualitative Study of the New Social Contract between Readers and Editors." This report captured the zeitgeist of the market-driven journalism movement and left an indelible mark on the way newspapers thought about their audiences.

One way of understanding the ethos of the market-driven journalism movement is to look closely at Ruth Clark's report as one of its defining texts. In 1978 Clark was hired to conduct a series of focus groups in twelve U.S. cities to try to understand what readers and nonreaders thought and felt about newspapers. A year later, she published the report, which was distributed by the ASNE-run Newspaper Readership Council. It became their most popular piece of research, selling thousands of copies. Even the *New Yorker* took note, discussing the report as the lead item in their "Talk of the Town" column.

Clark's mission had been to discern whether there was a growing communication gap between editors and newspaper readers. In the report, she states, "The overriding conclusion of this research is that there is indeed a gap—and a serious one at that."[42] According to the report, editors had been blinded by the consensus of news values shared among most of the other people with whom they rubbed shoulders. However, ordinary people—not professional journalists or the high-profile news makers with whom they mingled—did not share these values. Clark pointed to three major areas in which the worldview of news readers differed from that of editors. One was that readers felt a sense of "information overload," as news sources expanded and demands on their own time increased with two-income households and a greater variety of leisure-time opportunities. To help assuage information overload, Clark's report said readers wanted more news summaries, better indexing and formats that lent themselves to quick searches, and more information about what was being offered by other media.[43] Newspapers across the country, led most visibly *USA Today*, heeded these suggestions and started including more summaries, indexes, and detailed television listings.

The second theme that Clark found was that readers had started to expect a "new social contract" between them and their papers. Readers were no longer willing to accept professional judgments about the news agenda without having their own say in the matter. Clark's report used comments from her focus groups to describe some of the types of news that members of the public thought they were not getting enough of from their local newspapers and wanted as aspects of the new contract. The types of news that Clark's participants said they wanted to see in greater quantities included local news, especially "happy" local stories; stories to help readers "cope" with contemporary life by providing more consumer information; and stories that would allow readers to appreciate the vicarious experience of participating in events such as being at a courtroom hearing or sailing across the world. The report also included one other heading indicating what readers were looking for as part of the new contract: "Don't Just Tell Us about the World—Help Us Understand It." There was no further explanation of what this meant aside from four quotes, including these two that represent the main ideas:

> "The problem with national and international news is that things are so complicated and hard to follow."
> (a regular reader)
>
> "I wish they'd use more maps when they report foreign affairs. I never know exactly where the country is. Often a new name for a country springs up and it is hard to keep up."
> (a college-educated occasional reader)[44]

What is interesting about this section of the report is that it started to point toward a vision of what readers wanted that was quite different from the main thrust of the reader-centered news movement. The heading suggested, though spelled out in no detail, that readers might have wanted news reporting that provided a greater social or historical context to make news more meaningful for them. But this was not the lesson that newspapers took away from the Clark report.

The last theme that Clark highlighted received the most attention in the enthusiastic follow-up to her report. It was articulated in a section she titled "The Importance of 'Me.'" Speaking to an emerging zeitgeist, she argued that readers were becoming more focused on the self and their private lives and less interested in public matters. They were seeking information that would be directly relevant to their own everyday activities. She suggested that newspapers needed to assign much more coverage to the "self" beat, including stories about physical fitness, diet, nutrition, creativity, pop psychology, handling emotional problems, looking good and feeling good, and self-improvement.[45] This vision soon exploded in popularity in newsrooms across the country, and Reese Cleghorn, former dean of the University of Maryland School of Journalism, suggests the growth of "news you can use" was linked directly to the Clark report.[46]

Clark's report focused especially on a liminal category of readers, what she called "the occasional" reader. She identified this group as the most important target for newspapers' readership efforts. Much like political parties that choose a strategy of taking their base for granted while trying to appeal to independent voters, efforts to popularize news through a marketing orientation tended to center on enticing the occasional reader. Jeremy Iggers, a former staff writer at the *Minneapolis Star Tribune,* explained that their research had been showing that the paper's core constituency of readers who had a high interest in local politics could not "be driven away with a stick."[47] With this group considered secure, efforts to make the paper more appealing focused on different images of readers. The problem of the occasional reader could have sparked newspapers to search for compelling ways to tell the story of public life to people who had become disenchanted by newspapers' traditional political fare. It might have suggested that there were social issues and controversies that journalists were not covering and that coverage needed to be expanded beyond the issues defined by official voices. But these were not the implications of the Clark report. Instead, "Changing Needs" portrayed the occasional reader as someone turning toward inward concerns, looking for brevity and simplicity in news reports concerning public life.

Five years after Clark published her landmark report, she produced an update based on a different research methodology. This report, titled "Relating to Readers in the 80s: An Update on Changing Needs of Changing Readers," portrayed a dramatically different picture of what readers wanted. It found that audiences had swayed back toward wanting more traditional "hard" news from their papers. Clark characterized the attitude shift as, "Then it was *me, my life, my problems, my environment* and now it's *news, facts, basic information.*"[48] While Clark suggested the different attitudes that she had found reflected a change of the times, Bogart argued that it was a matter of using different research methods, as the second study had included a much larger sample and relied more on quantitative measures.[49] Whatever the reason for the difference in findings, the second report did not garner nearly as much attention or wield the same powerful influence as the previous one had. According to Charles Layton and Mary Walton, "The new report sank like a stone."[50] One of the unspoken reasons the first report might have had so much appeal, as Layton and Walton suggest, was that it found that what readers wanted was precisely what advertisers wanted them to want—lighter consumer-focused fare that would make for a more congruent vehicle for selling consumer goods.

Embracing Market Segmentation

The new marketing orientation led news organizations to think about their readers not as one single mass but as a coalition of numerous consumer segments. With the mass audience divided up into component parts, newspapers had to decide which segments were worth pursuing. Publishers had long been aware that newspapers appealed to different readers in different ways, but the market-driven movement greatly intensified their efforts to differentiate among groups of readers in terms of targeted appeals.[51] In part, this was because newspapers started pitching themselves differently to advertisers. For a long time, newspapers promoted themselves as a mass advertising medium that was uniquely capable of reaching almost everyone living in a particular city or region. By the 1970s, however, advertisers were already shifting their focus toward targeted marketing. Simultaneously, the readership problem made it more difficult for newspapers to claim to be universal. Market-driven journalism offered two types of responses to these challenges. One was to fight against the decline of readership, and this included not only everything else that was being done to popularize news but also the introduction of new products called "total market vehicles." These were typically weekly tabloids that mixed feature material with advertising, given freely to nonsubscribers.[52] By 1979 more than half of daily newspapers had a total market program in place.[53] The other response was that newspapers themselves began targeting specific groups. In *Presstime* Kaspar described this philosophy: "Modern market-oriented newspapers start with a definite group of people in mind and seek to supply that group's informational and entertainment needs."[54] This meant managers and editors needed to think about their newspapers in terms of appeal to specific groups. It also led to what became known as the "sectional revolution." Throughout the 1970s and 1980s, more and more newspapers created special sections designed to appeal to certain niches, and some of these sections would be distributed only in zones representing upscale consumers.

Getting past the notion of a single mass audience could have had some advantages for groups of readers that had long been ignored or underserved. Instead of treating all readers as interchangeable members sharing the same experiences and concerns, recognizing a greater diversity among groups of readers could have helped news producers to become more keenly aware of differences among the communities they served. The mass newspaper had long faced criticisms for poor coverage of issues of particular concern to women, communities of color, working-class communities, and other marginalized groups.

As discussed in the previous chapter, in the late 1960s and early 1970s social movements, women journalists, and journalists of color had organized to put pressure on news organizations to diversify their workforce and provide better coverage of communities that had been neglected by the high-modern professionalism. Leonard Downie and Michael Schudson assert that market pressures pushed papers to expand their definitions of news since the 1960s to include once-neglected news topics that could be of particular salience to women, communities of color, and other subordinated groups.[55] Still, it is important to distinguish between the role that market research played in these gains and that of other sociological factors, such as activism, changes in cultural attitudes, and more general economic shifts. Market-driven journalism advocates sometimes paid lip service to the cause of advancing journalistic diversity. However, they showed very limited interest in engaging with the calls put forward by feminists and other community activists to seriously address social and political concerns especially important to their communities. The most striking evidence of this is that literature supporting the marketing approach pays little attention to the issue of newspapers' systemic biases against subordinated groups.

Advertisers cared deeply about attracting female audiences, especially those in the upper middle class. Occasionally, they saw readers of color as potentially valuable. However, the market-driven journalism approach resulted in strategies for courting these groups primarily as consumer categories without unique social or political concerns. Simultaneously, market-driven journalism also promoted a logic of market segmentation that actually provided news executives with a rationale to further ignore communities of color and low-income communities, even in the face of research suggesting that people from these communities were often among the most loyal and devoted groups of readers.[56]

Advertisers saw upper-middle-class women as a particularly desirable demographic, and newspapers tried to find new ways to appeal to them. One tactic was to develop special sections intended to be especially relevant to the interests of women from upscale demographics. In the 1970s, sections with titles such as "Lifestyle," "Living," and "Style" appeared that were designed for such a purpose.[57] Some of these sections replaced what had been previously called "Women's Pages." The new lifestyle sections tended to move away from the older women's format, which focused especially on traditional homemaking topics. The new sections leaned more heavily toward purchasing rather than homemaking, with a greater emphasis on entertainment and style.

In a carefully researched study of newspapers' efforts to target women through special sections, Dustin Harp shows that editors and managers influenced by market research tried to reach out to women almost exclusively through constructing them as consumers, even as other news workers presented alternatives.[58] As the new sections began to appear, many women journalists were organizing and advocating for other types of changes, including hiring more women in positions of power, increasing coverage of social and political topics of particular relevance to women, and the integration of this content throughout the paper. Harp shows these demands met with little effective response, even in the 1990s, when newspapers became especially concerned about a dip in women's readership. During this slump, many newspapers influenced by the marketing approach reintroduced sections labeled as "Women's News." Some of the editors and journalists working on these sections indeed were able to appropriate resources to cover important stories that might have otherwise been ignored. Yet Harp documents that many women working in these sections felt they had to compromise their journalistic aspirations by catering heavily to consumer-oriented features and that such sections fostered a resentment for segregating "women's issues" apart from general news.[59]

When advocates of market-driven journalism took notice of communities of color, it was also because they seemed like they might be an appealing bloc of consumers to sell to advertisers. By the early 1980s, it was becoming clear that the numbers of Latino/as living in the United States was growing rapidly. Latino/as were also establishing themselves in the middle class. Marketers started to talk about the 1980s as the "decade of the Hispanic," and the whiff of a lucrative market started to interest newspapers that had not paid much attention to Latino/a communities previously. In competition with the established Spanish-language press, some Anglo newspapers began running columns, sections, or even editions in Spanish. However, many of these efforts faced criticism that they offered only superficial outreach to Spanish-speaking communities. Critics also argued such segmented targeting marginalized news (aside from crime) about Latinos/as and pushed it away from the general circulation.[60] Gannett shook up the Spanish-language newspaper market in 1981 when it purchased *El Diario–La Prensa,* then the largest Spanish daily in the United States. Publisher Manuel Bustelo promised, "Gannett believes in our community. That's why they acquired *El Diario* and put it in our hands as the first Hispanic link in the great Gannett chain."[61] However, when Gannett sold the paper in 1989, staffers reported that they had felt neglected by Gannett after initial hopes that the chain would bring more resources to the paper.[62]

A major study conducted in 1999–2000 by Northwestern University's Readership Institute offers one of the most glaring examples of the narrow interest marketers had in communities of color only as potential consumers. As part of a national readership survey of more than thirty-seven thousand people, the institute provided a subreport titled "How Newspapers Can Better Serve African Americans and Hispanics." The study included no discussions about unique political or social concerns associated with these groups. Using a standardized survey, it identified African Americans' top concern with editorial content to be a desire for "easy to read content," followed by an interest in "home, health, food, and travel." Latino/a readers were most interested in "easy to read content," with "community announcements, obituaries, and news about ordinary people" coming in second. Not surprisingly, given the rigid categories used by the survey, it found similar results among white readers. Research like this, reflecting the market orientation of its sponsor, has been unable to explore in any depth or nuance relationships between news organization and groups facing long histories of discrimination and marginalization. The finding most celebrated in the report had nothing to do with editorial content but everything to do with advertising. Pointing to survey results that indicated African American and Latino/a readers had more interest in advertisements than whites, the report proclaimed, "The implications are enormous. Newspapers have traditionally believed that the first step is building an audience and then selling that audience to advertisers. This finding clearly says that improving advertising is a key way to build an audience. In order to build Hispanic and African-American readership, the key questions may be what categories of advertising are most important to them and whether the newspapers can include more advertisers in the locations where they like to shop."[63]

While the marketing orientation occasionally led to such attempts to cater to communities of color in modes of address favored by advertisers, the larger momentum was that newspapers started limiting their circulation efforts only to readers perceived as desirable by advertisers. *USA Today* gained a populist image largely because it was ridiculed by journalists at more established and prestige papers. But this paragon of market-driven journalism had a business plan from the very start that targeted mostly affluent readers.[64] Many other newspapers stopped offering services to rural or distant subscribers because they calculated that delivery was too expensive and that advertisers did not see these people as quality customers. With a mandate to concentrate on upscale demographics, newspapers shied away from promotional efforts in working-class or poor areas or from thinking seriously about how to cover news most important to these communities.[65] In a 1979 interview about why the *Los Angeles Times* had not been devoting more attention to minority communities, a marketing and research specialist, John Mount, explained that his paper did not "approach marketing from a racial standpoint. It just happens that more affluent and educated people tend to be white and live in suburban communities."[66] Such comments reveal classist and racist assumptions embedded in marketing paradigms, assumptions of which practitioners are not necessarily aware. On the basis of its marketing strategy, the *Los Angeles Times* justified devoting less resources to covering nonwhite communities and decided against creating special sections for minority and low-income communities that it had been creating for more wealthy ones.

Thomas Leonard's *News for All* provides detailed documentation of the move that starts in the 1970s as newspapers across the country began backing away from lower-income readers. Through curtailing services, neglecting promotion, and not prioritizing in-depth coverage of communities seen as undesirable to advertisers, newspapers started to rid themselves of "unwanted readers." Reflecting on what a major shift this represented in the history of the U.S. press, Leonard writes, "The intoxicating thought that news was for all guided a press that reveled in its democratic spirit. The crash of this faith as journalists came to see multitudes of readers they did not want has been an unexpected and momentous change in the media of the twentieth century."[67] For advocates of market-driven journalism, such a change spoke only of advancing sophistication of the industry's uptake of market-segmentation strategies.

Diverging Responses to the Readership Problem

The remedy for the readership problem proposed by market-driven journalism was certainly not the only option available. In the last chapter, I described other paths journalists and activists had started to take in reaction to the crisis that high-modern journalism faced in the late 1960s and 1970s. Among those that flourished for a brief period in the late 1960s and early 1970s was a surge of experimentation in new journalism, an emphasis on investigative journalism that came along with the development of what Hallin called "critical professionalism," and activism among women and journalists of color to push for better coverage of their communities and more diverse newsrooms. It is impossible to say just how the news industry might have evolved if more resources and energy had been put behind these developments for a long period of time.

It was not only outside activists and young renegades who pointed to alternatives to market-driven journalism. There were even some business leaders and researchers working in the top echelons of the newspaper industry offering understandings of the readership problem and strategies for solving it that differed from the major thrust of the market-driven movement. Leo Bogart, for instance, argued that diminishing readership was an outgrowth of urban poverty and the collapse of civic infrastructure in inner-city communities. It had been in dense urban areas where modern newspapers had first thrived. Worries about how an increase in urban poverty would affect newspapers first came to the attention of the industry by the mid-1960s, even before declining readership had been widely recognized as a problem. Bogart urged news organizations to take an active role in urban revitalization. He pitched this message as a strategic effort to sustain relationships not only with urban readers but also with the financially shaky urban retailers who had been loyal advertisers. Aware that he needed to speak directly to their mutual financial interests, Bogart tried to convene a "high-level two-day seminar on the marketing implications of downtown urban decay" between major publishers and retailers in 1964.[68] In a memo to the head of the Newspaper Advertising Bureau, Bogart pitched his idea for the summit by saying, "The problems of urban decay have been of perennial interest to newspapers editorially, but they are also of vital importance to newspapers in their competitive fight against neighborhood weeklies, shoppers, mail circulators, and the electronic media. Yesterday I sat at lunch with newspaper people from Philadelphia and Cleveland who exchanged examples of how their established old-line downtown department stores were folding and having their business taken away by suburban discounters who do relatively little advertising in newspapers."[69]

Though this initial proposal failed to materialize, Bogart and others made repeated attempts over the coming years to convene newspaper groups to address the relationship between urban poverty and newspapers, mostly without success. Ed Wheeler, general manager of the *Detroit News* in 1964, articulated what might have been the prevailing sentiment among the industry; he reacted to Bogart's proposal by saying, "We've looked into this problem, and decided there's nothing we can do about it."[70] Two years before the Watts riots, the general manager of the *Los Angeles Times* told Bogart, "We don't have this problem in Los Angeles."[71] Yet when the Kerner Commission released a report in 1968 examining the causes of racial unrest, the commissioners placed significant blame on the news media, finding that "news media have failed to analyze and report adequately on racial problems in the United States and, as a related matter, to meet the Negro's legitimate expectations in journalism."[72]

Another theory for solving the readership problem was that newspapers simply had to make greater commitments to "quality" and put a greater effort toward living up to professional values. Advocates for this point of view were frequently professional journalists or editors who eyed marketing research with suspicion. One particularly outspoken proponent of this view was Lester

Markel, who had served in top editorial positions at the *New York Times* for more than forty years before he retired in 1968. Markel dismissed market-driven journalism as "Gallup editing" and called on newspapers to reinforce their professionalism, suggesting that a greater devotion to familiar professional standards would lead to the era of "a new newspaper."[73] Markel and others not only appealed to professionalism as an ideal, but also argued that it made good sense as a business strategy. They also drew on the logic of product differentiation, suggesting that newspapers needed to distinguish their product from what was available on television news. To do this, newspapers would have to establish themselves in readers' minds as the source for depth, accuracy, and thoroughness in reporting. *Washington Post* media reporter Howard Kurtz supported this view, adding that high-quality professional journalism would lead to long-term loyalty and readership. He warned, perhaps presciently, that the solutions proposed by editors and executives aligned with the market-driven approach might result in some short-term gains but would eventually leave readers feeling there was nothing uniquely valuable about newspapers.[74]

Other journalists protested the kinds of changes the marketing mentality was bringing to newspapers. Doug Underwood left the trade amid mounting frustrations with the direction newsrooms were taking in the 1980s and early 1990s. Speaking of the experience of reporters and editors, Underwood describes the shift brought on by market-driven journalism in these terms: "The daily newspaper business has undergone a remarkable transformation from the days when editors in green eyeshades made seat-of-the pants news judgments and readers were only noticed when they wrote a letter to the editor. Today's market-savvy newspapers are planned and packed to 'give readers what they want'; newspaper content is geared to the results of readership surveys, and newsroom organization has been reshaped by newspaper managers whose commitment to the marketing ethic is hardly distinguishable from their vision of what journalism is."[75] Some journalists felt their professional integrity was being compromised. Some thought newspapers were losing their civic purpose and they were not able to fulfill the motivations that had led them into the profession. Some wrote exposés of the discouraging and often ridiculous changes they saw taking place in newsrooms under the influence of marketing fever and corporate management.[76]

Shortcomings of Market Research

Did market-driven journalism succeed? Attempting to answer this question requires looking at different goals animating marketing visionaries—to keep papers profitable, to solve the readership problem, and to democratize the news media. Only on the first of these counts does it seem like a defensible position to suggest that market-driven journalism may have had some success. While a thorough investigation would require more analysis into the causal factors, the U.S. newspaper industry remained profitable throughout much of the 1980s and 1990s, though it did experience a significant downturn in revenue during the recession of the early 1990s. Advertising revenues for daily U.S. newspapers rose steadily throughout most of the 1980s and 1990s, and circulation revenue also increased during most of this time.[77] However, this was not due to flourishing readership. Total newspaper circulation per household continued to decline throughout this period (before massive digitization began in the early 2000s).[78] Whether market-driven journalism might have accelerated or slowed the pace at which newspaper readership would have declined otherwise is difficult to determine. But clearly, the influx of marketing research and market-driven newspapers did not reverse the readership problem.

Assessing the effect of the movement's goal of democratizing journalism requires a theoretical analysis rather than a purely empirical one. But, briefly, let's first look at some empirical data indicating the failure of market-driven journalism in this respect. If the marketing orientation in fact had rescued newspapers from a tyrannical control by elite editors, we could expect that this process would have led to greater levels of confidence and trust in the press. However, numerous surveys indicate that trust in the U.S. news media has plummeted since the early 1970s.[79] This research itself does not pinpoint the reasons for this decline—that is, they do not provide evidence that it is linked to market-driven journalism—but clearly there are no signs of a strong positive relationship.

More importantly, the reasoning used by advocates of marketing approaches to journalism, asserting their approach democratizes the news agenda, has significant flaws. Market research enticed news managers with the promise of a direct window into the desires and preferences of everyday people. Surveys or focus groups, so the thinking went, would provide a means through which readers could let editors know what they *really* wanted. Of course, marketing researchers and specialists themselves have known that it is not so simple. Christine Urban, who became one of the most sought-after newspaper market researchers, warned readers of *Presstime*, "Just having data does not marketing make. Someone has to analyze the data and figure out *why* people are saying or doing what they are."[80] In this section, I discuss two types of complications with conducting, interpreting, and responding to market research: epistemological and ontological. This is not to suggest that all marketing research is inherently flawed, though many researchers themselves have expressed significant concerns about the uneven quality of newspaper research relative to their own standards.[81] My point, however, is only that marketing research is not as democratic as its advocates sometimes proclaim; it does not serve purely as a transparent medium through which readers can express their true desires. More realistically, market research can be understood as a type of cybernetic system that incorporates feedback from readers to guide news managers toward their goals of making a profit.[82]

First, there are epistemological problems with market researchers' aspirations to serve as a mere relay for consumers' demands. No method of data collection, or mode of interpretation, simply represents *the* most accurate reflection of consumers' preferences. Market researchers debate which methods are most useful for which purposes.[83] In a postpositivist age, it is easy to recognize that the very design of research studies (for whatever the field) influences what the findings might be. For readership research, this might mean that the categories that researchers create for a survey, let's say about what respondents are looking for in news, define how the respondents can express themselves. One survey might ask whether readers want more news about "local politics," while another might ask whether readers want papers to offer more coverage of "debates about local civic matters—such as the allocation of local tax dollars and commercial zoning." These two choices might be meant to designate the same category of news, but they could lead to quite different answers from respondents. In focus groups, the questions posed by researchers will also frame the terms of discussion. After the data have been gathered, they need interpretation. The concepts, narratives, and expectations that are already familiar to the analyst inform interpretations through which she tries to make sense of data patterns.

Critics of market-driven journalism have argued that news managers and editors drawing lessons from market research have primarily used the research as justification to support preconceived notions about audience taste. Al Neuharth boasted that the market research conducted before the launch of *USA Today* had simply confirmed the hunches he always had.[84] Philip Meyer suggested, while he was a leading market researcher for Knight Ridder, that typically "editors point to research findings as mere restatements of common sense."[85] Alison Carper argues that market research is often used quite selectively by newspapers, not so much to find new information but to provide a justification for making changes that have already been conceived. Recounting an experience from her former employer *Newsday,* she describes a focus group of likely women readers conducted by consultants who had been told about the paper's idea for creating a "Women's Pages" section. According to Carper, the consultant seemed to only record responses when the women in the group made statements supporting prevailing theories about the appeal of a women's page, and the moderator followed up only on such responses.[86]

Beyond the biases that result from a lack of double-blind procedures, market researchers also face other problems familiar to social scientists, including questions about the generalizability of data from a laboratory or survey environment to real-world situations and difficulties selecting a representative sample of respondents. These types of biases and problems are not unique to market research, of course. But since much market research lacks a peer-review process and many of the findings are kept proprietary, market researchers are not likely to keep to the same standard of rigor as social scientists.[87] This is not necessarily a weakness, because, in the end, marketing clients are not paying for objective representations of what consumers "really want." If a market research firm helps provide evidence that a certain strategy—adding women's pages, for instance—could sell papers, then they have done their job for the client. This is true even if other strategies could also be used to mobilize readers. The research does not necessarily have to test "what readers really want" but rather should test the viability of a certain marketing strategy in a particular market environment. Newspaper companies are paying for information that uses feedback from consumers about what type of goods might be used to create value and profit for the company; such news products might not reflect what citizens would find most desirable in an ideal world.

The ontological complications with market research concern the nature of the objects it supposedly illuminates. Those who claim market research democratizes the news suggest it reveals readers' true preferences and interests. But what kind of reality do these preferences have? Where do they come from? Are readers' preferences deep expressions of individual autonomy, or are they fickle epiphenomena of historical and environmental conditions? Such questions get to the heart of the philosophical divide between what has been called "critical" and "administrative" research.[88] Theodor Adorno famously criticized the Princeton Radio Research Lab's study of listeners' "likes" and "dislikes." For Adorno, this research reflected only what kinds of tastes had been cultivated in an environment in which radio consistently "plugged" a certain kind of musical formula.[89] Adorno did not see this research as helping the industry meet radio listeners' desires because they were responding only to the desires that had been formed under restricted conditions, conditions in part imposed by the radio industry.

The same kind of critique can be applied to market research concerning popular tastes for news. Market researchers may see their results as the voice of sovereign individuals expressing preferences, as something equivalent to people making democratic choices to "elect" the news media. Yet using the election analogy begs the question of whether the constituents have been provided the means to make informed choices in such an election. The critical theory perspective suggests this is not necessarily the case, as legitimate democratic choices need to be formed in environments in which people experience a fuller sense of freedom, including an enriching public culture that offers citizens an exposure to a wide array of diverse voices, ideas, and sentiments.[90] Does making democratic choices about news first require an exposure to a broad range of different styles of and approaches to telling stories about public life? This would be a requisite condition to build an analogy between marketplace media choices and the ideal of elections driven by the choices of an informed citizenry.

C. Edwin Baker offers another ontological argument that questions standard assumptions about the preferences revealed by marketing research and consumer choices. Baker argues that when markets gauge preferences, "what is identified and measured is an artifact of the method used, and other methods are possible."[91] Marketers typically try to predict what Baker calls "market-expressed preferences," which identify what a person "wants at that moment *acting in the market.*"[92] But people's media preferences are multifaceted and relative to different situations. Arguably, much of the satisfaction that people draw from news has to do with a sense of sharing stories that link us to our communities. Merely placing a story in a prominent position on a newspaper or on a website might make it more interesting because its prominence indicates its likelihood to be a common point of reference.

News readers' preferences may differ in public and private situations, when made quickly or reflectively. Even when preferences seem impulsive, impulses can be primed by different types of environments. For instance, a person might make one type of magazine choice when checking out at a supermarket. But if that same person was asked to reflect on which magazines she would most like to read, she could answer differently. As Baker points out, we often have preferences about preferences. We might prefer to make different sorts of media choices than we often do in our typical environments. We may also prefer that our media environment would be altered so we would have different kinds of choices more readily available.

Market research does not provide a way to tackle these complexities or tell us which kind of preferences are the most "democratic." Researchers employed to figure out what kind of media people would prefer in their own ideal media environment could come up with very different findings than those investigating present market preferences. In fact, market researchers themselves have been puzzled by findings that news readers want seemingly contradictory things—stories with greater depth and shorter stories.[93] Perhaps reflective situations lead to a desire for greater depth and more hurried choices lead to a desire for brevity. Granting such complexity to consumer preferences means there is much at stake in deciding the legitimate means through which individuals can identify their preferences. Baker argues, "No neutral or logical principle indicates that one or another identification or measure of preferences is more accurate, legitimate or 'real.' Society's (or an analyst's) determination about which expressions to credit depends on the purpose of the identification and measurement. The choice can always be, and often is, contested. That is the stuff of politics."[94] Democratic politics is not only a matter of abiding by popular preferences, but also a contest over the settings and conditions in which citizens form and express their preferences.

• • •

As discussed in the previous chapter, there are many connections between popular forms of journalism and political culture. Several historians have argued that changes in dominant forms of journalism in the past can be understood, at least partly, as reactions to changes in political structures, habits, and norms. Richard Kaplan, for instance, demonstrates that the rise of the ideal of objectivity and the decline of the partisan press in the early twentieth century were at least partially a reflection of the waning influence that political parties had during this period.[95] Hallin shows that one of the conditions that allowed a high-modern style of journalism to flourish during the post–World War II period was a "liberal consensus" in which political and social elites in the United States shared a broad consensus over basic liberal values and Keynesian economic assumptions.[96] Similarly, the movement away from high modernism and toward market-driven journalism reflects some of the larger changes that were happening in U.S. political culture at the time.

Market-driven journalism came about at the same time as the ascendancy of what social critics and historians have called "neoliberalism" or "market fundamentalism."[97] It was a period characterized by an increasing faith in markets as the proper arbiter of all areas of social life. Political leaders from Republicans to New Democrats converged around a new consensus, quite distinct from the postwar liberal consensus, that government should prioritize the expansion of unencumbered markets and policy shifted toward support for deregulation, privatization, and the retrenchment of the welfare state. Political leaders increasingly embraced the model of the market and market competition as an almost universal template for governing social institutions. Beyond ruling elites, neoliberalism also took hold of the popular imagination, as the image of market competition as the paragon of democracy won over many hearts and minds. Thomas Frank captures this spirit and ideology with the term *market populism,* which he describes as the prevailing sense that "in addition to being mediums of exchange, markets are mediums of consent. With their mechanisms of supply and demand, poll and focus group, superstore and Internet, markets manage to express the popular will more articulately and meaningfully than do mere elections. By their very nature markets confer democratic legitimacy, markets bring down the pompous and the snooty, markets look out for the interests of the little guy, markets give us what we want."[98] This milieu celebrated freedom manifested through individual choice in a marketplace, and these sentiments combined with other attacks discussed in the last chapter on U.S. journalism's posture of social responsibility and professionalism. The theory of social responsibility posited that news organizations had a duty to support the public interest, something beyond their role as profit-seeking businesses. Yet with market populism in the air, the idea of professionals striving for a responsibility that went beyond fulfilling consumer demand became suspiciously elitist and paternalistic. For proponents of market-driven journalism, there were plenty of rhetorical resources to disparage claims that professionals should have the authority to decide what to put on the news agenda and how it should be presented.

These overarching trends in U.S. culture and politics set the stage for a shift away from journalism's high modernism, but, as this chapter illustrates, actors within the news industry gave market-driven journalism its specific form. Market researchers did not simply listen to "what readers wanted" in news; they and their allies in news management positions constructed a particular story about news audiences. From Ruth Clark's landmark research report onward, the audience image adopted by market-driven journalism's culture of production was of readers as consumers seeking self-gratification. These consumers wanted more health, sports, fashion, and consumer news, as well as entertainment and "happy" news. They had not turned away from politics and public life entirely, but their interest in these domains was limited. News consumers mostly wanted quick and easy-to-follow updates when it came to politics and current affairs. Perhaps not so coincidentally, this image of the audience happened to fit well with advertisers' desires for content conducive to their own marketing goals. It also justified a shift in power in the newsroom. Because professional journalists did not understand the needs of contemporary readers, executives and managers had reason to grab the reins and take more control.

Market-driven journalism did not mean that newspapers stopped covering politics or social controversy. As newspapers grew more profitable in the early

1980s, they also grew in average size—from 19.8 pages of editorial content in 1970 to 32.4 pages in 1986.[99] Bogart argues that national and world news coverage actually expanded somewhat during this period, though this kind of news became a smaller portion of the pie, as lifestyle news and other types of news in vogue with market-driven journalism grew at a much higher rate. Perhaps the more important consequence of the market-driven journalism movement is that it absorbed most of the energy directed toward trying to mobilize a larger readership. Other alternatives to high-modern journalism that had been building steam in the late 1960s and early 1970s—critical professionalism, new journalism, reporter activism—lost their momentum.

In short, market-driven journalism came out of a culture of production that took hold at the executive and management levels of much of the U.S. newspaper industry in response to the readership problem of the 1970s. The changes inspired by this movement were not simply responses to what consumers wanted; the movement played an essential role in the construction of a particular image of the news audience. Newspapers then invested resources to mobilize the very audience that marketers depicted. In other sectors of the commercial news world, other images of the news audience and strategies for mobilizing them would emerge. The next chapter turns to another group of news outlets—twenty-four-hour cable news channels—that have also tried to heed the call of audience desires. Cable news producers, however, have heard something quite different than newspapers in these demands.

CHAPTER 3

The Cable News Wars

Another Approach to Popularizing Commercial News

> Television is the great democracy where people vote with their eyes.
>
> —Reese Schonfeld, first president of CNN

On January 31, 2014, Bill O'Reilly told his viewers on *The Factor* just why President Obama had agreed to an interview with him the next day, Super Bowl Sunday. As O'Reilly explained, "Although the President sometimes criticizes Fox News, he knows the power of it. The Public Policy Polling Group recently surveyed registered voters about who they trust in TV news. Fox News won by a landslide." Peter Hart, writing for the left-leaning media watchdog group Fairness and Accuracy in Reporting, was quick to point out something obscured by O'Reilly's boast about public trust in Fox. Indeed, Hart agreed, the poll cited by O'Reilly found that more respondents named Fox News as their most trusted news source than any other source. Yet O'Reilly had neglected to mention that Fox News had also been named more frequently than any other news source as respondents' "least trusted" source.

Cable news can be a puzzling genre. It straddles a line between a "traditional" news format and something new. Given that much discussion about the future of news pivots on a distinction between mass-media news models and emerging forms in a new media landscape, where does cable news fit? Is it a harbinger of things to come in a fragmented media environment? Or might it be the latest effort of a more traditional news model trying to find relevance in a changing environment through modest reform? Like most of the legacy news outlets, the most popular cable news networks are all owned by major media conglomerates, they rely on professional journalists for much of their news gathering, and they share some common textual and aesthetic features with local television news and network news—from frequent shots of anchors behind desks to the use of many of the same kinds of sound bites and live shots.[1] Cable news networks have not entirely forsaken the ideology of high-modern journalism. Although some critics see cable news as an arena for partisan slant and rancor, for the time being at least the major cable news networks—CNN, MSNBC, Fox News—make some claim to offer nonbiased news coverage outside of specific commentary-based programs.[2] Even Fox News, the pioneer of partisan branding in cable, still clings defiantly to its slogan of "fair and balanced."

In other respects, cable news networks have been adopting a range of approaches to telling stories about public life that mark a pointed contrast with broadcast journalism's high-modern norms. Cable as a medium is not simply a new format with more time for news than broadcast television; cable news has been articulated to different programming strategies and different conceptions of audiences.[3] Broadcasters' news divisions come from a legacy in which news programming explicitly served as a public service to help satisfy FCC requirements that station licensees serve the public interest. Cable news does not have such a legacy, and profit making has always been its primary objective. As many television scholars have argued, the multichannel environment of cable has meant a potential for fracturing the monolithic "mass" audience, associated with the heyday of network television, into a system that focuses on targeting distinct niches.[4] As I will explore in more detail later, claims that cable news has given way entirely to strategies based on partisan appeal oversimplify the distinctiveness of cable news.

Yet even from the first days of CNN, cable news primarily targeted a niche audience. This is the group of heavy-news watchers—a group sometimes referred to as "news junkies."[5] The boundaries of this group have never been tightly fixed, and cable news has been recruiting news junkies as much as it has been catering to them. The portion of U.S. residents who watch cable news is not small. A 2010 study reported by the Pew Research Center study found that 39 percent of U.S. residents say they "regularly get news from a cable channel."[6] As Pew's documentation of growth and flux in the makeup of the cable audience indicates, these viewers were not simply waiting for cable news to appear. Since the late 1990s, the cable news audience has become more diverse and significantly larger than during CNN's first decade and a half. Even while the Internet has introduced much more competition—especially competition for cable news' long-standing forte of breaking news—the median size of the prime-time cable news audience (for CNN, Fox News, and MSNBC) climbed up until 2008.

While cable news has borrowed conventions from other news formats, it has also been cultivating its own forms of storytelling, some of which are in pointed opposition to the objective style that characterized twentieth-century print and broadcast journalism.[7] The differences between cable news and the norms of journalism's high-modern period have grown greatly since the beginning of the "cable news wars." The cable news wars began in 1996 when MSNBC and Fox News launched, challenging CNN as its first serious competitors in the U.S. market and stirring up a fight for ratings among the networks that led to programming innovations. The competition among these cable networks' prime-time programming has been most intense, and it has been in this area where differences between the presentation style of network news and cable news have come to the fore. Prime time cable hosts such as Bill O'Reilly, Sean Hannity, Lou Dobbs, and Rachel Maddow have crafted their personae in stark contrast to network news anchors. Not only are they more opinionated, but they also convey attitude and express emotion on a far wider spectrum than the broadcast stars of journalism's high-modern period. Even CNN's Anderson Cooper, who eschews the partisan identity often associated with MSNBC and Fox News, is promoted by CNN as a "fast-moving, surprising and provocative alternative to the typical network evening newscast."[8]

Arguably, cable news has been as influential of a force on U.S. political culture as new media formats such as blogs or Twitter. This chapter explores how cable news came to be a genre for telling stories about public life and current events with a unique set of conventions and stylistic emphases. Cable news, in a sense, has brought its own "media logic" to bear on U.S. politics—using this term to refer to how cable news provides a lens for making sense of politics that reflects a set of values and emphases.[9] The logic of cable news exceeds its own programming, as political campaigns, government officials, and other actors have adapted some of their own routines to perform on the terrain of cable news. The media logic of cable news naturalizes particular assumptions about politics, mostly important assumptions about wherein lies the drama, joy, and intrigue of political life. This chapter also examines that logic and the shared common sense about audiences and their desires that pervade cable news' culture of production.

The unique characteristics of the genre have become most pronounced during the prime-time programming of the three major U.S. cable news networks. At the time of this writing, the three networks seem to have settled on distinct identities in terms of ideological perspectives. Fox is more welcoming to conservative views, MSNBC supports mainstream Democratic to more progressive views, and CNN continues to claim to differentiate itself from its competitors through offering more balanced perspectives. Yet this apparent clarity among a spectrum of political identities has come into focus only since the late 2000s; its durability for the future is uncertain. While each network has sought to differentiate itself from the competition, the networks have come to share assumptions about what types of techniques and strategies they can use to raise their ratings and make their news more popular with desirable audiences. Indeed, each cable network plays its hand a bit differently, but they have mostly come to agree on the rules of the game and what is in the deck. This chapter analyzes the assumptions about winning audiences that have come to be pervasive among cable news decision makers. These shared assumptions manifest themselves in what I am calling the "industry popular," the discourse that has developed among cable news insiders structuring conversations about audience desire and what makes news popular.

Making Sense of Cable Chatter

While cable news networks have succeeded in becoming profitable and powerful political venues, they have also become frequent objects of disdain among media critics, politicians, and satirists. Many question whether the kind of journalism associated with the cable news wars contributes to healthy democracy. As the competition among the networks heated up, audiences grew, but cable news also increasingly faced criticism associating it with shouting matches, fearmongering, partisan vitriol, and sensationalism. Early in his presidency, Barack Obama singled out cable news as a form of media harmful to public discourse, referring to "cable chatter" and making comparisons between cable news and the staging of professional wrestling.[10] In the *American Journalism Review,* Paul Farhi has described the "cable news effect" as focusing the news agenda around one or two prominent stories of the day, often pertaining to political gaffes or partisan accusations. During political campaigns, Farhi says, cable news exerts its "biggest influence on the rest of the media. . . . Cable's intense and often immediate coverage of the day's big controversy forces candidates to fire back, which then compels the rest of the media to cover the response."[11]

Perhaps no one has been a more relentless critic of cable news than Jon Stewart, former host of Comedy Central's *The Daily Show.* Stewart found endless fodder for his brand of critical satire not only on Fox News but also on CNN and MSNBC. Stewart and his colleagues parodied not only particular cable hosts and personalities but also the style, tone, and patterned tropes of cable news coverage. Speaking to millions of viewers each episode, *The Daily Show,* now hosted by Trevor Noah, continually criticizes cable news for bolstering a fear-ridden and broken political discourse while failing as journalists to contribute a greater understanding of public issues. In a stunning 2004 rebuke, Stewart appeared on CNN's *Crossfire,* turning away from his typically humorous posture and pleading with the hosts to stop their program because it was "hurting America." Months after Stewart's appearance, *Crossfire* was canceled, and then–CNN president Jonathan Klein said he agreed "wholeheartedly with Jon Stewart's overall premise."[12] Yet *Crossfire*'s shouting-match format was only one of *The Daily Show*'s targets, and *Crossfire* itself was temporarily revived by CNN in 2013.

The popularity of *The Daily Show* suggests many people share frustrations with cable news and the political culture that it helps to shape. Why, then, has a style of journalism so widely criticized, even ridiculed, become so dominant on cable? There are, surely, many influences that have helped shape the texture of cable news programming. Yet to have an impact on cable news production, these factors have to work their influence through a key bottleneck in the circuit of culture—the institutional settings where a relatively small group of people are responsible for managing the cable news networks. This group has control over scarce resources necessary to produce, promote, and distribute cable news. My argument in this chapter is that cable news' culture of production has settled on a rather narrow vision of what it should be and what features can make it appealing to audiences. Other actors—such as audiences, advertisers, and political groups—clearly exert pressure to push news production in certain directions. Still, the influence of such pressures is filtered through the way the producers interpret and formulate their responses to these other actors.

The development of the culture of cable news production offers a way to think about why cable stations have not attempted more diverse and creative strategies for attracting news audiences. At the same time, this perspective helps to demonstrate how cable news producers have introduced a unique vision of how to popularize news, one that differs substantially from the market-driven newspaper movement. Both cable news producers and advocates of market-driven newspapers share a commitment to commercial imperatives and an emphasis on pleasing and attracting audiences. Both react against some of the ideals of high-modern journalism. Yet cable news producers and market-driven newspaper advocates conceive of their audiences' desires quite differently. As discussed in chapter 2, the market-driven newspaper movement has tended to see audiences as rational consumers, portraying them as self-interested readers seeking the most personal value from the time and money invested in news consumption. For market-driven newspaper advocates, potential readers are concerned primarily with getting an immediate, pragmatic value out of the news. The trend toward "news you can use" epitomizes this outlook on readers' desires, but this conception of the news audience has also pushed newspapers toward emphasizing other consumer conveniences such as light entertainment and amusement and short news summaries.

In contrast, efforts to popularize cable news have focused on hailing audiences not as parsimonious and calculating consumers but rather as "obsessive" viewers. Cable news places a greater emphasis on orchestrating news spectacles and presenting them in ways intended to evoke a compelling sense that viewers *need* to stay tuned to an urgent stream of information and commentary, even without an instrumental purpose for watching. The marketing approach to newspapers called on editors to cede their professional power and respond to the kinds of audience preferences revealed through surveys and focus groups. Such research has played a significantly less central role in justifying cable programming decisions than it has for market-driven newspapers. Instead, cable news has followed more closely to the intuitions of guru figures, including high-profile anchors and executives such as Fox New president Roger Ailes and Rick Kaplan, who served at different times as the president of CNN/U.S. and MSNBC.

Cable news has also elevated certain anchors and pundits to the status of stars and populist champions. These personalities have been cast as focal points for drawing audiences toward news programs to witness, or experience vicariously, emotional displays and ideological confrontations. So while newspapers weakened the editorial voice and autonomy of professional journalists to cater to popular interest as represented by market research, cable news turned toward amplifying the voices of particular kinds of news personalities.

In the sections that follow, I first offer a brief historical overview of the rise of cable news up to the start of the cable news wars. This section looks at how CNN established an approach to twenty-four-hour news programming that stuck close to many high-modern principles while the network fought to maintain its monopolistic position as the only cable news channel. That era ended in 1996, the year MSNBC and Fox News both launched. They did so on the heels of a news ratings bonanza spurred by the O. J. Simpson trial. With new competitors in the market, a ratings war began, and each network started seeking new programming strategies and tactics for keeping viewers, especially during times when there seemed to be no major breaking news events. The rest of the chapter looks at the cable news landscape since 1996. Through examining how cable news insiders have described their perceptions of what audiences want out of this genre, I highlight several themes that have come to define the industry popular for cable news.

CNN and the Birth of Cable News

One of cable news' origin stories centers on visionary individuals who launched CNN, the first all-news cable network. In his autobiography, Ted Turner tells a triumphant tale of the founding of CNN as a feat of entrepreneurial vision and gumption overcoming the disbelief of establishment media types. Turner had inherited a billboard company from his father and already earned a reputation as a cable pioneer in the late 1970s. Using satellites to transmit content from his Atlanta-based superstation to local cable operators across the United States, Turner had made millions working with the cable industry. Even with this track record, however, Turner believed his plan to create a twenty-four-hour news station was not taken seriously by the media establishment. The high cost of television news gathering, Turner's lack of experience in journalism, and his desire for an Atlanta-based headquarters (rather than the more conventional choices of New York or Washington, D.C.) made his plan sound highly improbable to experienced news executives. According to CNN's first president, Reese Schonfeld, Turner himself had no interest in news when he started CNN; he simply thought there was more money to be made in cable for news than in sports, movies, or entertainment because they had already been developed.[13]

For those more inclined to see structures rather than "great people" as the driving forces of history, twenty-four-hour cable news was something bound to appear with or without Ted Turner or Reese Schonfeld.[14] Given the technological, economic, and regulatory environment of the late 1970s and 1980s, it might have been inevitable that an all-news cable network would have arisen. By the late 1970s, cable systems were rapidly expanding, and operators needed more original programming. An all-news format seemed like an obvious choice to fill this airtime, especially as so many local television news programs—many relying heavily on marketing consultants—had proved to be quite profitable.[15] Local news programming was the source for a large percentage of many affiliates' profits. Turner himself sought assurance that no other media company was planning to launch a commercial cable news channel before he began to invest in CNN.[16]

Whatever the likelihood that another individual or company would have launched an all-news channel, once CNN got there first it was in a special position to shape what cable news would become. From 1980 to the launch of MSNBC in 1996, no competing all-news channels seriously challenged CNN's U.S. monopoly. CNN fought to keep it that way.

The only significant threat to CNN's position during this period came from a joint venture backed by ABC and Westinghouse. These two large companies made plans to work together to launch two rolling cable news channels. The first of these to launch was the Satellite News Channel, debuting in June 1982. SNC produced an eighteen-minute "news wheel," continuously cycling through the top stories of the day or hour. The second channel, which never actually made it onto television, would have been a more open news format, similar to CNN. Not only were these stations backed by financial giants that already had a vast news infrastructure—Westinghouse ran a twenty-four-hour radio news service in addition to ABC's television news—but they were courting cable operators by offering to give their programming away for free. CNN was charging fifteen cents per month per subscriber, a small but significant fee.

CNN's response to SNC reveals that the tactics for dominance in cable competition are often far removed from winning viewers' affection. Cable channels compete first over rights to gain availability to viewers. As CNN executives learned about plans for SNC, they scrambled to create their own news-wheel channel, initially called CNN2 (which later became Headline News).[17] CNN also set a discounted pricing system, giving cable operators an incentive to run both of their channels. The choice both entities made to run a headline-news format suggests they shared some of the same inklings about news audiences as the founders of *USA Today* and many of the market-driven newspaper advocates. The news-wheel approach was motivated by an image of news audiences as busy consumers wanting digestible bits of information. An expensive ad campaign branded SNC as "the Non-Stop News Machine." Many of the ads proclaimed, "Give us 18 minutes. We'll give you the world."[18] Such ads offered up the image of a news service and an impersonal machine programming to service viewers' instrumental needs. This type of promotion in no way forecast the personality-driven style of cable news that would later become its hallmark during the ratings wars.

CNN defeated SNC, not by proving itself more capable of satisfying audience desires, but through eliminating the competition. Settling an antitrust suit, CNN agreed to pay ABC and Westinghouse twenty-five million dollars to get out of the cable news business.[19] With the cable wires cleared of a competing news channel, this meant that the programming strategies adopted by CNN would define cable news, at least in the United States, for the first decade and a half of its existence.

The challenge of programming twenty-four-hour television news was significant. CNN producers were working without any one model to guide them. How would they fill all this time with television news? What styles of reporting and programming would the network rely upon? To answer these questions, CNN tapped into ideas from various news genres, especially all-news radio.

First and foremost, however, they accepted the basic ideals of high-modern journalism as the foundation of the CNN brand.

At the same time as U.S. newspapers and local news broadcasters were turning to marketing consultants and moving away from high-modern journalism, Turner sought to brand CNN as an innovative venue for a quite traditional form of news. He claimed to have done no market research prior to the launch of CNN, quipping that "Henry Ford didn't need focus groups to tell him that people would prefer inexpensive, dependable automobiles over horses."[20] He explained his vision of CNN's journalistic ethos by contrast with other television news sources: "While the networks and local news stations seemed to follow a 'if it bleeds, it leads,' rule centering their broadcast on murders, car wrecks, disasters, and the like, I wanted us to do more serious journalism and to go deeper into the most important issues of the day. I also wanted to present news in an unbiased fashion. . . . Schonfeld and I decided that on CNN, news would be the star, not our on-air people."[21] Turner's words, of course, need to be taken with a grain of salt. Roger Ailes and Fox executives too would later lay claim to following certain professional journalistic norms, namely, fairness and balance. Still, while Fox's strategic deviation from high-modern norms was obvious and provocative, CNN mostly sought to build its reputation by sticking quite close to traditional conceptions of objective journalism. Staking a claim to high-modern news values—rather than attempting to redefine them as Fox would do—was central to CNN's brand identity. Establishing CNN's credibility relative to conventional standards was perhaps more important for building relationships with potential sources and news makers than viewers. Turner and Schonfeld would regularly disparage the major network newscasts as irresponsible in public interviews; Schonfeld told one interviewer that he called the broadcast networks "strip-miners of the mind" because "they pander to the worst instincts."[22] Yet CNN tried to hire talent from many of the same network news broadcasts they were criticizing, even attempting to recruit Walter Cronkite.[23]

One obvious reason for CNN to adopt the mantra "news is the star" (later adopted as a slogan by al-Jazeera America) was because the network could not afford to hire many of the well-known news reporters and anchors they initially sought. They did hire Bernard Shaw, who had worked for CBS and ABC, and Daniel Schorr, who had worked for CBS and National Public Radio. Yet an important part of CNN's initial business model was to pay their personnel significantly less than the networks; not only their stars but also CNN's non-unionized workforce as a whole received lower pay than those working for other television news operations.[24] In significant respects, CNN's news-is-the-star branding indeed steered it toward a mode of news storytelling that put less emphasis on anchors than network news. Larry Smith conducted a content analysis comparing coverage of the 1988 national party conventions by CNN and all the broadcast networks. Smith's findings suggested that CNN indeed was embodying its ideal at this point. Compared with each of the broadcast networks, CNN devoted significantly less time to anchors and organized their narrative around an "event-centered framework rather than a 'talent-centered' one."[25] Such an approach would be dramatically reversed later on.

Until the late 1990s, CNN fashioned much of its ordinary programming as a television wire service, summarizing news stories in an hour cycle and updating them throughout the day.[26] A conventional "hard news" orientation helped CNN gain legitimacy with policy makers, so this kind of news remained the network's major programming emphasis, though it devoted time to sports, finance, and talk programming as well. Schonfeld described one of CNN's major strategies as "counter-programming," meaning CNN would offer something different from what was on other channels during the same time slot.[27] For instance, the broadcast networks were airing national news at the 7:00 p.m. hour, so CNN would offer national news at 6:00 p.m. and business news at 7:00 p.m. They did not have to offer the most popular type of news programming during a particular hour; they just needed to pick off a sufficient audience for their ratings to look respectable.

Some of CNN's programming choices showed its producers were drawing on similar perceptions of news audiences as the market-driven journalism movement. In a quest for "happy news," CNN featured periodic segments called "People & Places." The network dipped into the news-you-can-use motif with segments on cooking and a feature offering relationship advice from Dr. Joyce Brothers. Many of these features were run as segments embedded within CNN's regular news cycle, but it also set aside regular time specifically for shows focusing on sports news, financial news, and late-night talk shows. CNN also drew on perceptions about audiences stemming from radio and television talk show programming. Well-known pundits such as Barry Goldwater, Phyllis Schlafly, Ralph Nader, and Bob Novak were hired as CNN editorialists.[28] Though these voices appeared regularly, CNN maintained a sharp line between its news programming and editorializing.[29] One of CNN's most distinctive early programs was the political debate program *Crossfire,* which began in 1982. Yet *Crossfire* remained an anomaly unique from the bulk of CNN's pre-1996 programming. On the whole, CNN's pundits were guests, not hosts, and they filled only a small portion of the schedule. In 1985 CNN hired radio talk show host, and *USA Today* columnist, Larry King. *Larry King Live* became CNN's highest-rated program on a consistent basis. Despite King's impressive ratings, CNN executives did not rush to fill more airtime with the talk show formula, as they were concerned too much talk programming could damage CNN's reputation as a serious news outlet.[30]

CNN found ratings gold in another type of news—nonstop coverage of breaking events. Even in its early days, when its news-gathering capacity was vastly outmatched by the networks, CNN leveraged its advantage of being able to devote unrestricted airtime to coverage of live events. By the mid-1980s, as cable's reach had expanded and CNN was available in millions of homes, it had become clear that covering live events was the network's forte. In October 1987, CNN achieved its highest ratings yet by devoting itself to nearly nonstop coverage of the multiple-day rescue of "Baby Jessica" McClure, who had fallen down a twenty-two-foot well in Midland, Texas.[31] CNN's ratings spiked during the rescue. Some media critics saw this as a breakthrough for the network, though CNN already had a clear record of spikes around coverage of major breaking events, such as the hijacking of TWA Flight 847 and the Challenger space shuttle explosion in 1986.[32] CNN was banking on the appeal of "liveness," which TV scholars have discussed as one of the medium's key aesthetic values.[33] CNN's focus on breaking news and finding ways to inventively fill airtime with such events even when little new information was coming in became the network's greatest innovation. One telling, if hyperbolic, description of CNN's influence was that the network "redefined news as something that *had* happened to something that *is* happening."[34]

There was a problem, however, with depending on breaking events for ratings. When major events happened, CNN's ratings would soar. But without major news stories breaking, it would lose most of these viewers. This became known as "the CNN problem." The problem came most clearly into focus after the first Gulf War in 1991. The first Gulf War was a watershed moment for CNN. During the first few hours of the U.S.-led invasion, CNN was the only network with a correspondent reporting live from Baghdad. At certain times during the war, CNN was being watched by more people than were watching any other channel—broadcast or cable. Yet after the war, their ratings dipped back below prewar levels—with an average daily rating a fraction of what it had been during the war.[35]

Given the environment CNN was operating in during the early and mid-1990s, the CNN problem was not as dire as it might seem. The network, indeed, made limited efforts to develop more distinctive programs.[36] Still, though lower ratings on most days meant that CNN could not sell a very large audience to advertisers, its regular audience did have qualities that made it especially appealing to certain advertisers. CNN attracted a demographic that advertisers found otherwise hard to reach: older affluent males. Some advertisers were willing to pay premium prices because CNN appeared to be building trust among this group of men who were otherwise thought to not watch much television.[37] But more important, advertising revenue was only part of CNN's financial success. CNN's spikes during times of crisis led to a perception of broad consumer demand. This allowed CNN wide access to basic-cable tiers and gave it leverage to collect handsome subscriber fees from a large base. Even while CNN's management was concerned about its relatively low ratings outside of breaking events, the network was quite profitable. The year 1995 was an especially good one for CNN's ratings, with the O. J. Simpson trial a leading focal point. In fact, all-news cable was proving so profitable that several new entrants prepared to jump into the ring. The next year would bring remarkable change to the cable news landscape.

Shaking Up Cable News

If Ted Turner was the personality most associated with the first fifteen years of cable news, the last couple of decades have belonged to Fox News president Roger Ailes. Ailes has not had the same penchant for personal publicity as Turner, yet several writers and journalists have named him as a media mastermind, crediting him with upending the television news business, changing the landscape of U.S. political culture, and steering the Republican Party toward right-wing, media-driven populism.[38] Ailes got his start on television as a producer for *The Mike Douglas Show,* but he earned his national reputation as a media consultant for Richard Nixon in 1968. In the decades that followed, Ailes served in different capacities as a media consultant for numerous right-leaning politicians and became a key figure in a short-lived attempt to create a right-wing television news service in the mid-1970s. Later, Ailes enjoyed a stint as a Broadway producer. Yet it was through his work with conservative politicians that Ailes's televisual instincts became legendary. He was even shadowed for months by actor Richard Gere to prepare for a role in the 1986 film *Power* about the seedy world of political consultants. As Ailes's well-studied biographer Gabriel Sherman documents, one of his greatest talents has long been mobilizing white working-class resentment. In 1993 Ailes claimed to have left political campaigning and consulting for good and became president of NBC's new business news network CNBC, and he was slated to head up a new NBC-owned cable network, America's Talking. When NBC agreed to a deal with Microsoft to create MSNBC, Ailes discovered NBC executives did not want him associated with the new network. Just then, Rupert Murdoch was looking for someone to head his new news network, Fox News.

Three major events changed the map of U.S. cable news in 1996. CNN, along with the rest of the Turner Broadcasting System, was acquired by megaconglomerate Time Warner. MSNBC and Fox News both launched that same year, ending CNN's monopolistic reign. ABC had also been considering launching its own all-news cable network, though it was apparently dissuaded from doing so as Rupert Murdoch started paying hefty fees for access to cable subscribers. To many observers, MSNBC seemed to be the new entrant that should have given CNN the most worry. NBC, of course, already had a well-established television news division. And its partner Microsoft seemed capable of propelling MSNBC into the vanguard at the start of an era of digital convergence.

One advantage that CNN held over both the new entrants was that it was already available in more than sixty-five million homes. The opening salvos of the cable news wars would not be about winning over viewers' hearts and minds, or courting advertisers or news makers; the competition for cable access came first. Backed by the fortunes of Rupert Murdoch's News Corporation, Fox relied on an unorthodox tactic for gaining subscribers. Instead of charging cable operators a fee per subscriber, as was customary in the business, Fox offered "incentive payments," paying cable operators for access to subscribers. Fox's payments were rumored to be a remarkable figure—ten dollars or more per subscriber.[39] The incentive payments likely totaled significantly more than the initial budget of eighty to one hundred million dollars for the newsroom and production expenses estimated for the network's first year.[40]

News Corporation drew on its political capital, as well its deep pockets, to make sure that Fox News would be available to cable subscribers. Time Warner Cable owned the cable system serving most of New York City. Fox and MSNBC both desperately wanted access to New York City, but to do so they had to enter into complex negotiations with Time Warner Cable. According to Sherman, Time Warner Cable had initially indicated that it would allow both Fox and MSNBC a slot on the New York system. Negotiations became more complicated, however, and Time Warner executives, awaiting FCC approval of the merger with Turner Broadcasting, made a move to "let [FCC] regulators look tough and claim credit for busting CNN's cable news monopoly" by forcing them to carry a CNN competitor.[41] Yet as this process played out, Time Warner Cable decided it was going to offer a spot only to MSNBC and not to Fox. Murdoch was incensed and waged a powerful effort to make Fox News available in New York, including leveraging his political connections with Mayor Rudolph

Giuliani. The Giuliani administration tried to force a deal. He suggested that he would have turned one of the city's public, educational, and government access channels over to Fox News if the network was not otherwise offered carriage. A federal judge issued an injunction prohibiting Giuliani from appropriating PEG channels for Fox News, but Time Warner eventually agreed to carry News Corporation's Fox News as part of a deal between two conglomerates over the sale of a satellite operation company.[42]

Before their launch dates, MSNBC and Fox eventually managed to secure access to tens of millions of homes. Media reporters and cable news executives began to frame the competition among the networks as the "cable news wars."[43] Some of this framing was fueled by personal animosities. Ted Turner and Rupurt Murdoch had exchanged barbs, with Murdoch accusing CNN of liberal bias. Turner expressed contempt for News Corporation's tabloid-driven media empire, vowing that CNN would beat Fox News and squish Murdoch "like a bug."[44] While the "cable news wars" refrain appeared time and again in media reports about the industry, it has never been clear to what extent the cable news networks have actually been competing over the same viewers. From the late 1990s to early 2000s, the audiences grew for each of the networks, in part because of the expansion of cable.[45] The attacks of September 11th and the early years of the war in Afghanistan also seemed to boost ratings, not only during peak moments but also through setting a higher baseline of attention.[46]

While all the cable news networks were expanding their viewership in the early 2000s, Fox was racing ahead of the competition. By June 2002, Fox News was regularly beating CNN as the top-rated cable news channel, even though Fox was available in millions fewer homes. As news reports of Fox's rating victory broke, CNN spokespeople were quick to point out that CNN still had many more total viewers than Fox. Roger Ailes quipped back, saying he couldn't believe that CNN was boasting that "they have the larger number of disaffected viewers."[47] CNN, indeed, had more total unique viewers each month, but Fox had a higher average rating because its viewers stayed tuned in for much longer. The picture emerging from the ratings patterns was that Fox was doing something different that kept hold of its viewers' attention in ways that CNN and MSNBC were not. It was particularly during moments when there were no major breaking news events that Fox was trumping the other networks so handily, suggesting that perhaps the upstart network was finding a solution to the CNN problem. Executives at CNN and MSNBC were clearly taking notice. A new understanding of cable news was emerging among all the major players—any network that wanted to gain viewers, especially in prime time, had to do things differently. The networks were all trying to figure out what it was that viewers now wanted. Fox News represented Roger Ailes's hypothesis. With an eye on Fox's stunning growth, CNN and MSNBC were trying to come up with their own answers to this perennial question.

The Industry Popular of the Cable News Wars

Even if the cable news networks were not actually locked in a zero-sum game for the same viewers and profits, the cable news wars worked as a powerful framing device that influenced how each of the networks sought to mobilize their audiences. This frame brought the cable news networks together on a field of competition. It created opportunities for the networks to differentiate themselves from each other, while at the same time suggesting they were playing the same game, with more or less the same rule book. In this context, cable news started to define itself as a genre, and this genre looked quite different from the televisual news-wire vision that had served as the guiding template during CNN's monopoly era. While cable news continued to emphasize live, breaking events, Fox News and MSNBC at first, joined later by CNN, began building new programming strategies, especially during prime time.

The rest of this chapter analyzes how the cable news networks have been answering the question of how to bring audiences to their prime-time programming. I do so by examining a discourse I am calling the "industry popular" for cable news. By this, I am referring to the industry's patterned ways of speaking about cable news audiences and their desires. This discourse structures a field of possibilities for programming techniques and strategies recognized as viable options for appealing to cable viewers. It also feeds into how the networks fashion their brand identities.

The industry popular represents a kind of industrial common sense—a set of assumptions that is not entirely stagnant but helps stabilize the possibilities of the genre. It is an element of cultures of production that sustain the recognizability of popular genres. There is an industry popular for sitcoms, dramas, game shows, and reality show competitions, just as there is for cable news. Conventional assumptions about these genres indeed change over time, and there will always be deviations from the established norms. The assumptions of the industry popular are reflected not only in the ways cable news executives and producers speak but also in the larger discursive environment in which they are embedded. Media reporters and trade journalists, and frequently viewers and fans, draw on the industry popular to explain what is working, or not working, on cable news programs. While different people express a range of opinions on these questions, this discourse on cable news wars has settled into certain patterns. Particular assumptions about and schemata for conceptualizing the terrain of cable news and its popular audiences, which I explore below, have been repeated and encoded as the basic starting points of these conversations. These are the underlying assumptions and schemata that I analyze in the rest of this chapter. My approach follows from Gunther Kress's description of the functioning of discourse: "In relation to certain areas of social life that are of a particular significance to a social institution, [discourse] will produce a set of statements about that area that will define, delimit, and circumscribe what it is possible to say with respect to it, and how it is to be talked about."[48] Discourses do not have one-way relations to material realities, and I am not suggesting that the discourse about cable news and its audiences shapes reality entirely on its own. Ratings, for instance, have a force that is not entirely mutable by description. I do not want to de-emphasize the economic conditions that shape the context in which the industry popular is formed. Yet ratings, revenues, letters and e-mails from viewers, and every other form of feedback that producers encounter about the reception of their programs take on their meanings and impact only as their significance is interpreted by producers. The discourse of the industry popular provides the interpretative filter—though one that is itself provisional and open to change—for making sense of ratings and other forms of feedback on the success of cable news programming.[49]

One way to help understand cable's innovations in television news is through examining how cable news' culture of production has crafted specific "rules of the game" for competition and settled on certain notions of what qualities attract the news audiences they seek. Industry discourses tend to make sense of what kinds of programming might "work" with audiences through the lens of genre. Within the television production community as a whole, there is something akin to a meta-level industry popular encompassing the industry's common sense about what kinds of genres and formats might have popular appeal in the first place. This meta-level industry popular may also specify a style, or range of styles, associated with popularity across genres. One example of thinking about the industry popular at this level is television scholar John Caldwell's claim that in the 1980s, television producers began to understand their medium through a new framework, one that he calls "televisuality." Caldwell argues that with the rise of cable, the introduction of new digital technologies, and other broad cultural changes starting in the 1980s, mainstream U.S. television producers moved from "a framework that approached broadcasting primarily as a form of word-based rhetoric and transmission" to "a visually based mythology, framework, and aesthetic based on extreme self-consciousness of style."[50]

To understand insiders' assumptions about the possibilities for popularizing cable news, I searched through hundreds of articles describing the competition among cable news in trade and professional journals, such as *Broadcasting & Cable*, *Advertising Age*, and the *Columbia Journalism Review;* in the media pages of major newspapers, such as the *New York Times* and *Christian Science Monitor;* and in biographical and autobiographical accounts written by cable news insiders. I organized the repeated patterns that emerged within this discourse into four thematic clusters: creating anchor star power, infusing opinion or attitude into news, pursuing niche demographics, and popularizing content or visual style.[51] What these themes share in common with each other is a movement away from thinking about news audiences as the market-driven newspaper movement did, as practical, self-interested consumers. But they do not construct an image of cable news audiences as citizens drawn toward news because of a desire to participate in conversations on the public good. Instead, the cable news viewers are positioned as spectators captivated by personalities, opinionated fervor, and the sensational rush of news programming as drama and political theater.

Anchor Star Power

The discourse of the cable news wars takes for granted that star anchors are a pivotal dimension of the competitive struggle for winning over prime-time audiences; the story of the competition told through media reports and trade publications often places the search for stars at the center of the struggle for audiences.[52] Since the early days of broadcast news, certain anchors and reporters have, on occasion, achieved a starlike status. In his history of American television news, Steve Barkin argues that the celebrity status of anchors and reporters grew as television newsrooms became more profitable.[53] While promoting star anchors is not a practice unique to cable news, the cable news wars spurred a sharp increase of emphasis on the search for star anchors and reporters to draw audiences to news; cable news has also redefined the kinds of character and qualities associated with star anchors. The cable networks have proved themselves willing to sign multimillion-dollar celebrity anchor contracts and spend millions on promotional and branding campaigns revolving around anchors. Tellingly, top executives now talk publicly and enthusiastically about their investments in star anchors, no longer putting up any pretense that news is the only star.

One of the first moves made by MSNBC and Fox News to break into the cable news market was to hire well-known anchors. MSNBC was initially expected to be the more powerful of the two challengers to CNN because it had the star power of the *NBC Nightly News* staff at its command.[54] Walter Goodman, a TV critic for the *New York Times,* voiced his skepticism about MSNBC's first promotional tagline, "The Revolution Begins Here," by suggesting that it was news stars and not an innovative news style that MSNBC was promoting on cable, noting that the network was promoting NBC news stars "incessantly all day every day through the week; it was an NBC News iconography."[55] Yet MSNBC's strategy was somewhat hampered by the reluctance on the part of NBC's top broadcast anchors and reporters to appear on the fledgling network that started off with small audiences and an uncertain future.[56] As MSNBC later developed a branded identity oriented toward liberal and progressive politics (in terms of the mainstream U.S. political spectrum), many of NBC's broadcast stars sought to minimize their association with the liberal brand.[57] Upon its launch, Fox News also quickly entered the search for stars. One of their first major acquisitions of a well-known on-camera personality was Brit Hume, who had been a White House correspondent for ABC. Media reporters across the country saw Hume's agreement with Fox as a boost to its brand recognition and as a newsworthy event in itself.[58]

Star anchors and personalities have not just been a matter of importance for launching the new network; much of the competition for ratings among cable news networks has been understood as a battle of acquiring, leveraging, and creating star power. Competition over star anchors led to one of the most aggressive moments in the cable news wars when CNN hired away Paula Zahn from the Fox News channel. The nabbing of one of Fox's young anchors led to bitter recriminations from Fox, including a lawsuit Fox filed against Zahn for breach of contract that was quickly dismissed by a judge. Roger Ailes challenged the influence of Zahn's star power in a statement echoed throughout the world of media reporting, telling a *New York Times* reporter that in lieu of Zahn, "I could have put a dead raccoon on the air this year and gotten a better rating than last year. All our shows are up."[59] Soon Ailes executed his revenge against CNN by hiring away one of its own stars, Greta Van Susteren. Van Susteren's departure from CNN created even more publicity for Fox, as she publicly talked about corporate mismanagement at CNN and appeared on the cover of *People,* highlighting her new cosmetic surgery.[60]

Cable news networks have not only tried to bring in ready-made stars, but also invested their resources in grooming existing and new talent for the role. They have used several tactics to cultivate potential star anchors—giving them more prime-time airtime, featuring them in frequent promotions and advertisements, and having producers coach them and stage their performances to bring out the personal qualities believed to make them exceptionally appealing to audiences. One of the qualities producers have frequently tried to channel from potential star anchors has been a capacity for expressing populist indignation and anger. Much of the anger that has been channeled to produce cable news stars is directed against contemporary mediated political culture, an arguably ironic target. The most prominent example of this pattern is the development of Fox News' temperamental Bill O'Reilly. *The O'Reilly Factor* (1998–present) has been the highest-rated prime-time cable news program since the early 2000s. Signaling his own antipathy for the norms of media culture, O'Reilly proclaims his show to be "the no spin zone." While O'Reilly's initial ratings on Fox News proved disappointing, Ailes saw great potential in the former *Inside Edition* host. After some early floundering, Ailes reconfigured O'Reilly's program on Fox, moved him to a more prominent time slot, and coached him to become the populist star he soon became through what Ailes called an "evolutionary process."[61]

Attempts to position middle-aged white male anchors as populist heroes, often angry and fed up with political culture, have not been unique to Fox News. CNN helped transform Lou Dobbs from the wry but rather flat host of *Moneyline,* to which he had contributed since 1980, to an opinionated and unabashedly populist anchor of *Lou Dobbs Tonight* (2004–9).[62] Dobbs became widely known for his anti-immigration (and anti–free trade) rants, leading to protests against Dobbs's presence on CNN by Latino and immigrant rights groups.[63] The transparency of Dobbs's reincarnation for a ratings grab was obvious to many critics, as one *Dow Jones* reporter commented: "Because Dobbs is trying hard to craft an image and boost his show's ratings, it's never easy to know for sure where his television persona ends and his heartfelt beliefs actually begin."[64] MSNBC supported the transformation of Keith Olbermann from a somewhat quirky and charismatic sportscaster turned news anchor to the most vociferous cable news critic of the Bush administration (and critic of Bill O'Reilly).[65] Olbermann became host of what was the network's top-rated program to date. One danger of cultivating such stars is that such hot-blooded characters clash with bosses or turn toward extremes that start to worry networks about damaging the brand. Olbermann and Dobbs, along with Fox News superstar Glenn Beck, were released from their anchoring roles amid growing disputes between the stars and network management.

While women's presence in lead roles on cable news seems to be increasing somewhat since the start of the cable news wars, the genre's lead prime-time anchors have been disproportionately male. Yet there have been some attempts to position female anchors too as populist antianchors. CNN cast former NBC *Weekend Today* anchor Campbell Brown in such a role. When Brown was hired in 2008, then–CNN president Jonathan Klein described Brown's appeal as "common-sense journalism" that "wasn't built in a lab or concocted by consultants."[66] While Brown's persona was pitched as a contrast to what Klein referenced as the "histrionic" personalities of cable news, the arc of her program, *Campbell Brown: No Bias, No Bull* (2008–9), cast her in a similar role to what O'Reilly claimed to be—a no-nonsense everywoman seeking the truth in a manipulative world of media. Fox News' Ailes has offered a similar narrative about former corporate litigator Megyn Kelly, host of *The Kelly Files* (2013–present).[67]

Cable news networks also promote their anchors' star power through advertisements that accentuate personality factors that are supposed to draw viewers. To counter the image of itself as a stuffy network, on the heels of the 2004 election ratings boost CNN ran a series of ads trying to draw out the humorous side of its most well-known personalities at the time, including Christiane Amanpour, Wolf Blitzer, Anderson Cooper, Paula Zahn, Dr. Sanjay Gupta, and Lou Dobbs.[68] Like much of television entertainment, cable news networks have also tried to capitalize on sexualizing some of their female anchors and reporters. A minor controversy broke out when CNN's advertisement for Paula Zahn's *American Mornings* suggested that Zahn was provocative, smart, and, "oh yeah, just a little sexy," with an accompanying sound that many believed was a zipper. CNN denied the sound was a zipper and pulled the commercial off the air after a day.[69] Fox News has been less abashed about directing sexualized gazes toward their female anchors and pundits, clearly trying to sell staged sexiness.[70]

Cable news insiders understand star power as more than an ability to increase the networks' ratings while the star is on air. Stars may also help promote other programs through passing viewers off to an adjacent program or through one star grooming another. Rachel Maddow made regular appearances on MSNBC's *Countdown with Keith Olbermann* (2003–11) before she was given her own show, airing right after Olbermann's. Maddow's show started with exceptionally high ratings, and media journalists and MSNBC personnel attributed part of her quick success to her association with Olbermann.[71] More important than providing a boost to adjacent programming, however, the industry views stars as essential assets for establishing the brand identity.[72] Yet the frequency with which stars have been traded among the different networks indicates that the value of stars may impact a brand identity without uniquely contributing to a brand image. Their value has been at least somewhat transferable among brands. Even Glenn Beck, who became an icon for Fox News' right-wing base, rose to cable news prominence during a two-and-a-half-year stint on CNN's Headline News channel.

Espousing Opinion and Attitude

During prime time, all the cable news networks have tried to break away from the "straight" style of unemotional and detached reporting associated with the high-modern television journalism. Instead, they are embracing a form of journalism that puts a greater emphasis not only on commentary and opinion but also on style and attitude. The tendency toward highlighting attitude, emotion, and opinion on prime-time cable news can be at least partially distinguished from partisan branding strategies. Even CNN, which has generally tried not to be seen as a partisan network, has been scrambling since the early 2000s to fill its prime-time hours with programming that offers opinion, analysis, and talk formats rather than news summaries.[73] Conveniently, opinion-driven talk programming tends to be less expensive to produce than news reporting, especially news reporting that requires field operators and scattered news bureaus.

Infusing news with analysis and commentary is, of course, not a novel concept. Michael Schudson documents a movement among journalists in the 1930s, not long after the modern form of objective journalism had established its firm grip on the United States, calling for more "interpretative journalism."[74] Interpretative journalism appeared especially in Sunday editions and offered space for journalists to provide a narrative to give readers a greater understanding of context and the significance of the week's news. The "new journalism" movement of the late 1960s and 1970s, discussed in chapter 1, also reacted against the detached style of professional U.S. journalism to emphasize more subjective and emotional experience. Print magazines, television news magazine such as *60 Minutes,* news talk shows, talk radio, and other forms distinct from primary daily news sources have long offered a place for news blended with commentary and opinion. So what is most unique about the turn toward commentary and opinion in cable news is that it represents a shift in a media form that had established itself as primarily a place for straight reporting. To some, cable networks appear to be offering opinionated journalism as a substitute for rather than a supplement to the nightly television news report. Jonathan Klein, president of CNN/U.S. from 2004 to 2010, suggested this shift on his network had to do with the increasing availability of news headlines on the Internet: "For too long, CNN was a place where, come primetime, we kept on doing the same thing we've been doing all day. Keep giving you the headlines. And that was fine when we were the only game in town, now there's kind of another outlet for people to get their headlines on demand, and it's no longer cable news. It's the Internet."[75]

Many of cable news' prime-time shows still offer something like headlines, dealing with the day's top stories. However, they treat these stories differently from traditional broadcast journalism. The staid and detached delivery of high-modern anchors has been replaced on cable by anchors who play up their passions and frequently interweave reporting with commentary.

Cable news producers have developed a range of programming formats to fill the prime-time hours. Relatively few of the cable news prime-time shows follow a traditional talk show or round-table format in which a host and guests talk about a limited number of current issues without trying to cover the day's headlines (though examples of this genre included CNN's *Larry King Live* and *Piers Morgan*). The most prevalent format lies somewhere between a talk program and a nightly newscast, featuring hosts who cover most of what they identify as the day's top stories, while talking with guests and offering opinion and commentary. This format includes shows such as Fox's *The O'Reilly Factor* and *Hannity*, MSNBC's *The Last Word with Lawrence O'Donnell* and *Hardball with Chris Matthews*, and CNN's *Erin Burnett OutFront*.

Another common type of prime-time cable news program looks more similar to a traditional news broadcast with less emphasis on the host's opinions. However, even programs billed as less opinionated make a point not to imitate network news; rather, these programs stress the attitude and personality of their hosts. *The Fox Report*, hosted by Shepard (Shep) Smith, is an example of such a program. The Fox News website says Smith's "fast-paced and jam-packed anchoring is a glimpse into the future of television news" and boasts that Smith delivers a "pull-no-punches attitude to cover the stories of the day." Similar language for describing Smith—praising his pacing and snappy attitude—has been echoed by media reporters and even hosts at other networks.[76] Like several other Fox News personalities, Smith brought prior experience from work on the tabloid side of the industry; he had been a reporter for *A Current Affair*.

Perhaps the figure who reveals the most about cable's image of the new anchor is CNN's Anderson Cooper. While Cooper's programs have not proved to have the ratings draw of Bill O'Reilly, probably no other cable news figure has received as much consistent acclaim among media critics as Cooper. Nor have many other cable anchors been as heavily promoted by their employers. The image fashioned for Cooper is one that combines the elements of the traditional reporter with an expressive style unique to cable news. On the one hand, Cooper's image is one of a dogged correspondent dedicated to pursuing his stories even in the face of danger. He is well known for his on-the-ground reporting in war and disaster zones. Numerous CNN promotion spots include video footage of Cooper in chaotic or dangerous environments—standing next to military tanks, in the midst of protests, and reporting from disaster zones. On the other hand, Cooper's emotional sensitivity and willingness to break the pose of objectivity are what media critics and CNN producers say set him apart.

Cooper started making a name for himself as a reporter by sneaking into Burma, Vietnam, Somalia, and other conflict zones with a forged press pass to shoot freelance video.[77] But Cooper's career prior to cable news was not exclusively devoted to journalism; he had been hosting the reality television show *The Mole* just before he was hired by CNN. Cooper's most notable breakthrough came during Hurricane Katrina. As the extent of the devastation of the hurricane and its dismal aftermath was unfolding, CNN showed Cooper reporting from New Orleans nearly in tears. He became one of the first national reporters to aggressively question leading politicians about their apparent satisfaction with the government response to the calamity. Shortly after Cooper's Katrina coverage, CNN expanded his prime-time role. Jonathan Klein said in a *New York Times* interview, "He is the anchorperson of the future." Klein stressed that Cooper is "an anti-anchor person" and "all human. He's not putting it on."[78]

Because CNN is the cable news channel that has most consistently highlighted its commitment to preserving traditional news values, its programming may be the best indicator of how the genre as a whole has shifted since the start of the cable news wars. In 2007 CNN replaced Paula Zahn, the highly prized anchor the network lured from Fox years earlier. After the decision was announced, Zahn told the *New York Times*'s Jacques Steinberg, "We worked so hard to maintain a high quality of objective reporting on the air. Yet what has become clear when you look at the landscape, particularly in the 8 o'clock hour, it seems pretty obvious the audience is drawn to opinion-driven shows. That is not what I do."[79] While Steinberg stated that the decision to replace Zahn "was ultimately a function of ratings," her show's ratings had actually been rising. However, they had not been rising fast enough in comparison to those of her competitors at Fox and MSNBC for that hour. It was not the Nielsen ratings themselves that made the firing decision. The numbers spoke something meaningful only to producers ready with an interpretative schema in mind, one contrasting "straight news" to "opinion-driven talk" as the key to understanding audience preferences.[80]

Partisan Branding and Pursuing Niche Demographics

No other aspect of the cable news wars has sparked more public discussion and controversy than the rise of news programming designed to entice specific partisan audiences. The pioneer of the partisan strategy has undeniably been Fox News. Fox News built its brand around an appeal to conservatives convinced that mainstream media outlets have a liberal bias. The cultural and political impact of Fox News has been significant for multiple reasons. Fox News created a very prominent platform for certain right-wing voices and ideas that might not otherwise have found space in major media.[81] At times Fox has allowed some of these views to be promulgated without much scrutiny and seemingly led viewers toward accepting factual distortions favoring right-wing policies (such as the belief that Saddam Hussein was intimately connected with the September 11th attacks on the United States, a misconception that bolstered support for the U.S. invasion of Iraq).[82] One impressive study compared voting in areas where Fox News was and was not available from 1996 to 2000. The researchers found evidence suggesting Fox News was responsible for a 3–8 percent increase in Republican votes during a time when the Fox audience was still growing rapidly. Hence, it is not surprising that Democrats, progressives, and left-leaning critics have seen Fox News as a major force in ideological and electoral struggles in the United States. By the early 2000s, a wave of critics began producing well-documented critiques and revelations of conservative biases and misinformation in Fox News coverage.[83]

Fox News built its reputation as a right-wing network without directly proclaiming a political or ideological affiliation. In early interviews, Fox News executives and stars pitched the network as a source for news without bias, while implying CNN and the broadcast networks themselves were biased in favor of liberal views.[84] Accusing other networks of liberal bias, while staunchly claiming its own balance, seemed to be just the message to send to conservative viewers, especially as Fox also started drawing praise and special appearances from conservative and right-wing political figures and approbation from Democrats. During the long investigation of the sexual relationship between President Bill Clinton and White House intern Monica Lewinsky, Fox News became the network most dedicated to covering the scandal. Yet Ailes decidedly trod with some caution as the Clinton-Lewinsky revelations were breaking. He did not want it to seem that Fox was leading a crusade against Clinton; Ailes deliberately held back on scooping certain accusations of presidential misconduct until other major outlets had reported them.[85] Nonetheless, Fox kept a relentless focus on the story. It was a perfect way to blend the general pleasure of a sensational sex scandal with a more particular appeal to conservatives' passionate anger directed toward a morally corrupt, liberal president. Fox built up its programming schedule to devote more time to the Clinton scandal, even creating a short-lived show hosted by the conservative gossip writer Matt Drudge. Drudge had helped bring the first allegations against Clinton to light on his online aggregation site, *The Drudge Report.*

Fox News' ratings grew quickly from the Clinton scandal on, and by June 2002 Fox was consistently beating incumbent network CNN in both prime-time and total ratings. As Fox's dominance in the ratings persisted, cable news producers at MSNBC and CNN, along with media reporters, were trying to make sense of how Fox was engaging and growing such a large audience.[86] Industry insiders offered different interpretations of Fox's success. For some, Fox represented an early adopter of the more opinionated and attitude-infused style of news delivery that was coming to define cable news. Others saw the key to Fox News' ratings in its willingness to incorporate tabloid-style news content and hype-inducing graphics. Most prominently, the right-wing partisan bent of Fox News seemed be the wellspring of its success. But was that simply because Fox News had discovered the benefits of pursuing an ideological niche, or was it specifically because they had chosen a right-wing niche?

Many in the industry were not sure if a cable news network or even particular programs targeting a liberal or leftist niche could succeed in the same way as Fox had with viewers or advertisers. The argument coming from many leaders at Fox was that liberals already controlled most of the news media. Alternatively, some believed liberal viewers would not be drawn toward the same kind of invectives that seemingly enticed many Fox viewers to stay tuned to hosts like O'Reilly and Hannity. Furthermore, liberal perspectives, and especially further left perspectives, could clash with advertisers' interests or generate flak from the powerful right-wing institutions capable of mobilizing boycott campaigns. Air America, the left-progressive talk radio network that launched in 2004, faced such problems with advertisers.[87] In a remarkable story that received too little attention, a leaked memo from ABC Radio Networks revealed that almost ninety companies were taking part in an advertisers' blackout of Air America; ABC instructed all of its affiliates not to run ads from those companies during any syndicated Air America programming. This list included many major corporations, such as McDonald's, Microsoft, Hewlett-Packard, and Walmart. Those same companies were advertising on the Fox News Channel.

During the first years of the Bush presidency, CNN and MSNBC tried to follow Fox News' success by making their own attempts to target conservatives. In 2001 CNN tried to hire the king of conservative talk, Rush Limbaugh.[88] That summer Walter Isaacson, then new president of CNN, stirred controversy by making a series of visits to conservative lawmakers to see what the network might be able to do to assuage conservative hostility about CNN's alleged liberal bias.[89] MSNBC tried its hand at creating programs with a rightward bent, including *Alan Keyes Is Making Sense* (2002), featuring the conservative activist who had gained national notoriety for rhetorical flourish while participating in the Republican presidential debates of 2000. By 2003, MSNBC proved willing to put on a right-wing host even more incendiary than anyone at Fox News. They hired Michael Savage, who had built a reputation as a radio host for his raging attacks against women, the gay rights community, racial minorities, and liberals. Savage had even referred to MSNBC itself as "More Snotty Nonsense By Creeps" and degraded the network's anchor Ashleigh Banfield by calling her "the mind-slut with a big pair of glasses that they sent to Afghanistan."[90] Despite protests from gay rights activists and other groups, and even objections by NBC's Tom Brokaw, MSNBC went ahead with producing and airing *The Savage Nation.* The series aired for only a few months, as the network fired Savage after he told a caller he was a "sodomite" and said, "You should only get AIDS and die, you pig."[91]

The cable networks were much less aggressive in their attempts at niche targeting of liberal or progressive viewers, though many had contracts with commentators representing liberal perspectives. CNN and Fox tried to put liberals and conservatives in debate-oriented shows such as CNN's *Crossfire* and Fox's *Hannity and Colmes* or on special news panels. Jeff Cohen, the founder of the left-leaning media-watch organization Fairness and Accuracy in Reporting, served as a regular commentator for all three cable networks at different times from 1987 through 2003. Cohen argues that starting with the first years of *Crossfire,* cable news programs almost always pitted moderate liberals against more flamboyant conservatives.[92] Until MSNBC's new programming formula emerged in the mid-2000s, leftist populists only infrequently appeared as hosts or even regular guests on cable news. Fox News, surprisingly, deviated from this pattern in 1997 when they hired activist-rapper Chuck D as a regular commentator, leading to controversy among media critics over whether such a hire only signaled a move closer toward entertainment rather than news.[93]

In a bid to fight back against its last-place ranking in the cable news wars in the early 2000s, MSNBC created a prime-time talk show hosted by Phil Donahue, who frequently represented progressive and liberal perspectives. The network's handling of *Donahue* (2002–3) exemplifies the caution with which it approached the prospects of liberal or progressive programming. *Donahue* debuted just as the Bush administration was drumming up support for an invasion of Iraq. Cohen served as a senior producer for the show, and he wanted to pursue a liberal/left niche audience for the program, drawing up plans for an advertising campaign in progressive magazines. But according to Cohen, MSNBC management vetoed this approach. As the show began featuring debates about the rationale behind a U.S. invasion of Iraq, MSNBC demanded that Cohen and Donahue run more celebrity stories and make sure that more prowar than antiwar voices were present during discussion about the possible Iraq invasion.[94] MSNBC canceled the show in February 2003, claiming that low ratings were the reason. At the time, *Donahue* was the highest-rated show on MSNBC, though its ratings were still lagging significantly behind its competitors on CNN and Fox.[95] Later, an internal MSNBC memo was leaked, suggesting other reasons for the show's cancellation. The memo stated that Donahue presented "a difficult public face for NBC in a time of war" because the show was creating "a home for liberal antiwar voices at a time that our competitors are waving the flag at every opportunity."[96]

It was not until 2005 that MSNBC started moving toward bolder efforts to target liberal audiences. Bush's popularity was plummeting in the aftermath of the disaster of Hurricane Katrina and prolonged fighting in Iraq. Fox News' ratings were in a brief period of decline. Searching for new political narratives to resonate with their base, Fox News turned to what some critics saw as a desperate ploy by focusing substantial coverage on an alleged "war on Christmas" that holiday season.[97] MSNBC's Keith Olbermann, host of *Countdown with Keith Olbermann,* gained sudden attention for his sharp criticism of the Bush administration during his "Special Comment" segments that began appearing in the aftermath of Hurricane Katrina. Olbermann's special comments were designed to evoke the memory and mythology of Edward R. Murrow's famous editorial rebuke of Senator Joseph McCarthy and the demagoguery surrounding the anticommunist hearings he was leading. Yet Olbermann's delivery of these special comments weaved from a Murrowesque tone of stately authority to moments of fevered invective, at one point telling President Bush to "shut the hell up."[98] As Olbermann's ratings shot up in the wake of his special comments, MSNBC's Phil Griffin told the *New Yorker* that "all of the sudden, [Olbermann] took off . . . in ways that MSNBC never had a show take off."[99] Television critics quickly started drawing comparisons between Olbermann and Bill O'Reilly. Olbermann consistently baited O'Reilly with attacks, repeatedly nominating O'Reilly for his "Worst Person in the World" segment, and O'Reilly's counterpunches may have given a further boost to Olbermann's ratings.[100]

Olbermann's ratings clearly pointed to a new branding strategy for MSNBC, and it started to reshape its image into an anti-Fox network targeting Democrats. The network began adding more shows led by hosts representing liberal views, starting with *The Rachel Maddow Show* (2008–present), followed by programs such as *The Ed Show* (2009–15), *The Last Word with Lawrence O'Donnell* (2010–present), and *PoliticsNation with Al Sharpton* (2011–present). Even as MSNBC added these new programs, the network remained ambivalent about how far to pursue liberal branding. Around the launch of *The Rachel Maddow Show,*

MSNBC sought to portray itself as a network distinguished by its willingness to engage more liberal views but not as a liberal network. Maddow, an AIDS activist and Rhodes scholar, emphasized in interviews that while her show would be opinionated and not rooted in traditional notions of objectivity, it was not meant to be a partisan format. Maddow told one reporter, "I certainly have beliefs and opinions, just like anybody does. . . . But I don't have an agenda. This wasn't like, great, an opportunity to impose 'X' on the world. I think of this as a chance to talk about the news on TV for an hour each day."[101] MSNBC was rebranding itself as "The Place for Politics" at that time for the 2008 election. For debates, conventions, and election night, MSNBC removed opinionated hosts Chris Matthews and Keith Olbermann from anchor positions to maintain clarity between MSNBC's commentary programs and their commitment to objective-style news.[102] However, by 2010 the network moved to more fully embrace a liberal-progressive brand and adopted another slogan, "Lean Forward," intended to strengthen the progressive association with the brand.[103]

The ascendancy of liberal voices on MSNBC as a counterbalance to the conservatism of Fox News quickly led to speculation that cable news may be evolving into a reconstituted form of the partisan press.[104] Yet it remains an open question whether a partisan divide on cable news will persist or exactly how cable news networks will be willing to negotiate tensions between promoting leftist or progressive views and advertising interests, organized conservative backlash, and executive ideology. MSNBC's "Lean Forward" identity was adopted as a business strategy in a particular political situation. Unlike 2002, when the antiwar views occasionally expressed on *Donahue* would have found little support among Democratic elites, MSNBC's programs representing liberal views draw heavily on interviews from elected Democrats.[105] MSNBC hosts have criticized the Obama administration on issues such as domestic spying and lack of movement toward climate change—issues where there are a sizable number of elected Democrats taking oppositional stances toward presidential policy. However, MSNBC's liberal programs have not shown a willingness to confront the same range of news stories found on noncommercially supported leftist news programs like Pacifica's *Democracy Now!* In contrast, Fox News has brought views from deep within conservative think tanks, talk radio, and the conservative blogosphere into the spotlight of major media.[106]

Perhaps some of the limits of commercially branded progressive cable news were revealed by Cenk Uygur, who created the left-oriented webcast *The Young Turks* and hosted *MSNBC Live* for six months in 2011. Despite a significant increase in ratings while Uygur hosted *MSNBC Live,* he was not offered a continued prime-time hosting role. Uygur cut ties with the network, claiming that

Phil Griffin had told him that "he'd been talking to people in Washington, and that they did not like my tone."[107] Uygur also reported that Griffin had told him that MSNBC represented "the establishment" and the new host needed to act like it.[108] Griffin himself has suggested he wants to create a brand for MSNBC that is not centered on progressive politics but one oriented toward a lifestyle branding identity that can be integrated with other Comcast-owned cable networks. According to a profile of Griffin by *New Republic* writer Rebecca Dana, Griffin sees MSNBC "covering fashion, entertainment, sports, and food, and he imagines an audience coming to his anchors not just for their takes on the immigration bill, but also for their restaurant recommendations or their take on the summer blockbuster."[109]

To sum up, Fox News introduced the strategy of building a partisan brand and targeting a conservative niche. After years of Fox dominance in ratings competition, MSNBC has made a move toward a type of counterprogramming featuring programs oriented toward liberal perspectives, though it has deployed this strategy with considerably more timidity than Fox News has with its conservatism. For both of these networks, the most overtly partisan programming has gone hand in hand with a talk-oriented format, rather than formats focusing on more expensive package pieces or investigative units. This programming has remained primarily focused on immediate news events of the day and reaction. Some hosts, especially MSNBC's Rachel Maddow, Chris Hayes, and Melissa Harris-Perry, have made efforts to provide historical and sociological context surrounding current events. Yet the kind of partisan branding that has come to define cable news emphasizes takedowns of ideological opponents, as well as the warmth and charm of anchor personalities, more than other types of appeal.

The cable news networks still make selective claims to represent balanced journalism, albeit a style that differs starkly from the norms of broadcast television's high modernism. To the critics of Fox News, its slogans "Fair and Balanced" and "We Report, You Decide" may only appear, at best, as laughable and ironic or, at worst, authoritarian "lies" told by "lying liars."[110] Yet accurate or not, the claims of independence from party and ideology seem to play almost as important a role for much of cable news programming as for high-modern journalism. Many of cable's loudest hosts who have most flaunted their penchant for attitude—including Bill O'Reilly, Lou Dobbs, Chris Matthews, Campbell Brown, and Erin Burnett—have proclaimed their independence from any political party or single ideology.

It also remains true that pursing partisan niche audiences is only part of the story for cable news. Each network has been trying to build coalition audiences. A report by the Pew Research Center in 2012 found that 33 percent of

Fox viewers consider themselves moderate (23 percent) or liberal (10 percent), and 22 percent say they are Democrats. The same survey found 32 percent of MSNBC viewers identify as conservative, with 16 percent of the networks' viewers identifying as Republican and 24 percent as independent.[111] An earlier study from 2009 by Pew found that 33 percent of "regular" Fox News viewers identify as Democrats. There could be all sorts of reasons these viewers would watch Fox, including ironic or oppositional viewing. Still, the significant portions of MSNBC and Fox viewers who do not align with the primary political persuasion of the respective networks suggest an important reason neither network is willing to make outright claims to represent a particular political perspective.

There are also other dimensions to cable news' niche-segmentation strategies, including age demographics. Since 1980, seniors have made up a large share of the cable news audience. A 2010 survey found that the average viewer's age was sixty-five for Fox News, sixty-three for CNN, and fifty-nine for MSNBC.[112] Advertisers pay the most for viewers ages twenty-five to fifty-four—known in the industry as "in the demo"—so the cable news networks have all been trying to build younger audiences while retaining their older loyal ones. Though Fox News and MSNBC both launched with promises to appeal to younger viewers than CNN, such promises have not been fulfilled.[113] MSNBC sought to capture the attention of younger viewers through quickening the pace of the newscast, staging more dramatic visual displays, and even creating a set that had the appearance of a Starbucks-style café.[114] Each of the networks have also experimented with visual styles, online interactivity, and hiring younger stars to attract younger viewers.[115] Still, cable news networks seem reluctant to pursue younger viewers at the expense of older ones.[116] While the demo represents the most generally prized advertising demographic, cable news networks also have the option of pursuing advertisers who want to reach older and wealthier viewers, an audience who can be hard to reach through other outlets.[117] Prime-time cable news' frequent commercials for retirement services and certain pharmaceuticals suggest they often target older markets.

Last, the cable news networks, as mentioned previously, generally target viewers with especially strong interest in news, a psychographic group sometimes referred to as "news junkies." Yet here again, the cable news strategy has not been one of exclusive focus. As with many niches, the boundaries of this group are not well defined. The search for news junkies is as much a process of recruitment—finding new ways to hook viewers into news—as it is of discovery. Cable news networks benefit from spikes in audiences representing a larger group than their core news junkies during elections and breaking news events. Though such spikes do not necessarily lead to more income from advertising sales, they give the networks leverage in negotiating with cable operators and bringing in subscription revenue. As the networks have established themselves, subscriptions have generally accounted for a more stable and often larger portion of revenues than advertising.[118]

Popularizing Presentation Style, Content, and Interactivity

Cable producers have also looked beyond anchors and personalities for other techniques to heighten the emotional intensity of news. One key element has been arresting visual displays and presentational styles. Fox News and MSNBC in particular led the way with experimenting with bold graphic interfaces and jolting audio effects. Part of this philosophy is simply that more sensual stimuli keep audience attention. The news crawl—a streaming text with news updates running across a portion of the screen—that runs during much of the cable news programming is one example of efforts to provide constant stimulation. Television news programs had experimented with crawls during times of crisis before they became a regular feature of cable news. The big-three cable stations all started making more regular use of tickers to cover nonemergency news as they transitioned out of crisis coverage of the September 11th attacks.[119] The ticker itself became the subject of media accounts. Although critics differed in how they highlighted the potential for the ticker to yield information overload, all framed the device as a mechanism for quickening the pace of incoming information or catching the attention of visually hungry viewers.[120]

In talking about efforts to popularize the content and visual style of cable news, industry discourses tend to borrow much of their vocabulary and concepts from other genres. In particular, much of this discourse relays understandings about audience tastes derived from entertainment television and tabloid print journalism. Industry leaders and media reporters frequently pose questions about whether cable news should embrace more tabloid-oriented strategies for ratings gains. Other critics argue cable news has already become too much like tabloids. But what are the characteristics of "tabloid" news? The term *tabloid* suggests catering to a category of taste placed lower on a hierarchy of cultural capital than high-brow or "quality" news.[121] However, this term has not been used consistently to denote specific practices.

One tabloid-like strategy for popularizing cable news content is sensationalizing, or hyping, its presentation. Sensationalizing involves heightening the sense of urgency or importance of a topic through conveying a strong emotional or visceral reaction to it; the quality of that affective intensity might be characterized as anything from shock to fear to moral condemnation. Different types of stories can be presented sensationally, including topics frequently associated with more "hard" news (such as a war or economic troubles) and those associated with "soft" news (such as kidnappings or celebrity scandals). There are similarities between this kind of presentation sensationalism in cable news and the kind of sensationalism Michael Schudson says Joseph Pulitzer brought to the New York newspaper world of the 1880s. In Schudson's analysis, "sensationalism meant self-advertisement," and its techniques in the 1880s included more illustrations, boasting of circulation numbers, and larger and more prominent headlines.[122] For cable news, news stories are self-promoted through other devices such as attention-grabbing banners like "Countdown to War," thumping music introducing a story, and the emotional expressiveness and language used by the on-screen personality, conveying the urgency and intensity of the story.

Another strategy associated with tabloidization is devoting coverage to stories believed to evoke popular interest that do not coincide with professional news values, which tend to privilege a traditionally circumscribed political arena. Stories focusing on entertainment news, celebrity, scandal, and isolated crimes are especially prevalent examples. In the late 1990s, some representatives from MSNBC and Fox News offered justifications for focusing on more entertainment news and scandal as part of an effort to democratize news agenda setting. Eric Sorenson, then president of MSNBC, articulated this sentiment in a 2000 interview: "To an 18-year-old, *news* might be that 'Erin Brockovich' is No. 1 at the box office. *News* might be that 'N Sync has the hottest album at Tower Records. *News* might be that there's a cool *new* Web site that allows you as an Internet consumer to download an MP3 to your hard drive. . . . When we're applying our decision-making apparatus to the flow of all the *news* that's coming across the transom every day, we're thinking of it from a 25- to 54-year-old point of view, and we don't make any bones about that."[123] However, cable news producers have long recognized limits to focusing too much attention on entertainment and scandal. Industry insiders have worried that too much crime and entertainment content could damage their brands, even if it might bring short-term ratings gains.[124] Content studies conducted by the Pew Research Center's State of the News Media have consistently shown that cable news stations focus much more on political stories than celebrity- or entertainment-related stories. Cable producers see their audiences as primarily interested in traditional "hard" news, though scandals tend to get a lot of coverage when they become part of an ongoing narrative with breaking developments.[125] Rebranding efforts by the cable news networks in the mid- to late 2000s put an even greater focus on political news and other forms of traditional news.[126]

Cable networks have also attempted to forge closer ties with viewers through trying to integrate online interactivity and cable news. In the mid-late 1990s, as MSNBC and Fox were rolling out their programming and promotions to challenge CNN, *convergence* was a powerful buzzword used by industry leaders and media reporters. This term, of course, can take on different meanings—but the meanings that were especially salient for cable news leaders were the promises that Internet and cable properties could integrate television and interactive experience, share content, and boost each other's ratings and profits. At the star-studded announcement of the MSNBC partnership, which took place in the studio of *Saturday Night Live* in 1995, Tom Brokaw and Bill Gates appeared via satellite on giant screens onstage. The event was orchestrated as a spectacle to suggest an unprecedented experiment in digital convergence for journalism. NBC president Bob Wright promised that "NBC and Microsoft have come together to create news for the next millennium. . . . Both the cable and online services will be fully integrated with NBC television in an interlocking chain of news and information delivery that meets all levels of viewers' needs."[127] Bill Gates proclaimed that both companies believed "in a world of interactivity," and they were going to bring "this interactive world in integration with the broadcast."[128]

Yet the actual operation of cable news convergence efforts has hardly proved to be as dramatic or innovative as suggested by the rhetoric of the 1990s. MSNBC, during its first few years, tried to brand itself as a tech pioneer and put a tech-culture spin on some of its programs, especially *Internight* (1996–99) and *The Site* (1996–97). Though these programs sometimes featured responses to viewers' e-mail and promoted the MSNBC website—and *The Site* featured many tech news stories—it would be hard to argue they were truly pioneering new types of interactive experiences with cable audiences.

MSNBC scaled back on its branding focus as a convergence innovator, but all the cable news networks have continued to incorporate elements of online interaction in their prime-time programming.[129] Most of this has been along the lines of featuring viewer questions or comments sent by e-mail or social media, airing viewers' tweets about a breaking event on a ticker, or conducting instant polls online. This kind of online integration can give the sense of a participatory news environment, but it involves only user-generated content that is carefully controlled and selected by paid cable news staff. The most ambitious effort for user-generated content on cable news has been CNN's iReport, which allows citizen journalists to upload stories and videos on the iReport site, and CNN journalists will vet certain stories with fact-checking. These sources can be marked with a tag saying "CNN verified" on the iReport site, and some are used as sources by CNN's television reporters. Still, the iReporters provide a very small portion of the sources cited on air, overwhelmingly less than politicians and other official sources. CNN's citizen journalists do not set the news agenda, but CNN editors may selectively pluck content from the user-generated site when it suits their needs.[130]

The Horizons of Cable News

In introducing this chapter, I framed cable news as straddling a line between traditional news media and new media. Considering the programming strategies that have been central to their outreach efforts, cable news also seems to trouble other divisions often used to map the news media terrain: niche versus mass media, tabloid versus quality journalism, and news versus entertainment. The cable news networks have been searching for the loyal niche audience who will keep their average audience ratings high. Yet such audiences are not well defined, and the need to appeal to a mass subscriber base, including subscribers who may be only infrequent viewers, continues to serve as a check on cable news networks adopting a tightly focused narrowcasting model. So, cable news continues trying to formulate programming with an appeal to both broad audiences and more specific niches. In seeking this popular appeal, cable news has incorporated only limited doses of the classic characteristics of tabloid journalism associated with the likes of programs such as *A Current Affair* or *Inside Edition*. Still, they have also moved away from traditional notions of "quality" journalism in the high-modern tradition.

Cable news programming also challenges any clear distinction between news and entertainment. Many writers have argued that, especially in a contemporary environment saturated with popular culture, entertainment and political engagement can intermingle; the flourishing of civic culture may even depend on integrating entertainment values with political engagement.[131] In an analysis centering on satiric news programs, Jeffrey Jones argues that "entertaining politics offers a *cultural* site where new issues, languages, approaches, and audiences' relationships to politics on television are occurring."[132] For Liesbet van Zoonen, fusing entertainment with politics offers the most promising escape from a modernist and elitist political sphere that "will hear and allow only one proper political mode of expressing public concerns and conflict, which is characterized by informed judgment, impersonal reaction, and rational debate."[133]

Given the polarized positions of cultural populism and purist rationalism invoked around questions of politics and entertainment, I want to draw clearly what I see as some of the implications of this examination of the industry popular of cable news.[134] The argument I am making is not that cable news networks put too much effort into making news entertaining and appealing. Rather, the problem I think this analysis can illuminate is that there is not enough diversity in cable's efforts to make news and the story of public life a compelling, rich, and popular genre, especially in the high-profile prime-time news programming I explore here.[135] The commercial market has largely failed to provide the funding and promotion for experimentation beyond the confines of the narrowly conceived industry popular.[136] There are some alternatives to the big-three cable networks in the United States, including al-Jazeera America, BBC World News America, Glenn Beck's TheBlaze network, RT (formerly Russia Today), and the now-defunct Current TV. Yet these networks have all faced major disadvantages compared to the big-three cable stations in terms of cable carriage, cross-media promotion opportunities, and funding (though al-Jazeera and BBC have quite substantial resources). As of yet, they simply cannot compete with Fox, MSNBC, and CNN in terms of not only gaining loyal viewers but simply gaining exposure and awareness among U.S. viewers.

At both its best and its worst, cable news programming produces political theater and dramatizes public life. Cable news is polarizing, popular, and, at times, populist. The way cable news stages politics and current events as an arena of breaking events and conflict, narrated by charismatic anchors, thundering with intense sounds and exploding visuals, may help make news exciting and compelling. But might there be other creative ways to produce compelling news for a twenty-four-hour television format? Clearly, the growth of cable news' popularization techniques comes out of competition for ratings and profits. Cable networks have no public interest obligations, and the commercial and corporate nature of the cable news networks means they cannot put a mission to invigorate public life ahead of financial gain. Surely, some of the programming tactics discussed in this chapter could be part of a vision for popular news articulated to a mission to promote an expanded popular interest and participation in civic life. Yet while cable news networks have been keen to differentiate themselves from high-modern journalism in many respects, they have only exaggerated certain tendencies targeted by some of professional journalism's sharpest critics. Instead of expanding news agenda setting and framing power much beyond the scope of government officials, the guests and voices heard on cable news networks orbit closely around elected officials, party activists, and campaign strategies. Cable news networks have, on the whole, only exacerbated modern journalism's tendency toward horse-race coverage and a focus on political strategy and maneuvering rather than exploring perspectives and issues.[137] Cable news has not aimed at expanding popular interest in public life but rather has catered to what producers perceive to be an array of existing niche interests.

News organizations seeking to broaden popular investment in democratic life would need to explore questions such as the following: How can we tell stories about political life that can help elucidate connections between the personal and the political? How can we bring into view links between everyday life experiences and opportunities and collective decision making? Can news media stir popular passions for political engagement and for mobilizing collaborative publics? How can news organizations include better coverage coming from perspectives representing marginalized groups and viewpoints? Might news organizations be able to strike a chord of popular resonance by moving away from the tendency to define news in concert with official sources?[138] Unsurprisingly, voices posing such questions are missing in industry discourses on popularizing cable news. By showing how a limited set of notions has set the horizon for what the industry deems as viable for cable news, my analysis here suggests that the forms and styles of news that circulate on cable are not inevitable; today's cable news is not simply a response to consumer demand or an expression of U.S. "culture" writ large. Another popular is possible.

CHAPTER 4

Popularizing News 2.0

The front page of the internet.
—Reddit.com

Mission: Democratization of news media and extending the consumption of news into a conversation.
—Newsvine.com

On the night of the 2012 national election, Barack Obama appeared live on the social news site Reddit. It was to be the last campaign stop of his career as a presidential candidate. As a website popular especially among young men, Reddit was a good place for Obama to make one last push to get a group of sometimes reluctant voters out to the polls. Yet Obama's attention to Reddit was not only about demographics. Since his first year as president, Obama's administration experimented with building more connections with citizens over social media and cultivating an image of a president exploring the frontiers of digital democracy. Obama participated in several electronic town halls—hosted by Reddit, Google Hangout, Twitter, Facebook, LinkedIn, and on whitehouse.gov—to respond directly to questions posed by users. What marked these occasions as different from town hall forums hosted by broadcast or cable news outlets was that the questions Obama faced were curated not by CNN or NBC producers but by ordinary users. The social media town halls allowed users themselves to vote on which questions (posed by fellow users) the president should address. For some, Obama's willingness to open himself to citizen-curated questions signaled a bold embrace of the potential of new media. Describing Obama's first virtual town hall, an Associated Press report stated with characteristic matter-of-factness, "The event allowed him to speak directly to Americans through the Web, bypassing the filter of the news media."[1] Yet for critics, Obama's turn toward social media looked suspicious; perhaps his embrace of these platforms was less about direct connection with citizens and more in keeping with the administration's desire to control its message. The social media visits could be viewed as a turn to venues where he could avoid scrutiny from seasoned political reporters.

Electronic town halls where users both formulate and select questions for public officials represent one vision of digital media obviating the gatekeeping function once performed by professional journalists. But hopes of replacing media gatekeeping with online collective intelligence have extended far beyond such town halls. The migration of news online has led to even more intense pressure for professional editorial discretion to yield to user demand, especially as new tools have created more sophisticated and immediate feedback loops between media outlets and users.

There are many approaches for putting users in charge of the digital news agenda. Visit almost any major English-language news website today, and you'll be offered an option that lets you sift through the top stories ranked by "most e-mailed," "most commented on," or simply "most popular" among users. News organizations from the *Washington Post* to Buzzfeed to local news sites are increasingly relying on audience metrics to make decisions about what to publish and, in some cases, what segment of an audience to direct to a particular story.[2] Some of the types of information about readers' activity that were relatively expensive and time-consuming to attain through offline market research can be gathered online instantly, with little cost. News outlets frequently use audience metrics to rank published stories; such metrics also serve as indicators of what types of stories should be produced in the first place. On one extreme, Demand Media, Journatic, and other content mills monitor Web search terms to decide what topics are worth assigning to their (woefully underpaid) freelance writers.[3] Topics are chosen by algorithmic analysis of popular search terms.

Social media have become important filters directing flows of attention around news and current events. A 2014 study conducted by the Media Insight Project found that "fully 4 in 10 Americans say they got news in the last week from social media."[4] The study's authors concluded that though few now rely only on social media for news, "social media is becoming an important tool for people across all generations to discover news." Many upstart news outlets recognize this, of course, and they have been working intensely to build audience engagement strategies around social sharing of news items. Well-known online news outlets such as Upworthy and Buzzfeed have built their core identities around efforts to promote the spreadability of their news.

Long-established news organizations too are recognizing the crucial role that social media play in driving traffic and, in effect, serving as a second level of editors for the popular news agenda. In May 2014, a revealing report titled "Innovation" was leaked from inside the *New York Times*. A team of *Times* leaders had spent six months focusing intensely on internal and industry research and interviews. Their final report urged that the paper needed deep cultural and institutional changes to reverse course, as it was falling behind in "the art and science of getting our journalism to readers." The report detailed how competing outlets, from the *Guardian* to the *Wall Street Journal* to the *Huffington Post*, were breaking with traditional news routines and building extensive audience-engagement strategies. The most compelling argument used to persuade colleagues that the *Times* needed to make major shifts, which would disrupt complacency with familiar newsroom practices, pointed to figures showing a dramatic decline in home-page visits. In 2013 the number of home-page visitors on the *Times* site had fallen to close to half the number of such visitors in 2011. Yet this was not because readers were leaving the *Times* website as a whole; overall page views remained relatively steady, but users were no longer relying on front-page editors to select the news for them. Instead of heading to the home-page stories selected by editors, the authors said, "Readers are finding and engaging with our journalism in vastly different ways. More readers expect us to find them on Twitter and Facebook, and through email and phone alerts."

For digital optimists, such signs point to an age in which those Jay Rosen has so famously described as "the people formerly known as the audience" are asserting an unprecedented role in news circulation.[5] In this chapter, I focus on one vision for how online technologies are enabling a handoff of editorial and curatorial power from editors to users—social news sites. I have chosen to analyze social news in particular because it represents perhaps the most idealistic model for users to democratize editorial power. As sites based on collaborative filtering, social news sites represent microcosms of the larger vision for the Web as a whole to serve as a collaborative filter for news. Although the term *social news* has somewhat fuzzy boundaries, it is primarily used to describe aggregation websites—such as Reddit, Slashdot, and Newsvine—where users can submit content from all over the Web. Users vote items up and down in prominence, and most of these sites also host comments that are themselves curated by users. Many of the items linked to on the most popular social news sites might not even fit their users' definitions of "news," though all such sites place an emphasis on timeliness and include significant activity in categories traditionally recognized as news. At heart, social news sites exemplify a form of *collaborative filtering* for determining news priorities. Defined broadly, collaborative filtering entails organizing, recommending, and sorting Web content based on algorithmically processed user feedback. Collaborative filtering can rely on feedback that has been recorded surreptitiously. Amazon, for instance, might recommend a book for you based on its record of what other users who have similar purchase histories to yours have bought. Social news sites offer a feedback mechanism that seems more appealing as a form of democratic activity, since they ask for the users' conscious participation in the filtering process (though some sites also incorporate traces of user activity that might not be consciously revealed by users). Participating in social news can feel a lot like voting in an election for the news agenda, one that is constant and ongoing.

Social news is not only a filtering technique employed by a handful of successful news aggregators. It also represents the most believable adaptation of today's technologies to realize a long-running dream of setting a news agenda based on audience interest. More boldly than other online news formats, social news sites have tapped into the affordances of online communication to practice their own version of the "new social contract" between news editors and audiences that Ruth Clark called for in 1979. As discussed in chapter 2, Clark told editors that newspaper readers were no longer willing to simply be told what was news; they wanted to have a say in defining it. For Clark, market research provided readers a chance to have their input heard. Today, social news sites make that promise in a more radical way.

Two popular—though conflicting—notions contribute to the appeal of collaborative filtering. One is its populist element. Collaborative filtering seemingly offers a way to aggregate peer judgments as an alternative to professional expertise for deciding the most important news stories, the best books, the quality of movies, and so on. The other aspect of its appeal, however, relies on an aura of technical ingenuity and trust in technological expertise. Collaborative filtering requires designers to make all sorts of decisions about how feedback will be collected, calculated, distributed, and displayed. This filtering relies on algorithms embedded with many value choices. Yet popular engagement in such design decisions is, to say the least, severely limited. Instead, there often appears to be a widespread faith in programmers and Silicon Valley to make decisions about the mechanisms through which culture gets sorted and assessed.[6] This type of faith in the algorithmic architecture seems pervasive across platforms for sharing news and other content—whether it involves social news rankings, Facebook news feeds, or trending topics on Twitter.

Collaborative filtering is one way in which techniques for creating and sharing news online are challenging what scholars refer to as the "cultural authority" of professional journalists. This authority has rested on the power of professional journalists to define news, set the daily news agenda, and decide how it should be prioritized and presented.[7] For digital optimists, the decline of this cultural authority monopolized by professionals and the dispersal of power among ordinary Web users represent a promising development and indicate that the Web is democratizing news in a profound way.

This chapter analyzes collaborative filtering as a digital-age model for popularizing and democratizing news and draws comparisons between it and previous postprofessional news models, especially the market-driven newspaper movement discussed in chapter 2. I look at how social news sites developed under the influence of the open-source movement, while legacy news organizations were grappling with how to build their own online news structures and routines. I also probe claims that social news represents a model of democratizing the news agenda. Although social news sites have something valuable to contribute to the public sphere, I suggest that the vision behind social news shares many of the same assumptions and shortcomings as the market-driven news paradigm. Like market-driven news, social news sites also grasp at the elusive figure of exogenous consumer demand.

The Networked Public Sphere, Collaborative Filtering, and Democratic Gatekeeping

As discussed in chapter 1, early-twentieth-century news organizations started embracing the notion that journalists were members of a profession with a special capacity to make objective judgments about news. By the middle of the century, journalistic professionalism became the dominant normative model for how a myriad of world events and perspectives could be winnowed down in the scarce space of the news hole. The move toward professionalization coincided with a transformation in news markets across the United States. Many cities and towns experienced a transition from a news market characterized by multiple competing partisan newspapers to one controlled by a single daily paper that claimed to be able to represent all views fairly. The model of professional news, which evolved out of these circumstances and peaked with journalism's "high-modern" form, has faced increasing challenges since the late 1960s. From the underground press of the 1960s and 1970s to market-driven newspapers to cable news, a variety of journalistic models and forms have challenged the ideology of professionalism.

Despite the long series of hits against high-modern journalism, popular narratives about online news tend to envision the Internet itself as the first radical departure from the expert-driven mentality of professionalism. Accounts of online innovations eroding the control of professional gatekeepers too rarely acknowledge resistance to professionalism preceding the Web. This runs the risk of suggesting that the future of news appears to be a matter of technological development. Consider, for instance, this description of the impact of digital technology in Dan Gillmor's influential book *We the Media:*

> Technology has given us a communications toolkit that allows anyone to become a journalist at little cost and, in theory, with global reach. Nothing like this has ever been remotely possible before.
>
> In the 20th century, making the news was almost entirely the province of journalists; the people we covered, or "newsmakers"; and the legions of public relations and marketing people who manipulated everyone. The economics of publishing and broadcasting created large, arrogant institutions—call it Big Media. . . . Big Media, in any event, treated the news as a lecture. We told you what the news was. You bought it, or you didn't. . . . Tomorrow's news reporting and production will be more of a conversation, or a seminar.[8]

Gillmor invokes the metaphor of news as a lecture versus conversation, which has had many iterations among advocates for demand-driven journalism. Although he acknowledges talk radio as a precursor to a more participatory style of news, like many bloggers and social media entrepreneurs, he suggests that the interactive capacities of the Web have played the defining role in decentering professional authority.

In crafting a narrative about new technologies' challenge, there are always choices to make between emphasizing claims of continuity or claims of rupture. Within popular discussions about the state of news in the United States, I think it is fair to say the most pervasive stories about what the Internet means for journalism highlight rupture. Popular books on online journalism tend to point to ways interactive technologies and easy access to publishing empower ordinary users and consumers. This kind of story is reflected especially by writers such as Jay Rosen, Jeff Jarvis, and Clay Shirky.[9] A couple strands of journalism scholarship, however, have pointed toward important continuities amid the rise of online news. Political economists have pointed out that many of the same media companies still produce most of the news that people actually encounter online. News ethnographers have looked at how professional journalists have adapted new technological possibilities in ways that try to preserve, or negotiate a degree of preservation of, many of their existing professional routines and values.[10] I want to look at another form of continuity—how the demand-driven ideal of postprofessional journalism has been adapted and extended in the face of emerging technological possibilities.

The last several chapters of this book have made the argument that digital technologies are far from the sole forces responsible for the declining grip of professionalism in U.S. news. Major efforts to reimagine how news could be defined by consumer demand rather than editorial expertise were well under way by the time online news became a significant factor. Nonetheless, the Internet has indeed opened new possibilities for alternative modes of news production and distribution. These possibilities stem not only from technological development—in design as well as investments in areas such as broadband infrastructure and consumer marketing—but also from the political imagination that has been embedded in ways of speaking and thinking about the significance of an Internet era. While notions of cyberdemocracy were common throughout the 1990s, by the mid-2000s a particular and powerful discourse associating the Internet with participatory democracy came into focus around Web 2.0, or "the social Web." Much of this discourse celebrates images of horizontal or peer-to-peer communication networks (sometimes called distributed networks) as democratic alternatives to hierarchical and bureaucratic forms of organization.[11] Daniel Kreiss, Megan Finn, and Fred Turner refer to this way of understanding the affordances of social media as the "peer-production consensus," which they argue has been echoed in large swaths of digital media scholarship as well as more popular discourse.[12] They note a pervasive sense that Internet-enabled networks of peer production provide more egalitarian, more democratic, and ultimately more gratifying and empowering regimes of cultural production than industrialized and bureaucratic models of cultural production.

Of all the domains that have witnessed a rise in recent experiments in peer production, claims about peer production democratizing culture have perhaps been strongest in regards to journalism. The most celebrated innovation has been the rise of "citizen journalists," the growing cadre of ordinary people using blogs, photo- or video-sharing sites, and social media sites (especially Twitter) to share their own bits of news and commentary. But amateur access to publishing alone does not signify a systemic shift in flows of news and information. Merely being able to publish news and views in a potentially public location is not itself a new opportunity dependent on the Internet. Posting information to a lonely website is not all that different from posting a printed pamphlet on a lamp pole, bulletin board, or other public location where it might not receive any notice. The Web post and lamp pole start to look much less similar when flows of attention on the Web make it possible for an ordinary citizen's blog post, video, or photo to be circulated, linked to, or otherwise incorporated into a larger, more dispersed, and more complex network of civic information. Without search engines, social networks, social news and bookmarking sites, news aggregators, and other networked linkages, the lonely Web post would never seem very promising.

To understand the crucial role of online filtering mechanisms in optimistic visions of online democracy, we can look at legal scholar and network theorist Yochai Benkler's model of "the networked public sphere." Benkler has been one of the most influential and thoughtful scholars writing about how the Web is evolving to create new, and more democratic, dynamics regulating flows of news and information. Benkler's *The Wealth of Networks* (2006) speaks to the optimism of the Web 2.0 zeitgeist about networked culture. He argues that the fundamental architecture of emerging networked communications "improves the political public sphere," and so he argues for the democratic advantages of networked media over twentieth-century mass-media systems.[13] Benkler wants to show that the Internet represents a democratizing technology without relying on the same kind of digital utopianism characteristic of the early 1990s. Key to his argument is the recognition that, if its democratic promise is to be realized, the networked public sphere not only must allow freer access to publication than mass media, but also needs democratic mechanisms for filtering and circulating the abundance of information (including opinion and discussion) that it makes available.

Benkler seeks to challenge what he sees as two recurring concerns about online democracy. On that one hand, skeptics have charged that the Internet is too chaotic, too unorderly, and too decentralized; thus, it creates a space where all can speak, but "the central point of failure becomes the capacity to be heard," rendering its democratic potential ineffective. On the other hand, another set of critics suggests the Internet actually has a tendency toward too much centralization and concentration—with companies like Google directing outsize portions of the traffic and a pervasive "winner-take-all" effect where the most popular online producers monopolize online attention.

In contrast to these two views, Benkler argues for what he readily calls a "Goldilocks position . . . [that] the observed use of the [Internet] exhibits an order that is not too concentrated and not too chaotic."[14] Collaborative filtering plays a central role in what Benkler sees as the solution to balancing abundant chaos and concentration online. He points to specific websites—including the photo-sharing site Flickr and social news site Slashdot—that use collaborative filtering to curate news and information. These serve as examples of native Web solutions to the problem of navigating informational abundance—they provide peer evaluation and recommendation processes to sift attention-worthy items from the forgettable for different communities of users. Yet collaborative filtering does not just take place at the level of individual websites in the networked public sphere. Benkler's account suggests the Internet as a whole acts as a collaborative filter. While acknowledging an uneven spread of attention, he proposes that most of the Internet is so interlinked that if an important story starts almost anywhere on the Web, it can be filtered up to more prominent websites, passing through particular online communities based on special interests to more general larger ones.

For sophisticated digital optimists like Benkler, there is no place for the illusion that the online abundance means the end of news filtering. What they see, however, is one paradigm of gatekeeping—journalistic professionalism—being replaced by another one that is more egalitarian, participatory, and democratic. Whether the term *gatekeeping* even applies to this participatory filter is controversial. Axel Bruns argues that peer recommendation constitutes a distinctly different form of "gatewatching" rather than gatekeeping.[15] In any case, selecting and prioritizing certain news stories over others remain essential because even though the Internet's capacity for storing information is near limitless, popular attention remains a scarce resource.

Collaborative filtering is the mechanism that enables a collective form of peer editing.[16] Collaborative filters can sort news based on what Pierre Levy calls collective intelligence.[17] In the minds of advocates, collaborative filtering democratizes news by allowing editorial decisions to be made by everyday users and the collective subject they form when their feedback is given expression through algorithms (a collective intelligence, wise crowd, and the like) rather than a few designated editors. In another influential book speaking optimistically about a growing participatory culture, Henry Jenkins draws a contrast between knowledge produced by collective intelligence versus what he refers to as "the expert paradigm." Clearly, the professional model of journalism epitomizes the expert paradigm. For Jenkins, the emergence of a more democratic and participatory culture is tied to a shift from the expert paradigm to collective intelligence.[18] In such a media culture, the once stark lines demarcating media consumers from producers are fading.

Creating Online News and Making It Social

The financial crisis U.S. news began facing in the mid-2000s coincided, roughly, with a significant uptick in the availability of online news and a surge in blogs and new forms of social media providing opportunities for amateurs to share and recommend news. The timing of the industry's financial crisis lent some credence to the view that legacy news organizations were proving themselves to be stuck in the past and maladaptive to the digital media environment. In the burgeoning blogosphere, especially among a popular group of bloggers, legacy news outlets were dubbed "dinosaur" media. By invoking the rhetoric of dinosaur media and other epithets implying the obsolescence of established news media, bloggers were reacting against the dismissive attitudes of some journalists who characterized blogging and other forms of citizen journalism as sloppy, unreliable, and driven by emotion and hype rather than information and analysis.[19] They were also aggrandizing these rising formats, painting a contrast between a new generation of digital news makers—a youthful and savvy one—and a moribund old press that had lost touch with the evolving cultural norms of the media landscape. While arguably amateur bloggers and paid journalists have come to a greater recognition of each other's strengths since the mid-2000s, stereotypes of legacy media outlets as digitally inept and citizen journalists as disorderly and unreliable continue to serve as influential frames for understanding contemporary news dynamics. In this section, I offer a brief overview of the historical circumstances surrounding the rise of social news sites in the United States. Their rise, however, is tied to the migration of news online generally, including news provided by established media companies. It is important to show that the growth of online news media has not demonstrated a quick cultural shift in which established news media simply lost their popular appeal. Rankings of top news sites online consistently show most of the most popular online news destinations are affiliated with legacy news organization representing newspapers, cable news, or network news outlets.[20] Established news organizations have lost a significant degree of their leverage to monetize their news products and commodity audiences online, but this change does not mean there is no longer a popular taste or consumption demand for the type of news produced by such outlets.

While established news outlets have not usually been at the forefront of devising innovative ways to use Web capacities for sharing news, they have not been entirely resistant to such efforts. Pablo Boczkowski has written the most comprehensive history of the digitization of U.S. daily newspapers. He approaches U.S. newspapers as a culture of production—or in his words a "culture of innovation"—characterized by "a combination of defensive, reactive, and pragmatic traits" during the early period of digital exploration before widespread Internet adoption in the mid-1990s.[21] By this, Boczkowski means that news organizations tended to follow perceived trends rather than attempt to initiate new ones (reactive), focus on maintaining their existing domains rather than venturing into new areas (defensive), and mostly focus on "the short-term well-being of what was identified as core business, rather than more idealistically pursuing projects that seemed promising but could pay off only in the long term." This characterization largely fits with the image of established news organizations as cautious and adverse to digital innovation unless under pressure. Through a careful analysis of statements made by leading figures in the news industry during this time, Boczkowski demonstrates the defensive, reactive, and pragmatic quality of some of the reasoning news leaders used to justify investments in digital experiments during this time. Yet Boczkowski, along with other digital news historians, also provides evidence showing that daily newspapers were among the first major investors in creating cultural content in online formats.[22] So while newspapers executives might have justified their digital experiments on defensive and reactive bases, they also helped mobilize and promote new digital formats well before widespread Internet access in the United States.

Between 1981 and 1986, more than two dozen U.S. newspapers began offering videotex services, an interactive technology that used phone or cable lines to transmit data for display, usually as text, on a television set or monitor.[23] Major news chains such as Times-Mirror and Knight Ridder made sizable investments in these systems and helped promote a consumer market for them.[24] Videotex did not prove to be a fiscally successful technology for newspapers, and the industry lost millions of dollars through these investments. Still, these experiments seem to have inspired U.S. newspapers to take an early interest in creating screen formats for news. The Newspaper Advertising Bureau set up a New Technology Department and joined other newspapers and the Associated Press in a pilot study of CompuServe in the early 1980s. Startext, a system created by a partnership between the *Fort Worth Star-Telegram* and the Tandy Corporation in 1982, appears to have been the first experiment of a media company providing digital space for user-generated news. Startext users connected from home modems and could access much of the paper online as well as contribute their own movie reviews, commentary, and more.[25]

During the dot-com boom in the mid- to late 1990s, major U.S. news organizations, especially newspapers, were establishing their online presences at a rapid pace. Before widespread access to the Web, many papers partnered with online services such as CompuServe, Prodigy, and American Online. Until 1995 commercial activity was restricted on the Internet, which had been developed by public funding for the military and later by university researchers. When major news companies began to move online, most of what they featured on their sites became known as "shovelware," news content taken from elsewhere (especially print copy) and simply moved online. As Ben Scott has observed, however, even the first generation of shovelware allowed for innovations in the way news could be accessed: online news stories were grouped together topically, related stories within the publication were often connected with hyperlinks, some stories included hyperlinks to original source material, and archives became easily accessible.[26] For the first time outside of a library periodical room, users could access news from outlets around the world, or at least from anywhere that had developed Internet infrastructure. These innovations could be felt on an experiential level by millions of users. As Scott also notes, the growth of online news also gave the news industry an opportunity to deploy the rhetoric of digital empowerment and revolution. Such appeals helped divert energy from mounting criticism of media companies' declining investment in public service news.

In the early 2000s, newspapers and some television news organizations started enhancing their online offerings and aiming for something beyond a repackaging of print content. More news sites began to incorporate multimedia. A study of eighty U.S. newspaper websites found that only 7 percent had video in 1997, compared to 44 percent in 2003.[27] Shortly thereafter, video became almost ubiquitous on major newspaper sites. A challenging question for traditional news sources has been how to integrate interactive features of online media. Startext was a very early example of an interactive space set up by established media. But this level of interactivity was not carried over to most early websites run by established news outlets. At first, the opportunity to e-mail reporters was one of the few interactive attributes of online journalism. By the mid-2000s, more news sites were adding comment sections for certain articles. Some news sites started to make space to host readers' blogs, though these were cordoned off from the rest of the material. At about the same time, many sites started introducing the "most popular" widgets, but this allowed users only to recommend, indirectly, stories from the host site. Later, legacy news outlets were participating in social media through Facebook accounts, encouraging (sometimes requiring) staff to maintain Twitter accounts, adding more interactive features, and embedding sharing buttons on their websites.

While online news sites run by major media companies acted somewhat slowly and cautiously to tap into the interactive social capacities of Internet sites, other producers began experimenting with alternative ways to create and distribute news online. The first social news site that gained widespread attention was Slashdot, which started out as a website linking to stories about technology-related news. In 1997 Rob Malda, a Hope College student known online as CmdrTaco, started a site first called "Chips & Dips," soon to become Slashdot. *Slashdot* was a play on words—a befuddling trick for Web newcomers, who would still pronounce every character when talking about the URL of a website. Malda and many early Slashdot followers proudly aligned themselves with the geek community. Its tagline was—and remains—"News for nerds, Stuff that matters." The website's following built upon a shared interest in the open-software movement and, perhaps even more important, a deep resentment of Microsoft. At first, Malda posted links to Web stories having to do with Linux, hacking, video games, *Star Wars,* and other items relating to geek culture.

Malda's interest in the open-software movement led him to start thinking about how to run a website inspired by the same collaborative ethic. As he began receiving many e-mails from followers suggesting links to stories, he started allowing other users to contribute to the site. As it continued to grow, he developed a system for assigning users "moderation power" in order to filter content on the site in an orderly and cyberdemocratic manner. The Slashdot system awarded users with certain types of moderation power based on their usage patterns and the feedback their own contributions had received. Moderator status was not something users could possess permanently, but it was rewarded on a temporary basis and distributed randomly among those who were eligible.[28] In the late 1990s, this was a very unusual way of running a website. But Slashdot quickly gained recognition among early Web adopters and tech advertisers. By its second year of operation, it had more than one hundred thousand hits a day.

Slashdot gained a high profile in the tech community, becoming a frequent topic of discussion in *Wired.* Then, imitators soon followed. New sites sprang up that introduced somewhat different models for filtering news stories and other Web items through peer collaboration. In 2003 a Carnegie Mellon graduate created del.icio.us (later Delicious) and introduced "social bookmarking" and "tagging" into the vocabulary of social Web culture. Originally, the focus of Delicious was to provide users with a way to keep track of websites that they had visited and wanted to remember by marking them with key terms (tags).[29] But Delicious also allowed users to share their bookmarks with each other, providing a way to navigate the Web based on user-generated tags. Delicious created a "most popular" page and pages that would allow users to follow trending topics.

Digg launched in 2004 and became the first social news site to gain widespread popularity beyond Slashdot's core technology community. Like Slashdot, Digg users submitted links and headlines to news items from across the Web. Unlike Slashdot, on Digg the links submitted by Digg users appeared directly on the site without the approval of any moderator or staff member. Digg users could vote directly on the prominence of news items, as the site helped pioneer the soon-to-be-ubiquitous social "like" buttons (or in Digg's case "Digg" or "unDigg"). While moving away from Slashdot's exclusive focus on technology news and tech culture, Digg remained mostly focused on timely news-related items, and Digg's category pages, including business, technology, politics, and science, helped to maintain such an emphasis. Digg's rise to popularity illustrates the kind of accidents and coincidences that can be key to a successful social media site. The site received a boost into mainstream attention from an unlikely source: Paris Hilton's cell phone was hacked in 2005, and the data were published online. A Digg user posted a link to the cell phone data, and as the story made its way to the top of Digg's home page, Digg became the top hit on Google and Yahoo! for people searching for "Paris Hilton cell phone hack."[30] Hundreds of thousands of users visited Digg for the first time, overwhelming its servers and slowing down the site severely.

After the Hilton incident, Digg rode a quick wave of success. By late 2005, it was attracting more than a million monthly visitors and several times as many a year later.[31] Newspapers and magazines around North America ran hundreds of articles about the site, and several reported rumors that established tech companies were offering to buy Digg for hundreds of millions of dollars.[32] In 2006 *Businessweek* featured a cover image of Digg's youthful-looking founder, Kevin Rose, wearing a backward hat and headphones with a story titled "How This Kid Made $60 Million in 18 Months."[33] Other social news sites established themselves around this same time, and several were bought by major media companies. Reddit, which would eventually displace Digg as the most popular social news site, was founded in 2005 by a pair of twenty-two-year-old students at the University of Virginia. Its founders' initial vision was that Reddit would be even less focused on technology than Digg and that a simple visual format would attract a wider array of visitors.[34] Reddit was purchased by Condé Nast in 2006. Newsvine, another popular social news site, was also founded in 2005, and it was acquired by MSNBC in 2007. While Digg led the pack as the most visited social news site for many years, by 2010 it was faltering in part because of user disappointment surrounding a major redesign. By 2012 Reddit overtook Digg as the most visited social news site. Later that year, Digg sold its domain name and brand to another company that turned the site into a different kind of news-aggregation site.[35]

Social news sites, and many fans and media commentators, have boasted that they had finally found a way to democratize news. Many of the top sites emphasize the theme that social news provides a democratic alternative to traditional editors. Newsvine's Facebook profile declares its mission as follows: "Democratization of news media and extending the consumption of news into a conversation."[36] Digg's early website pushed the theme of the power of users over editors: "From the biggest online destinations to the most obscure blog, Digg surfaces the best stuff as voted on by our users. You won't find editors at

Digg—we're here to provide a place where people can collectively determine the value of content and we're changing the way people consume information online. How do we do this? Everything on Digg—from news to videos to images—is submitted by our community (that would be you). Once something is submitted, other people see it and Digg what they like best."[37]

Even journalists working for legacy news organizations started writing about social news as a democratization of journalism. For example, the *Christian Science Monitor* ran a story about social news sites under the heading "Who Controls the News? On the Web, You Can."[38] The *Chicago Tribune*'s Internet critic Steve Johnson suggested, "[Digg is] news democratized, or maybe it's just the flavor of recent months."[39] The Pew Center's Project on Excellence in Journalism (PEJ) produced a special report on Digg and other user-driven news sites, asking, "If someday we have a world without journalists, or at least without editors, what would the news agenda look like? How would citizens make up a front page differently than professional news people?"[40] For the time period they studied, the PEJ report found that the user-driven news agenda appeared "more diverse, yet also more fragmented and transitory than that of the mainstream news media."[41] Even writers who were quite skeptical of social news seemed fascinated with the idea that there is something democratic about how these sites work.

Examining the Social News Approach

Claims that social news sites "democratize the news" deserve careful consideration. While offering a critique of social news as a satisfying model for building a democratic news media, I want to suggest that their appeal cannot be reduced only to the attraction of the digital sublime. Although the allure of a technological fix for democracy surely plays a role, the promise of social news speaks to a demand-driven vision for democratizing news that predates social media. Social news sites represent an attempt to streamline the feedback loop between popular interests and editorial decision making. This is the same kind of feedback loop that market researchers have wanted to harness, though they have faced methodological and epistemological hurdles, as discussed in chapter 2. With real-time feedback, the possibility of greater numbers involved in direct participation, and arguably more transparency between user participation and editorial agenda making, the social news model has some real differences and advantages over the market research model.

The basic premise of social news advocates is sensible: the claim is that they democratize news by allowing all to partake in a collaborative decision-making process to set the news agenda. Social news gives users a certain kind of voting rights in regard to the news agenda. The kind of voting offered by social news might even appear to be a more radical form of democracy than elections for political representatives. Social news users are not electing representatives to make decisions for them; they are participating in something that looks more like direct democracy where a popular referendum on news priorities is always taking place. The market research approach, in contrast, requires additional steps of mediation. In most traditional market research scenarios, researchers first collect feedback through surveys, observations, or focus groups; then it is the researchers who must construe generalizations about what *kinds* of news or *qualities* of news stories a population prefers. In the social news model, there is no need for these kinds of generalizations—user feedback directly impacts the ranking of particular items.

Direct democracy has often been held up as an ideal and a model for solving many of the problems of representative democracy.[42] In this respect, social news—and collaborative filtering more generally—strikes a chord resonant with long-standing populist sensibilities. The vision of social news sites is also based on aggregative model of democracy—a model that defines democracy as a process of decision making driven by individual preferences.[43] There are other paradigms that assume robust democracy requires not just a counting of individual preferences. Models of deliberative and agonistic democracy call for ensuring specific kinds of communication and discourse that allow popular preferences to take shape in contexts in which these preferences are informed by facts, reasoning, and empathetic engagement with multiple perspectives. While social news sites do allow for comments and host discussion about linked items, the paradigm embedded in their voting procedures falls much closer to aggregative democracy: individual users' votes, rather than the outcome of a deliberation, determine the placement of an item.

In this section, I explore several specific problems that surface as social news sites attempt to "apply" democracy to news. None of this analysis suggests social news sites are antithetical to democracy. Rather, I want to show why social news sites do not merely offer transparent reflections of popular interest in news—even among their limited groups of users. This is not because such sites employ an insidious or malevolent process of shaping user demand. Rather, if we accept the premise that media environments influence popular tastes and desire, then any mechanism for making such desire manifest is inescapably particular and selective in how it operationalizes its measures of popular interest. The analysis that follows illustrates aspects of this process on social news sites. Closely examining how social news sites mobilize their publics shows they take a somewhat different approach from market research to try to set a news agenda based on popular interest. Yet even with the immediacy and heightened interactivity of digital media, these sites are still unable to simply mirror popular news interest.

The remainder of this chapter puts into question three assumptions tied to claims that social news sites can democratize news: collaborative filters can create dependable and value-free measures of popular choice, social news sites can engage diverse and heterogeneous groups of users, and users' preferences for news are ontologically grounded independently of the way they are mediated. Interrogating these assumptions suggests that social news does not simply hand power over to "the people," but rather it too mobilizes users in particular ways.

Framing Votes

In democratic elections, the rules and protocols governing the electoral process need to be open to public scrutiny and debate to maintain legitimacy. This does not necessarily mean that it leads to a consensual process. But even in an era that widely celebrates the privatization of government services, it is hard to imagine that a push to have private companies run elections and decide on their basic protocols and eligibility requirements would be taken seriously. In regards to social news sites, however, the fact that site owners usually make unilateral decisions about voting protocols has hardly dampened enthusiasm.

When a person "votes" for a news item on a social news site, what does this mean? Does it mean she finds the item enjoyable? Has she found something that makes her laugh? Does it mean she thinks the topic of the story is important news? Does it mean that she not only thinks the story is important, but also thinks the link conveys valuable and important information about it? Does it mean that she thinks that others will find the story interesting?

All social news sites frame the meaning of votes. Site owners are not able to dictate exactly how users employ the affordances of the site, and sites leave room for a good deal of ambiguity about what a vote means. Yet all these sites help frame the meaning of votes through both their description and their architecture. During the peak of Digg's popularity, it nudged users toward voting for items they thought would appeal to other users. As Digg's FAQ explained, "If your submission rocks and receives enough Diggs, it is promoted to the front page for the millions of our visitors to see."[44] Reddit's FAQ suggests an up vote is for "good" content and a down vote is for "junk." A section on "reddiquette" provides more explicit instructions. This section says users should not vote down on an item just because they disagree with its viewpoint, nor should they vote for an item based on its title or headline alone. It also advises that the titles of posts should be "factual and opinion-free," and the voters should exercise their power to moderate "based on quality, not opinion. Well-written and interesting content can be worthwhile, even if you disagree with it."[45] Newsvine's site includes a code of honor, calling on users to respect each other, avoid self-promotion, and use informative rather than sensational headlines.

Of course, the explicit statements made on these FAQ pages do not have an omniscient power to control how everyone uses the site. However, sites have more forceful ways of influencing user norms through their code (or site architecture) and terms of services.[46] One way to think about how code shapes the voting process is that designers determine the configuration of the voting levers. Some sites allow up and down votes, for instance, while others allow only up votes. Some sites have created levers more intricate than binary up or down options. On Slashdot the voting protocols require user-moderators to tag comments with a descriptive adjective such as *informative* or *flame bait*. Adjectives considered positive by the site designers lead to a higher rating and vice versa for the negative ones. Social news sites also intervene through reward and punishment systems meant to preserve the harmony of the community and regulate users to stay within the terms of service. Reddit allows users to accumulate "karma" points through contributing links and comments that receive a favorable reception among their user base. Slashdot has a reputation system that rewards users by increasing their potential to influence the site if their contributions conform to its users' dominant values. The former Digg built a reputation system that at one point allocated significant control of front-page stories to so-called power users, those users who had long track records of successful contributions.[47] Social news sites can eject or ban users who are not following their intended protocols. Reddit uses a practice it calls "shadowbanning," making it so a banned user's posts can be seen only by herself or himself. In 2014 Reddit shadowbanned a user with the handle Unidan, who was one of the site's most popular and karma-rich users, for setting up multiple accounts to down-vote adversaries and up-vote himself.[48]

The full significance of the framing power of social news sites might come into clear view by looking at an outlier in the social news field—NewsTrust .net. NewsTrust is a nonprofit social news site founded in 2005 that cultivates a different voting sensibility than many other sites. NewsTrust initially received support from many foundations and individual donors, including the MacArthur Foundation, the Omidyar Network, Open Society, the Sunlight Foundation, the Mitch Kapor Foundation, and Craig Newmark, and in 2012 it was acquired by the Poynter Institute. It has partnered with a number of major media outlets as well as academic journalism programs. Its mission is to help "people find good journalism online. Our web review tools let you rate the news based on journalistic quality, not just popularity. Based on member ratings, we feature a daily selection of top rated news and opinions on our free site. We're non-profit, non-partisan, and committed to helping citizens make informed decisions about democracy."[49]

NewsTrust has designed a set of voting protocols that attempt to operationalize these values. Instead of ranking items based on simple up or down votes, NewsTrust users rate stories based on a number of different dimensions. Depending on a user's level of experience, she will be asked to evaluate news items based on different review forms for each of two categories of news: fact-based items and opinion items. The shortest review form asks each user to say whether a story is fair, whether it is factual, and then whether she recommends it. The longest form has a total of eighteen dimensions, including judgments about whether a story cites expert sources, provides a balanced viewpoint, and is "enterprising," which an FAQ explains as meaning, "Does this story show initiative? Courage? Did the author or publication take risks gathering and publishing this story? Were significant resources involved?"[50]

While NewsTrust offers a way for more people to play a role in the editorial process than with traditional publications, the site's structure tries to preserve traditional journalistic values and train amateurs in how to emulate professional journalism's standards. NewsTrust is an example of a "pro-am" (professional-amateur) experiment in online news, an approach that has been gaining attention from nonprofit and foundation funders. In addition to the longer review forms, NewsTrust also contains online training for developing what it identifies as "news literacy," including a guide on how to "Think Like a Journalist" and "Crap Detection 101."

Clearly, NewsTrust attempts to shape the activity of users on the site. It is a social news site that is interactive and participatory, but it is not hard to see how the action of users on this site is bound by a set of constraints. Yet these are what Anthony Giddens would call "enabling constraints."[51] NewsTrust's protocols do not merely limit users' actions; they also make a certain type of interaction possible. NewsTrust's voting mechanism enables users to enact a particular form of citizenship corresponding to a well-established set of journalistic values. In essence, NewsTrust offers a training ground for cultivating what might be professional journalism's ideal type of reader.

Some people surely find the professional news values promoted by NewsTrust appealing. The site attempts to counter several of the most prevalent complaints that have been lodged against online news sites—charges that they traffic in unverified rumors and create clusters of like-minded people unwilling to expose themselves to diverse viewpoints. Still, the NewsTrust model will surely have its critics. This model may smuggle in questionable aspects of professional news values, such as deference to official sources. It could also limit broad participation because its requirements could be seen as too arduous or incongruent with the habits of many Internet users.

Thinking about the particularity of the interactivity embedded in NewsTrust's design can help illuminate the particularity of all social news sites. Reddit enthusiasts may claim that users on their site face fewer constraints and thus have more freedom than users on NewsTrust. Yet such a view offers only a narrow understanding of freedom in a negative sense—focusing only on what types of activity a site censors without regard to what it positively cultivates. Consider this situation from the perspective of a regular NewsTrust user. Let's call her Alisa and assume she accepts the basic norms and values encoded in NewsTrust. If Alisa ventures over to Reddit, she may find it a frustrating experience. She will be able to make judgment calls about what she votes for based on her own quasi-professional news values, but she will not find herself in a community that gives back to her the kinds of recommendation and filtering she values. Reddit may not create the conditions for democratic news that Alisa desires.

My argument here is that the norms for interaction and the way voting is framed on social news sites matter. Social news sites are encoded with different values and voting structures, and they produce quite different forms of interactivity, sharing, and collective judgment. While users indeed give life to these sites, the site design provides a structure that shapes the possibilities and probably trajectories of user engagement.

Counting Votes: #AlgorithmProblems

Social news sites rely on algorithms for calculating user feedback and translating raw inputs into a ranked order for the prominence of stories and comments. These ranking algorithms are more complex than a simple tabulation of votes. The ranking algorithms often take into account factors such as how many votes a certain item has received in a particular time period and the time lapse since its first posting. The algorithms of some sites factor in characteristics about users; users who have voted for popular items in the past might have more say than newbies or users whose tastes do not appear to align as well with the site.

Most social news sites keep secret the algorithms they use to rank stories, comments, and the visibility of subgroups, though Reddit has been a notable exception in being relatively open about its ranking algorithms. One major reason for this secrecy is to prevent "gaming," a practice in which users or groups of users try to exert an inordinate amount of influence to bring certain items to the top of the page or hide them. The biggest gaming threat often comes from spammers or marketers who try to use their resources to organize online voting strategies to get certain stories to the front page. Because of the massive influence wielded by the top social news sites, an item appearing near the top of the ranking may be able to send tens of thousands, or even more, users to a Web page.

While the threat from public relations gaming is real, it is very difficult, perhaps impossible, to distinguish between organized groups of gamers promoting something for financial interests and groups of users orchestrating coordinated voting campaigns for other reasons—such as political groups trying to promote or demote a certain cause. This is both a technical challenge and a philosophical quandary. The philosophical quandary is that such algorithms must embed value choices promoting a certain vision of the ideal form of citizenship that can be exercised on the site. For most of the top social news sites, the preferred style of citizenship idealizes an atomistic individual—someone who votes according to their own preferences and judgment without being part of an organized campaign.

Major sites such Reddit, Hacker News, and Slashdot all include instructions to users discouraging them from trying to coordinate voting campaigns for links or comments, and many social news sites make participating in such efforts an offense warranting a user's eviction. Reddit says it will ban users who engage in a "vote ring," occurring when members agree "to vote on certain things together, either a specific submission, a user, a domain, or anything like that."[52] This rule is well known among major users of the site, and it has raised some thorny questions. For instance, the subreddit (a group of users formed to discuss a certain topic) known as /r/shitredditsays was formed to identify Reddit posts that are "bigoted, creepy, misogynistic, transphobic, racist, homophobic, or just reeking of unexamined, toxic privilege." Considering that Reddit is largely a male-dominated site, it is unsurprising this subreddit has received a lot of criticism from other users. Many have accused shitredditsays of being an organized voting brigade, though the shitredditsays home page explicitly tells users not to mass down-vote content appearing on the site.[53] As the rules currently stand, subreddits like shitredditsays cannot encourage down-voting (or up-voting) content without risking bans.

Social news sites can also try to penalize coordinated voting campaigns through algorithms designed to detect and counter such practices. Given the secrecy of their algorithms, many social news sites do not publicly reveal whether they attempt to do this. The former Digg designed its algorithm to give more weight to disconnected groups of users than ones who appeared to be working in concert after a voting ring known as the Digg Patriots—dedicated to keeping "liberal" content off top pages—was revealed. Tarleton Gillespie has documented something similar in how Twitter identifies "trending" topics.[54] During the period of Gillespie's research, Twitter's trending-topics algorithm privileged topics that were accelerating in discussion among users without known links to each other. Citing an example of a controversy over possible Twitter censorship, Gillespie suggests this aspect of Twitter's trending algorithm offers one possible explanation for why #OccupyWallStreet never appeared on the trending list, despite large spikes in its frequency. Gillespie argues that Occupy activists may not have realized that the values embedded in Twitter's algorithm, not specific human intervention, may have made it unlikely for #OccupyWallStreet to achieve trending status. This indeed might be construed as a form of "censorship."

The algorithms that determine prominence on social news sites entail responses to more value-laden questions beyond how they judge coordination among voters. For just a few examples, social news algorithms must choose whether to factor in the established reputation of users, whether incoming up votes or links from items appearing on more obscure websites receive more weight than very popular ones, whether content labeled in all subcategories will be treated equally, and how the prominence of an item on one subcategory or list on a site might affect its ranking on other subcategories or lists on the same site (for instance, Reddit has separate lists for "rising," "top," and "front page" items). Across all social news sites I have encountered, timeliness matters. Social news algorithms tend to favor news that appears to be "breaking" on the site. They can do this by including decay functions in their algorithms that weigh against items that have already been on the site for extended periods of time. This approach resonates with professional news outlets' emphasis on breaking stories, yet clearly both cases reflect editorial decisions prioritizing particular news values.

The Recursivity Problem

Collaborative filtering revolves around a certain irony: the filter decides what content users are exposed to, while, at the same time, users collectively decide what content passes through the filter. This creates conditions that could, in extreme circumstances, lead to a recursive loop. Once an item starts to make it to a prominent place on a social news site, many more users will encounter that item and will be much more likely to vote for it compared to an item buried deep in the site. Social news sites can mitigate these recursive tendencies through various strategies: ejecting items after a certain amount of time, weighing against votes received while in the most prominent positions, directing users to supplemental currents of news items not sorted through the same kind of collaborative rankings (such as a "rising" list in addition to a most popular), and so forth. Yet even though social news sites are clearly able to avoid the trap of a completely stalled loop, they do not fulfill the ideal of creating a playing field in which every news item submitted has an equal shot at making it to the top pages. On social news sites, like the rest of the Web, certain items will receive much more attention because of their placement in high-traffic areas. Of course, for many social news sites, users can also submit votes for news items while surfing the Web, but this stream of votes gives an advantage to content appearing on highly trafficked Web pages.

In this respect, social news sites share a problem in common with Web search engines. Search engines like Google order their results based, in part, on which sites receive the most links (especially from sites that themselves receive high numbers of incoming links). As a site moves to the top of common search results, it also tends to receive more attention and more links.[55] Thus, a recursive pattern can form. This problem has been referred to as a type of search-engine bias, "Googlearchy," "the-rich-get-richer," or the "winner-take-all" effect.[56] Matthew Hindman describes one especially rigorous study that explored linking patterns across an array of online political communities discussing topics such as abortion, gun control, and the U.S. Congress. The researchers used search bots to crawl through hundreds of thousands of sites and links, creating a map of links representing discussion about these topics on the Web. They found exponentially steep differences between the number of links the top sites received compared to the vast majority of sites. For example, in one sample of 1,015 sites discussing abortion identified through a bot crawl seeded by a Google search, the top site received 31.1 percent of the inbound links, the top-ten sites received 70.6 percent of links, and the top 50 sites received 88.8 percent of links. This is an extremely top-heavy distribution. Of the twelve discussion communities they investigated, each composed of between about 500 and 3,000 individual websites, the concentration of links was uniformly very high, with the top 50 sites in each community receiving more than 70 percent of the inbound links.[57] This same top-heavy pattern held even among the subcommunities of sites supporting one particular viewpoint (that is, similar distribution even among sites taking a pro–gun control stance). What does this suggest about Web traffic and search engines? In reviewing his own research and other studies, Hindman argues that all evidence points to "the conclusion that profound inequalities in links define search engine visibility and patterns of traffic."[58]

Although I have not been able to find any empirical studies specific to social news sites, the same general dynamic—high visibility begets higher visibility—that is true of search engines holds true in principle for social news sites. Both Google and social news sites create filters determined by users' activity, while they simultaneously influence the very patterns of their users' activity. Social news proprietors can creatively engineer algorithms to influence ranking patterns in different ways, but for rankings to give every item equal attention and opportunity (prior to filtering) would require a radical departure in terms of user expectations. Users would have to agree to rate randomly selected content so that the initial layer of exposure is not skewed by prior rankings or ratings. Yet such a scheme would require asking users to sacrifice time rating unfiltered content. Would users be willing to put in such voluntary efforts? This approach is not impossible to imagine, but it would require cultivating an online community with a strong commitment to a value-driven vision of democratic news.

Social Exclusivity

If social news sites are an important part of a networked public sphere, as well as harbingers of the potential of such a public sphere more generally, they should not simply reproduce the exclusions and communicative power imbalances of the mass media age. Enthusiasm for "networked" or "participatory" news is underwritten by a hope that interactivity will make participating in news and public discussion more appealing to diverse groups of citizens and lead to broader engagement in public life than known under the regime of mass media. The aspiration for a universal appeal is reflected in how social news sites promote themselves. Newsvine, for instance, claims to be "an instant reflection of what the world is talking about at any given moment."[59] Many media critics and scholars, of course, recognize that the online world, including social media, is plagued with many of the same divisions and inequities as the offline world.[60] Nonetheless, visions of a burgeoning participatory culture often assume that the fact of interactivity and the dialogical affordances of digital media empower everyone and can draw in social groups who had been most neglected by mass media.[61]

What can social news sites tell us about the prospect of creating an inclusive, networked public sphere? I want to suggest two criteria for evaluating social news sites in terms of their capacity for enhancing social inclusivity. First, they should offer platforms for diverse publics to work collaboratively to set a common news agenda. Second, they should help mobilize broad groups of users to take an active interest in engaging with news and public life. Looking at this first criterion, I want to use the phrase "common news agenda" cautiously. As Nancy Fraser has powerfully argued, under conditions of social inequity and stratification, democracy needs multiple public spheres, including spaces for peer-to-peer dialogue among marginalized groups and those representing particular viewpoints.[62] Still, as Fraser also points out, a democratic media system also requires a flow of ideas and information across different groups. Scholars disagree on the relative emphasis to place flows of discourse across more heterogeneous publics versus discourse within publics formed around particular identities, such as gender, race, and sexual orientation. Yet few would disagree that a democratic media system needs an infrastructure that exposes socially and politically dominant groups to perspectives and expressions of experience coming from marginalized groups and minority viewpoints. Professional journalism has not set a high bar in this regard. Critics have documented persistent patterns in professional journalism excluding views in ways that reinforce gender, racial, sexual, and class subordination and limited exposure to critical views of U.S. policy.[63] Nonetheless, looking at popular social news sites does not suggest that substituting the editorial logic of collaborative filtering bodes well for overcoming the tendency for dominant publics to have little exposure to minority or marginalized views.[64]

It is difficult to accurately judge the actual user base of social news sites today. Nonetheless, there has been a strong and persistent sense that popular websites most associated with voting news, such as Reddit, Slashdot, and the former Digg, are male-dominated spaces (see examples of feminist bloggers' criticism of these sites below). In contrast, social bookmarking spaces, such as Pinterest and Delicious, which do not focus on events considered to be news by their users or take the same approach to ranking items by votes, have been widely perceived as feminine spaces. The major social news sites—which clearly traffic in many types of conversations that even users would likely not describe as "news"—especially attract male users affiliated in some way with "geek culture."

Of course, present-day demographics merely provide a snapshot of who is using social news sites at this particular time. For some critics and scholars, relatively privileged groups represent early adopters exploring the frontiers of digital culture. Henry Jenkins argues that the cultural practices of such early adopters offer the "best window" on the future because "these elite consumers exert a disproportionate influence on media culture."[65] However, there are many reasons to believe that the practices of early adopters might not offer such a good window for predicting the uptake of social news sites among groups of users with less cultural and economic capital.

One reason to be cautious about expectations of expanding social news participation is that such sites have often proved to be inhospitable spaces for people from underrepresented groups to share views and experiences. For example, Digg, Slashdot, and Reddit have all faced criticism from feminist bloggers and others for fostering an atmosphere of sexism that makes them unwelcome spaces for women and users identifying as lesbian, gay, bisexual, transgender, or queer.[66] Echoing complaints voiced elsewhere, Irin Carmon, a writer on the prominent feminist blog *Jezebel,* wrote, "It's no secret that Digg is a terrible place for women, whether as conversation topics, authors, or participants."[67] Writing for another blog, Lauren Orsini wrote, "Is Reddit sexist? It hardly seems worth an argument: It is . . .," while offering tips coming from women who use Reddit about how to navigate the site in ways that reduce encounters with hostile sexism.[68] As mentioned previously, a popular subforum on Reddit is dedicated to identifying sexist, racist, transphobic, homophobic, and other bigoted speech commonly found elsewhere on the site. Sometimes site administrators have taken steps to remove abusive users, yet sometimes site administrators themselves have contributed to alienating women. For an April Fools' joke mocking a quest for increasing female readership, Slashdot creators changed the site's color scheme to pink and changed their tagline from "News for nerds, Stuff that matters" to "OMG!!! Ponies!!!"[69]

The prejudices and hostility that users who are not white heterosexual males have faced on some social news sites clearly represent a negative force pushing against the uptake of social news among more diverse groups of users. Yet the challenge of diversifying social news may be just as much a matter of the lack of pull forces drawing new users toward social news as those pushing them away. For some of the tech writers most enthusiastic about online news, the idea of being able to vote and discuss news stories online might seem like a universally attractive feature of news in a participatory culture—a feature that simply accords to the nature of human preferences. But with closer scrutiny, the special kind of social satisfaction and pleasure that comes from this particular type of interactive participation seems to be an acquired one. Like the pleasures of polo, chess, or basketball, enjoying participation in social news relies on developing certain tastes and skills through certain experiences. These experiences and resultant tastes are often unequally distributed across lines of gender, race, class, and other social divisions. In a unique history of the Internet, Thomas Streeter shows how a changing set of romantic notions about cyberspace greatly influenced who used the Net and how they used and added to it. Streeter suggests that a feeling of "self-motivated exhilaration" drew many white male engineering types into computing during the 1980s and 1990s. This feeling was not simply an effect of networked computing in general. Rather, Streeter argues that the kind of spellbinding and compelling experiences some people had with early networked computers stemmed from a certain *habitus*—a term sociologist Pierre Bourdieu uses to describe a social environment cultivating particular kinds of personal dispositions—that forged romantic associations with online activity.[70] It was not only men of a particular class background who had the capacity to experience such exhilaration in connections with computing. But Streeter helps to illustrate how social circumstances made it much more likely for certain groups of midlevel professional men, rather than women or working-class men or executive-level men, to be disposed toward such feelings. Similarly, participating in social news debates may also be dependent on a set of dispositions that are not cultivated in the same fashion across gender, race, socioeconomic, and other social identities.

To focus on gender for a moment, consider the stark gender gap in contributor participation that has long persisted on *Wikipedia,* even though it is one of the most well-known and visited sites on the Internet. In the most comprehensive study to date, a group of researchers found that only about 13 percent of *Wikipedia* contributors were women in 2010.[71] A major study of contributors to open-source software suggests an even more dismal gender gap, estimating that only 2 percent of open-software contributors are women.[72] There are surely many layers to explaining these trends, and there are likely parts of this story that researchers simply do not yet understand. Still, it is clear that in addition to the hostility and lack of encouragement women all too often find in such heavily male-dominated environments, there are also diffuse socialization forces contributing to such gendered differences.[73] The concept of habitus helps to understand how such patterned social differences are maintained through individual choices and actions without suggesting that dispositions or habits are fixed in essential ways. Contemporary conditions might make it more likely that men, for instance, will be more inclined to participate in social news (especially when the norms of social news interactivity have been initially formed by largely male groups of users). Yet it is certainly possible that such a link between gender and social news participation could change.

To address its own gender gap, the Wikimedia Foundation has started to support programs designed to cultivate broader participation among women. Educators and activists have hosted *Wikipedia* editing parties to encourage women and underrepresented groups of users to participate. Yet in the largely commercial sphere of social news, we might not see many of these types of investments dedicated to expanding participation across groups unless they are deemed strategic advertising targets. In fact, commercial media companies are all the more likely to put their investments behind Web services that target groups of users assumed to already have particular sets of tastes. Recommendation algorithms developed by such companies also push us toward material assumed to be appropriate for our gender, class background, race, political orientation, and other such identity profiles.[74] The point here is not that social news will necessarily always be male dominated or dominated by people of a particular age range and educational background. Yet if the current demographic trends are going to change, we cannot simply assume these changes will be driven by broader groups of users flocking toward a universal appeal of collaborative news editing. Rather, new groups of users will likely need to be mobilized and cultivated.

Social News as a Model for the Future of News

Online publishing has opened profound and new possibilities for how news can be produced, edited, circulated, and curated by users. Social news sites offer one example of a creative approach for filtering and sorting the vast amounts of news and information made available online. They represent an idealistic iteration of a larger trend as online news organizations of all stripes incorporate sophisticated forms of audience feedback into their publication and editorial routines and media organizations as a whole anxiously hope for incoming links from sharing various types of platforms like Facebook, Flipboard, Twitter, and Reddit. For many news producers, quantified audience feedback, often in the form of Web metrics, is becoming a driving influence behind story placement and selection.[75] Content mills like Demand Media try to tap into the pulse of popular interest algorithmically by monitoring trends in search terms and cheaply producing stories crafted to show up in search results for these terms. Social news sites operate on a model of site-to-user and user-to-user feedback that is more transparent and clearly feels a lot more like democratic participation than such surreptitious approaches to user feedback.

It can be alluring to believe that democracy works best when power is realized only through an aggregation of individual choices. If the promise of social news sites to democratize news was only a marketing ploy invoked by a small batch of websites, its limited vision of democracy would be of little significance. However, the belief that the collaborative nature of the Web will democratize media lies at the heart of a pervasive optimism about the development of online news and online media generally. This optimism stems from a sense that in the competitive environment of the Internet, the pursuit of popular interest will drive all sorts of experiments and lead to a richer and superior news media. In the conclusion, I examine contemporary discourses on the future of news. Arguably, the most influential position in discussions about the future of news suggests that the best way to handle today's crisis in journalism is to let the Web develop its own solutions. No need, proponents say, for collective deliberation about what norms a democratic media should strive for; rather, we should just trust the outcomes of the online economy/ecology. The dynamics of the Web, from such a view, have a fundamental drive toward greater democracy. The social news model, as an idealistic vision of collaboratively filtering news, offers a normative exemplar of native Web solutions to democratizing news.

However, it would be a mistake to accept the notion that social news represents popular preferences, as if merely reflecting an independent reality. This sort of thinking animates claims that these sites democratize news, as a similar way of thinking backed market researchers' claims to do the same for newspapers and other news formats. In each case, news organizations—whether news producers or aggregators—help stage the conditions in which audiences and users make their choices. The fact that the design of online spaces shapes users' activities is not a problem in itself; it is a corollary of understanding humans as creatures profoundly influenced by our environments rather than as atomistic selves. The danger in accepting, too easily, claims that social news sites democratize news is not that such sites fail to live up to the ideals of autonomous individualism. Rather, the problem is that pitching the democratization of news online only as a matter of satisfying existing demand forecloses other questions. It nudges us away from ethical questions about how to build media environments in which we make our choices about what kind of news matters to us and our communities. The satisfaction of measuring individual interest under a constrained set of circumstances should not keep us from engaging questions that lead to complex, and inevitably contentious, discussions about how to build a media system better equipped to support democratic life.

CONCLUSION

Beyond the Phantom Public

When I was first conceiving of this project in early 2009, a shock wave of panic was reverberating throughout much of the U.S. news industry. Newspapers' revenues were tumbling faster than ever, and news organizations across media were making deep cuts in staff to unprecedented levels. At the same time, speculation about and debates over the future of news were exploding—on blogs, in magazines and journalism reviews, and at conventions and conferences hastily being assembled. In the intervening years, the downward slope of investment in traditional news media has softened, at least according to some measures, but the sense that the U.S. news media are in the midst of a fundamental shift has only grown stronger. Debates about the future of news continue. There was a brief moment when calls for very sizable new streams of public funding for news resources were entertained by elected officials.[1] But such thinking fights against even stronger political currents. The dominance of neoliberal ideology among U.S. policy makers—favoring market-based provisions for all public needs—has largely persevered, despite the Great Recession.[2] Tea Party–fueled deficit panic helped shift U.S. political discourse away from a moment in which many political leaders talked openly about the failures of the free market and the need for public stimulus. Still, no solutions to the journalism crisis have been settled on, and many options remain open. As discussion and struggles over the future of news continue, there is more need than ever for tough scrutiny of demand-driven philosophies of news. There is also more need for attending to the dynamics of how to make news popular by creating opportunities for building news institutions that can articulate compelling, informative, and engaging stories of public life to broad publics.

In taking up the questions at the center of this book, I wanted to bring some of the intellectual resources of critical media studies to debates about the future of news. It is hard to imagine a more exciting time to be studying journalism than when we face unique opportunities for imagining and building news media that might be very different from the past. The changes taking place in news media concern not only content but the very modes through which people engage the media in everyday life and the ways media connect individuals to larger communities. Although interactive media are not inherently destined to level hierarchies of power, it is certainly possible that societal appropriations of new media technologies could mean a reworking of the infrastructure that regulates which ideas and visions circulate from point to point in our media system. The question is how crucial decisions at this critical juncture will be made and what course they will set for the years to come.

Media scholars have more opportunities than ever to contribute to public discussions about these matters. This may be a rare moment when media scholars' ideas can travel quickly beyond the normal circuits bounded by academic discipline.[3] However, critical media scholars have taken an uneven interest in participating in this pivotal moment. Many scholars residing in journalism departments and those working in the political economy tradition have indeed added their voices to these debates. Yet few of the concepts or concerns that have been most developed in cultural studies and critical approaches to popular culture have made their way into these public discussions. The role of media organizations in popularizing news and stimulating broad interest in public life has received too scant attention in the future of news debates.

In this conclusion, I want to draw out some implications of the previous chapters and make a case for what insights a critical understanding of recent models for popularizing news can offer contemporary discussions about rebuilding media institutions. I focus on three types of arguments that run throughout this book: a historical argument about the contemporary conjuncture of U.S. journalism, a theoretical argument about the nature of media power, and a practical argument about the role of popularization in building an infrastructure for digital-age media. This separation between history, theory, and praxis is only analytic. Each of these lenses provides different ways of seeing the importance of the popularization of news and the interdependent relationship between news institutions and publics.

Historical Argument: Postprofessional News and the New Phantom Public

The three models for popularizing news explored in chapters 2–4 each represent attempts to provide an alternative to the high-modern conception of professional journalism. Despite working in different media, coming to prominence at different times, and taking hold in quite different corners of the landscape of U.S. media, each has tried to rewire the connection between news producers and consumers. For market-driven newspapers, this meant using focus groups and other research methods as lines of communication for readers to tell editors what they wanted out of the newspapers. Market-driven newspapers also made polling more prominent, searched for colorful quotes from ordinary citizens, and sometimes expanded opinion pages, all as part of their efforts to empower readers and give them a voice in setting the news agenda. Cable news has taken a more demagogic approach. Cable news producers position the talking heads of their networks as stand-ins for popular audiences themselves. High-modern newscasters sought to present themselves, more or less, as neutral observers who could bracket all their own particular emotions, attitudes, and identities while on air. The stars of cable news, in contrast, flaunt emotion and attitude. But they frequently do so as a populist gesture, intending to signify that they embody and represent popular sensibilities breaking through the confines of institutional (professional) journalism and politics. Lastly, social news sites try to erase professional editors completely. Instead, they interpellate their users as voters who can set the news agenda and replace editors through their own inputs into algorithmically coded collaborative filters.

Each of the new approaches to journalism renounces the high-modern insistence that professional discretion provides the best means for setting the news agenda and deciding how to present it. These models also reject the philosophy of trusteeship—the doctrine of institutional social responsibility—that became so central to U.S. journalism's self-conception after the Hutchins Commission's report. Such a philosophy assumes professional journalists to be the guardians of "the public interest," an interest of which members of the public themselves may or may not be aware. Demand-driven journalism, in contrast, rejects the notion that journalistic professionals have a special capacity to discern such a public interest and opts instead for techniques that aggregate signs of individual interests.

The models of demand-driven news examined here can be grouped together as belonging to a period of "postprofessional" journalism. This does not mean that professionals have disappeared or that all professional standards have been lost; rather, it suggests there has been a general shift in the operative philosophy of news organizations. News organizations no longer idealize professional judgment as *the most legitimate* means for resolving the many puzzles and conundrums of democratic journalism. The trustee model has lost its hegemonic position in favor of attempts to put consumer preferences in the driver's seat behind the engine of news making. The loss of hegemony of high-modern ideals has not been evenly distributed; prestige publications such as the *New York Times,* the *Washington Post,* and a handful of other large metropolitan daily newspapers, as well as journalism schools, can still provide something of a bastion for professional ideals. Broadcast national news has not given up entirely on high modernism, either. Nonetheless, a faith in professionalism no longer holds nearly the same sway in news production as it once did, especially among those making decisions about how to allocate the vast resources and promotional leverage of major media companies.

Grouping market-driven newspapers, cable news, and social news sites together as belonging to a postprofessional period of U.S. journalism runs counter to narratives positing the Internet as a singular force prompting a rupture in modern journalism. It has become a familiar story that the Internet, sweeping into the world of news with the promise of interactivity and demolishing barriers to entry, precipitated a crisis for twentieth-century news models with a frenzy of creative destruction. According to this story, the Web empowered users to become their own editors and citizen journalists, whereas previously they had been mute audience members under the thumb of professionals who had monopolized the means of mass communication. My argument does not imply that the migration of news online is not historically significant. Undeniably, digital, mobile, and online media open promising affordances for new types of news, and they have been significant factors in catalyzing a financial crisis for established media industries. However, this book shows that news organizations have been shifting away from professional autonomy and trying to incorporate feedback from consumers for decades before Internet services became widely available. Many of the experiments with online news that seem most radical, such as social news sites, represent an extension and intensification of earlier trends rather than a break from the past. Looking at this process from a critical and historical lens also shows that dethroning professional journalists and seeking greater audience participation have not solved the problems of democratic journalism. Indeed, I find it convincing that building a more democratic news media calls for overcoming the monopoly once held by major news organizations over media production and distribution as well as their monopoly of cultural authority to define news. But dissolving such bottlenecks of concentrated power is not enough. Democratic news media also require the creation of new structures and institutions.

The postprofessional period has been characterized by a search for models of journalism based on the idealized notion of marketplace democracy in which consumers can pursue their self-interest without bureaucrats or public interest–minded experts making choices for them. Market-driven newspapers, cable news channels, and social news sites have all sought to justify their means for selecting and presenting news as responses to popular demand. In making such a case, they conjure what I call a "phantom public" as an alibi supposedly responsible for their own mobilization choices.

This notion is inspired by Walter Lippmann's *The Phantom Public* (1927). Lippmann invoked the specter of a phantom public to criticize the image of the public projected by the dominant understanding of democratic thinkers of his time. Within media studies, Lippmann became an icon representing elitism and doubt in the civic and intellectual competence of ordinary people.[4] However, several recent scholars have challenged this memory of Lippmann.[5] Michael Schudson argues that Lippmann was skeptical not so much of ordinary citizens' abilities, but of the very model of citizenship idealized during the Progressive Era. As Schudson puts it, this model was based on an ideal of the "omnicompetent citizen," who pursued knowledge about every issue of civic importance in order to make informed judgments. Indeed, Lippmann thought that his contemporaries' concept of democracy, which he saw encoded in civics textbooks, among other places, asked citizens "to yield an unlimited quantity of public spirit, interest, curiosity, and effort."[6] This seemed to be an impossible expectation, and Lippmann searched for a way of imagining democracy that would not demand a public composed of extremely self-sacrificing individuals.

If the dominant model of democracy during Lippmann's time assumed a public of omnicompetent citizens with boundless civic motivation, today's vision of democracy shared by postprofessional news outlets projects a very different image of the public. Contemporary news organizations imagine their public(s) as consumers seeking satisfaction for specific informational and entertainment desires.[7] This imaginary public exercises much more discretion about civic participation than that of Lippmann's day; rather than eagerly waiting to follow up on every bit of information thrown its way, this public expects news organizations to serve its preferences and desires. What makes this public a phantom is not an overestimation of its competence or propensity for civic virtue, but rather the assumption that it exists as a fully formed entity with a set of preferences already fixed.

Today's phantom public knows what it wants, and it needs news organizations to understand its preferences and cater to them. On the level of professed ideals (that is, on an ideological level), postprofessional journalism claims news should be driven by the demands of audiences or consumers. Yet as I have shown in chapters 2–4, these news organizations help mobilize their audiences; they cultivate and promote distinct types of attachment to news. Market research, channel ratings, and online voting mechanisms provide opportunities for feedback from audiences, but, at the same time, news producers shape the activity of these active audiences. Decades of agenda setting and framing research provide clear evidence that what topics news media present and how they are presented affect citizens' assessment of what matters to them.[8] What is wrong is not that news organizations are mobilizing publics, stirring up interest in particular issues and topics, and facilitating certain kinds of attachment to current affairs. But when media's power to activate audiences is denied and organic public preferences are said to be in control, the political struggles over media mobilization and the contests over the conditions in which publics take shape remain hidden.

Theoretical Argument: Media Power as Mobilization

This book builds upon and extends a framework for understanding the power of news institutions in contemporary circuits of culture. I have been arguing that news producers have a pivotal role in cultivating and mobilizing popular interest in aspects of public life. They help build the architectural backdrop of our everyday lives in ways that make certain issues, stories, and political tropes common points of reference among members of different publics. News producers, surely, must respond to pressures from audiences, advertisers, and political actors. However, such pressures are not entirely deterministic, and the system leaves considerable leeway for news organizations to interpret external demands and strategically adapt their responses to them. I have focused especially on how news organizations have responded to perceived audience demands—investing their resources in ways that help mobilize the very demands they claim to be serving. A normative media model that justifies its democratic appeal solely as a response to consumer preferences fails when those very preferences are staged by the institutions supposedly responding to them.

The concept of mobilization calls for further theoretical development, but here I want to suggest a few ways that it provides a useful avenue for conceptualizing a type of media power. Mobilization offers a different vantage point than some of media studies' more familiar approaches to power—namely, through the concepts of ideology and governmentality. Media scholars have appropriated all these concepts for diverse purposes. Yet, on the whole, ideology and governmentality, along with certain interpretations of hegemony focused on struggles over cultural meanings, have all lent themselves to a focus on how media institutions negotiate or impose the will of those who control them onto the consciousness, beliefs, subjectivity, or affective registers of media consumers. Ideology and hegemony have provided different frameworks for understanding how individual users negotiate meanings and identity constructions through media texts. The governmentality perspective has been taken up to analyze how media texts provide training resources for subjects to enact different practices of self-governance upon themselves.[9] The concept of mobilization, however, turns the focus toward the role that media play in facilitating social connections (rather than individual dispositions, affects, or beliefs) through providing key platforms for the formation of connected groups or publics.

Recognizing that media structures can both enable and prevent public mobilizations shows that media institutions wield "productive" and "repressive" mechanisms of power. Michel Foucault has argued that conventional understandings typically approach power as a repressive force and "identif[y] power with a law that says no," such that "power is taken above all as carrying the force of a prohibition."[10] Many media scholars and cultural theorists have turned toward Foucault's "productive" vision of power to examine how subjects are molded into active and productive citizens, rather than repressed, by regimes of power. Foucault's division between productive and repressive approaches to power is useful, though Foucault hardly stands alone in offering ways to conceive of power as a productive force that can shape human subjectivities. Exploring the power of media in terms of mobilizing publics offers one way to analyze media's productive power. It suggests that media structures help shape publics and democratic constituencies. Mobilization points toward thinking about struggles over media power not only as the question of whether big companies or cliques of professional journalists monopolize media resources. Rather, it suggests that when societies make decisions about how to structure their media, they are setting some of the basic parameters for what kinds of political cultures and participation will be possible. Decisions about media structures have a constitutive or ontological influence on the kinds of publics that can flourish. Hence, media structures are never purely neutral; it is not an option to create a media system that simply reflects a society's inherent political character because that character itself will be conditioned by its media structures. This is the productive side of the power of media institutions and structures. At the same time, the concept of mobilization can also help analyze their repressive power. Media institutions can also prevent or constrain attempts at mobilizing publics from succeeding when they regulate resources critical to activating popular mobilizations.

Using mobilization as a critical concept also avoids reproducing the myth of audiences as "cultural dupes" or describing the power of media organizations as simple manipulation. This perspective suggests that media organizations hold key resources integral to the process of generating publics and promoting particular modes of citizenship. News sources devote significant labor and capital to put together a convenient package of information and narrative available for consumers that they cannot easily substitute. To draw on an example from chapter 2, the package assembled by market-driven newspapers facilitated a consumer-oriented mode of citizenship; these papers provided news resources that encouraged readers to follow items of immediate pertinence to daily life and scan other news updates just enough to feel they were keeping pace with others. Not only did market-driven newspapers interpellate individual readers as citizen-consumers, but they provided a shared point of reference to anchor this particular culture of citizenship. In other words, individuals read the paper not only for its direct content but as a gauge for knowing what other community members were thinking about, talking about, which events they would be participating in, and so forth.

The typical characterization of communication media like newspapers and television news programs as "one-to-many" or "hub-and-spoke" mass media structures obscures the fact that they also serve as nodal points for connecting communities and creating possibilities for shared conversational topics and coordinated action. Hence, *even "old media" have always had some of the networked qualities of social media platforms;* broadcast news, newspapers, and radio facilitate certain types of peer-to-peer connections (for example, conversations about news, showing up at the same time to a rally or ball game), while they also serve as centralized forms of communication. Recognizing the networked qualities of mass media also helps explain some of the "mass" qualities of online media. Even though the ease of online publishing means there are vastly more potential news publishers than ever before, evidence suggests that much of users' attention tends to amass around a relatively small number of extraordinarily popular platforms and sites.[11] At least part of the reason for such concentration stems from "network effects"—the ways in which the value a user derives from a particular media source depends on the popularity of that source with other users in their community. Popular media outlets help synchronize and connect publics. Since much of public life depends upon complex coordinated activity, news media play a central role in determining whether attempts to mobilize people around particular issues, candidates, and social movements will or will not seem credible and significant. Voices and issues ignored or marginalized by key media institutions face a tremendous disadvantage in public mobilization.

The trustee philosophy of high-modern journalism had provided a temporary, but flawed and unsustainable, solution to a puzzle of setting a democratic news agenda: leave it to seasoned professionals, who claimed to be able to stand outside of politics, to provide an authoritative account of the messy reality of political contest. Postprofessional journalism proposes a different tactic: if the press is a governing institution, then it should be beholden to the dictates of public demand. But if public opinion itself takes shape in a coconstitutive relationship with news media, how can public opinion provide a foundation for deciding the fundamental features of the press system itself? This is the question facing postprofessional journalism for which none of the models I have explored has provided an answer.

This problem parallels a similar quandary about the relationship between the public and other branches of representative government. For some time, democratic theorists tended to view elected representatives as mere proxies delegated by their constituents to stand in for their own preferences during legislative decision making. From such a view, elected representatives are supposed to respond to (rather than shape or influence) their constituents' policy preferences. What political theories call a "mandate" or "delegate" theory of representation assumes that representatives should base their own decisions on the will or mandate of their constituents.[12] A trustee model of representation, in which elite legislators represent the public interest as paternalistic figures responsible for the public rather than responsive to it, has been the traditional alternative to the mandate model.[13] However, a number of progressive democratic theorists have recently started to move toward an alternate understanding of representation that political theorist Lisa Disch refers to as "the constructivist turn."[14] This theory of representation is worth exploring because the problem of the relationship between the public and political representatives (as "elite communicators") reflects some of the same tensions between the public and news outlets.

One impetus prompting political theorists to rethink normative theories of democratic representation comes from empirical studies. On the one hand, contemporary survey and ethnographic research suggests that ordinary citizens generally appear to be more competent in terms of holding stable and coherent political opinions than researchers once thought. On the other hand, this research also suggests that citizens' opinions depend mightily on the way political leaders and elites frame and present issues. The constructivist turn represents a fundamental shift in thinking about how people make political choices, as Disch explains:

> Research in public opinion and political psychology has taken what researchers call a "constructionist" or "constructivist" turn . . . from a rational individualist to an environmental or contextual account of preference formation. The former holds individuals to define their preferences according to needs, desires, and values that are fixed prior to political contests and relatively impervious to political influence. The latter contends that preferences are constituted in the communication that occurs during decision making, implying that choice is as much something that institutions effect as it is something that an individual makes.[15]

Disch advocates that normative political theory follow this turn too. She suggests giving up the mandate theory of democratic representation in favor of "a mobilization concept of representation." Drawing on Ernesto Laclau and Chantal Mouffe's understanding of how political rhetoric and language give shape to social antagonisms and alliances, Disch suggests the process of political representatives needs to "participate in forming demands and social cleavages, not merely to reflect them."[16] In this vision, the normative role of political representatives is not to simply carry out the will of their constituents, or to act as enlightened trustees making decisions for them. Instead, political representatives are integral in stimulating the way publics imagine themselves and their shared aims, thus playing a constitutive role in preference formation while they are still held accountable for the success of their advocacy.

Mobilization, I want to suggest, is a key concept for thinking about the role of both media institutions and political representation in democratic societies. The more clearly the mobilization capacity of media is identified, the more difficult it becomes to sustain a neoclassical understanding of media markets catering to exogenous consumer demand.

But can mobilization be differentiated from manipulation or coercion? No, not by itself. This remains a vexing challenge for developing a normative concept of democratic journalism or representation as mobilization. Disch proposes that "reflexivity" is one important criterion for distinguishing communicative circumstances that foster manipulation from those that encourage democratic mobilization. By reflexivity, she means a condition in which no one party reserves the right to speak, as the public and every individual have formal and informal means of communication to contest the agendas of powerful groups. Perhaps most important, Disch argues that reflexivity requires that "the political communications of advocacy groups, mass media, and opinion shapers would be in competition with one another so as to mitigate passive absorption of elite communications."[17] Disch's vision of reflexive representation offers some helpful guidelines for thinking about a way out of a state of U.S. journalism caught between an ideological reliance on consumer preferences and the trusteeship of professionalism. Reflexivity suggests a need for a media infrastructure that makes it easy for people and groups to access communicative means to initiate or maintain mobilizations. It also points to a need to foster and cultivate a public disposed to broad exposure to an expansive range of views and mobilization efforts.

Toward Praxis: Popularization and the Future of News

There is little question that, since the mid-2000s, U.S. news organizations have been facing a genuine crisis that threatens to shake up the long-standing model of funding news mostly through advertisements directed at a broad audience. The Pew Research Center estimates that the total revenue supporting newsgathering operations in the United States dropped from $94–$95 billion in 2006 to $63–$65 billion in 2014, a decline of almost a third of total news revenue in less than a decade.[18] Their estimate takes into account news gathering across print, digital, television, and radio, along with both nonprofit and commercial revenue streams. Newspapers have been hit the hardest by this financial crisis. From 2006 to 2010, the combined online and print advertising revenue for newspapers fell 48 percent.[19] These losses, not surprisingly, have meant media companies have made enormous cuts in the investments they make in collecting and selecting news. Between 2000 and 2010, the newspaper industry slashed about 30 percent of the money it had been spending each year on reporting and editing capacities.[20] The trend suggests that newspapers' newsroom investments will likely continue to diminish. For funding paid reporting, newspapers are of paramount importance. The Pew Research Center estimates that even as late as 2009, newspapers were still providing about 90 percent of the funds spent on professional reporting in the United States.[21] National broadcast news divisions too have made deep cuts to their own newsroom budgets. By 2010 network newsrooms employed fewer than half the numbers they had in the 1980s.[22] Jobs in digitally native news organizations have been growing, with the Pew Center noticing an especially fierce uptick in hiring among digital news organizations in 2013. Still, there are absolutely no signs suggesting that digital-based news organizations, or any other type of news organization, are hiring paid reporters at levels that could come close to matching newspaper losses.[23]

Since 2009 several government bodies have convened their own hearings or meetings on questions about the future of news, including the House Judiciary

Committee, the Senate Commerce Committee, the Federal Trade Commission, and the FCC. One reason the Senate hearing attracted special attention was because David Simon, former *Baltimore Sun* reporter and creator of HBO's *The Wire,* offered an especially brutal assessment of U.S. newspapers. He squarely blamed the industry for its own demise, saying the newspaper industry had "butchered itself and did so at the behest of Wall Street," as publishers ran in hot pursuit of short-term earnings, slashing newsroom investments while losing public trust. As Simon emphasized, major divestments in news capacity had begun in earnest even while newspapers were reaping profit margins that would be considered exceptionally high compared to most other industries.[24]

As painful as the circumstances that led to these discussions have been for recently unemployed and underemployed journalists, these kinds of conversations indicate a rare opportunity to believe that the future of journalism does not have to look much like the past. This is a moment that clearly offers possibilities for what Robert McChesney describes as a critical juncture, a point in time when organizational and policy decisions, along with everyday media habits, form along new lines likely to set a path that will define the parameters of media development for a long time to come.[25] As the old saying goes, today's crisis in journalism represents not only a threat but also an opportunity—a chance to build a media infrastructure more capable of facilitating a vibrant and engaged democratic culture. Although building such a media system is clearly a tall task under any conditions, it will be especially unlikely if, in the midst of all sorts of disruption and change in U.S. news media, the flawed vision of demand-driven journalism continues as the dominant alternative to the (ever-shrinking) professional news model.

In this section, I offer a framework for making sense of numerous responses to the current crisis of journalism by dividing them into three categories: *traditionalist, entrepreneurial-ecosystem,* and *critical activist.* Each of these represents a different attitude toward the critical juncture facing journalism. The groupings I propose here divide reactions to the crisis in journalism based on assumptions about *the process by which normative questions about democratic news institutions should be answered.* The traditionalists look to what has seemingly worked in the past to answer this question. The evolutionary-entrepreneurial approach looks to competition in the online marketplace or ecosystem. The critical activist approach declares that conscious and collective efforts need to be made to build a media infrastructure capable of supporting democratic life and governance. These approaches also diverge in their responses to the editorial philosophies of high-modern and demand-driven journalism.

Few discussions of the future of journalism have even recognized demand-driven journalism as a historical trend or connected the similarities in its philosophy across formats such as *USA Today* and online news practices like social news and monitoring audience metrics. I argue that the critical and historical analysis offered in this book can help highlight problems with traditionalist and, most especially, with the entrepreneurial reactions to journalism's crisis. These perspectives tend to ignore the ways that news organizations mobilize popular interest in news. If news organizations play such a critical role in shaping popular interests, then the space for meaningful democratic participation in news media cannot be limited to exercising consumer demand within a media environment defined by commercial forces (and some limited philanthropic ones). Rather, I offer support for what I am calling the critical activist response to the journalism crisis. This approach opens the door for popular participation not only at the level of exercising consumer demand but in making decisions about structuring the media environment in which we make our news choices.

Traditionalist Approaches

The traditionalist response seeks to find ways to preserve existing models of journalism. Traditionalists tend to have reverence for high-modern journalistic ideals, or at least certain aspects of them. This does not mean traditionalists are against all forms of innovation. Rather, they believe existing models of journalism offer something that has a unique social value, and they propose concerted efforts to preserve whatever aspects of familiar journalistic practices or institutions they deem worthy of enduring. Some traditionalists seek to secure funding for large-scale commercial news organizations beholden to professional ideals; others see the future in a hybrid news system with a central role for both commercial and nonprofit news organizations supporting professional journalism. Conceptions of just what characterizes "professional" journalism also differ among the traditionalists. Many of them do not hold tightly to the ideal of objectivity, though they tend to value paid reporters and fact gatherers and news institutions not aligned with particular ideological or partisan perspectives. Most of the traditionalists' ideas for the future of news revolve around trying to find a "business model" that can continue to fund traditional professional journalism. Among the ideas for how this might be accomplished are charging users fees for online subscriptions to news websites, creating systems for micropayments, establishing a cooperative bargaining unit among news sources to garner higher advertising rates, directing news organizations to branch out into other services such as local printing and direct marketing as new sources for commercial journalism subsidies, and preventing online aggregators or others from repurposing news stories and siphoning away media company online traffic and revenue through more stringent enforcement of copyright.[26]

Creating online paywalls for newspapers has become one of the central tactics for newspaper companies to try to preserve revenue. There has been a vigorous debate in the newspaper industry surrounding paywalls.[27] Some industry leaders suggest newspapers made a grave mistake by allowing content to be free on the Internet in the first place, setting the expectations that news content should always be free.[28] Others, however, fear that "putting content behind a pay wall can stunt online audience growth, because those who cannot or do not want to pay to access a newspaper's content will go elsewhere for news and information."[29] Although only a few papers such as Little Rock's *Arkansas Democrat-Gazette* and the *Wall Street Journal* required online readers to pay for full access in the mid-2000s, paywalls have been surging since 2011. The *New York Times* introduced a new kind of paywall system that year, charging for full access while allowing free access to a limited number of stories and to stories shared through social media. By July 2013, the Pew Research Center reported that 450 of the 1,380 U.S. daily newspapers had some kind of paywall on their websites.[30] Increases in subscription revenue have not stemmed overall losses for newspapers. They have, however, moved online newspapers a step closer to becoming an elite medium.[31] Critics within and outside the industry have voiced a concern that tinkering with paywalls and other marginal income sources can too easily serve as a distraction from facing more fundamental challenges in the news industry.[32]

From the traditionalist perspective, the fundamental problem posed by the financial crisis is to find strategies for preserving aspects of mid- to late-twentieth-century journalism. Advocates differ on just what aspects of this tradition should be saved. When making the case for their distinctive contribution to public life in the emerging media landscape, many spokespeople for legacy media news companies emphasize the public service role of legacy news organizations. This does not mean these advocates signal a resurgence of the high-modern ideals. Rather, they tend to stress the social value of high-quality journalism. Some advocates of the traditionalist approach have no problem equating high-quality journalism with a market-driven mentality of giving consumers what they want. Walter Isaacson, for instance, supports his argument for a pervasive micropayment system by saying, "I love journalism. I think it is valuable and should be valued by its consumers. Charging for content forces discipline on journalists: they must produce things that people actually value. I suspect we will find that this necessity is actually liberating."[33] This view has been put most boldly by Rupert Murdoch. Testifying before the Federal Trade Commission, Murdoch proposed three key steps for legacy news organizations to thrive: "First, media companies must deliver the news media consumers want—and do it in the ways that best fit their lifestyles. That means we must innovate like never before. Second, we need to do a better job of persuading consumers that high-quality, reliable news and information does not come free. Good journalism is an expensive commodity. Finally, the government needs to clear the path for companies to invest and innovate—by reducing unnecessary regulation and eliminating obstacles to growth and investment."[34] Murdoch's approach, however, represents a selective understanding of what constitutes government regulation. While he argues for relaxing the FCC ban on media companies owning both a newspaper and a broadcast television station in certain markets, he also calls for more vigorous regulation along another dimension—copyright enforcement to prevent aggregators from claiming fair-use rights to pull excerpts from published news stories.

Other advocates representing a traditionalist perspective speak of the need to preserve certain journalistic traditions without justifying them on the basis of consumer wants. For some, this means opening possibilities for greater nonprofit support for journalism. One of the most influential calls for this approach can be found in "The Reconstruction of American Journalism," coauthored by Leonard Downie, former executive editor of the *Washington Post,* and Michael Schudson. The key element Downie and Schudson wish to see preserved is what they call "accountability journalism." By this they mean "reporting, analysis, and investigation" that are "pursued collaboratively by stable organizations that can facilitate regular reporting by experienced journalists, support them with money, logistics, and legal services, and present their work to a large public."[35] Downie and Schudson openly embrace many of the new forms of news and public discourse blossoming online, but they stress that "what is paramount is preserving independent, original, credible reporting, whether or not it is popular or profitable, and regardless of the medium in which it appears."[36] Among other remedies, Downie and Schudson call for making it easier to designate news outlets as nonprofits, encouraging partnerships between news organizations and universities, collecting FCC license fees designed to support a fund for local news, and encouraging philanthropic organizations to support continuous reporting rather than special journalism projects.

Entrepreneurial-Ecosystem Approach

This approach frames networked media as an evolving, decentralized communication system that will itself sort out the best solutions for journalism's crisis—at least in the long term. Proponents of this approach place their faith in entrepreneurial ingenuity to devise innovative ways of producing and sharing news and public conversation in the new media landscape. Their hopes for entrepreneurial activity are combined with a belief in an online ecosystem that will sort out the best approaches. Hence, this view suggests that those forms of journalism that survive and thrive in online competition for attention and resources will have proved themselves most fit to fulfill social needs in a digital age. Proponents of this approach do not believe any special efforts should be made for favoring existing institutions. Instead, they tend to see the Web as a complex, seemingly self-correcting, system bound to produce a more robust news ecology better suited to contemporary social and cultural needs.[37] Journalism scholar Mark Deuze describes this basic philosophy when he says, "Technological innovation and adoption processes can be seen as evolutionary in a Darwinian sense, in that whichever technology—as in: device, code or protocol—is dominant at any given point in time is not necessarily the 'best,' but rather the more 'fitting' with the prevailing culture."[38] If media environments have an inherent tendency toward progressive evolution, then preserving the values of professional journalism should not be a priority, especially not if it entails tinkering with the online ecosystem.

Entrepreneurial advocates often employ a rhetoric that characterizes existing news institutions as elitist and maladaptive entities, trying to hold on to the cultural authority they once monopolized. Undoubtedly, these frustrations are rooted in genuine concerns and resonate with the long history of criticism of the professional model of journalism. Yet these critics tend to overlook the prominence and problems of the history of demand-driven journalism. In the *Columbia Review of Journalism,* Dean Starkman offers his own characterization of what I am calling the entrepreneurial-ecosystem approach; he calls it "the future of news [FON] consensus," pointing to a group of public intellectuals who have been highly influential in public discussions of the future of news, especially Clay Shirky, Jeff Jarvis, and Jay Rosen. Starkman incisively describes this mode of thought: "At its heart, the FON consensus is anti-institutional. It believes that old institutions must wither to make way for the networked future. . . . And let's face it, in the debate over journalism's future, the FON crowd has had the upper hand. The establishment is gloomy and old; the FON consensus is hopeful and young (or purports to represent youth). The establishment has no plan. The FON consensus says no plan *is* the plan. The establishment drones on about rules and standards; the FON thinkers talk about freedom and informality." Advocates of this perspective argue that democracy does not need newspapers, legacy news organizations, or even journalism as we have known it. Rather, this perspective suggests, as Clay Shirky argues, "When we shift our attention from 'save newspapers' to 'save society,' the imperative changes from 'preserve the current institutions' to 'do whatever works.' And what works today isn't the same as what used to work."[39] The emphasis here is not on appropriating newly available technologies and their affordances to achieve a vision of the public good but rather experimenting with entrepreneurial ventures. Those experiments that survive—meaning they find sustainable funding—are the ones believed to be most suited for the ecosystem.

For most who take this approach, the evolving news system appears to be one that will be more democratic than the fading paradigm of mass media. A digital, networked era of journalism, they predict, will blur hierarchical distinctions in the news world, such as the chasm between professional reporter and ordinary citizen. Seen from this perspective, the Web has several characteristics that make it destined to foster a superior system for news. First, it creates a platform for distribution that greatly lowers barriers of entry for new voices to share news and become part of the mediated public sphere. Second, optimists tend to believe the Web can leverage collective intelligence, meaning that scattered individuals can communicate over the Web to create news or informational mosaics in nonhierarchical coordination with each other.[40] As discussed in the last chapter, this vision is reflected in Yochai Benkler's normative-empirical concept of the "networked public sphere." Benkler argues that the capacity of networked media can lead to a greater total productive potential and increase the autonomy of individuals to gather and produce information by themselves or in loose collaborations.[41] Social news sites are one example of such collaborative projects made possible by the Web. Last, proponents of the entrepreneurial approach argue that the Internet simply leads to increased consumer choice and informational abundance.

I refer to this as the "entrepreneurial-ecosystem" approach to solving the crisis of journalism. In this vision, entrepreneurial creativity generates new ideas about how to produce, share, and finance news; competition for survival in the news ecosystem ferrets out which solutions are best suited for the media environment. One of the strengths of this perspective is its acknowledgment of the impossibility of predicting exactly what new journalistic practices and forms might arise in the changing environment. Who could have predicted ten years ago that a 140-character microblogging platform would become a central news source for many breaking events? How can we understand what creative new appropriations and developments in digital media will become major contributors to our flows of news and public discussion five or ten years from today? Any perspective on the future of news that cannot acknowledge and accommodate significant unknowns for the future strains credibility. The entrepreneurial-ecosystem approach takes the unpredictability of future innovation as a central premise. Advocates ask us to believe that something will work and, whatever that something is, it will lead to a more vibrant and democratic media system than we could dream up through centralized planning.

The metaphor of the *media ecosystem* inspires this kind of imagination. The ecosystem metaphor has become widespread since the mid-2000s. This metaphor is put to different uses with quite different emphases. In the natural sciences, the concept of an ecosystem is used to study intertwined fates of various species of plants, animals, microorganisms, and even geological structures like the properties of a soil that are connected together in webs of mutual influence and dependence. Thinking ecologically offers a way to link together different levels of analysis—from individual to species to whole ecological systems. One of the strengths of importing the ecosystem metaphor into the media is that it can highlight interdependence among media outlets—that is, why the growth of local blogs, niche online news sources, or a platform like Twitter influences the whole field of news media, including metropolitan newspapers, local television news, and so on. This notion can also lead us to recognize how media systems have their own emergent properties that cannot be explained by reference only to individuals or individual institutions. Another strength of this metaphor is that it points to the increasing diversification of news sources online; *the news media* no longer needs to refer to a handful of well-established institutions.

The metaphor of the ecosystem, however, can also lead to reification and mystification. Referring to a "media ecosystem" risks ascribing a natural order—either a static or a dynamic, evolving one—to a particular set of media relations. There has been a long history in the United States of naturalizing commercial media relations; as McChesney has documented, market thinkers have been largely successful in making sure that "the operating assumption in most discussions of the U.S. media system is that media are a natural province of the market."[42] The ecosystem metaphor risks furthering the notion that an online world dominated by commercial forces represents the natural order. Much like the metaphor of an "organic society," so common among late-nineteenth- and early-twentieth-century sociologists, the ecosystem metaphor brings the interconnectedness and interdependence of a media system to attention while downplaying struggles over power.

The ecosystem metaphor is frequently deployed in ways that smuggle in the assumption that the digital media system will naturally develop toward an equilibrium point of optimal flourishing and diversity. Stephen Berlin Johnson, a popular writer and tech guru, spelled out this vision in a speech at the 2009 South by Southwest Festival, the text of which circulated widely on his popular blog. Johnson's speech introduced a conceit around the notion of an informational ecosystem, as he compared the state of the ecosystem for technology news from the 1980s to the present. Johnson recalled his college days in the 1980s when he would wait anxiously at the bookstore for monthly issues of *Macworld.* Back then, Johnson says, technology news was a "barren desert." With the rise of the Web, new tributaries and flows of information opened up, quickly spiraling out until a lush rain forest evolved. The rapid growth of technology news on the Internet led Johnson to make this prediction:

> [The ecosystem of technology news] is the old-growth forest of the web. It is the sub-genre of news that has had the longest time to evolve. The Web doesn't have some kind [of] intrinsic aptitude for covering technology better than other fields. It just has an intrinsic tendency to cover technology *first,* because the first people that used the web were far more interested in technology. . . .
>
> So this is what the old-growth forests tell us: there is going to be more content, not less; more information, more analysis, more precision, a wider range of niches covered. You can see the process happening already in most of the major sections of the paper: tech, politics, finance, sports.[43]

Johnson, along with other tech enthusiasts, offers insight on the unpredictable and decentralized processes of innovation that can take shape online. Yet they often take a leap of faith and put their trust in Web ecology as an optimizing system.

For those subscribing to the entrepreneurial-ecosystem vision of the future of news, the media ecosystem often ends up looking more like the fabled free market of Adam Smith than the hybridized human-built and biological ecosystems of today's Anthropocene. For many contemporary environmental activists, the solution to the problems of humans' environmental impact is not to be sought in trying to return to a state of nature prior to human intervention. Rather, for political ecologists who view "ecological systems as power-laden rather than politically inert," the normative course for environmental action relies on coordinated, democratic, and well-informed human efforts.[44] In contrast, Web faithful like Johnson predict that networked media ecosystems can solve the problems of democratic journalism by their own innate logic; informational provisions will grow as organic responses to competitive environments, inciting businesses and nonprofits to creatively satisfy users' interests in news. Instead of public debates about what types of news will best serve democratic needs, Web enthusiasts ask us to think along the lines of Jeff Jarvis, who poses the question (as a book title) *What Would Google Do?*[45] From this outlook, the problem of democratic journalism is an entrepreneurial problem. It is a matter of thinking like Google and devising innovative forms of journalism that can succeed in the Web environment. Like the evolutionary mechanism, success means survival and proliferation. It might be a matter of making a profit, or it might be a matter of devising sustainable nonprofit structures. In any case, proponents do not believe the future of democratic journalism calls for coordinated movements dedicated to political, social, or cultural change; rather, the future calls for entrepreneurs with keen intuitions about the nature of the emerging Web culture. While entrepreneurial-ecosystem proponents tend to speak of revolution and unpredictable futures, their faith in a better news system ultimately remains anchored to the philosophy of demand-driven journalism. News media evolve toward a superior state, in this vision, because entrepreneurs are vigorously competing to satisfy users' needs and desires.

Critical Activist Approaches

The critical approach to the journalism crisis proposes that this juncture should be a moment of deliberation on what purposes journalism needs to serve in democracy and how best to build an infrastructure to suit those ends. This perspective goes against deeply ingrained ways of understanding the modern U.S. news system as an institution that, while of great importance to politics, can be governed apolitically. The governance of the media was supposed to be "apolitical" in that, at least since the aftermath of World War II, the prevailing ideology was that there was no need for public debate or scrutiny regarding basic structural questions of the media system. Instead, a combination of market factors and professional experts upholding self-regulation would keep news media functioning properly. As discussed in chapter 1, Victor Pickard documents how this apolitical outlook came to dominate thinking about the news in the United States since the mid-1940s after the deflation of a wave of media reform activism. The reliance on market forces and self-regulation (that is, social responsibility) was the outcome of what Pickard calls "a postwar settlement" in which news organizations implicitly promised to uphold the professional standard and, by doing so, deflected calls for state intervention.[46]

Since the postwar settlement, freedom of the press has largely been understood in the United States as a negative liberty. If press freedom is a negative liberty, the state's only duty is to refrain from censorship or interference; there is no guarantee that citizens have access to a media system that widely circulates diverse views or cultivates popular engagement in public life.[47] Proponents of the critical activist approach to the crisis tend toward reframing freedom of the press in terms of positive liberty, suggesting the state (or other civic collectives) has an obligation to build an infrastructure for a public media sphere that gives citizens and social groups an opportunity to broadly circulate their views.

The critical activist approach is not incompatible with an enthusiasm for creative, even entrepreneurial, experimentation. Yet unlike the entrepreneurial-ecosystem approach, supporters of the critical activist approach argue for a need to build media structures and networks of institutions with normative goals in mind, and, typically, they see the need for public investment to support democratic media. Victor Pickard, Josh Stern, and Craig Aaron, for instance, exemplify this view when they suggest the crisis of journalism calls for the need to develop a "national journalism strategy." They believe such a strategy could ensure that "public and foundation dollars are being invested in projects that will result in the kind of journalism democratic societies require."[48] Jessica Clark and Patricia Aufderheide are thinking along the same lines when they suggest that even in a competitive online environment, special funding needs to be devoted to building a sophisticated and interactive public media system (public media 2.0) to engage and mobilize communities to partake in democratic life: "Building dynamic, engaged publics will not be a top agenda item for any business. Neither will tomorrow's commercial media business models have any incentive to remedy social inequality. Participation that flows along today's lines of access and skill sets will replicate past inequalities. If public media 2.0 looks less highly stratified and culturally balkanized than the public media of today, it will be because of conscious investment and government policy choices."[49] The main difference between the entrepreneurial-ecosystem approach and the critical activist one is that they hold differing notions of successful solutions to the current crisis of journalism. Proponents of the critical activist approach want to find ways to build a journalistic infrastructure that lives up to normative expectations arrived at through public consideration.[50] Proponents of the entrepreneurial approach see success in whichever projects thrive and survive in the Web ecosystem; successful media in this vision succeed presumably because they best fulfill users' wants and fit with the evolving norms and expectations of digital culture. From the entrepreneurial-ecosystem perspective, the answer to the journalism crisis lies in entrepreneurs trying to figure out how to create media forms that will survive in the conditions set by the emerging media environment, whereas for those coming from the critical activist approach the very conditions of the media environment should not be accepted as given but rather scrutinized and debated.

Like any set of categories, the framework I put forward here offers a particular lens for viewing debates about the future of news—one that emphasizes how normative decisions about news infrastructure should be made. There are, of course, other ways of dividing up the debate, and this framework itself could be broken into numerous subcategories within each approach. Although I have

Three Approaches to Responding to the Crisis of U.S. Journalism

	Traditionalist	Entrepreneurial-ecosystem	Critical activist
Foundation of normative ideals	Ideals for news based on professional norms or what media companies have learned about market preferences	"Ideals" emerge based on what kinds of news thrive in media ecosystem	Ideals identified through reflective public deliberation on the needs of democratic media
Policy goals	Government policy should protect ailing industry (e.g., increasing copyright enforcement, loosening cross-ownership bans)	Government policy should prevent established companies from monopolizing emerging media (e.g., support for Net neutrality, intellectual property reform)	Government policy should help build investment in media infrastructure (e.g., support for public media or nonprofit start-ups, public investment in broadband)
Favored economic model	Corporate capitalism (for some, supplemented with philanthropy)	Competitive capitalism/ entrepreneurial capitalism (for some, supplemented with social entrepreneurialism and commons-based production)	No single economic model, but greater interest in public financing

referred to proponents who fall under each of these categories, this framework is based on ideal types, as I have divided up the approaches based on philosophical orientations that some participants in the future of news debates do not always adhere to clearly or consistently.

A Future for Popular News?

The period of postprofessional journalism has been characterized by tactics for avoiding public discussion and debates about the role media should play in democracy. Its guiding ideology has been that individual choice and consumer demand can answer this question. This solution invokes a phantom public and fails to acknowledge that the very news environments supposedly shaped by popular demand simultaneously mobilize and structure that demand. Glorifying individual choice provides an alluring fantasy that everyone is an autonomous agent who can choose her own media. With the practically infinite channel capacity of the Internet, this fantasy may seem to be closer to reality than ever. However, if individual choice is in many respects an environmental and institutional effect, if our media environment conditions our preferences, if the most ubiquitous and convenient media we are unwittingly exposed to are largely chosen by institutional arrangements, then the image of the autonomous consumer fades. There is no denying consumer agency on both individual and collective levels. However, in this book, I have tried to illustrate how consumer demand is shaped, channeled, and molded. The "to each his own" philosophy of the libertarian theory of the press crumbles when there is no way to escape collective decisions about creating news institutions in which people's choices inherently impinge on one another. In other words, building media institutions is an inescapably political task.

None of the historical moments that I have explored in this book exemplify a "golden age" when media institutions devoted significant resources and experimented creatively to try to promote broad engagement in public life. Still, there are a number of indications that, as more news moves online, news media may further neglect such a responsibility and cater even more exclusively to a smaller, mostly privileged group of news consumers. Empirical evidence suggests there is a growing "knowledge gap" regarding news and public affairs. Whereas some people indicate they are consuming news and information in the digital age more voraciously than ever before, there are also signs that a growing number of people are always going "newsless" and not checking in with any news sources on a typical day.[51]

The most innovative segment of the news industry, new online media companies, has been increasingly focused on targeting affluent people with high levels of formal education and preexisting interests in news. For example, the site *Vox.com* launched in 2014 with a mission, in the words of editor Ezra Klein, to provide "crucial contextual information necessary to understand what's happened" through explanatory journalism.[52] Such a mission represents a hopeful vision of one kind of journalism that might (or might not) thrive in the niche-oriented world of online news. Yet such idealistic visions tend to be articulated to outlets aiming to primarily serve educated and wealthy groups of users. *Vox* describes its audience base to advertisers as "a covetable community of young yet affluent decision makers who are highly influential in both their personal and professional circles."[53] Patch.com, which coordinates a network of hyperlocal news services in hundreds of U.S. communities, provides another example. Though Patch makes use of the egalitarian language of community empowerment, its business plan revolves around launching sites primarily in high-income communities. Patch uses a method for deciding where to launch new locations not in response to local initiatives, but "based on an algorithm that examines fifty-nine factors, including potential advertising revenue, income, voter turnout, and retail spending."[54] Even *Gawker,* one of the most lively tabloid-oriented online news sites, pitches itself to advertisers through claims to serve an upscale group of users. On a page designed for potential advertisers, *Gawker* boasts statistics that show 80 percent of its audience has been enrolled in college and more than half (of its predominantly single and eighteen- to thirty-four-year-old audience) live in households making more than fifty thousand dollars a year.[55] Many of the best-known nonprofit news sites, such as *MinnPost* and *Voice of San Diego,* have also primarily catered to affluent groups predisposed toward heavy news consumption.

There is a chicken-and-egg problem here. Investors in high-quality news sources target educated audiences because they believe these audiences are the most interested in such forms of news (as well as the most desirable to advertisers or most likely to pay subscriptions or donate to nonprofits). Yet continual targeting of such groups and not others means that all sorts of media outlets are investing resources in cultivating upper-middle-class interest in news while not cultivating other groups' interest in news. There are indeed online experiments that aim to serve more diverse groups—such as the *Twin Cities Daily Planet,* which brings together voices from ethnic, labor, feminist, and other alternative news organizations along with local bloggers in Minneapolis and St. Paul. While such efforts point toward promise for popular mobilization online, they are receiving an extremely small sliver of the financial resources in the world of online news, much smaller even than higher-profile philanthropic efforts primarily serving more elite audiences.

This growing news gap only further highlights the need for building a media system that provides incentives and resources for creating news that promotes interest in public life and opportunities for meaningful participation across class, gender, race, sexual identity, and other social divisions. News organizations need to bring a far wider array of issues and voices into the public sphere and create compelling and convenient opportunities for engagement. There is little reason to believe such a system will simply evolve by itself without organized and conscious efforts. We cannot continue grasping onto the same faith, so pervasive since the 1970s, that competition and spontaneous consumer demand will drive the development of democratic news media.

Notes

Introduction

1. Quoted in Bob Garfield, "Getting Desperate," *On the Media from NPR*, February 20, 2009, http://www.onthemedia.org/transcripts/2009/02/20/04.

2. The term *audience* has become increasingly troubling for many media scholars. For a further discussion of problems with the concept of audience, see Jack Bratich, "Amassing the Multitude: Revisiting Early Audience Studies," *Communication Theory* 15, no. 3 (2005): 242–65. As the growth of digital media has made more media experiences interactive, some have felt the notion of audience seems increasingly antiquated. In place of the notion of audience, terms such as *users, participatory cultures,* and *publics* seem to suggest a more respectful and empowering way to figure those journalism scholar Jay Rosen calls "the people formerly known as the audience." Jay Rosen, "The People Formerly Known as the Audience," *Pressthink*, June 27, 2006, http://archive.pressthink.org/2006/06/27/ppl_frmr.html. Nonetheless, I continue to use the term *audience* as one way to designate the addressees of news media and the communities that interpret news. There are two reasons for this. First, it seems to me that suggesting the notion of audience has become obsolete in a digital age expresses far too much optimism that power asymmetries between institutional producers and everyday citizens have been eradicated by technology. Second, I employ terms such as *audiences, users,* and *publics* to suggest they share something in common and that none of these identities can entirely cleave themselves of each other's meanings. Clearly, these terms are not entirely interchangeable; rather, they conjure distinct senses pointing to the same or similar referent(s). At play here are competing ways of

making sense of media circulation from an industry point of view, from the experience of users immersed in net culture, and from a standpoint concerned about democratic citizenship and the public sphere.

3. For a critique of the way in which the addiction metaphor has been mobilized in antitelevision rhetoric, see Jason Mittell, "The Cultural Power of an Anti-television Metaphor: Questioning the 'Plug-In Drug' and a TV-Free America," *Television & New Media* 1, no. 2 (2000): 215. For an example of how the concept of addiction troubles rational-choice economists, see this attempt to go to great lengths to try to make sense of addiction within the neoclassical paradigm: Gary S. Becker and Kevin M. Murphy, "A Theory of Rational Addiction," *Journal of Political Economy* 96, no. 4 (1988): 675–700.

4. Mary Walton, "Investigative Shortfall," *American Journalism Review* (September 2010), http://www.ajr.org/article.asp?id=4904; Paul Starr, "Goodbye to the Age of Newspapers (Hello to a New Era of Corruption)," *New Republic,* March 4, 2009, http://www.newrepublic.com/article/goodbye-the-age-newspapers-hello-new-era-corruption#; Steve Waldman and the Working Group on the Information Needs of Communities, "Information Needs of Communities: The Changing Media Landscape in Broadband Age," Federal Communication Commission, June 2011, http://www.fcc.gov/infoneedsreport.

5. Dean Starkman, "Confidence Game," *Columbia Journalism Review* (December 2011), http://www.cjr.org/essay/confidence_game.php.

6. Dan Gillmor, *We the Media: Grassroots Journalism by the People, for the People* (Sebastopol, Calif.: O'Reilly, 2006), xii–xiii. For other versions of this rupture narrative, see Axel Bruns, "Gatewatching, Not Gatekeeping: Collaborative Online News," *Media International Australia, Incorporating Culture & Policy* 107 (2003): 31–44; Mark Deuze, "The Changing Context of News Work: Liquid Journalism and Monitorial Citizenship," *International Journal of Communication* 2 (2008): 848–65; Jeff Jarvis, *What Would Google Do?* (New York: Collins Business, 2009); and Yochai Benkler, *The Wealth of Networks: How Social Production Transforms Markets and Freedom* (New Haven, Conn.: Yale University Press, 2006).

7. Immanent critique has been a central, even defining, method for critical theory. Although many critics still draw on this method today, the term itself seems to have become less common in discussion of contemporary critical and cultural methods. For an overview, see Robert J. Antonio, "Immanent Critique as the Core of Critical Theory: Its Origins and Developments in Hegel, Marx and Contemporary Thought," *British Journal of Sociology* 32, no. 3 (1981): 330–45.

8. Mark Fowler and Daniel Brenner, "A Marketplace Approach to Broadcast Regulation," *Texas Law Review* 60 (1982): 210.

9. John Dewey, *The Public and Its Problems: An Essay in Political Inquiry* (Athens: Ohio University Press, 1954); Michael Warner, *Publics and Counterpublics* (New York: Zone Books, 2005).

10. R. W. McChesney, *The Problem of the Media: US Communication Politics in the Twenty-First Century* (New York: Monthly Review Press, 2004), 18.

11. Daniel Sullivan, "Business Service Model Promotes Better Newspapers," *Newspaper Research Journal* 27, no. 4 (2006): 69.

12. For further discussions of the challenges to professional journalism in the late 1960s and 1970s, see Daniel C. Hallin, *We Keep America on Top of the World: Television Journalism and the Public Sphere* (New York: Routledge, 1994), 170–80; Michael Schudson, *Discovering the News: A Social History of American Newspapers* (New York: Basic Books, 1978), 176–94; and Doug Underwood, *When MBAs Rule the Newsroom: How the Marketers and Managers Are Reshaping Today's Media* (New York: Columbia University Press, 1995), 38–54.

13. Hallin, *We Keep America on Top of the World,* 170. Kevin G. Barnhurst and John Nerone, on the basis of their own extensive primary research about newspaper form, also outline a period of "high modern" journalism that begins to transform into a "late modern" period starting around the 1980s. Kevin G. Barnhurst and John Nerone, *The Form of News: A History* (New York: Guilford Press, 2001).

14. W. Joseph Campbell, *The Year That Defined American Journalism: 1897 and the Clash of Paradigms* (New York: Routledge, 2006), 19.

15. Leo Bogart, *Preserving the Press: How Daily Newspapers Mobilized to Keep Their Readers* (New York: Columbia University Press, 1991).

16. Paul Du Gay, ed., *Production of Culture/Cultures of Production* (London: Sage, 1997); John Caldwell, *Production Culture: Industrial Reflexivity and Critical Practice in Film and Television* (Durham, N.C.: Duke University Press, 2008). David Nord proposes a similar concept he calls "communities of production" in *Communities of Journalism: A History of American Newspapers and Their Readers* (Urbana: University of Illinois Press, 2001).

17. Caldwell, *Production Culture,* 2 (emphasis in the original).

18. Simon Cottle, "Media Organisation and Production: Mapping the Field," in *Media Organisation and Production* (Thousand Oaks, Calif.: Sage, 2003), 11.

19. For an advocate of such a view, see Bruce M. Owen, "Confusing Success with Access: Correctly Measuring Concentration of Ownership and Control in Mass Media and Online Services," *Stanford Law and Economics Olin Working,* Paper no. 283 (May 2004): http://papers.ssrn.com/sol3/papers.cfm?abstract_id=545302. C. Edwin Baker refers to this approach as the "standard model" among economists, by which he means the neoclassical assumption that competition leads to "preference-maximizing [media] production and distribution." C. Edwin Baker, *Media, Markets, and Democracy* (New York: Cambridge University Press, 2002), 7. For a critical review of how major industry spokespeople have made this argument, see Eileen R. Meehan, *Why TV Is Not Our Fault: Television Programming, Viewers, and Who's Really in Control* (Lanham, Md.: Rowman & Littlefield, 2005), 1–27.

20. For classic sociological studies demonstrating this principle, see Gaye Tuchman, *Making News: A Study in the Construction of Reality* (New York: Free Press, 1978); and Herbert Gans, *Deciding What's News: A Study of "CBS Evening News," "NBC Nightly News," "Newsweek," and "Time"* (New York: Vintage Books, 1980).

21. Paul Hirsch, "Processing Fads and Fashions: An Organization-Set Analysis of Cultural Industry Systems," *American Journal of Sociology* 77, no. 4 (1972): 639–59; Andrzej Huczynski, "Explaining the Succession of Management Fads," *International Journal of Human Resource Management* 4, no. 2 (1993): 443–63.

22. Ross Andrew, *No Respect: Intellectuals & Popular Culture* (New York: Routledge, 1989), 52.

23. Andreas Huyssen, *After the Great Divide: Modernism, Mass Culture, Postmodernism* (Bloomington: Indiana University Press, 1986), 48.

24. Barbie Zelizer, "When Facts, Truth, and Reality Are God-Terms: On Journalism's Uneasy Place in Cultural Studies," *Communication and Critical/Cultural Studies* 1, no. 1 (2004): 109.

25. With the uptake of semiotics and what became known as the "cultural turn" across much of communication studies, media theorists tended to pay relatively little attention to the role of media in coordinating social action or in identifying the value individuals find in media not just for the pleasures of content but for its promises of social connection as well. A more recent surge of interest in social and sociological theory among media theorists—including field theory and actor network theory—along with emerging questions about the appropriation of social media among social movements are bringing questions of coordinated social action back to the forefront of media studies' scholarly agenda. For instance, see W. Lance Bennett and Alexandra Segerberg, *The Logic of Connective Action: Digital Media and the Personalization of Contentious Politics* (New York: Cambridge University Press, 2013).

26. James Carey, *Communication as Culture: Essays on Media and Society* (Boston: Unwin Hyman, 1989), 30.

27. Sydney Shanberg, "More and More, Newspapers Follow TV," *Seattle Times*, May 23, 1991, A17, quoted in Underwood, *When MBAs Rule the Newsroom*, 56.

28. Victor Pickard, *America's Battle for Media Democracy: The Triumph of Corporate Libertarianism and the Future of Media Reform* (New York: Cambridge University Press, 2014).

29. Brian McNair, "Journalism and Democracy," in *The Handbook of Journalism Studies*, edited by Karin Wahl-Jorgensen and Thomas Hanitzsch (New York: Taylor & Francis, 2008), 237.

30. Quoted in Jay Rosen, "'We'll Have That Conversation': Journalism and Democracy in the Thought of James Carey," in *James Carey: A Critical Reader*, edited by Eve Stryker Munson and Catherine A. Warren (Minneapolis: University of Minnesota Press, 1997), 191.

31. James Curran, "What Democracy Requires of Media," in *The Press*, edited by Geneva Overholser and Kathleen Hall Jamieson (New York: Oxford University Press, 2005), 120.

32. These are the functions that prominent journalism scholar and activist Robert McChesney says journalists must seek to fulfill. McChesney, *Problem of the Media*, 57.

33. Daniel Hallin, "Neoliberalism, Social Movements and Change in Media Systems in the Late Twentieth Century," in *The Media and Social Theory*, edited by David Hesmondhalgh and Jason Toynbee (New York: Routledge, 2008), 43–58.

34. See Daniel Hallin, "The Passing of the 'High Modernism' of American Journalism Revisited," *Political Communication Report* 16, no. 1 (2006), http://frank.mtsu.edu/~pcr/1601_2005_winter/commentary_hallin.htm; McChesney, *Problem of the Media;* Underwood, *When MBAs Rule the Newsroom;* and Bob Franklin, *Newszak and News Media* (New York: Arnold, 1997).

35. McChesney, *Problem of the Media,* 67–88; Dan Schiller, *Objectivity and the News: The Public and the Rise of Commercial Journalism* (Philadelphia: University of Pennsylvania Press, 1981); Mary Vavrus, *Postfeminist News: Political Women in Media Culture* (Albany: State University of New York Press, 2002).

36. Tuchman, *Making News;* Barbie Zelizer, "Journalists as Interpretive Communities," *Critical Studies in Media Communication* 10, no. 3 (1993): 219–37; Mark Fishman, *Manufacturing the News* (Austin: University of Texas Press, 2014).

37. See Kevin Glynn, *Tabloid Culture: Trash Taste, Popular Power, and the Transformation of American Television* (Durham, N.C.: Duke University Press, 2000); Catharine Lumby, *Gotcha: Life in a Tabloid World* (St. Leonards, New South Wales: Allen & Unwin, 1999); and John Langer, *Tabloid Television: Popular Journalism and the "Other News"* (London: Routledge, 1997).

38. Catharine Lumby, *Bad Girls: The Media, Sex and Feminism in the 90s* (St. Leonards, New South Wales: Allen & Unwin, 1997), 117.

39. See Samuel Bowles, "Endogenous Preferences: The Cultural Consequences of Markets and Other Economic Institutions," *Journal of Economic Literature* 36, no. 1 (1998): 75–111.

Chapter 1. A View from Somewhere

1. Spiro Agnew, "Television News Coverage," Des Moines, Iowa, November 13, 1969, http://www.americanrhetoric.com/speeches/spiroagnewtvnewscoverage.htm.

2. James Carey, "The Problem of Journalism History," in *James Carey,* edited by Munson and Warren, 91 (see introduction, n. 30). This essay was first published in 1974.

3. Schudson writes, "'Objectivity' is the chief occupational value of American journalism and the norm that historically and still today distinguishes US journalism from the dominant model of continental European journalism." Michael Schudson, "The Objectivity Norm in American Journalism," *Journalism* 2, no. 2 (2001): 149.

4. Whether journalists ever achieved full professional status is a question open to debate. See Howard Tumber and Marina Prentoulis, "Journalism and the Making of a Profession," in *Making Journalists: Diverse Models, Global Issues,* edited by Hugo de Burgh (London: Routledge, 2005), 58–74. The notion of "professionalism" that I invoke throughout this chapter is not an argument that journalists indeed achieved full professional status; rather, it is that the ideal of professional judgment became a way for news companies to justify their claims to objectivity and cultural legitimacy.

5. According to Marion Marzolf, journalists feared writing favorable reviews of Seldes's very popular books of press criticism because of publishers' intense scorn for him. At least one journalist who did write a favorable review was fired. Marion

Marzolf, *Civilizing Voices: American Press Criticism, 1880–1950* (New York: Longman, 1991), 141.

6. While Streckfuss offers the most rigorous account of journalistic "objectivity" coming to be a consistently used term in his analysis of the writing of journalistic trade magazines and associations, Maras notes that Charles Ross's textbook *The Writing of New* (1911) had described "objectivity" as a key quality of modern reporting some years earlier than the uses discovered by Streckfuss. Richard Streckfuss, "Objectivity in Journalism: A Search and a Reassessment," *Journalism Quarterly* 67, no. 4 (1990): 973–83; Steven Maras, *Objectivity in Journalism* (Cambridge, U.K., and Malden, Mass.: Polity, 2013); Charles Ross, *The Writing of News: A Handbook* (New York: Henry Holt, 1911).

7. Carey, "Problem of Journalism History," 88.

8. Robert E. Park, "The Natural History of the Newspaper," *American Journal of Sociology* 29, no. 3 (1923): 273–89.

9. Donald Shaw, "News Bias and the Telegraph: A Study of Historical Change," *Journalism Quarterly* 44, no. 1 (1967): 3–12. See further discussion of this theory in Andrew Porwancher, "Objectivity's Prophet: Adolph S. Ochs and *New York Times*, 1869–35," *Journalism History* 36, no. 4 (2011): 186–95.

10. In his later work, Schudson agrees with the assessment that most U.S. newspapers remained largely partisan long after the heyday of the penny press. Michael Schudson, *The Sociology of News*, Contemporary Societies (New York: W. W. Norton, 2003), 80.

11. David Mindich, *Just the Facts: How "Objectivity" Came to Define American Journalism* (New York: New York University Press, 2000), 18–20; Schiller, *Objectivity and the News*, 8–10 (see introduction, n. 35); Richard Kaplan, *Politics and the American Press: The Rise of Objectivity, 1865–1920* (New York: Cambridge University Press, 2001), 10–12.

12. Hazel Dicken-Garcia, *Journalistic Standards in Nineteenth-Century America* (Madison: University of Wisconsin Press, 1989), 97.

13. Schiller, *Objectivity and the News*, 46.

14. Schudson, *Discovering the News*, 107 (see introduction, n. 12).

15. According to Peter Novick, there was a similar division among "internalists" and "externalists" in accounting for objectivity as an ideal in the discipline of history. Peter Novick, *That Noble Dream: The "Objectivity Question" and the American Historical Profession* (New York: Cambridge University Press, 1988), 9.

16. For an overview of modernism's influence on journalistic objectivity, see Barbara Kelly, "Objectivity and the Trappings of Professionalism, 1900–1950," in *Fair & Balanced: A History of Journalistic Objectivity*, by Steven R. Knowlton and Karen L. Freeman (Northport, Ala.: Vision Press, 2005).

17. Schudson, *Discovering the News*, 71.

18. See also Stuart Ewen, *Captains of Consciousness: Advertising and the Social Roots of the Consumer Culture* (New York: McGraw-Hill, 1976), chap. 2.

19. Streckfuss, "Objectivity in Journalism," 975.

20. Ibid.

21. Kaplan's work follows up on one of the themes that came out of Nerone's "Mythology of the Penny Press" and Schudson's critical response to that piece. Schudson himself has followed this trajectory somewhat by suggesting that the new objectivity of the Progressive Era complemented the new duties and cognitive tasks that citizens were being called to perform by the Progressive model of "informed citizenship." The model of informed citizenship was an ideal not only espoused by Progressives but put into practice by a number of electoral reforms such as the primary (replacing the caucus) and the Australian ballot (that is, the introduction of secret ballots that ended the practice of being able to submit as a ballot a party-produced "ticket" in support of all of the party's candidates). It's worth noting, however, that the connection Schudson draws between the press and politics is still mediated through the experiential world of the average citizen-newspaper reader. The citizen now experiences political participation as an independent voter, and this experience correlates with the newly prominent "informational" model of news. Kaplan's model is more top-down. For him, the shift toward objectivity reflects not so much the experiential consciousness of average citizens but the realignment of power and possession of symbolic resources. Kaplan, *Politics and the American Press;* John Nerone, "The Mythology of the Penny Press," *Critical Studies in Mass Communication* 4, no. 4 (1987): 376–404; Schudson, "Objectivity Norm in American Journalism," 160–61.

22. For further analysis of the culture of nineteenth-century politics, see Michael E. McGerr, *The Decline of Popular Politics: The American North, 1865–1928* (New York: Oxford University Press, 1986); and Michael Schudson, *The Good Citizen: A History of American Civic Life* (New York: Free Press, 1998). These histories challenge recent claims that postmodern political cultures represent a turn from an ideological to an affective logic in politics.

23. Kaplan, *Politics and the American Press,* 150.

24. Ibid., 150.

25. Tuchman, *Making News* (see introduction, n. 20); Gans, *Deciding What's News* (see introduction, n. 20).

26. Kaplan also makes this argument. Kaplan, *Politics and the American Press,* 142.

27. Douglas Birkhead, "News Media Ethics and the Management of Professionals," *Journal of Mass Media Ethics: Exploring Questions of Media Morality* 1, no. 2 (1986): 30.

28. A. J. Kaul, "The Proletarian Journalist: A Critique of Professionalism," *Journal of Mass Media Ethics* 1, no. 2 (1986): 47–48.

29. Kaplan provides an excellent overview of the economics of consolidation of this era as well as the cultural and political conditions creating possibilities for newspaper consolidation. Kaplan, *Politics and the American Press,* 123–30.

30. Schiller, *Objectivity and the News,* 185.

31. In addition to the sources discussed below, see this assertion in Streckfuss, "Objectivity in Journalism," 982.

32. Marzolf, *Civilizing Voices,* 50–61.

33. Ibid., 50.

34. Upton Sinclair, *The Brass Check,* 222, quoted in Schiller, *Objectivity and the News,* 188.

35. McChesney, *Problem of the Media,* 59 (see introduction, n. 10).

36. Ibid., 66.

37. Ibid., 63.

38. Jay Rosen, "Beyond Objectivity," *Nieman Reports* (December 22, 1993), http://www.highbeam.com/doc/1G1-15003456.html.

39. Hallin, "Passing of the 'High Modernism'" (see introduction, n. 34).

40. Streckfuss, "Objectivity in Journalism."

41. Marzolf offers a detailed overview of press criticism in the 1930s. She emphasizes that one major theme of press criticism during this era was the question of whether the press's influence was "waning." This concern arose because much of the press was perceived to be against FDR and the New Deal, yet he proved very popular among voters. Marzolf, *Civilizing Voices,* 133–48.

42. Pickard, *America's Battle for Media Democracy,* 126 (see introduction, n. 28).

43. Marzolf, *Civilizing Voices,* 138.

44. Ben Scott, "Labor's New Deal for Journalism: The Newspaper Guild in the 1930s" (Ph.D. diss., University of Illinois, 2009).

45. Ibid., 35.

46. Gwenyth L. Jackaway, *Media at War: Radio's Challenge to the Newspapers, 1924–1939* (Westport, Conn.: Greenwood Press, 1995).

47. Kaul, "Proletarian Journalist," 52.

48. Marzolf, *Civilizing Voices,* 149–50; Victor Pickard, "'Whether the Giants Should Be Slain or Persuaded to Be Good': Revisiting the Hutchins Commission and the Role of Media in a Democratic Society," *Critical Studies in Media Communication* 27, no. 4 (2010): 391–411.

49. Quoted in Marzolf, *Civilizing Voices,* 164.

50. Commission on Freedom of the Press, *A Free and Responsible Press: A General Report on Mass Communication: Newspapers, Radio, Motion Pictures, Magazines, and Books* (Chicago: University of Chicago Press, 1947), viii.

51. Earlier drafts of this report had included more radical recommendations, such as suggestions that government subsidize loans or delivery for start-up competitors or the institution of a radio tax to fund a greater sphere of nonprofit media. However, more cautious members of the commission feared that such recommendations would be used to smear its reputation or even link the commission to communist ideology. Pickard, *America's Battle for Media Democracy,* 152–89.

52. The term *social responsibility* theory was applied by Fred S. Siebert, *Four Theories of the Press: The Authoritarian, Libertarian, Social Responsibility, and Soviet Communist Concepts of What the Press Should Be and Do* (Urbana: University of Illinois Press, 1956).

53. Victor Pickard, "Reopening the Postwar Settlement for U.S. Media: The Origins and Implications of the Social Contract between Media, the State, and the Polity," *Communication, Culture & Critique* 3, no. 2 (2010): 171.

54. For the most insightful and fullest account of the outcomes of 1940s battles over media reform, see Pickard, *America's Battle for Media Democracy*.

55. For an insider's account of the deferential culture among professional journalists in the 1950s, see James Boylan, "Declarations of Independence," *Columbia Journalism Review* 25, no. 4 (1986): 29–45. See also James Aucoin, *The Evolution of American Investigative Journalism* (Columbia: University of Missouri Press, 2005), 42–83.

56. Aucoin, *Evolution of American Investigative Journalism*, 51.

57. Godfrey Hodgson, "The Ideology of Liberal Consensus," in *America in Our Time* (Garden City, N.Y.: Doubleday, 1976), 67–98.

58. Abe Peck, *Uncovering the Sixties: The Life and Times of the Underground Press* (New York: Pantheon Books, 1985).

59. Michael Massing, "The Rise and Decline of Accuracy in Media," *Nation* 243, no. 7 (1986): 200–214.

60. Kerwin Swint, *Dark Genius: The Influential Career of Legendary Political Operative and Fox News Founder Roger Ailes* (New York: Union Square Press, 2008), 59–75; Gabriel Sherman, *The Loudest Voice in the Room: How the Brilliant, Bombastic Roger Ailes Built Fox News—and Divided a Country* (New York: Random House, 2014), 97–107.

61. For the best account of how the news industry came to perceive a crisis with declining readership, see Bogart, *Preserving the Press* (see introduction, n. 15).

62. See ibid.

63. When television broadcasters faced criticism from the FCC's Newton Minnow and others for failing to provide programming in the public interests, the networks turned to their news divisions and documentary production units to stake their public service claims. See Michael Curtin, *Redeeming the Wasteland: Television Documentary and Cold War Politics* (New Brunswick, N.J.: Rutgers University Press, 1995).

64. Michael J. Socolow, "'We Should Make Money on Our News'": The Problem of Profitability in Network Broadcast Journalism History," *Journalism* 11, no. 6 (2010): 675–91.

65. Ibid., 677.

66. For a thorough, though decidedly celebratory, history of the influence of news consultants and market research firms on local television news, see Craig Allen, *News Is People: The Rise of Local TV News and the Fall of News from New York* (Ames: Iowa State University Press, 2001).

67. For discussions of these links, see Schudson, *Discovering the News*, 187–88; and John Hellmann, *Fables of Fact: The New Journalism as New Fiction* (Urbana: University of Illinois Press, 1981). In his history of U.S. literary journalism, Hartsock argues there was not anything "new" and distinguishing about the formal elements of this style of journalism. He suggests that "it would be easy in the hubris of [the sixties] generation to examine the form [of new journalism] as having a claim to our attention and being distinctive in its own right." John C. Hartsock, *A History of American Literary Journalism: The Emergence of a Modern Narrative Form* (Amherst: University of Massachusetts, 2000), 191.

68. Aucoin, *Evolution of American Investigative Journalism*.

69. Ibid., 82.
70. Boylan, "Declarations of Independence," 38–39.
71. Ibid., 39.
72. James Aronson, "Mediations," *Antioch Review* 29, no. 3 (1969): 438.
73. Boylan, "Declarations of Independence," 39.
74. Ibid., 38.
75. Alice Fahs, *Out on Assignment: Newspaper Women and the Making of Modern Public Space* (Chapel Hill: University of North Carolina Press, 2011).
76. Carolyn L. Kitch, *Pages from the Past: History and Memory in American Magazines* (Chapel Hill: University of North Carolina Press, 2005), 94.
77. For discussions of organizing efforts among African American journalists in the late 1960s and 1970s, see Wayne Dawkins, *Black Journalists: The NABJ Story* (Sicklerville, N.J.: August Press, 1997), 1–39; and Patricia Newkirk, *Within the Veil: Black Journalists, White Media* (New York: New York University Press, 2002), 69–96.
78. Dawkins, *Black Journalists,* 2.
79. Aronson, "Mediations," 439.
80. Dawkins, *Black Journalists,* 8.
81. David Halberstam, *The Powers That Be* (New York: Alfred A. Knopf, 1979), 400. Zelizer references this same passage from Halberstam and makes her own case that during the sixties and early seventies, "the more general concerns about the shifting boundaries of cultural authority presented journalists with specific professional challenges, new practices, and alternative ways of legitimating themselves." Barbie Zelizer, *Covering the Body: The Kennedy Assassination, the Media, and the Shaping of Collective Memory* (Chicago: University of Chicago Press, 1992), 20.
82. Gwyneth Mellinger, *Chasing Newsroom Diversity: From Jim Crow to Affirmative Action* (Urbana: University of Illinois Press, 2013), 52–73.
83. Hallin, "Neoliberalism, Social Movements and Change," 49 (see introduction, n. 33).
84. Boylan, "Declarations of Independence"; Hallin, "Neoliberalism, Social Movements and Change"; Robert McChesney and John Nichols, *The Death and Life of American Journalism: The Media Revolution That Will Begin the World Again* (Philadelphia: Nation Books, 2010), 47; Underwood, *When MBAs Rule the Newsroom,* 38–54 (see introduction, n. 12).
85. Barnhurst and Mutz provide evidence that newspapers have been offering longer stories with more context and less of a singular focus on events. They see this as a long-term trend in changes in reporting throughout the twentieth century. Kevin Barnhurst and Diane Mutz, "American Journalism and the Decline in Event-Centered Reporting," *Journal of Communication* 47, no. 4 (1997): 27–53.
86. See Gwyneth Mellinger's analysis of the failure of the American Society of Newspaper Editors to reach the goals it had set for newsroom integration and diversity between 1978 and 2000. Mellinger, *Chasing Newsroom Diversity.*
87. Sally Lehrman, "The Danger of Losing the Ethnic Media," *Boston Globe,* March 5, 2009.

Chapter 2. Bringing Marketing into the Newsroom

1. The most compelling evidence for how widely recognized this problem had become was the willingness of so many newspapers across the country to contribute to the Newspaper Readership Project. See Bogart, *Preserving the Press,* chap. 2 (see introduction, n. 15).

2. Howard Kurtz, "Yesterday's News: Why Newspapers Are Losing Their Franchise," in *Reinventing the Newspaper: Essays by Frank Denton and Howard Kurtz,* by Frank Denton and Howard Kurtz (New York: Twentieth Century Fund Press, 1993), 76.

3. Ibid.

4. Hugh J. Martin, "Measuring Newspaper Profits: Developing a Standard of Comparison," *Journalism & Mass Communication Quarterly* 75, no. 3 (1998): 500–517; Stephen Lacy and Hugh I. Martin, "Profits Up, Circulation Down for Thomson Papers in 80s," *Newspaper Research Journal* 19, no. 3 (1998): 63–76.

5. The surge in newspapers' interest in market research in the 1970s has been widely noted. See Bogart, *Preserving the Press,* 95–97; Underwood, *When MBAs Rule the Newsroom,* 38–54 (see introduction, n. 12); and Alison Carper, "Marketing News," in *Politics and the Press: The News Media and Their Influences,* edited by Pippa Norris (Boulder, Colo.: Lynne Rienner, 1997), 45–66.

6. Frank Denton, "Old Newspapers and New Realities: The Promise of the Marketing of Journalism," in *Reinventing the Newspaper,* by Denton and Kurtz, 61–112.

7. George Albert Gladney, "The McPaper Revolution?," *Newspaper Research Journal* 13, nos. 1–2 (1992): 54–71.

8. The most prestigious papers, such as the *New York Times* and the *Washington Post,* adopted aspects of such marketing strategies only on a very selective basis. Their reluctance to embrace the market-driven paradigm may explain why journalism scholars—so often focused on the most high-profile newspapers—have often overlooked the importance of the market-driven newspaper movement. These prestige papers seem to have been pursuing a strategy called "the class appeal" that focused on establishing a brand associated with an educated and cosmopolitan readership. See Denton, "Old Newspapers and New Realities," 30.

9. Leonard Downie Jr. and Michael Schudson, "The Reconstruction of American Journalism," *Columbia Journalism Review* (October 19, 2009), http://www.cjr.org/reconstruction/the_reconstruction_of_american.php?page=all.

10. By the 1980s, as John Nerone puts it, "the news industry orphaned the working-class market while it was still profitable." John Nerone, "The Death (and Rebirth?) of Working-Class Journalism," *Journalism* 10, no. 3 (2009): 354.

11. Although I discuss explicitly only a few historians who have marked this shift specifically with the language of "high modernism," other journalists and scholars have identified the 1970s as a turning point in the news industries through descriptions that largely concur with Hallin, Barnhurst, and Nerone. See McChesney and Nichols, *Death and Life of American Journalism,* 47 (see chap. 1, n. 84); Underwood, *When MBAs Rule the Newsroom,* 38–54; and James Hamilton, "The Market and the Media," in *The Press,* edited by Overholser and Jamieson, 351–71 (see introduction, n. 31).

12. Barnhurst and Nerone, *Form of News,* 20–24 (see introduction, n. 13).

13. Ibid., 303.

14. I analyze the contradictions of market research later in this chapter. An especially incisive critique of how the news industry generally accepted a simplistic view of readers despite the complex findings of market research can be found in Charles Layton, "What Do Readers Really Want?," *American Journalism Review* 21, no. 2 (1999).

15. Barnhurst and Nerone, *Form of News,* 306.

16. Ruth Clark, *Changing Needs of Changing Readers: A Qualitative Study of the New Social Contract between Newspaper Editors and Readers* (Reston, Va.: American Society of Newspaper Editors, 1979).

17. Underwood, *When MBAs Rule the Newsroom,* x.

18. Clark, *Changing Needs of Changing Readers,* 3.

19. For overviews of some of these various findings, see Layton, "What Do Readers Really Want?"; and Philip Meyer, "A Struggle with the News Research Puzzle," *Presstime* (December 1982): 5–9.

20. See the contrast between Ruth Clark's 1979 readership report and her 1984 findings. "Readers Now Want Hard News, New Clark Study Says," *Presstime* (May 1984): 52–53.

21. Bogart, *Preserving the Press.*

22. A *p-value* is used to determine whether a set of data meets significance for rejecting—as improbable—a hypothesis that there is no codependent relationship between variables.

23. The term *audience image,* referring to cultural producers' conception of their audience, comes from James Ettema and David Whitney, "The Money Arrow: An Introduction," in *Audiencemaking: How the Media Create the Audience* (Thousand Oaks, Calif.: Sage, 1994), 1–18.

24. These figures come from Bogart, *Press and Public,* 16.

25. Ibid., 23.

26. Bogart put forward the argument that broad sociological factors were behind the decline of newspaper readership in *Press and Public.*

27. Thomas Leonard, *News for All: America's Coming of Age with the Press* (New York: Oxford University Press, 1995), 179–82.

28. Carole Wurzelbacher, "Despite Industry Problems, Japanese Print Readership Remains High," *Editors Weblog,* June 9, 2010, http://www.editorsweblHog.org/newsrooms_and_journalism/2010/06/despite_industry_problems_japanese_print.php; Jyrki Jyrkiainen, "The Finnish Media Landscape," in *European Media Governance: National and Regional Dimensions,* edited by Georgios Terzis (Chicago: Intellect Books, 2007), 97–111.

29. Bogart, *Preserving the Press,* xi.

30. Edwin Emery, *History of the American Newspaper Publishers Association* (Westport, Conn.: Greenwood Press, 1970). For an account of the role the ANPA played during

the "media war" between newspapers and radio news outlets, see Jackaway, *Media at War* (see chap. 1, n. 46).

31. Michael O'Neill, "Foreword and Summary," in *Changing Needs of Changing Readers*, by Clark, 2.

32. A catalog of these materials can be found in Bogart, *Preserving the Press*, 286–99.

33. "Readership Institute: About Us," Readership Institute, accessed October 18, 2010, http://www.readership.org/institute/institute.asp.

34. Everette E. Dennis and David L. Stebenne, "Requiem for a Think Tank," *International Journal of Press/Politics* 8, no. 2 (2003): 11–35.

35. Rick Kaspar, "Marketing News," *Presstime* (December 1984): 20.

36. Alison Carper refers to this reasoning as the "business imperative" argument. Carper, "Marketing News."

37. Denton, "Old Newspapers and New Realities," 7.

38. Quoted in Bogart, *Preserving the Press*, 147.

39. James Batten, "America's Newspapers: What Are Our Prospects?" (Press-Enterprise Lecture Series, Riverside, Calif., April 3, 1989), http://www.pe.com/reports/lecture/misc/1989_hays_batten.pdf.

40. Among the most important of the institutions providing this training was the American Press Institute and the Management Center at the Poynter Institute. For a detailed discussion of think tanks, academic programs, and other institutions that became the knowledge centers of the market-driven journalism movement, see Underwood, *When MBAs Rule the Newsroom*, 83–94.

41. Karen Freeman, "Ruth Clark, 80, Pollster Who Changed an Industry," *New York Times*, March 7, 1997, http://www.nytimes.com/1997/03/07/us/ruth-clark-80-pollster-who-changed-an-industry.html.

42. Clark, *Changing Needs of Changing Readers*, 11.

43. Ibid., 12.

44. Ibid., 14.

45. Ibid., 15.

46. Reese Cleghorn, "Ruth Clark Changed the World of News," *American Journalism Review* (April 1997), http://www.ajr.org/article.asp?id=1146.

47. Conversation with the author, Minneapolis, June 8, 2008.

48. "Readers Now Want Hard News," 52.

49. Bogart, *Preserving the Press*, 143.

50. Charles Layton and Mary Walton, "Missing the Story at the Statehouse," *American Journalism Review* (August 1998), http://www.ajr.org/article_printable.asp?id=3280.

51. For an early example of newspapers using special content to target specific groups, see Dustin Harp's discussion of New York newspapers in the 1890s attempts to entice women readers. Dustin Harp, *Desperately Seeking Women Readers: U.S. Newspapers and the Construction of a Female Readership* (Lanham, Md.: Lexington Books, 2007), 22–24.

52. While the stated aim of such vehicles was "total" coverage of a paper's city or metropolitan area, they were sometimes distributed only to neighborhoods with desirable income levels. Bogart, *Preserving the Press,* 158.

53. Elise Burroughs, "Modern Marketing Makes Its Mark," *Presstime* (December 1981): 8.

54. Kaspar, "Marketing News," 21.

55. Downie and Schudson, "Reconstruction of American Journalism."

56. Leonard, *News for All,* 173.

57. Leo Bogart, "Newspapers in Transition," in *American Media: The Wilson Quarterly Reader,* edited by Philip S. Cook, Douglas Gomery, and Lawrence Wilson Lichty (Washington, D.C.: Woodrow Wilson Center Press, 1989), 53.

58. Harp, *Desperately Seeking Women Readers,* 31–52.

59. Ibid., 53–114.

60. David Rambo, "Newspapers Ponder Course for 'Decade of the Hispanic,'" *Presstime* (April 1982): 47–48.

61. Quoted in ibid., 49.

62. Michael Fleming and Karen Freifeld, "Spanish Newspaper Sold to Publisher?," *Newsday,* August 31, 1989.

63. Readership Institute, "How Newspapers Can Better Serve African Americans and Hispanics," *Impact Study* (2003): 7, http://www.readership.org/consumers/data/african_hispanic.pdf.

64. Allen Neuharth, *Confessions of an S.O.B.* (New York: Doubleday, 1989).

65. Leonard provides an extensive documentation of ways in which newspapers began shedding "unwanted readers" starting in the 1970s. Leonard, *News for All,* 168–74.

66. Félix Gutiérrex and Clint Wilson, "The Demographic Dilemma," *Columbia Journalism Review* (February 1979): 53.

67. Leonard, *News for All,* 150.

68. Bogart, *Preserving the Press,* 43.

69. Ibid., 42–43. Bogart made his first attempt to convene this summit in 1964, but he would make other unsuccessful attempts to convene an industry group around the same concern later.

70. Ibid., 43.

71. Ibid.

72. Otto Kerner, "Report of the National Advisory Commission on Civil Disorders," 1968, http://historymatters.gmu.edu/d/6553/.

73. Philip Meyer, "In Defense of the Marketing Approach," *Columbia Journalism Review* 16, no. 5 (1978): 60; Bogart, *Preserving the Press,* 109–11.

74. Kurtz, "Yesterday's News."

75. Douglas Underwood, "Reporting and the Push for Market-Oriented Journalism: Media Organizations as Businesses," in *Mediated Politics: Communication in the Future of Democracy,* edited by W. Lance Bennett and Robert M. Entman (Cambridge: Cambridge University Press, 2001), xviii.

76. James D. Squires, *Read All about It! The Corporate Takeover of America's Newspapers* (New York: Times Books, 1994); Howard Kurtz, *Media Circus: The Trouble with America's Newspapers* (New York: Times Books, 1993).

77. Rick Edmonds, Emily Gustin, and Tom Rosenstiel, "Newspapers: Building Digital Revenues Proves Painfully Slow," State of the News Media, 2012 (Pew Research Center, Project for Excellence in Journalism, February 11, 2013), http://stateofthemedia.org/2012/newspapers-building-digital-revenues-proves-painfully-slow/.

78. Martin Langeveld, "Moderating Declines: Parsing the NAA's Spin on Newspaper Circ Data," Nieman Journalism Lab, May 4, 2010, http://www.niemanlab.org/2010/05/moderating-declines-parsing-the-naas-spin-on-newspaper-circ-data/.

79. Jonathan M. Ladd, *Why Americans Hate the Media and How It Matters* (Princeton, N.J.: Princeton University Press, 2011).

80. Burroughs, "Modern Marketing Makes Its Mark," 5.

81. Meyer, "Struggle with the News Research Puzzle."

82. Cybernetics is the study of feedback-enhanced control systems that became a popular field, especially for military application, in the mid-twentieth century. Mark Andrejevic refers to "cybernetic systems" as processes that incorporate feedback from an environment to reach a goal that has been determined by a programmer. He draws on this concept as a way to caution against a tendency to see any form of communicative interaction, especially between media producers and consumers, as an attribute of democratic media. While Andrejevic's own focus has been geared toward online interactivity, the concept of a cybernetic system applies equally well to offline marketing research. Cybernetic interactivity fosters relationships in which users take part in helping creators achieve a predecided goal. Participants enhance the means, but do not necessarily have a say in the end goals, of the communication process. Andrejevic distinguishes this type of cybernetic feedback from democratic interactivity in which the end goals of the communication system are collaboratively decided upon by the participants. Mark Andrejevic, *iSpy: Surveillance and Power in the Interactive Era* (Lawrence: University Press of Kansas, 2007), 44.

83. For instance, focus groups started to become popular among news researchers in the late 1970s, but many researchers saw them as highly unreliable. Bogart offers some criticism of focus-group methods and argues that they became popular among editors because of their cost-effectiveness and their occupational fondness for quotations. Bogart, *Preserving the Press,* 135–36.

84. Peter Prichard, *The Making of McPaper: The Inside Story of "USA Today"* (Champaign, Ill.: Spotlight Press, 2007).

85. Meyer, "Struggle with the News Research Puzzle," 5.

86. Alison Carper, *Paint-by-Numbers Journalism: How Reader Surveys and Focus Groups Subvert a Democratic Press* (Cambridge, Mass.: Joan Shorenstein Center, Harvard University, John F. Kennedy School of Government, 1995), 10.

87. Meyer also suggests market research suffers from a lack of theory such that the cumulative findings of researchers are not being used to build a consistent and

coherent understanding of the readership problem. Meyer, "In Defense of the Marketing Approach."

88. For notable discussions of this divide, see Todd Gitlin, "Media Sociology: The Dominant Paradigm," *Theory and Society* 6, no. 2 (1978): 205–53; and Paul Lazarsfeld, "Remarks on Administrative and Critical Communications Research," in *Studies in Philosophy and Social Science* 9 (1941): 2–16.

89. Susan Cavin, "Adorno, Lazarsfeld & the Princeton Radio Project, 1938–1941" (American Sociological Association annual meeting, Boston, July 31, 2008), http://www.allacademic.com/meta/p237089_index.html.

90. One of the most influential visions of the type of environment required for democracy is Jürgen Habermas's theory of the public sphere. Jürgen Habermas, *The Structural Transformation of the Public Sphere: An Inquiry into a Category of Bourgeois Society* (Cambridge, Mass.: MIT Press, 1989). Habermas's specific theory of the public sphere has been scrutinized and criticized, but even many of his critics endorse the idea that democracy requires something along the lines of a public sphere—institutional structures, media systems, discursive space, or an environment that makes democracy possible through giving public opinion the chance to form under a set of normative conditions. See Craig Calhoun, ed., *Habermas and the Public Sphere* (Cambridge, Mass.: MIT Press, 1992); and Chantal Mouffe, "For an Agonistic Public Sphere," in *Radical Democracy: Politics between Abundance and Lack,* edited by Lars Tonder and Lasse Thomassen (Manchester: University of Manchester Press, 2005), 191–205.

91. Baker, *Media, Markets, and Democracy,* 63 (see introduction, n. 19).

92. Ibid., 83.

93. Layton, "What Do Readers Really Want?"

94. Baker, *Media, Markets, and Democracy,* 64.

95. Kaplan, *Politics and the American Press* (see chap. 1, n. 11).

96. Hallin, "Passing of the 'High Modernism'" (see introduction, n. 34).

97. David Harvey, *A Brief History of Neoliberalism* (New York: Oxford University Press, 2007); Lisa Duggan, *The Twilight of Equality: Neoliberalism, Cultural Politics, and the Attack on Democracy* (Boston: Beacon Press, 2004).

98. Thomas Frank, "The Rise of Market Populism: America's New Secular Religion," *Nation* 271 (2000): 13–19.

99. Bogart, "Newspapers in Transition," 53.

Chapter 3. The Cable News Wars

1. Not all cable hosts remain locked behind desks. CNN's Wolf Blitzer, for instance, has a penchant for standing and moving around the studio to point at maps, charts, graphs, and even the occasional hologram. Relying less on a technological edge, Glenn Beck spent much of his time on his Fox News program standing to make use of his famous chalkboard.

2. Interestingly, the term *objectivity* appears less frequently in discussions about cable news. Perhaps "objectivity" connotes a bland neutrality that cable news is trying to distance itself from while its journalists still seek to lay claim to some form of professional grasp on truthfulness and comprehensiveness in their coverage.

3. Amanda D. Lotz, *The Television Will Be Revolutionized* (New York: New York University Press, 2007).

4. See Lynn Spigel and Jan Olsson, eds., *Television after TV: Essays on a Medium in Transition* (Durham, N.C.: Duke University Press, 2004); Jonathan Gray, Jeffrey P. Jones, and Ethan Thompson, *Satire TV: Politics and Comedy in the Post-network Era* (New York: New York University Press, 2009); and Lotz, *Television Will Be Revolutionized.*

5. One important difference between the market orientation of cable news and local television news stations pertains to their different audience strategies. Craig Allen has carefully documented that the marketing consultants most responsible for developing the concept of "eyewitness news" and other market-driven local TV news innovations steered stations away from journalistic forms believed to be most appealing to upscale audiences. Instead, these consultants urged a more personality-driven and consumer-focused form of news believed to be more appealing to a much larger class segment they identified as "the middle majority." Cable news, on the contrary, has tended to focus not only on upscale audiences demographically but also, psychographically, on those with especially high interest in political news. See Craig Allen, "News Directors and Consultants: RTNDA's Endorsement of TV Journalism's 'Greatest Tool,'" *Journal of Broadcasting & Electronic Media* 51, no. 3 (2007): 424–37.

6. Pew Research Center for People and the Press, "Americans Spending More Time Following the News," September 12, 2010, http://people-press.org/2010/09/12/americans-spending-more-time-following-the-news/.

7. By "cable news" here, it is important to note, I am referring to a genre and style of news found on the major U.S.-based cable networks—MSNBC, Fox News, and CNN. Because these stations have developed a unique style of news presentation, it has become common for journalists, politicians, and ordinary viewers to talk about "cable news" in reference to these major channels only. This way of speaking about "cable news" does not include the whole gamut of all-news stations available on cable, which include a tremendous variety across the globe, including an estimated seventy all-news cable channels based in India alone and scores of channels in the United States, many of which are local, like Your News Now in Buffalo, New York. See Stephen Cushion, "Three Phases of 24-Hour News Television," in *The Rise of 24-Hour News Television: Global Perspectives,* edited by Justin Lewis and Stephen Cushion (New York: Peter Lang, 2010), 23.

8. "CNN Programming Schedule," CNN, accessed February 4, 2011, http://www.cnn.com/CNN/Programs/.

9. The notion of "media logic" has typically been invoked to refer to a prevailing logic across almost all commercial media institutions, as when Altheide and Snow

first used the term to refer to a pervading "mass media logic." I am narrowing the scope here to focus on the mediating influence of just the cable news genre. David L. Altheide and Robert P. Snow, *Media Logic* (Beverly Hills, Calif.: Sage, 1979).

10. Peter Hamby, "Obama Brushes Off 'Petty and Trivial' Cable Chatter," *CNN Politicalticker* (blog), March 26, 2009, http://politicalticker.blogs.cnn.com/2009/03/26/obama-brushes-off-petty-and-trivial-cable-chatter/; Jonathan Martin, "President Obama, White House React to 'Cable Chatter,'" *Politico*, July 22, 2010, http://www.politico.com/news/stories/0710/40041.html.

11. Paul Farhi, "Cable's Clout," *American Journalism Review* (September 2008), http://ajrarchive.org/Article.asp?id=4574.

12. Bill Carter, "CNN Will Cancel 'Crossfire' and Cut Ties to Commentator," *New York Times*, January 6, 2005, http://www.nytimes.com/2005/01/06/business/media/06crossfire.html.

13. Maurice Schonfeld, *Me and Ted against the World: The Unauthorized Story of the Founding of CNN* (New York: Cliff Street, 2001), 15.

14. As cultural-business historian and Turner biographer Eric Guthey puts it, a structural perspective would lead to the conclusion that "someone would have eventually created a superstation and a CNN even if Turner had not existed." Eric Guthey, "Ted Turner's Media Legend and the Transformation of Corporate Liberalism," *Business and Economic History* 26, no. 1 (1997): 189.

15. Allen, *News Is People* (see chap. 1, n. 66).

16. Ted Turner, *Call Me Ted* (New York: Grand Central, 2008), 160–61.

17. Hank Whittemore, *CNN: The Inside Story* (Boston: Little, Brown, 1990), 199–203.

18. Philip Dougherty, "Advertising: 'Nonstop News Machine,'" *New York Times*, June 18, 1982.

19. Turner, *Call Me Ted*, 200.

20. Ibid., 161.

21. Ibid., 165–66.

22. James Traub, "The Nonstop News Network," *Columbia Journalism Review* 20, no. 2 (1981): 61.

23. Turner, *Call Me Ted*, 166.

24. "Union Seeks to Organize Turner's Cable News Network," *Wall Street Journal*, January 8, 1982, http://global.factiva.com/redir/default.aspx?P=sa&an=j000000020020326de1800ulh&cat=a&ep=ASE.

25. Larry David Smith, "How the Dialectical Imperative Shapes Network News Content: The Case of CNN vs. the Entertainment Networks," *Communication Quarterly* 40, no. 4 (1992): 338–49.

26. Former CNN president Sid Bedingfield used the term *television wire service* to describe how CNN thought of its programming in an interview with me on January 17, 2011. This characterization is consistent with accounts from CNN executives in Turner, *Call Me Ted*; Whittemore, *CNN: The Inside Story*; and Peter Waldman, "Media: CNN Rechannels Efforts to Achieve Premier Status," *Wall Street Journal*, October 16,

1989, http://global.factiva.com/redir/default.aspx?P=sa&an=j000000020011116dlagoortw&cat=a&ep=ASE.

27. Schonfeld, *Me and Ted against the World,* 75–76.

28. Turner, *Call Me Ted,* 187; Traub, "The Nonstop News Network," 58.

29. Whittemore, *CNN: The Inside Story,* 45.

30. Sid Bedingfield, interview with the author, Skype, January 17, 2011.

31. Monte Plott, "Rescue Gets CNN Top Ratings," *Atlanta Journal,* October 23, 1987.

32. Phil Rosenthal, "CNN's Big News Is Its 10 Years of Success," *Los Angeles Daily News,* June 1, 1990; P. Waldman, "Media."

33. See Elana Levine, "Distinguishing Television: The Changing Meanings of Television Liveness," *Media, Culture & Society* 30, no. 3 (2008): 393–409; and Jérôme Bourdon, "Live Television Is Still Alive: On Television as an Unfulfilled Promise," *Media, Culture & Society* 22, no. 5 (2000): 531–56.

34. Lucy Küng-Shankleman, *Inside the BBC and CNN: Managing Media Organisations* (London: Routledge, 2012), 79.

35. Stephen Battaglio, "Calm after the Storm," *Adweek* (March 9, 1992).

36. "CNN Tries Promo Hook," *Advertising Age* (March 16, 1992); P. Waldman, "Media."

37. John M. Higgins, "D'Alba Keeps Fighting for CNN," *Broadcasting & Cable* 135, no. 42 (2005): 40.

38. Several writers have devoted books to the influence of Roger Ailes. The most probing and well-researched is Gabriel Sherman's epic biography, *Loudest Voice in the Room* (see chap. 1, n. 60). Other accounts of Ailes and his influence can be found in Scott Collins, *Crazy Like a Fox: The Inside Story of How Fox News Beat CNN* (New York: Portfolio, 2004); Swint, *Dark Genius* (see chap. 1, n. 60); and David Brock, Ari Rabin-Havt, and Media Matters for America, *The Fox Effect: How Roger Ailes Turned a Network into a Propaganda Machine* (New York: Knopf Doubleday, 2012). The most favorable account of Ailes can be found in Zev Chafets's authorized biography, *Roger Ailes: Off Camera* (New York: Penguin, 2013).

39. Les Brown, "How CNN's Rivals Got into the Coop," *Television Business International* (September 1, 1996); Elizabeth Jensen and Mark Robichaux, "TCI Will Carry 24-Hour News Created by Fox," *Wall Street Journal Europe,* June 26, 1996; Sherman, *Loudest Voice in the Room,* 184–86.

40. Bill Carter, "TCI Reaches Deal with Fox to Carry All-News Channel," *New York Times,* June 25, 1996, http://www.nytimes.com/1996/06/25/business/the-media-business-tci-reaches-deal-with-fox-to-carry-all-news-channel.html.

41. Sherman, *Loudest Voice in the Room,* 205.

42. Collins, *Crazy Like a Fox,* 100–106; Sherman, *Loudest Voice in the Room,* 204–19.

43. See Collins, *Crazy Like a Fox.*

44. Ibid., 68.

45. Jim Forkan, "News Nets Jockey in Demo Derby," *Multichannel News* 22, no. 5 (2001): 26; Ed Martin, "Ratings Bumps Have CNN, Fox, MSNBC Claiming Victory," *Advertising Age* 70, no. 16 (1999): 18–22.

46. Alan Breznick, "War Ratings Boost Channels," *Advertising Age* 74, no. 20 (2003): C94.

47. Bill Carter, "Moves by Fox and CNN Signal a New Push for New Audiences," *New York Times*, January 4, 2002, http://www.nytimes.com/2002/01/04/business/moves-by-fox-and-cnn-signal-a-new-push-for-new-audiences.html.

48. Gunter Kress, "Ideological Structures in Discourse," in *Handbook of Discourse Analysis: Discourse Analysis in Society*, edited by T. A. Van Dijk (London: Academic Press, 1985), 28.

49. The industry popular offers a variation on cultural studies' concern with "the popular" as a central concept at the heart of contemporary cultural struggles. Stuart Hall argues that the popular could be understood as "those forms and activities which have their roots in the social and material conditions of particular classes; which have been embodied in popular traditions and classes." By employing the term *industry popular*, I intend to shift the focus away from the question of which cultural forms, images, or traditions are rooted most with the groups Hall refers to as the popular classes. Instead, the industry popular turns toward how media industries interpret, respond to, and mobilize their own of notion of the popular. The concept helps pose the question: what cultural forms (specifically of news) do media industry discourses frame as having the potential for popular appeal? Stuart Hall, "Notes on Deconstructing the Popular," in *People's History and Socialist Theory*, edited by Raphael Samuel (London: Routledge & Kegan Paul, 1981), 235.

50. John Caldwell, *Televisuality: Style, Crisis, and Authority in American Television* (New Brunswick, N.J.: Rutgers University Press, 1995), 4.

51. My method started with searching for stories about the competition among the cable news networks using search terms such as *cable news war* or *CNN MSNBC Fox ratings* in databases such as LexisNexis, Factiva, and EBSCO Communication and Mass Media Complete. I supplemented these searches with ones that zeroed in on moments that I knew would raise questions about cable news choices, such as when particular programs were canceled or a new executive was hired. I also turned to several books that mostly offered biographical or autobiographical accounts of the cable news wars, including Jeff Cohen's *Cable News Confidential: My Misadventures in Corporate Media* (Sausalito, Calif.: PoliPointPress, 2006), Scott Collin's *Crazy Like a Fox*, and Gabriel Sherman's *Loudest Voice in the Room*. Although my research focuses on written discourses, I was able to conduct several interviews of former cable news leaders for background and contextualization. I spoke with Sid Bedingfield, former executive vice president and senior manager of CNN/U.S.; former CNN/U.S. president Jonathan Klein; Jeff Cohen, a former senior producer of MSNBC's *Donahue* and a former contributor to CNN, Fox News, and MSNBC; and former CNN chief White House correspondent and *Newsmaker Sunday* host Charles Bierbauer. The themes I highlight here reflect my own interpretation, of course, of what has been most central to the industry discourse. All the themes I identify have been repeated prominently across multiple sources.

52. For just a few examples of the scores of articles that frame star power as a key element of the cable news competition, see Bill Carter, "Bitterness and Posturing as Rivalries Resurface in Fight for Cable News," *New York Times,* June 3, 1996; Sean Callahan, "Fox Hounds Rivals into a Star Search," *Advertising Age* 73, no. 23 (2002): 4, 14; Mike Tierney, "Ads Accent CNN Stars' Lighter Side," *Atlanta Journal-Constitution,* November 16, 2004; Brian Stelter, "Fresh Face on Cable, Sharp Rise in Ratings," *New York Times,* October 21, 2008; Ned Martel, "Outfoxing Fox," *Los Angeles Times,* March 6, 2005; and Stuart Elliott, "As Television News Enters the Post-Lewinsky Era, Fox Pushes a 'Powerful Prime Time' Campaign," *New York Times,* March 8, 1999. Fox News president Roger Ailes makes this point: "Crisis drives news. When there's no crisis, then it's up to a star to bring people in." Quoted in Steve Donohue, "With Ailes at Helm, FNC Ascends," *Multichannel News* 22, no. 23 (2001): 8.

53. Steve Barkin, *American Television News: The Media Marketplace and the Public Interest* (Armonk, N.Y.: M. E. Sharpe, 2003), 16.

54. Collins, *Crazy Like a Fox,* 70.

55. Walter Goodman, "New and Familiar Faces in News Channel Debut," *New York Times,* July 23, 1996.

56. Collins, *Crazy Like a Fox.*

57. Alessandra Stanley, "MSNBC as Fox's Liberal Evil Twin," *New York Times,* August 31, 2012.

58. For examples of such coverage, see Associated Press, "ABC's Brit Hume Turns to Fox," *Boston Globe,* December 11, 1996; and John Carmoody, "Hume Moves to Fox," *Seattle Times,* December 11, 1996.

59. Quoted in Collins, *Crazy Like a Fox,* 81. See also Bill Carter, "Fox Loses Round in Its Suit over Anchor's Move to CNN," *New York Times,* May 1, 2003.

60. Verne Gay, "A Foxy Move: Greta Van Susteren's Departure from CNN Has Left Her Former Employer Nervous," *Newsday,* June 29, 2003, D12.

61. Marvin Kitman, *The Man Who Would Not Shut Up: The Rise of Bill O'Reilly* (New York: Macmillan, 2008), 169.

62. Anne Becker, "CNN Adds More Dobbs," *Broadcasting & Cable* (October 10, 2006), http://www.broadcastingcable.com/news/programming/cnn-adds-more-dobbs/29590.

63. Michael Kinsley, "The Twilight of Objectivity," *Pittsburgh Post-Gazette,* April 7, 2006; Ken Auletta, "Mad as Hell," *New Yorker,* December 4, 2006.

64. Jon Friedman, "CNN's Lou Dobbs Is the Anti–Brian Williams," *Dow Jones News Service* (November 9, 2007).

65. Peter J. Boyer, "One Angry Man," *New Yorker,* June 23, 2008.

66. Howard Kurtz, "Brown's CNN Role: A Matter of Opinion," *Washington Post,* October 21, 2008, http://www.washingtonpost.com/wp-dyn/content/article/2008/10/20/AR2008102003296.html?sub=AR.

67. Andrea Morabito, "Fox News Moving Megyn Kelly to Primetime," *Broadcasting & Cable* (July 2, 2013), http://www.broadcastingcable.com/news/programming/

fox-news-moving-megyn-kelly-primetime/66013; Brian Stelter, "Fox News Anchor Megyn Kelly Renews Contract," *New York Times,* May 7, 2013, http://www.nytimes.com/2013/05/08/business/media/fox-news-anchor-megyn-kelly-renews-contract.html; Brian Lowry, "With Megyn Kelly Move, Fox News Makes a Cosmetic Change," *Daily Variety,* September 17, 2013.

68. Tierney, "Ads Accent CNN Stars' Lighter Side."

69. Lisa deMoraes, "CNN Caught In 'Zipper' Ad for Paula Zahn," *Washington Post,* January 8, 2002.

70. For example, Sherman reports that a senior Fox News executive told him that Ailes once complained about anchor Catherine Crier's attire, saying, "Tell Catherine I did not spend x-number of dollars on a glass desk for her to wear pant suits." Sherman, *Loudest Voice in the Room,* 238.

71. Matea Gold, "MSNBC's New Liberal Spark Plug," *Los Angeles Times,* September 29, 2008; Stelter, "Fresh Face on Cable, Sharp Rise in Ratings."

72. Many writers take this as a tacit assumption, but for an explicit endorsement of this connection, see Rob Owen, "News Teams Establishing Brands," *Cincinnati Post,* May 26, 2003.

73. Jim Rutenberg, "In an About-Face, CNN Turns to News Talk Shows to Polish Its Ratings," *New York Times,* January 1, 2001.

74. Schudson, *Discovering the News,* 187–88 (see introduction, n. 12).

75. Martel, "Outfoxing Fox."

76. Peter Johnson, "Will Fox News' Success Force Competitors to Take Sides? Experts Predict More Partisan Cable News," *USA Today,* November 22, 2004; Elizabeth Jensen, "An Anchorman with Attitude: Fox News Channel's Shepard Smith Hasn't Let an On-Air Gaffe Put a Dent in His Career Arc," *Los Angeles Times,* December 13, 2002; Matea Gold, "At Fox News, He's the Man in the Middle," *Los Angeles Times,* October 8, 2006.

77. David Hirschman, "Suddenly Ubiquitous CNN Personality on Burma, Anchoring, and the Perils of Celebrity Jeopardy," *MediaBistro* (blog), May 11, 2004, http://thoroughlyandersoncooper.blogspot.com/2011/05/where-were-you-7-years-ago.html.

78. Elizabeth Jensen, "An Anchor Who Reports Disaster News with a Heart on His Sleeve," *New York Times,* September 12, 2005.

79. Jacques Steinberg, "Paula Zahn to Leave CNN, Replaced by Campbell Brown," *New York Times,* July 25, 2007.

80. In 2010 Campbell Brown also left CNN, citing low ratings and an inability to "compete with the opinion-mongers that dominate cable news in prime time" as her own reasons for leaving. Brian Stelter, "CNN Anchor to Depart, Weary of the Cable Bombast," *New York Times,* May 18, 2010.

81. Brock, Rabin-Havt, and Media Matters for America, *Fox Effect.*

82. Steven Kull, Clay Ramsay, and Evan Lewis, "Misperceptions, the Media, and the Iraq War," *Political Science Quarterly* 118, no. 4 (2003): 569–98.

83. Alexandra Kitty, *Outfoxed: Rupert Murdoch's War on Journalism* (documentary), (Disinformation, 2004); Al Franken, *Lies and the Lying Liars Who Tell Them: A Fair and Balanced Look at the Right* (New York: Dutton, 2003); Brock, Rabin-Havt, and Media Matters for America, *Fox Effect.*

84. For examples, see John Meroney, "The Fox News Gamble," *American Enterprise* (September 1, 1997); Karen Donovan, "Fox News Channel Seeks Its Niche," *Crain's New York Business* (September 22, 1997); and "Led by Roger Ailes Fox's News Hounds Give Chase," *Broadcasting & Cable* (September 15, 1997).

85. Sherman, *Loudest Voice in the Room,* 230.

86. Jane Levere, "The Fox News Channel Tops CNN's Audience, and Casts Its Eyes toward Its Advertising Rates," *New York Times,* January 30, 2002; Ken Auletta, "Vox Fox: How Roger Ailes and Fox News Are Changing Cable News," *New Yorker,* June 26, 2008; P. Johnson, "Will Fox News' Success Force Competitors to Take Sides?"; Richard Linnett, "Fox Trumpets Victory over CNN," *Advertising Age* 74, no. 28 (2003): 8.

87. Maria Aspan, "Some Advertisers Shun Air America, a Lonely Voice from Talk Radio's Left," *New York Times,* November 6, 2006.

88. Jim Rutenberg, "Seeking Sizzle at CNN," *New York Times,* August 15, 2001.

89. Collins, *Crazy Like a Fox,* 169–70; Maureen Dowd, "CNN: Foxy or Outfoxed?," *New York Times,* August 15, 2001.

90. Howard Kurtz, "Protest Letters to MSNBC Draw Savage Response," *Washington Post,* March 5, 2003.

91. Brian Lowry, "Savage Gets the Boot after On-Air Anti-gay Outburst," *Los Angeles Times,* July 8, 2003.

92. Cohen, *Cable News Confidential,* 22.

93. Eric Deggans, "Rapper as TV Journalist? Media Critics Shake Heads," *St. Petersburg (Fla.) Times,* June 29, 1997; Joe Schlosser, "Rapper Hired by Fox News," *Broadcasting & Cable* (May 19, 1997).

94. Cohen, *Cable News Confidential,* 165.

95. Bill Carter, "MSNBC Cancels Phil Donahue," *New York Times,* February 26, 2003, http://www.nytimes.com/2003/02/26/business/media/26PHIL.html.

96. Cohen, *Cable News Confidential,* 186; Tom Shales, "A Media Role in Selling the War? No Question," *Washington Post,* April 25, 2007.

97. Sherman, *Loudest Voice in the Room,* 312–13; Daniel Denvir, "A Short History of the War on Christmas," *Politico,* December 16, 2013, http://www.politico.com/magazine/story/2013/12/war-on-christmas-short-history-101222.html.

98. Keith Olbermann, *Countdown with Keith Olbermann,* MSNBC, May 21, 2008.

99. Boyer, "One Angry Man."

100. Bill Carter, "MSNBC's Star Carves Anti-Fox Niche," *New York Times,* July 11, 2006.

101. Gold, "MSNBC's New Liberal Spark Plug." See also Bill Carter, "MSNBC Changes Prime-Time Lineup," *New York Times,* August 20, 2008; and Stelter, "Fresh Face on Cable, Sharp Rise in Ratings."

102. Brian Stelter, "MSNBC Takes Incendiary Hosts from Anchor Seat," *New York Times,* September 8, 2008.

103. Brian Stelter, "With Tagline, MSNBC Embraces a Political Identity," *New York Times,* October 4, 2010.

104. John Harwood, "If Fox Is Partisan, It Is Not Alone," *New York Times,* November 2, 2009.

105. This observation comes from my own viewing of *The Rachel Maddow Show, The Ed Show, All in with Chris Hayes,* and *PoliticsNation with Al Sharpton.* These programs do sometimes offer progressive perspectives that would have been difficult to find on major networks before MSNBC started pursuing this strategy. Nonetheless, though they have been critical of the Obama administration at times when progressive Democrats have questioned his compromises, they tend to stay within views and voices acceptable to mainstream Democratic officials, while not remaining in lockstep with Democratic talking points.

106. Seth Ackerman, "The Most Biased Name in News: Fox News Channel's Extraordinary Right Wing Tilt," *Extra!,* August 2001, http://www.fair.org/index.php?page=1067.

107. Brian Stelter, "Sharpton Close to Being MSNBC Anchor," *New York Times,* July 20, 2011.

108. Griffin responded that his comments about "people in Washington" had not been referring to government officials, but rather MSNBC employees had been having trouble booking guests on Uygar's program because of his aggressive tone. Ibid.; Paul Harris, "Young Turk Burns Bridges with MSNBC," *Guardian Unlimited,* September 9, 2011.

109. Rebecca Dana, "Slyer than Fox," *New Republic,* March 25, 2013, http://www.newrepublic.com/article/112733/roger-ailes-msnbc-how-phil-griffin-created-lefts-fox-news.

110. Franken, *Lies and the Lying Liars Who Tell Them.*

111. Pew Research Center for People and the Press, "State of the News Media, 2012," September 27, 2012, 44, http://www.people-press.org/2012/09/27/in-changing-news-landscape-even-television-is-vulnerable/.

112. James Hibberd, "Fox News Has Oldest Cable Audience," *Hollywood Reporter* (blog), November 30, 2010, http://www.hollywoodreporter.com/blogs/live-feed/fox-news-oldest-cable-audience-54230.

113. Greg Braxton, "News with Attitude on 'Fox Files,'" *Los Angeles Times,* December 3, 1998.

114. Collins, *Crazy Like a Fox,* 131; Howard Kurtz, "Is Fox's News Channel Cable-Ready?," *Washington Post,* October 14, 1996.

115. David Bauder, "Networks Woo Youth with Popular Anchors," *Chicago Tribune,* December 8, 2003.

116. For an example of a discussion of this dilemma, see Jim Rutenberg, "CNN Aims at Young Viewers as It Revamps News Format," *New York Times,* August 5, 2001.

117. Higgins, "D'Alba Keeps Fighting for CNN"; Joe Flint, "Bush Cable Ads Aim to Solidify 'Partisan' Vote," *Wall Street Journal*, August 26, 2004.

118. In 2013 all the networks saw greater revenues from subscriptions than advertising. Looking at data from Pew Reports going back to 2006 shows that Fox News sometimes earned more in advertising revenue, but subscription revenues caught up as they renegotiated fees based on the network's ratings. Jesse Holcomb and Amy Mitchell, "Cable: A Growing Medium Reaching Its Ceiling" (Pew Research Center, Project for Excellence in Journalism, 2013), http://stateofthemedia.org/2013/cable-a-growing-medium-reaching-its-ceiling/#competition-for-audience-beyond-the-major-news-channels.

119. Robert Strauss, "Tough on the Old Ticker? The Constant Crawl along the Bottom of the Screen on Cable News Channels Keeps Us Up to Date but May Be Information Overload," *Los Angeles Times*, December 31, 2001.

120. Ken Kerschbaumer, "Cut the Clutter," *Broadcasting & Cable* 134, no. 44 (2004): 22; Deborah Potter, "The TV Ticker Parade," *American Journalism Review* 24, no. 7 (2002): 7; Robin Finn, "Writing Miniature Messages for a Maximum Medium," *New York Times*, August 18, 2005; Allison Romano, "Ticker Embedded in News," *Broadcasting & Cable* 132, no. 31 (2002): 26.

121. Colin Sparks and Peter Dahlgren, eds., *Tabloid Tales: Global Debates over Media Standards* (Lanham, Md.: Rowman & Littlefield, 2000).

122. Schudson, *Discovering the News*, 95.

123. Kelly Heyboer, "Cable Clash," *American Journalism Review* 22, no. 5 (2000): 20.

124. For an example of how these tensions have played out at Fox, see Sherman, *Loudest Voice in the Room*, 241–43.

125. Martel, "Outfoxing Fox."

126. Stelter, "With Tagline, MSNBC Embraces a Political Identity"; John Cook, "'Crossfire' Demise Another Attempt to Redefine CNN," *Chicago Tribune*, January 9, 2005.

127. Quoted in Collins, *Crazy Like a Fox*, 9. See also Steve McClellan, "The New Name in News: MSNBC," *Broadcasting & Cable* (December 18, 1995).

128. Quoted in Stephen Battaglio, "Microsoft Paying NBC $220 Mil in News Pact," *Hollywood Reporter*, December 15, 1995.

129. Microsoft grew disenchanted with the partnership, selling off its stake in the television side of MSNBC in 2005 and selling its remaining investment in the online site in 2012.

130. For further discussion, see Farooq A. Kperogi, "Cooperation with the Corporation? CNN and the Hegemonic Cooptation of Citizen Journalism through iReport.com," *New Media & Society* 13, no. 2 (2011): 314–29.

131. Stephen Duncombe, *Dream: Re-imagining Progressive Politics in an Age of Fantasy* (New York: New Press, 2007); Jeffrey P. Jones, *Entertaining Politics: Satiric Television and Political Engagement*, 2nd ed. (Lanham, Md.: Rowman & Littlefield, 2009); Liesbet van

Zoonen, *Entertaining the Citizen: When Politics and Popular Culture Converge* (Lanham, Md.: Rowman & Littlefield, 2005).

132. Jones, *Entertaining Politics,* 14.

133. Zoonen, *Entertaining the Citizen,* 16.

134. I invoke these positions only to note that they serve as the framework in which much of the discussion about political entertainment has taken place. That said, few writers would actually claim to represent either of these two poles. Those leaning more to the populist direction usually portray the rationalist position as the dominant discourse. Those leaning more toward the rationalist pole tend to portray themselves as working against a dominant commercial-capitalist media logic.

135. Cable news networks have tried some programming experiments, mostly outside of prime time, such as news comedy shows and original documentary films, that I have not discussed in this analysis as they have not been as central to the industry-popular discourse.

136. It might be helpful to make an analogy between the claim I am making here and the argument made in *Dreamworlds 3*, Sut Jhally's trenchant critique of the representation of female sexuality in the music video industry. In a crucial line that frames his critique of the industry, Jhally says, "The real issue is not that there is too much discussion of sex but that there is not enough." As I have seen in class discussions, this line puzzles some students who initially try to understand *Dreamworlds 3* as a more familiar "antisex" or moralistic argument. Yet Jhally explicitly argues that the problem he sees in music videos is not the expression of sexuality and desire; rather, it is that "there is simply not enough diversity in the stories of sexuality that circulate in the culture." As he shows through countless clips, the tropes and images defining female sexuality in music videos seem awfully repetitive. In something of the same way, my analysis points to the limited range of tactics that cable news networks repeatedly use to try to entice audiences. The problem with these tactics is not that they are entertainment gimmicks and therefore inherently debased; rather, it is that there is not enough ingenuity and creative experimentation in trying to present compelling stories about public life for diverse audiences. *Dreamworlds 3: Desire, Sex, and Power in Music Video,* directed by Sut Jhally (Northamptom, Mass.: Media Education Foundation, 2007).

137. Hallin notes that broadcast television in the 1970s and 1980s moved toward a greater emphasis on political strategy and what he calls the "inside-dopester" perspective, commenting on political strategy and performance rather than substantive issues. By commenting on political strategy, television journalists found a vantage point to judge politics from a "technical" perspective, allowing them to avoid the appearance of supporting political values. Hallin perceptively notes such a perspective follows from a commitment to find space for journalistic expertise while maintaining the ideology of objectivity. Yet cable news hosts who have forsaken objectivity have become even more focused on strategy than broadcast news commentators. For cable news, the strategic maneuvering frame serves not as a buffer against value-laden intervention

but as a dramatizing frame to make politics a sport. Hallin, *We Keep America on Top of the World,* 133–52 (see introduction, n. 12).

138. Professional journalism has often been criticized for its overreliance on government officials and prominent individuals to set the news agenda and provide the sources of knowledge in most news stories. For a well-researched review of critiques of the relationship between professional journalists and official sources, see McChesney, *Problem of the Media,* 67–71.

Chapter 4. Popularizing News 2.0

1. Phillip Elliott, "Obama Fields Range of Questions at Internet Event," Associated Press, March 26, 2009, http://www.highbeam.com/doc/1A1-D975S4FO0.html.

2. Angela M. Lee, Seth C. Lewis, and Matthew Powers, "Audience Clicks and News Placement: A Study of Time-Lagged Influence in Online Journalism," *Communication Research* 41, no. 4 (2014): 505–30; C. W. Anderson, "Between Creative and Quantified Audiences: Web Metrics and Changing Patterns of Newswork in Local US Newsrooms," *Journalism* 12, no. 5 (2011): 550–66; Nikki Usher, "Al Jazeera English Online," *Digital Journalism* 1, no. 3 (2013): 335–51.

3. Nicole S. Cohen, "From Pink Slips to Pink Slime: Transforming Media Labor in a Digital Age," *Communication Review* 18, no. 2 (2015): 98–122.

4. Media Insight Project, "The Personal News Cycle: How Americans Choose to Get News," March 17, 2014, http://www.americanpressinstitute.org/publications/reports/survey-research/personal-news-cycle/.

5. Rosen, "People Formerly Known as the Audience" (see introduction, n. 2).

6. For discussions of algorithmic culture and the faith in technocracy behind it, see Ted Striphas, "Algorithmic Culture: 'Culture Now Has Two Audiences, People and Machines'—Futurists' Views," *Medium,* accessed October 31, 2014, https://medium.com/futurists-views/algorithmic-culture-culture-now-has-two-audiences-people-and-machines-2bdaa404f643; and Siva Vaidhyanathan, *The Googlization of Everything (and Why We Should Worry)* (Berkeley: University of California Press, 2012).

7. See Matt Carlson, "Blogs and Journalistic Authority: The Role of Blogs in US Election Day 2004 Coverage," *Journalism Studies* 8, no. 2 (2007): 264–79.

8. Gillmor, *We the Media,* xii–xiii (see introduction, n. 6).

9. I discuss the influence of these writers in conversations about the future of news in the conclusion. See also Starkman, "Confidence Game" (see introduction, n. 5).

10. C. W. Anderson, *Rebuilding the News: Metropolitan Journalism in the Digital Age* (Philadelphia: Temple University Press, 2013); Jane B. Singer, "Ethnography of Newsroom Convergence," in *Making Online News: The Ethnography of New Media Production,* edited by Chris A. Paterson and David Domingo (New York: Peter Lang, 2008), 157–70; Pablo J. Boczkowski, *Digitizing the News: Innovation in Online Newspapers* (Cambridge, Mass.: MIT Press, 2004).

11. See, for example, Clay Shirky, *Here Comes Everybody: The Power of Organizing without Organizations* (New York: Penguin, 2009); Benkler, *Wealth of Networks* (see introduction,

n. 6); and Henry Jenkins, *Convergence Culture: Where Old and New Media Collide* (New York: New York University Press, 2006).

12. Daniel Kreiss, Megan Finn, and Fred Turner, "The Limits of Peer Production: Some Reminders from Max Weber for the Network Society," *New Media & Society* 13, no. 2 (2011): 243–59.

13. Benkler, *Wealth of Networks,* 10.

14. Ibid., 239.

15. Axel Bruns, "The Active Audience: Transforming Journalism from Gatekeeping to Gatewatching," in *Making Online News,* edited by Paterson and Domingo.

16. I use the term *collaborative filtering* broadly, referring to any method of sorting and ordering information online through tools designed to register feedback based on peer activity. Sometimes *collaborative filtering* is used to specifically designate personalized recommendations based on user data.

17. Pierre Lévy, *Collective Intelligence: Mankind's Emerging World in Cyberspace* (Cambridge, Mass.: Perseus Books, 1999).

18. Jenkins, *Convergence Culture,* 52–54.

19. Tim P. Vos, Stephanie Craft, and Seth Ashley, "New Media, Old Criticism: Bloggers' Press Criticism and the Journalistic Field," *Journalism* 13, no. 7 (2012): 850–68; Jay Rosen, "Why 'Bloggers vs. Journalists' Is Still with Us," *Pressthink,* March 4, 2011, http://pressthink.org/2011/03/monsters-of-the-newsroom-id-why-bloggers-vs-journalists-is-still-with-us/.

20. Jane Sasseen, Kenny Olmstead, and Amy Mitchell, "Digital: By the Numbers," State of the Media, 2013, http://www.stateofthemedia.org/2013/digital-as-mobile-grows-rapidly-the-pressures-on-news-intensify/digital-by-the-numbers/.

21. Boczkowski, *Digitizing the News,* 20.

22. See Adrienne Russell, *Networked: A Contemporary History of News in Transition* (Cambridge: Polity, 2011); David Carlson, "The History of Online Journalism," *Digital Journalism: Emerging Media and the Changing Horizons of Journalism* (2003): 31–55; and Ben Scott, "A Contemporary History of Digital Journalism," *Television & New Media* 6, no. 1 (2005): 89–126.

23. Boczkowski, *Digitizing the News,* 20–29; Carlson, "History of Online Journalism."

24. Carlson, "History of Online Journalism," 38; Bogart, *Preserving the Press,* 159 (see introduction, n. 15).

25. Carlson, "History of Online Journalism," 45.

26. Scott, "Contemporary History of Digital Journalism."

27. J. D. Greer and D. Mensing, "The Evolution of Online Newspapers: A Longitudinal Content Analysis, 1997–2003," in *Internet Newspapers: The Making of a Mainstream Medium,* edited by Xigen Li (Mahwah, N.J.: Lawrence Erlbaum, 2006), 23.

28. "Slashdot FAQ," Slashdot, accessed June 4, 2015, http://slashdot.org/faq/.

29. James Surowiecki, "Joshua Schachter, 32," *Technology Review* (2006), http://www.technologyreview.com/tr35/Profile.aspx?Cand=T&TRID=432.

30. Richard MacManus, "Interview with Digg Founder Kevin Rose," *ZDNet* (blog), February 1, 2006, http://www.zdnet.com/blog/web2explorer/interview-with-digg-founder-kevin-rose-part-1/108.

31. Miguel Helft, "Young Internet Producers, Bankrolled, Are Seeking Act II," *New York Times*, September 25, 2006, http://query.nytimes.com/gst/fullpage.html.

32. The *Washington Post* reported that Google was about to purchase Digg for two hundred million dollars in 2008. *Businessweek* reported that Yahoo! had tried to buy the company in 2006. Michael Arrington, "Google Walks Away from Digg Deal," *Washington Post*, July 26, 2008.

33. Sarah Lacy and Jessi Hemp, "Valley Boys: Digg.com's Kevin Rose Leads a New Brat Pack of Young Entrepreneurs," *Businessweek*, August 14, 2006, http://www.businessweek.com/magazine/content/06_33/b3997001.htm.

34. Richard Adams, "Innovations: Reddit.com," *Guardian*, December 8, 2005, http://www.guardian.co.uk/technology/2005/dec/08/innovations.guardian weeklytechnologysection1.

35. Joseph Walker and Spencer E. Ante, "Once a Social Media Star, Digg Sells for $500,000," *Wall Street Journal*, July 13, 2012.

36. "Newsvine Info," Facebook, accessed June 14, 2011, http://www.facebook.com/newsvine?sk=info.

37. "Digg: About Us," Digg, accessed May 10, 2009, http:/digg.com/about/.

38. Tom Regan, "Who Controls the News? On the Web, You Can," *Christian Science Monitor*, September 26, 2007.

39. Steve Johnson, "They Can Digg It: Sites Let People Decide News," *Chicago Tribune*, July 14, 2006.

40. Pew Research Center, Project for Excellence in Journalism, "The Latest News Headlines—Your Vote Counts," September 12, 2007, http://www.journalism.org/node/7493.

41. Ibid.

42. John Haskell, *Direct Democracy or Representative Government? Dispelling the Populist Myth* (Boulder, Colo.: Westview Press, 2001).

43. There are many categorical systems for describing different types of democracy. For discussions emphasizing differences between aggregative, deliberative, and agonistic democracy, see Jürgen Habermas, "Three Normative Models of Democracy," *Constellations* 1, no. 1 (1994): 1–10; Paul Starr, "Democratic Theory and the History of Communications," in *Explorations in Communication and History*, edited by Barbie Zelizer (New York: Routledge, 2008), 35–45; and Mouffe, "For an Agonistic Public Sphere" (see chap. 2, n. 90).

44. "What Is Digg?," n.d., accessed June 10, 2011, http://about.digg.com/about.

45. "Redditquette," n.d., http://www.reddit.com/help/reddiquette.

46. For further discussion of how software code and online design shape the norms of online culture, see Lawrence Lessig, *Code: And Other Laws of Cyberspace, Version 2.0* (New York: Basic Books, 2006); and Alexander R. Galloway, *Protocol: How Control Exists after Decentralization* (Cambridge, Mass.: MIT Press, 2004).

47. Michael Calore, "Digg Fights Top Users for Control," *Wired,* accessed April 7, 2009, http://www.wired.com/science/discoveries/news/2006/09/71750; Rand Fishkin, "Top 100 Digg Users Control 56% of Digg's Homepage Content," *Moz Blog* (blog), July 20, 2006, http://moz.com/blog/top-100-digg-users-control-56-of-diggs-homepage-content.

48. Fernando Alfonso, "How Reddit's Most Popular User Fell from Grace," *Daily Dot,* July 31, 2014, http://www.dailydot.com/news/reddit-unidan-shadownban-vote-manipulation-ben-eisenkop/.

49. "About NewsTrust.net," *NewsTrust* (blog), accessed June 15, 2011, http://blog.newstrust.net/2011/06/baltimore-as-seen-through-the-prism-of-different-media.html.

50. "More Review Questions," *NewsTrust,* accessed August 24, 2014, http://newstrust.net/guides/more-review-questions.

51. Anthony Giddens, *New Rules of Sociological Method: A Positive Critique of Interpretative Sociologies* (Stanford, Calif.: Stanford University Press, 1993).

52. "What Constitutes Vote Cheating and Vote Manipulation?," Reddit, accessed August 24, 2014, http://www.reddit.com/wiki/faq#wiki_what_constitutes_vote_cheating_and_vote_manipulation.3F.

53. For a discussion of this subreddit and its detractors, see Robin Ward, "Crawling the Downvote Brigades of Reddit," *Evil Trout* (blog), January 16, 2013, http://eviltrout.com/2013/01/16/crawling-the-downvote-brigades-of-reddit.html.

54. Tarleton Gillespie, "Can an Algorithm Be Wrong?," *Limn* 2 (2012), http://limn.it/can-an-algorithm-be-wrong/.

55. J. Cho and S. Roy, "Impact of Search Engines on Page Popularity," *Proceedings of the 13th International Conference on World Wide Web* (2004): 20–29.

56. Matthew Hindman, *The Myth of Digital Democracy* (Princeton, N.J.: Princeton University Press, 2009); Brenton Malin, "A Very Popular Blog: The Internet and the Possibilities of Publicity," *New Media & Society* 13, no. 2 (2011): 193; Cho and Roy, "Impact of Search Engines."

57. Hindman, *Myth of Digital Democracy,* 45–54.

58. Ibid., 56.

59. "Newsvine," *Newsvine,* accessed May 10, 2011, http://www.newsvine.com/.

60. Aimée Morrison finds a clever way to track changes in scholarly attitudes about the egalitarian and liberatory nature of cyberspace by mapping changes in reactions to John Perry Barlow's famous essay declaring, among other things, that cyberspace would be without racism, sexism, and class differences. Aimée Hope Morrison, "An Impossible Future: John Perry Barlow's 'Declaration of the Independence of Cyberspace,'" *New Media & Society* 11, nos. 1–2 (2009): 53–71.

61. Speaking to such hopes in his influential book, Jenkins argues that groups of early adopters who are "are disproportionately white, male, middle class, and college educated" offer the "best window" for understanding where a participatory convergence culture is heading. He acknowledges the troubling participation gaps in online

media and suggests that different social groups will adapt and modify the practices of the early adopters. Jenkins, *Convergence Culture,* 23.

62. Nancy Fraser, "Rethinking the Public Sphere: A Contribution to the Critique of Actually Existing Democracy," *Social Text,* nos. 25–26 (1990): 56–80.

63. For example, see Gwyneth Mellinger's account of how the American Society of Newspaper Editors failed to achieve their stated aspirations of reflecting the demographics of the U.S. population at large. Mellinger, *Chasing Newsroom Diversity* (see chap. 1, n. 82).

64. Nancy Fraser's landmark essay "Rethinking of the Public Sphere" clearly illustrates the need for multiple publics to have an opportunity to remain partially distinct from one another whenever social inequality and oppression exist. Fraser affirms the indispensability for democratic theory of the concept of a public sphere that is distinct from both the state and the marketplace. While she faults Habermas's early account of the liberal public sphere for its relative lack of attention to the exclusions of the liberal public sphere, she also argues for the need for multiple public spheres to offer spaces for counterpublics to form, so that groups facing subordination and oppression can articulate group interest and negotiate group identity. Yet, as Fraser recognizes, the need for multiple public spheres (including those of particular counterpublics) does not negate the need for a heterogeneous public sphere or spheres, which will mediate flows among publics. See also Nicholas Garnham, "The Media and the Public Sphere," in *Habermas and the Public Sphere,* edited by Calhoun (see chap. 2, n. 90).

65. Jenkins, *Convergence Culture,* 23.

66. For example, see Mariya Lysenkova, "Sexism on Reddit," *Geek Feminism Blog,* September 22, 2009, http://geekfeminism.org/2009/09/22/sexism-on-reddit/; mystery_guest, "Sexism Runs Rampant on Reddit (and Maybe the Rest of the Social Web)," *Daily SEO Blog,* June 12, 2008, http://www.seomoz.org/blog/sexism-runs-rampant-on-reddit-and-maybe-the-rest-of-the-social-web; Jen Nadeau, "Is Digg Sexist?," *Change.org,* December 22, 2008, http://news.change.org/stories/is-digg-sexist; and Saabira Chaudhuri, "Digg Bans 20–30 Users for Hate Speech in Response to Fast Company's Women in Web 2.0," *Fast Company* (blog), November 14, 2008, http://www.fastcompany.com/blog/saabira-chaudhuri/itinerant-mind/diggs-beth-murphy-talks-about-sites-culture-and-policies.

67. Irin Carmon, "Boys Will Be Boys: The Problem with Digg," *Jezebel,* May 25, 2010, http://jezebel.com/5531991/boys-will-be-boys-the-problem-with-digg.

68. Lauren Orsini, "Why Reddit Is Sexist—and What to Do about It," *Daily Dot,* December 23, 2011, http://www.dailydot.com/society/reddit-sexist-twoxchromosomes/.

69. Carmon, "Boys Will Be Boys."

70. Thomas Streeter, *The Net Effect: Romanticism, Capitalism, and the Internet* (New York: New York University Press, 2010), 123.

71. Ruediger Glott, Philipp Schmidt, and Rishab Ghosh, "*Wikipedia* Survey: Overview of Results," United Nations University, March 2010, http://www.ris.org/uploadi/editor/1305050082Wikipedia_Overview_15March2010-FINAL.pdf.

72. Rishab Ghosh et al., "Free/Libre and Open Source Software: Survey and Study," International Institute of Infonomics, University of Maastricht, the Netherlands, June 2002, http://www.flossproject.org/report/FLOSS_Final4.pdf.

73. Research points to this conclusion for a related question of why there continues to be such a gender gap in the fields of science, engineering, and technology. Catherine Hill, Christianne Corbett, and Andresse St. Rose, "Why So Few? Women in Science, Technology, Engineering, and Mathematics," American Association of University Women, 2010, http://www.aauw.org/resource/why-so-few-women-in-science-technology-engineering-mathematics/.

74. Eli Pariser, *The Filter Bubble: What the Internet Is Hiding from You* (New York: Penguin, 2011).

75. Anderson, "Between Creative and Quantified Audiences"; Pablo J. Boczkowski, *News at Work: Imitation in an Age of Information Abundance* (Chicago: University of Chicago Press, 2010); Usher, "Al Jazeera English Online."

Conclusion

1. Victor Pickard, "Return of the Nervous Liberals," *Communication Review* 18, no. 2 (2015).

2. For discussions of the resilience of neoliberal policy after the Great Recession, see Nolan McCarty, Keith T. Poole, and Howard Rosenthal, *Political Bubbles: Financial Crises and the Failure of American Democracy* (Princeton, N.J.: Princeton University Press, 2013); and Jamie Peck, Nik Theodore, and Neil Brenner, "Neoliberalism Resurgent? Market Rule after the Great Recession," *South Atlantic Quarterly* 111, no. 2 (2012): 265–88.

3. For example, in June 2011, the FCC released its own report on the future of news and media (under the conceptual framework of the "information needs of communities"), and at the heart of the 475-page report is the assumption that the United States faces a "critical juncture" in making key decisions about media policy that will shape future developments. This is the same concept proposed by Robert McChesney that I discuss in the introduction. S. Waldman and the Working Group on the Information Needs of Communities, "Information Needs of Communities," 8 (see introduction, n. 4).

4. Was Lippmann just an elitist who believed everyday people were unfit to rule? Without faith in an informed citizenry to keep democracy on track, Lippmann saw a more important role in democratic governance for experts specializing in procedural knowledge gathering. Lippmann's reliance on experts and his skepticism about the abilities of the mass public contributed to his reputation as an elitist among later communication scholars, especially cultural historian and essayist James Carey. Carey believes Lippmann's thinking was extremely influential in U.S. journalism, and he calls Lippmann's *Public Opinion* "the founding book of modern American journalism," but also detrimental to a democratic press. According to Carey, Lippmann's views led to a press system that "confirmed the psychological incompetence of people to participate" in democracy while discouraging public conversation and making journalists

and experts into the de facto bearers of public opinion. See James Carey, "The Press, Public Opinion, and Public Discourse: On the Edge of the Postmodern," in *James Carey*, edited by Munson and Warren, 245 (see introduction, n. 30). Schudson takes Carey and others to task for carelessly representing Lippmann and promoting him as a mythic elitist and antidemocrat. Michael Schudson, "The 'Lippmann-Dewey Debate' and the Invention of Walter Lippmann as an Anti-Democrat, 1985–1996," *International Journal of Communication* 2 (2008): 1031–42.

5. See Sue Curry Jansen, "Phantom Conflict: Lippmann, Dewey, and the Fate of the Public in Modern Society," *Communication and Critical/Cultural Studies* 6, no. 3 (2009): 221–45; Nathan Crick, "The Search for a Purveyor of News: The Dewey/Lippmann Debate in an Internet Age," *Critical Studies in Media Communication* 26, no. 5 (2009): 480–97; and Schudson, "'Lippmann-Dewey Debate.'"

6. Walter Lippmann, *The Phantom Public* (New Brunswick, N.J.: Transaction, 1993), 14.

7. Schudson himself has suggested a vision of contemporary citizenship, what he calls "monitorial citizenship," that shares some of the same assumptions about news consumers as demand-driven journalism. Schudson's monitorial citizens scan the news and informational environment widely, looking for news that matters to their personal good as well as listening for alarm bells pertaining to the greater public good. Schudson does not offer this concept as a definitively normative one, though as the concept has traveled in conversations in media studies and political science, it has been taken as a normative one, while the focus of monitoring has narrowed even more tightly on self-interest. In any case, monitorial citizenship suggests citizens come to news sources with preconceived notions of what they are looking for rather than an expansive curiosity or flexible sense of what matters. Schudson makes a convincing case that monitorial citizenship should not be castigated as always civically inadequate. Yet while the monitorial concept is meant to offer a more realistic vision of citizenship, it fails to capture important aspects of real citizen-news interaction, namely, the ways in which news media help shape citizens' concerns and interest. The consistent findings of agenda setting and framing research alone suggest that monitorial citizenship is not an accurate description of real-life news consumption practices. Schudson, *Good Citizen* (see chap. 1, n. 22). For more vigorous defenses of monitorial citizenship as a normative claim, see John Zaller, "A New Standard of News Quality: Burglar Alarms for the Monitorial Citizen," *Political Communication* 20, no. 2 (2003): 109–30; and Deuze, "Changing Context of News Work" (see introduction, n. 6).

8. Maxwell E. McCombs and Donald L. Shaw, "The Evolution of Agenda-Setting Research: Twenty-Five Years in the Marketplace of Ideas," *Journal of Communication* 43, no. 2 (1993): 58–67; David H. Weaver, "Thoughts on Agenda Setting, Framing, and Priming," *Journal of Communication* 57, no. 1 (2007): 142–47.

9. See Laurie Ouellette and James Hay, *Better Living through Reality TV: Television and Post-welfare Citizenship* (Malden, Mass.: Blackwell, 2008); Jack Z. Bratich, Jeremy Packer, and Cameron McCarthy, *Foucault, Cultural Studies, and Governmentality* (Albany:

State University of New York Press, 2003); and Toby Miller, *Technologies of Truth: Cultural Citizenship and the Popular Media* (Minneapolis: University of Minnesota Press, 1998).

10. Michel Foucault, *Power/Knowledge: Selected Interviews and Other Writings, 1972–1977* (New York: Pantheon Books, 1980), 119.

11. Hindman, *Myth of Digital Democracy* (see chap. 4, n. 56).

12. For especially lucid discussions of this problem in theories of democratic representation, see Hanna Fenichel Pitkin, *The Concept of Representation* (Berkeley: University of California Press, 1972); and Andrew Rehfeld, "Representation Rethought: On Trustees, Delegates, and Gyroscopes in the Study of Political Representation and Democracy," *American Political Science Review* 103, no. 2 (2009): 214–30.

13. See Pitkin, *The Concept of Representation.*

14. Lisa Disch, "Toward a Mobilization Conception of Democratic Representation," *American Political Science Review* 105, no. 1 (2011): 100–115.

15. Ibid., 102.

16. Ibid., 107.

17. Ibid., 111.

18. Jesse Holcomb and Amy Mitchell, "News Revenue Declines Despite Growth from New Sources," Pew Research Center, March 26, 2014, http://www.pewresearch.org/fact-tank/2014/04/03/news-revenue-declines-despite-growth-from-new-sources/.

19. Pew Research Center, Project for Excellence in Journalism, "State of the News Media, 2011: Newspapers, Data," http://stateofthemedia.org/2011/newspapers-essay/data-page-6/.

20. Pew Research Center, Project for Excellence in Journalism, "State of the News Media, 2011: Overview," http://stateofthemedia.org/.

21. Pew Research Center, Project for Excellence in Journalism, "The State of the News Media: Overview, 2010," http://www.stateofthemedia.org/2010/overview_key_findings.php.

22. Pew Research Center, Project for Excellence in Journalism, "State of the News Media, 2011: Network News, Essay," http://stateofthemedia.org/2011/network-essay/.

23. Pew Research Center, Project for Excellence in Journalism, "Key Indicators in Media & News," State of the News Media, 2014, March 26, 2014, http://www.journalism.org/2014/03/26/state-of-the-news-media-2014-key-indicators-in-media-and-news/.

24. David Simon, "Hearing on the Future of Journalism," 2009, http://commerce.senate.gov/public/?a=Files.Serve&File_id=9392d321-43e8-4053-bdbb-466070864d5e.

25. Robert W. McChesney, "Be Realistic, Demand the Impossible: Three Radically Democratic Internet Policies," *Critical Studies in Media Communication* 31, no. 2 (2014): 92–99.

26. For a review of such proposals, see Victor Pickard, Josh Sterns, and Craig Aaron, "Saving the News: Toward a National Journalism Strategy," Free Press, 2009, 28–32, http://www.freepress.net/files/saving_the_news.pdf; and Walter Isaacson, "How to Save Your Newspaper," *Time,* February 5, 2009, http://www.time.com/time/business/article/0,8599,1877191,00.html.

27. See Paul Berger, David LaFontaine, and D. J. Siegel, "The Free v. Paid Online Content Debate," Newspaper Association of America, March 2009, http://www.davidlafontaine.com/case-studies/final-pdf-paid-content.pdf.

28. Isaacson, "How to Save Your Newspaper"; David Lazarus, "Free News Online Will Cost Journalism Dearly," *Los Angeles Times*, December 26, 2007, http://www.latimes.com/business/la-fi-lazarus26dec26-column.html.

29. Berger, LaFontaine, and Siegel, "Free v. Paid Online Content Debate," 5.

30. Rick Edmonds et al., "Newspapers: Stabilizing, but Still Threatened," State of the News Media, 2013 (Pew Research Center, July 18, 2013), http://www.stateofthemedia.org/2013/newspapers-stabilizing-but-still-threatened/.

31. Media Insight Project, "Personal News Cycle" (see chap. 4, n. 4).

32. For scholarly criticism, see Victor Pickard and Alex T. Williams, "Salvation or Folly?" *Digital Journalism* 2, no. 2 (2013): 195–213. For discussions of this concern coming from within the industry, see Berger, LaFontaine, and Siegel, "Free v. Paid Online Content Debate."

33. Isaacson, "How to Save Your Newspaper."

34. Rupert Murdoch, "From Town Crier to Bloggers: How Will Journalism Survive the Internet Age?," 2009, 4–5, http://www.ftc.gov/opp/workshops/news/docs/murdoch.PDF.

35. Downie and Schudson, "Reconstruction of American Journalism," 11 (see chap. 2, n. 9).

36. Ibid., 12.

37. For other examples of such an orientation, see Steven Berlin Johnson, "Old Growth Media and the Future of News," *Stevenberlinjohnson.com*, 2009, http://www.stevenberlinjohnson.com/2009/03/the-following-is-a-speech-i-gave-yesterday-at-the-south-by-southwest-interactive-festival-in-austiniif-you-happened-to-being.html; Dave Winer, "The Reboot of Journalism," *Scripting News* (blog), March 19, 2009, http://scripting.com/stories/2009/03/19/theRebootOfJournalism.html; Clay Shirky, "Newspapers and Thinking the Unthinkable," *Clay Shirky* (blog), March 13, 2009, http://www.shirky.com/weblog/2009/03/newspapers-and-thinking-the-unthinkable/; and Jarvis, *What Would Google Do?* (see introduction, n. 6).

38. Mark Deuze, "Liquid Journalism," *Political Communication Report* 16, no. 1 (2006), http://frank.mtsu.edu/~pcr/1601_2005_winter/roundtable_Deuze.htm.

39. Shirky, "Newspapers and Thinking the Unthinkable."

40. See Jenkins, *Convergence Culture* (see chap. 4, n. 11).

41. For specific arguments about networked media and new opportunities for individual autonomy, see Benkler, *Wealth of Networks*, 8–9 (see introduction, n. 6).

42. McChesney, *Problem of the Media*, 18 (see introduction, n. 10).

43. S. Johnson, "Old Growth Media and the Future of News."

44. Paul Robbins, *Political Ecology: A Critical Introduction* (Malden, Mass.: John Wiley & Sons, 2011), 13.

45. Jarvis, *What Would Google Do?*

46. Pickard, *America's Battle for Media Democracy* (see introduction, n. 28).

47. Ben Scott, "A Broad, Positive View of the First Amendment," in *The Case against Media Consolidation*, edited by Mark D. Cooper (New York: Donald McGannon Center for Communication Research, 2007), 39–62; Pickard, "Reopening the Postwar Settlement for U.S. Media," 170–89 (see chap. 1, n. 53).

48. Pickard, Sterns, and Aaron, "Saving the News." For another example of scholar-activists proposing models for public funding for new models of journalism, see McChesney and Nichols, *Death and Life of American Journalism*, 157–212 (see chap. 1, n. 84).

49. Jessica Clark and Patricia Aufderheide, "Public Media 2.0: Dynamic Engaged Publics," Center for Media and Social Impact, 2009, http://cmsimpact.org/sites/default/files/documents/pages/publicmedia2.0.pdf.

50. What are these normative expectations, and where will they come from? This question exceeds the scope of this book. To add a few thoughts, I believe that proponents of the critical activist approach need to have dual commitments for setting normative expectations for democratic media. On one hand, they should be committed to "process norms," meaning that the ends of democratic journalism should be arrived at through a process of democratic communication. On the other hand, such a process entails that groups or individuals propose and advocate for specific norms for journalism that accord with their own notions of democratic life. Thus, proponents of the critical activist approach will advocate for specific norms and put those norms forward as provisional and in need of public scrutiny.

51. A report by the Pew Research Center found that 14 percent of people in 1998 reported getting no news on a typical day, compared to 19 percent in 2008. The increase was more dramatic for people between the ages of eighteen and twenty-four, with 25 percent going newsless on a typical day in 1998 and 34 percent in 2008. As with all surveys, however, these findings need to be interpreted cautiously. It is not clear if the survey would have picked up on outlets such as *The Daily Show* in counting news sources. Also, there's no way to control for the possibility that different events unfolding in 1998 and 2008 might account for some of the differences. Yet together with other evidence, these data help to suggest a pattern of a growing knowledge gap. See Pew Research Center for People and the Press, "Audience Segments in a Changing News Environment: Key News Audiences Now Blend Online and Traditional Sources," August 17, 2008, 5, http://people-press.org/files/legacy-pdf/444.pdf. For further discussion of the growing knowledge gap, see Markus Prior, *Post-broadcast Democracy: How Media Choice Increases Inequality in Political Involvement and Polarizes Elections* (New York: Cambridge University Press, 2007).

52. Ezra Klein, "Vox Is Our Next," *Verge*, January 26, 2014, http://www.theverge.com/2014/1/26/5348212/ezra-klein-vox-is-our-next.

53. "Vox Advertising," *Vox Media*, accessed January 10, 2015, http://voxmedia.com/brands/vox.

54. Ken Auletta, "You've Got News," *New Yorker*, January 24, 2011, 34.

55. "Advertising *Gawker* Media: *Gawker* Profile," *Gawker Media*, accessed July 2, 2011, http://advertising.gawker.com/gawker/.

Index

ANTHONY M. NADLER is an assistant professor of media and communication studies at Ursinus College.

THE HISTORY OF COMMUNICATION

Selling Free Enterprise: The Business Assault on Labor and Liberalism, 1945–60 *Elizabeth A. Fones-Wolf*
Last Rights: Revisiting *Four Theories of the Press* *Edited by John C. Nerone*
"We Called Each Other Comrade": Charles H. Kerr & Company, Radical Publishers *Allen Ruff*
WCFL, Chicago's Voice of Labor, 1926–78 *Nathan Godfried*
Taking the Risk Out of Democracy: Corporate Propaganda versus Freedom and Liberty *Alex Carey; edited by Andrew Lohrey*
Media, Market, and Democracy in China: Between the Party Line and the Bottom Line *Yuezhi Zhao*
Print Culture in a Diverse America *Edited by James P. Danky and Wayne A. Wiegand*
The Newspaper Indian: Native American Identity in the Press, 1820–90 *John M. Coward*
E. W. Scripps and the Business of Newspapers *Gerald J. Baldasty*
Picturing the Past: Media, History, and Photography *Edited by Bonnie Brennen and Hanno Hardt*
Rich Media, Poor Democracy: Communication Politics in Dubious Times *Robert W. McChesney*
Silencing the Opposition: Antinuclear Movements and the Media in the Cold War *Andrew Rojecki*
Citizen Critics: Literary Public Spheres *Rosa A. Eberly*
Communities of Journalism: A History of American Newspapers and Their Readers *David Paul Nord*
From Yahweh to Yahoo!: The Religious Roots of the Secular Press *Doug Underwood*
The Struggle for Control of Global Communication: The Formative Century *Jill Hills*
Fanatics and Fire-eaters: Newspapers and the Coming of the Civil War *Lorman A. Ratner and Dwight L. Teeter Jr.*
Media Power in Central America *Rick Rockwell and Noreene Janus*
The Consumer Trap: Big Business Marketing in American Life *Michael Dawson*
How Free Can the Press Be? *Randall P. Bezanson*
Cultural Politics and the Mass Media: Alaska Native Voices *Patrick J. Daley and Beverly A. James*
Journalism in the Movies *Matthew C. Ehrlich*
Democracy, Inc.: The Press and Law in the Corporate Rationalization of the Public Sphere *David S. Allen*
Investigated Reporting: Muckrakers, Regulators, and the Struggle over Television Documentary *Chad Raphael*
Women Making News: Gender and the Women's Periodical Press in Britain *Michelle Tusan*
Advertising on Trial: Consumer Activism and Corporate Public Relations in the 1930s *Inger L. Stole*

Speech Rights in America: The First Amendment, Democracy, and the Media
Laura Stein
Freedom from Advertising: E. W. Scripps's Chicago Experiment *Duane C. S. Stoltzfus*
Waves of Opposition: The Struggle for Democratic Radio, 1933–58 *Elizabeth Fones-Wolf*
Prologue to a Farce: Democracy and Communication in America *Mark Lloyd*
Outside the Box: Corporate Media, Globalization, and the UPS Strike *Deepa Kumar*
The Scripps Newspapers Go to War, 1914–1918 *Dale Zacher*
Telecommunications and Empire *Jill Hills*
Everything Was Better in America: Print Culture in the Great Depression *David Welky*
Normative Theories of the Media *Clifford G. Christians, Theodore L. Glasser, Denis McQuail, Kaarle Nordenstreng, and Robert A. White*
Radio's Hidden Voice: The Origins of Public Broadcasting in the United States
Hugh Richard Slotten
Muting Israeli Democracy: How Media and Cultural Policy Undermine Free Expression
Amit M. Schejter
Key Concepts in Critical Cultural Studies *Edited by Linda Steiner and Clifford Christians*
Refiguring Mass Communication: A History *Peter Simonson*
Radio Utopia: Postwar Audio Documentary in the Public Interest *Matthew C. Ehrlich*
Chronicling Trauma: Journalists and Writers on Violence and Loss *Doug Underwood*
Saving the World: A Brief History of Communication for Development and Social Change *Emile G. McAnany*
The Rise and Fall of Early American Magazine Culture *Jared Gardner*
Equal Time: Television and the Civil Rights Movement *Aniko Bodroghkozy*
Advertising at War: Business, Consumers, and Government in the 1940s *Inger L. Stole*
Media Capital: Architecture and Communications in New York City *Aurora Wallace*
Chasing Newsroom Diversity: From Jim Crow to Affirmative Action *Gwyneth Mellinger*
C. Francis Jenkins, Pioneer of Film and Television *Donald G. Godfrey*
Digital Rebellion: The Birth of the Cyber Left *Todd Wolfson*
Heroes and Scoundrels: The Image of the Journalist in Popular Culture
Matthew C. Ehrlich and Joe Saltzman
The Real Cyber War: The Political Economy of Internet Freedom *Shawn M. Powers and Michael Jablonski*
The Polish Hearst: *Ameryka-Echo* and the Public Role of the Immigrant Press
Anna D. Jaroszyńska-Kirchmann
Acid Hype: American News Media and the Psychedelic Experience *Stephen Siff*
Making the News Popular: Mobilizing U.S. News Audiences *Anthony M. Nadler*

The University of Illinois Press
is a founding member of the
Association of American University Presses.

University of Illinois Press
1325 South Oak Street
Champaign, IL 61820-6903
www.press.uillinois.edu

at yourself or your children through the wrong lens, you will never end up where you intended to go.

We all have core beliefs that affect how we think, how we respond or react, and how we make decisions. The culture is loud, invasive, and influential in the formation of these beliefs about ourselves, our children, and our family. God's view, however, which is found in the Bible, gives us a different, true, and effective way of viewing parenting that will impact everything we do in a transformative and positive way.

Parenting is not a to-do list, though there are many things we must do as parents. Neither is parenting a set method, though in the process of parenting you may choose to adopt certain methods. Parenting is also not a project with a beginning and an end. Parenting is a relationship. And relationships only succeed when we have a clear, true understanding of ourselves as well as the other people involved. *Learning Trust, Finding Treasure* will help you to understand truths about your relationship with your children that will strengthen not only the bond you have with your children, but also your personal walk with God, your understanding of God's Word, and your ability to trust that He is at work in both you and your children to bring about His perfect will as you follow Him.

I find that contrasts and comparisons often help me to understand truth. For example, the culture tells me I should do whatever makes me happy, but Jesus tells me to deny myself and follow Him because "… whoever wants to save his life will lose it; but whoever loses his life for My sake will find it" (Matthew 16:25). If I am living only for my own satisfaction and happiness, I will not have my eyes on Christ and will miss out on the joy of glorifying Him with my life. The culture also hates the concept of sin and finds correction offensive. But God's Word says, "One who is on the path of life follows instruction, But one who ignores a rebuke goes astray" (Proverbs 10:17). So much of what we hear in our culture is the opposite of what is right, good, and true. This goes for parenting ideas and philosophies as well.

In this study, I will be helping you see what a parent's role and responsibilities are according to God's Word, and what they are not. God has clearly given us instructions for how to raise our children. When we follow Him, we can trust Him with the results in our children's lives.

A few basics things for you to understand before you begin:

1. The principles outlined in this study apply to both moms and dads. However, I am a mother, so I primarily address mothers throughout the book. My examples will be about mothering.

2. This study presumes the Bible is a reliable, true, and trustworthy resource for instruction. It does not try to prove the Bible's reliability to those who do not believe what it says or recognize it as authoritative. There are, however, many other resources available that do teach why you can trust God's Word is true.

3. To get the most out of this study, I pray you would take the time to read the chapters and then answer the study questions in a thoughtful and intentional way, letting God speak to you through His Word. Each chapter has five days of questions for you to complete, setting a pace of working through one chapter per week.

Chapter 1

What Is the Point of Parenting?

Remember the first moment that little bundle was placed in your arms? In that instant, you changed! You became someone's mother—an honor and a title that profoundly impacted the rest of your life.

Motherhood may be exactly what you wanted and hoped for, or it may be a surprise. Regardless, the title "mom" carries with it much weight. Before the moment motherhood began for you, you may have determined what kind of mother you did *not* want to be; you may have focused on what kind of mother you *did* want to be; or maybe you hadn't given it much thought at all. However, whether you felt prepared, the baby arrived, and the journey began.

I have never met a woman that set out to be a bad mom. Almost every mother I encounter desires to do a good job for her children. She sets out with the best of intentions, a fully committed heart, and a keen sense of responsibility. She is optimistic about her chances of doing this job well. Hope is usually the sweet fragrance that accompanies birth, and it seems as though all is bright and beautiful. Even in the face of tough news at birth, like disabilities or health problems, most mothers rise to the challenge with the desire to manage any hardship with strength and commitment, determined to be the best mom they can be for this baby they already love so much.

However, in spite of the desire to mother well, every mom hits a wall at some point. Postpartum blues may cause some moms to face discouragement particularly early in their journey. Other moms are caught off guard with toddler tantrums, while others do not experience serious struggles until their children are in their tweens or teens. Some mothers have several children, and only one out of the bunch gives them a hard time. Others have four out of four (or more) that test their every move and challenge their every word, every minute of every day. Each family is unique in the mix of personalities, circumstances, ages, abilities, attitudes, and cultural leanings.

With so many differences among us all, how can anyone give advice about parenting? Well, God can. The reason God can is because He created us for a purpose, and that purpose is to glorify Him (1 Corinthians 10:31). We as Christians believe that when we live according to God's Word, we are blessed (John 14:23). Making an eternal impact on others for the Gospel of Jesus Christ is the primary goal of our lives (Matthew 28:18-20) and should influence our parenting (Deuteronomy 6:4-7). However, somehow in the hustle and bustle of life, that often fails to happen according to our intentions.

Could that be because we are looking at ourselves and our God-given responsibilities incorrectly? Maybe we have believed things about parenting that are not true, and therefore our ability to follow through is thwarted by these pervasive but ineffective beliefs. Or maybe we never really understood that God has a plan for parents because we were never taught the Bible contained such practical advice. Wherever you may find yourself on the spectrum today, it is never too late to gain a biblical perspective of parenting and renew your mind to God's truths.

You may be thinking, "Well, no matter what the Bible has to tell me about it, I know I am not going to be a perfect parent." You are right! Except for God Himself, there is no perfect parent, and even Adam and Eve completely disobeyed. **So the goal of studying what God says about parenting is not to help you become a perfect parent, but rather to ensure you are on the right track.** If you board a train going the wrong direction, it won't matter how well you behave on that train—how well you follow directions, how nice you are to other passengers, how educated you are about trains—you will still end up at the wrong destination.

That is why I am writing this study. Many well-meaning moms with good hearts are doing the best they can to be great parents, but they have the wrong perspective on what being a good parent is. They have donned the wrong glasses, boarded the wrong train, chosen the wrong goals, or have made the wrong assumptions. So with this in mind, let me ask you an important question: According to the Bible, what do you think a parent's *primary* responsibility is?

____

____

You may have answered with "to love unconditionally" (which is necessary) or "to protect" (which is needed) or "to nurture" (which is vital). But, according to God's Word, the *primary* responsibility of a parent is *to teach* (Deuteronomy 6:5-7). Are you surprised? Stop and think about your childhood. Do you have memories of watching your parents when you were little? Children are by nature avid learners and curious sponges that tend to soak up whatever they observe. Whether moms and dads are actively teaching or not, their children are learning from them. By action or inaction, parents teach.

By correct or incorrect behaviors, attitudes, and responses, children are taught because they are watching in order to learn.

Can you think of some things that are a part of your behavior because you imitated your parents? I get my love of old movies from my dad and my desire for a clean, organized home from my mom. I also got my temper from my dad and my love of God's Word from my mom. My mother taught me intentionally. My dad also taught me constantly, but he was unaware of it. **Just because someone does not intend to influence another does not mean the impact of their life is irrelevant.**

Rather than looking back after 20 years to discover that your children learned a whole lot from you that you never intended to impart to them, wouldn't it be better to set out to intentionally teach them the things God desires you to teach? Every day there are opportunities to teach your children truths from the Bible that will equip them to handle themselves and the world around them. Consider Deuteronomy 6:5-7: "You shall love the Lord your God with all your heart and with all your soul and with all your might. These words, which I am commanding you today, shall be on your heart. You shall teach them diligently to your sons and shall talk of them when you sit in your house and when you walk by the way and when you lie down and when you rise up."

This certainly describes a day in the life of a mom! As we sit with our children, walk with them, talk, eat, and ride in the car with them, play with them, lay them down for sleep, and wake them up in the morning, God says we can speak of Him, His love, His truths, and His promises. If we can grasp this as our job, we can find all sorts of creative ways to incorporate teaching God's Word to our children as part of everyday life.

When we ignore our children or fail to give them the positive, reinforcing, encouraging attention they need, we are teaching them to gain attention through negative behavior. They may be receiving negative attention, but to them it is better than nothing. When your children act up, ask yourself, is this because of something I have taught them? Parenting takes focused time and planning. Think about what they need to learn according to their age. Whether that is a Bible verse or a chore that needs doing or how to behave better, figure out ways to instruct them as you go about your daily life together.

2 Timothy 2:24-26 says, "The Lord's bond-servant (that's you and me if we are believers) must not be quarrelsome, but be kind to all, able to teach, patient when wronged, with gentleness correcting those who are in opposition, if perhaps God may grant them repentance leading to the knowledge of the truth, and they may come to their senses and escape from the snare of the devil, having been held captive by him to do his will." What a great picture of parenting! We are instructed here to be able to teach, to avoid being uptight and argumentative, and to be patient and gentle toward our children when we correct them. Children are so often "those who are in opposition," but by our obedience, they may "escape from the snare of the devil"! It is a powerful thought that we, by carefully teaching our children truth, are preparing their hearts to know God better and understand His ways. So the first principle we need to learn is this:

The Point of Parenting Is Teaching, not just Caretaking

Many parents believe that as long as they keep their children safe, giving them food, shelter, and an education, as well as doing the things that allow them to be relatively happy, then they've done a good job. But our primary task in our relationship with our children is to teach them. Of course, this includes teaching them how to act, be a friend, obey, be responsible, do well in school, cooperate, manage emotions, and respect others. But it also means teaching them God's Word so they can hide it in their hearts and be equipped when they are faced with challenges. There are a lot of resources out there to help you plant the Word of God in your children's hearts. **Just remember that children are automatic learners, so if you are not intentionally teaching, then they will look to others for answers to their questions and learn from them.** "Others" may be the television, friends, Google, or any number of influences that do not believe the way that you, a Christian, believe.

Let me give you an example of intentional teaching. Imagine your little boy is being unkind to his sister. You could just say, "Stop being mean to her!" But if you intend to teach, you could pull your son into your lap, open your Bible, and read Ephesians 4:32, which says, "Be kind to one another, tender-hearted, forgiving each other, just as God in Christ also has forgiven you." Then you could engage with your son by asking him what he thinks "tender-hearted" means. What are ways he can be tender and kind to his sister? What is forgiveness? Does he need to forgive her for anything or ask her to forgive him? Pray with him, and ask Jesus to help him learn how to treat his sister according to God's Word. Then challenge him to show her kindness in some tangible ways. Finally, clearly explain what the consequence will be if he is unkind to her again. (Yes, consequences are needed; we will get to that more later.)

Does that seem like a long process? Surprisingly, it doesn't take more than a few minutes. If you are prepared, have thought about appropriate verses ahead of time, and are ready to step in when needed, you will find this kind of teaching exercise with your children can easily become part of your routine. If you accept that you are called to be their teacher, you will embrace that role and spend time thinking about what your children are ready to learn.

One wise mother once told me, "If your children are aggravating you, it is probably your fault." Well, that may sound like a harsh thing to say, and you may be thinking, "Children are just aggravating sometimes!" But that statement was life-changing for me as a mom. Instead of thinking I needed to stop being aggravated, I started thinking about what I had failed to teach them that was impacting their behavior.

Were they whining all the time? How could I teach them not to whine and give them tools for how to communicate without whining? Were they picking on each other? How could I teach them to love one another and care for one another instead? I discovered as I was diligent to teach, they responded well to my instruction and often surprised me in how quickly they would change their behavior. I tried to be creative and innovative, using games, charts, play-acting, discipline, whatever it took to get the point across and instill the applicable Bible verses in their hearts. Pretty soon with lots of patience good habits set in, and they only needed reminders here and there to choose the better responses and attitudes they had been taught. I also found my children were happier and our whole family life ran more smoothly when they were successfully equipped with better ways to handle life's relationships and challenges.

Another key ingredient in being an excellent teacher of your children is to understand who they are and how they learn. Some children learn by doing. Some are visual learners, some auditory, and some need to imitate to learn. Regardless, learning for most children is an active process, especially when it comes to matters of the heart.

Understanding your children's personalities and learning styles takes time. Sometimes it takes trial and error! My firstborn is a girl, very verbal and intellectual. She was (almost) always able to learn by having something clearly explained to her. My second child was an active boy. I tried using words to explain what I needed him to learn, but words didn't make an impact. I had to be strategic to teach him lessons with actions and clear consequences that would get his attention—and yes, it took a lot of trial and error. My third child was extremely sensitive. She was sorry and crying before I even knew what she had done. I learned to wait until she was calm before talking through what had happened so that she could learn how to handle it better the next time. My fourth child had learning disabilities and cognitive delays. After much experimentation, I figured out that charts were the best way to help him learn. He loved seeing the stars go up every day and could feel proud of the choices he had made.

Once you spend time observing, praying, and listening in order to see the hearts of your children, you will gain insight. When you understand your children's strengths, weaknesses, learning styles, and personalities, you will find yourself adapting your parenting to what works best for them. You will be more appropriate in your approach (Proverbs 15:23) and more understanding of their struggles. You will also have more wisdom to tackle their issues (Proverbs 14:33a). When you seize those teachable moments and follow through with teaching your children, persevering with intentional connection while building your relationship with them, you will not regret it. **You are laying a foundation for your children's character that is vital for their future, and you are planting seeds in their hearts that prepare them to know and believe in the Gospel of Christ.**

The second principle to tackle in this chapter is the following:

The Point of Parenting Is Training, not Tolerating

Proverbs 22:6 says, "Train up a child in the way he should go, even when he is old he will not depart from it." This is a verse we as Christian parents hold onto with all our hearts, isn't it? We trust that if we are diligent to show our children the way, the truth, and the life (John

14:6) when they are young, they will hold to the straight and narrow when they are older.

My four children did not all take a smooth path to becoming Christian adults. While they were all taught and trained as children to follow Jesus and to love His Word, three of the four turned their back on Him completely for a while, getting lost in the tangled lies of this world and trying to make things work on their own. By the grace of God and His faithfulness, all three embraced Christ as their Savior and Lord in their teens and 20s and walk with Him today. I hope that encourages you!

God's work in our home has been nothing short of miraculous, and He has been gracious and kind to continue the work He started in my children's hearts when they were small. Has that happened to all the children of godly parents I know who raised their children to love the Lord? No. Is that verse an absolute promise, a guarantee, that all children who are trained to go the right way will definitely go that way? No. But it is a strong encouragement they will, and it is very often true they do.

While Proverbs 22:6 is not a promise, it is a general truth. The reason it is not a promise is that our children have their own free will to accept Christ as their Savior and obey Him, or not. They may choose to ignore the truth of the Gospel or to rebel against it. You may think, "What is the point of doing all this teaching and training if there isn't a guaranteed outcome?"

Well, do you wear a seatbelt? A practical example of a general truth is that by wearing a seatbelt, you will generally be kept safer while traveling in a car. Does wearing a seatbelt prevent all injuries in every car accident? No. Does wearing a seatbelt always prevent death? No. But in general, most injuries that happen during a car accident are reduced in severity by the wearing of a seatbelt. "An apple a day keeps the doctor away" is another general truth. Do all people who eat fruits and vegetables every day avoid all health problems? No. Do all people who eat fruits and vegetables every day live long lives? No. But in general, those who eat healthful foods have healthier bodies and are able to fight illnesses more effectively. While Proverbs 22:6 is not an absolute guarantee, if you as a mom focus on what it means to train up your child, you will be working out the part of the verse that is most applicable to you.

"The general truth contained in Proverbs 22:6 says that if a parent works hard to train his or her children to live a godly lifestyle, then it is likely that the children will continue to walk in those ways throughout their lives. The phrase "to train up a child in the way he should go," contextually, in the proverbial genre, means that parents need to be dedicated to teaching their children to live moral and godly lives. Training involves more than instruction—it also includes living out our lives in front of our children, modeling godly morals. It includes giving children practice and correction to help them learn the godly lifestyle. It requires dedication on the part of parents. In fact, the whole focus of this proverb is on the parent, not the child" (Mohler, 2007).

This is not to say that if children depart from God in their adult years that the parents did not train them up in the right way. Nor is it to be assumed that if children walk with God as adults, their parents necessarily trained them according to the Scriptures in their early years. But it is a general truth that "challenges parents to raise their children well and offers hope that the probable outcome will be glorious" (Mohler, 2007).

So how is training children different from teaching them? Well, teaching is communicating clearly what you want your children to understand and why. Training is helping them implement in practical ways what you have taught them. For example, if I want to teach my small children how to share, I must first teach them about sharing: "God says that sharing is loving and unselfish. When we play together, we want to share with one another so that everyone can enjoy playtime. The Bible says, 'Instruct them to do good, to be rich in good works, to be generous and ready to share' in 1 Timothy 6:18. So when you play with Legos today, I want you two to work together and share the pieces with each other." The opportunity for training comes when the children you have taught to share start fighting over the Legos. What should you do? A parent who is ready to train will intervene. It may require going back over the verse, helping them solve their problem, correcting their behavior, or facilitating apologies before encouraging them to try again.

We fail to train when we simply teach the principle but then give up when the children can't seem to follow through. If we get aggravated, separate the children for peace and quiet, and quit on the idea of them doing what we asked, we have missed the opportunity to train. **Children need our help to understand in real life how principles work. Just like children must practice to learn to read and write, they also need to practice how to share, be kind, and show love. Many things we want to teach are difficult for children (and for us!) at first.** We tend to have the expectation they will automatically know what to do, but learning new behaviors, such as sharing, can be uncomfortable and unpleasant. Children need to practice it enough to experience the benefit of getting along. Once they understand it is more fun to share while playing, they will develop that new habit.

God does not want us to train our children in the way they want to go, or the way they naturally would go, or the way we need them to go. He says to train them in the way they "should go," which is God's way (check Appendix A for verses you can use with your children). This kind of training takes time in God's Word planning, pondering, repeating, developing effective consequences, and reinforcing. It requires recognizing what is lacking, deciding it is the right time developmentally to begin teaching a certain principle, praying for wisdom, and choosing a course of action.

Training a child takes intentional energy! If that makes you feel tired, just think about when you were teaching your children to walk. It was so exciting to see them try to take their first steps. Did you stop and say, "Oh, not now. I am too busy to teach walking now." No, of course not! When your children were ready to learn to walk, you plopped on the floor, held out your arms, and said, "Come to Mommy! You can do it!"

As you trust God to give you wisdom as a mom, the areas of your children's lives where you need to train can be just as obvious if you understand it is your job and you are paying attention to their needs. If your children struggle with whining, disrespect, or disobedience, these are all signals they are asking for your help. They will not know how to behave correctly unless you teach them what is right and then also show them how to do what you expect them to do.

Each child of yours will need to be trained differently. Each one may learn different skills at different times, need more emphasis on some things than others, require more repetition than the other ones, or be more challenging than others. Each child is unique and deserves to be trained according to his or her needs. But what we do not want to do is simply tolerate our children. In today's culture, being tolerant is considered the right attitude and approach toward everything. But think about that for just a moment. If you and I were friends and you overheard someone asking me about you, and I said, "Oh, well, I tolerate her," how would you feel? The implication is that I put up with you; I simply endure my time with you. It is an insult.

God did not give us our children to tolerate them, to grit our teeth and get through our time with them. No, God gave us our children to teach and to train in the way they should go. And guess what? He also gave us our children to enjoy them (Psalm 113:9; Proverbs 15:20; 23:24; 27:11). Yes, that's right! Children who are taught and trained to be kind, loving, polite, responsible people who love God are enjoyable to be around!

So we are called to do much more than simply tolerate our children. There is a lot of stuff our kids are going to throw our way that we should not tolerate at all. There are words, behaviors, attitudes, and actions that are not glorifying to God and should not be allowed to persist in our children's hearts. When your children misbehave, do you find yourself constantly saying, "I need more patience and tolerance"? Well, you do need patience to discipline without anger, to repeat yourself without frustration, and to train with gentleness. But we as Christians are called to be intolerant of a lot of things (Revelation 2:19-21; Ephesians 4:25-31). Do not think you simply need tolerance. Be aware you need to train your children! **If you are simply tolerant of your toddler, you may be surprised what you will tolerate in your teenager. In many cases, you are not supposed just to "let it go." You may need to let go of the right to lose your temper but not of the responsibility to deal with your children's behavior.**

Chapter 1 Study Questions:

What Is the Point of Parenting?

Day One

1. Read Deuteronomy 11:18-21.

    a. How does God intend for the truth to be passed from generation to generation?

    ______

    ______

    b. What is the primary thing God wants you teaching your child?

    ______

    ______

    c. What environment do you believe is best for children to learn spiritual truth?

    ______

    ______

2. Read John 16:12-15, and list all the Holy Spirit's jobs mentioned in this passage.

    ______

    ______

3. It can be an overwhelming thought that God wants you to teach your children. However, remember He has not left you helpless. He has sent the Holy Spirit to be your teacher as you parent your children. You can ask for His help! Look up the

following Scriptures, and write down what you learn about the Holy Spirit.

a. Ephesians 4:30

____

____

b. 1 Corinthians 6:19

____

____

c. 2 Timothy 1:13-14

____

____

d. Acts 13:52

____

____

Day Two

Are you a caretaker of your children? Of course you are! But you are not only a caretaker. You are something much greater. You are a parent. And you are the only one who can be their parent. No one else can take your place. Others can take care of your children, but only you are their mom. However, God does value caretakers! So let's take a look at what the Scriptures say about being a caretaker.

1. What does the parable of the Good Samaritan in Luke 10:30-37 teach us about who we should care for?

 ____

 ____

2. What do the following verses say about whom and what we should care for, guard, or rescue?

    a. Proverbs 4:23 ______________________________

    b. Proverbs 13:3 ______________________________

    c. 1 Corinthians 12:24b-26______________________

    d. 1 Thessalonians 2:7__________________________

    e. James 1:27 ________________________________

    f. Psalm 82:4__________________________________

3. As you are a caretaker of yourself, your own children, and those the Lord puts in your path, you are an example to your children of how Jesus would act toward others. Write out Acts 20:35:

 ____

 ____

4. Take notice of the following order of priorities and how they are supported by the Scripture:

    a. If you do not care for yourself, you cannot effectively care for your family. What is the second part of the commandment found in Matthew 22:39? How are you caring for yourself?

____

____

b. If you do not care for your family, you cannot effectively care for others. See John 17:6-12. How did Jesus demonstrate His priorities in this passage?

____

____

____

c. Caretaking can be a full-time, exhaustive effort. In addition, there is no end to the needs of the world (John 12:8a). But you are called to walk with God and to serve your family first. There will be seasons when you will not have the time or the energy to pour into the community because your family will require all you have. There will also be seasons when you can train your children by caring for others in a context that involves them. Eventually, you will be able to contribute more into the world because your family responsibilities will have significantly eased. How did Jesus train His disciples to care by involving them in the following passages?

Matthew 19:14 ______________________________________

____

Matthew 17:14-21 ___________________________________

____

Luke 7:11-15

Luke 21:1-4

d. If you choose to busy yourself with service and caretaking outside of your family during a season when God has given you children as your primary responsibility, your availability to the wide, needy world will render you unavailable to those God has given you to teach, train, and protect. You will be running the risk of sacrificing generational, eternal fruit for the temporary satisfaction of good works that may be outside God's highest calling on your life. Read Luke 10:38-42 and Matthew 6:33 for examples of seeking God's priorities versus staying busy with good works, and write down your thoughts.

Day Three

Read 2 Timothy 2:24-26, and answer the following:

1. You, as a believer, are the "Lord's bond-servant." List the ways you are instructed to respond to others in verses 24-25a:

   a.

b. ______________________________

c. ______________________________

d. ______________________________

e. ______________________________

2. If you view these verses as instructions to you as a mom, who is it that is often in opposition to you?

____

____

3. What are the goals, then, of your correction as stated in verses 25b-26?

   a. ______________________________

   b. ______________________________

   c. ______________________________

   d. ______________________________

4. When your children are being disrespectful, disobedient, and belligerent, it is not natural to respond as Timothy instructs us.

   a. Read Galatians 5:16. What does it tell us to do so that we do not respond with anger, frustration, disgust, or disrespect?

   ____

   ____

b. Make note of when you are most frustrated with your child. What makes you the most irritable? What pushes your buttons?

____

____

c. What are some ways you can stop yourself in these frustrating moments with your children and choose to walk in the Spirit? (Hint: Training your child can reduce those frustrating moments.)

____

____

5. Even though we may think our anger will get the results we want, Timothy says our patience, kindness, and gentleness is more effective when correcting another. Anger can motivate changes in behavior, but it will not produce lasting changes in the heart. Read James 1:19-20. How does it correlate with 2 Timothy 2:24-26?

____

____

6. Pray and ask the Lord to help you remember to walk in the Spirit when you are tempted to respond with aggravation this week. Choose one of the above passages to memorize.

Day Four

Read Proverbs 22:6, and answer the following questions:

1. Write in your own words what you think it means to train a child.

    ____

    ____

2. Did your parents train you?

    ____

    a. How effective was their training? ______________

       ____

       ____

    b. How was their training not effective? ___________

       ____

    c. In what ways do you wish your parents had trained you or prepared you better?_________________________

       ____

       ____

    d. Does the idea of "training" your children seem strange or unusual to you?______________________________

    e. If so, think of the people in your children's lives that will be training them in all sorts of ways as they grow and develop.

Whose training do you want to have the most influence in their lives? ______________________________

____

3. What is the way your children should go? Look up the following verses, and write how you think they answer that question:

   a. Matthew 16:24 ______________________________

   ____

   b. John 14:6 ______________________________

   ____

   c. Psalm 119:9 ______________________________

   ____

   D. Proverbs 2:20 ______________________________

   ____

The Lord will be faithful to teach you the way your children should go as you trust Him and seek His face, one day at a time (Jeremiah 29:13). Let God teach you as you spend time with Him in His Word and in prayer. Seek the wisdom of parents that have gone before you. Understand God is personally interested in training you so that you can train your children.

Day Five

1. Define tolerance: ______________________________

   ____

   ____

2. "Tolerance" has become a cultural buzzword. How do you think its meaning has been misused or abused? ________________

____

____

3. What things is our culture completely intolerant of while insisting we should all be tolerant? ____________________________

____

____

4. Many parents find themselves just tolerating their children, longing for their next break from them, not enjoying them at all. At times parents may feel like their children are dreaded obligations.

    a. Have you ever felt this way? ________________________

    b. Did your parents feel this way about you? _____________

    ____

    c. Do you think this is just how parenting is because kids are hard to deal with? ______________________________

    d. If you see your children differently, write out how you see them and feel about them in general. ________________

    ____

    ____

5. Does God tolerate sin? ______________________________
   Explain your answer and support it with Scripture. ________

   ____

   ____

6. When we love someone, we are called by God to go far above and beyond mere tolerance. Read 1 Corinthians 13, and list all the things present in people who love as God calls them to love:

   ____

   ____

   ____

   ____

7. Loving people also means we promote and encourage only what is best for them and do not tolerate anything that would harm or lead them astray. Read the following verses, and list the things we are commanded not to tolerate:

   a. Ephesians 4:17-32 ______________________________

      ____

      ____

   b. 2 Timothy 3:2-5 ________________________________

      ____

      ____

8. Journal and pray right now. Confess the sins in your heart that you have become tolerant of and have made excuses for. Ask for the Lord's forgiveness and for the wisdom and strength to walk in the light. Then ask God for the ability to know what not

to tolerate in your children and how to train them effectively so they can avoid the destructive force of sin in their lives.

Chapter 2

What Is the Purpose of Parenting?

In Matthew 28:19, the Lord Jesus spoke to His disciples before He left this earth saying, "Go therefore and make disciples." Because those first-century Christians obeyed this command, we have access to the Gospel today. This instruction, to go and make disciples, is for believers today as well. The definition of a disciple is "someone who adheres to the teaching of another. It is a follower or a learner. It refers to someone who takes up the ways of someone else" (Parnell, 2014). Once we are followers of Jesus, He wants us to make disciples by helping others understand the Good News of His life, death, burial, and resurrection so that they too will follow Him, walk with Him, and then share the Gospel with others.

I often meet mothers who want to obey God by sharing the Gospel with others. When I tell them they have unbelievers in their own homes whom they are called to disciple, they look a bit stunned. As mothers, we often become so close to our children we forget they are unbelievers! You may assume your children are going to heaven because they seem innocent or because they were baptized as an infant. However, God's Word tells us that salvation comes through faith.

Each of us is called to "repent and believe in the gospel" (Mark 1:15), to receive Jesus (John 1:12), to believe in Him for eternal life (John 3:15-16; 6:47), to obey Him (John 3:36), to hear His Word (John 5:24), and to believe that Jesus is the Christ, the Son of God (John 11:27). It is not possible for infants to have faith. It is possible for parents to have faith and to pray for their babies, but children must come to Jesus of their own accord when they are old enough to understand their sin is a problem and they need Jesus to save them. (See Appendix B for a simple outline of the Gospel.) Your children need to hear the truth of the Gospel as a constant theme in your home, and after they have received that Gospel for themselves, they need to be brought up—or discipled—in the truth so that they can grow in their Christian faith toward spiritual maturity (Ephesians 4:11-16).

The Purpose of Parenting Is Discipling, not Distracting

So, what is discipleship, and how does it differ from teaching and training? In the time of Christ, when Jesus had disciples, they literally followed Him. They did life together. They ate together, walked together, served together, and dwelt together. They were not only listening when Jesus taught, but they were also watching how He handled situations, how He treated people, what He did with His time, and how He managed His life. In essence, Jesus' disciples learned who He was.

This is actually very similar to how children interact with parents. Our children do life with us, and it is our job to be intentional in demonstrating God's way as we go. When we are discipling our children, we are not only teaching them, we are also tutoring them, coaching them, and giving them life lessons about how God's Word should be applied each day.

You may think that you do not handle every situation like Jesus would, so it would not be good for every moment to become a teachable one. But if you think that way, you have forgotten the whole point of the Gospel. Again, we will not be perfect parents, but because of Jesus, every moment—even the imperfect ones—can become opportunities for discipleship.

Consider this example: Julie is having company over for dinner, but her day is not going according to plan. The baby is being fussy, her toddler refuses to take a nap, and her four-year-old decides to paint the wall with peanut butter. Somehow, in the midst of this, Julie still manages to get her recipe together and in the oven on time. Frantically, she cleans up the peanut butter, picks up toys, and makes herself look somewhat presentable. Fifteen minutes before her guests arrive, Julie checks the oven. Much to her dismay, the dinner is still cold and raw. In all the stress, Julie forgot to turn on the oven! This is the last straw in a long and trying day, and she loses it. Julie cusses and kicks the stupid oven, stomping around the kitchen with her hands on her head, completely frustrated and furious. Then she realizes her four-year-old is watching her every move, and she feels bad about the example she is setting.

If Julie stops there and storms off, she has taught her child what to do when he has a bad day. He also will kick at things and use the same colorful language the next time he is frustrated. However, if—after she has calmed down—she pulls her son close, humbles herself, and explains that she got angry, her words and actions were inappropriate, and she was wrong in the way she responded, she is seizing an opportunity to disciple her son. When she confesses that she is a sinner too, that she sometimes fails to obey God, and that she needs Jesus' help to do what is right, she is reminding her child of the Gospel. When she apologizes, asks for his forgiveness, and prays with him seeking the Lord's forgiveness, she is demonstrating what we are supposed to do when we mess up. If she explains those words are not right to use (Colossians 4:6) and tells her son that he will receive consequences if he uses them, she has discipled him. She has taught him God's ways, using her error as an example. Julie has humbled herself, making him aware that even though she is imperfect, God's truth still needs to be obeyed. In the process of discipling her child, she is encouraging him to learn and apply the truth, not just because it is taught but because it has been put into context as a practical, useful part of the day.

You may wonder, what should Julie do if, during this discipling process, the company shows up? Well, the child is the priority. The moment is key, and once it passes, the opportunity to impact her son in this situation will be gone. By graciously offering her friends something to drink and explaining she has something to take care of, she has shown that little boy he is her priority. Then Julie can return in a few minutes, laugh about forgetting to turn on the oven, order pizza, and enjoy her friends.

One of the most foundational biblical principles you are expected to teach your child, and then support with training and discipleship, is to obey you. It is a hard lesson, and one that requires teaching again and again. However, this is one clear commandment to children in God's Word: Obey your parents (Ephesians 6:1-2). **If you do not expect your children to obey you, you are failing to teach them the one thing God has asked of them. In other words, you are not helping them to obey God.** Obeying parents is important because it prepares children to obey God. By asking your children to obey you, teaching them to submit to you, and expecting them to respect you, you are training them to submit to the Lord.

Some may argue that children are not robots and therefore should not be expected to obey because it limits their freedom. But I have found obedient children are happier because they know healthy boundaries. In general, children like structure and are more content when they know what to expect. Just like a teacher cannot run a classroom without guidelines, a home needs the children's cooperation in order to run smoothly. What should a home's guidelines be? Well, there are some obvious ones spelled out in the Bible, like what kind of words should and shouldn't be used (Psalm 19:14), what kind of actions are acceptable and unacceptable (1 Peter 3:8-9), and what kind of attitudes glorify God (Philippians 2:5-7). There are also boundaries set according to parents' preferences and convictions.

When considering guidelines, or boundaries, I like to think of the game of football. There are all kinds of actions allowed during a football game. There is running, passing, tackling, defending, blocking, and even flying through the air! But if there were no lines on the field, none of those activities would make any sense. The game is played and enjoyed within a certain set of rules and expectations. The quarterback doesn't spend time trying to make a touchdown by running into the stands because that would be out of bounds and a complete waste of time and energy. What if every time there was a huddle, the rules changed? The game would get so complicated it would not even be a game anymore. Oftentimes, children spend energy wearing their parents down with manipulation, whining, and begging because the boundaries have not been made absolutely clear. Rather than just following through, time is wasted as they vie for control and try to get their way. As a result, nothing actually gets done, not even the thing the family wanted to do for fun.

If children know disobedience will result in consequences, they will more than likely decide rebelling is not worth it and settle down and enjoy life within the set boundaries. What should those consequences be? That is for you as parents to decide with God's Word as your guide and according to your family's values. As you choose how you will discipline your children and what consequences you will administer, remember they should be clear, consistent, and effective. Consequences should make an impact in such a way that the child does not want to repeat the offense.

Not every child needs the same type of consequence, and not every child responds the same way. In general, actions speak louder than words. Words—a firm "no" or a stern conversation—are not consequences. Following through with action is what makes an impact. Pray and seek wise counsel. **As you persevere, God will be faithful to give you the wisdom you need to choose discipline effectively. Remember that punishment stops, consequences teach, and encouragement starts.**

There are strong-willed children who never seem to obey, submit to boundaries, or respond to consequences. For some children, no matter how consistent their parents are, they are going to resist in disobedience, time and again. Even so, if you find yourself the parent of such children, God says you are still responsible to keep teaching, training, discipling, giving consequences, and not caving in to their demands. You are responsible, regardless, to discipline their behavior when they refuse to be obedient, even when it doesn't seem to make a difference.

Whether you experience the immediate reward of their obedience or not, you are teaching your children who is in charge and that you will obey God and do what is best for them even if they don't like it. You are reminding your children that you expect obedience, that life will go better for them if they obey, and that you are not willing to change your convictions just because they refuse to learn. Stick to it! I can tell you from experience that even if you do not see an immediate change in their hearts, they are learning more than you think, they are understanding more than they say, and they are getting more truth into their hearts than they admit. Remember they start small for a reason, and it is definitely easier to teach, train, and disciple when they are little. This sets the foundation of truth for them to return to when they are older. If you are steadfast when they are little, they will learn you mean what you say, and they will not easily forget that as a teenager.

The culture has taught us to expect little from children. They are presented as wild, out-of-control, unteachable little people that always cause trouble and never do what they are told. But the truth is, you can have high expectations of your children, and they can learn to obey you and love God. When your children know what you expect, and they meet your expectations, their self-esteem is built up. If a mom expects nothing, or very little, she is either saying she is incapable of handling her children or her children are incapable of handling themselves. When children reach higher and accomplish what Mom asks, they feel strong, capable, and believed in. Then Mom has the opportunity to praise and be proud of them. The fact that a mom asks these things of her children means she believes in them. If she never asks challenging things of her children, they never have an opportunity to try, and therefore, never have an opportunity to prove themselves to her. If Mom expects obedience and receives it, she will spend more time reinforcing obedience than punishing disobedience, which is what we all prefer.

My fourth child was adopted at age six from Central Asia. He came to us with a history of neglect and abuse, severe developmental delays, cognitive challenges, and without any understanding of family life or relationships. To say the least, raising him was a daunting challenge. But in spite of the struggles, it was remarkable how well this son was able to meet my expectations when I made them clear. However, he was extremely clever in his ability to convince others that he could not follow the rules. While he could sit completely still for me for the full hour-and-a-half Sunday morning church service, he convinced his Sunday school teacher he was hyperactive and incapable of following directions in her class. She found him uncontrollable. Then she observed this boy when I was in the room. He was a completely different, calm, well-behaved child. As delayed and challenged as he was in every area of his life, most of his behavior was all about expectations and consequences. He was perfectly capable of doing what was right. He just needed to know it was worth it.

In summary, children who obey live in a world full of the rewards of their own actions. Quick obedience means less whining, less arguing, and less time spent on consequences. It means a smoothly running household where family members understand their roles and responsibilities so that chaos, misunderstandings, and frustrations are minimized. Teaching, training, and discipling require effort, commitment, and perseverance. But the work is worth it! It may take weeks, months, or even years, but you will eventually experience the fruit of your labors as you seize your responsibility with all your heart and choose to follow through.

The purpose of parenting is discipling, not distracting. Distracting means occupying your children with an activity instead of expecting them to obey. Distracting, or redirecting, is what caretakers (babysitters, teachers) do with an unruly child, not what parents should do, except in rare situations. Confusion abounds when caretakers try to act like parents and parents act like caretakers!

For example, a parent may believe her child is incapable of waiting in a restaurant, so she brings along an iPad to keep the child occupied. What is wrong with this picture? Well, considering God wants us to teach, disciple, and foster a close relationship with our children, it is actually this parent's job to teach her child to sit still and wait patiently in the restaurant. Distraction will not build character. Even though it is definitely easier for the parent in the short term, it can be harmful for the child in the long term.

This parent could seize the moment to invest in the child and enjoy her, but instead she has encouraged her to pull away from the family and into passive entertainment. This little girl may actually want her parent's time and attention. She may feel shoved aside or unimportant when handed a device to keep quiet and busy. Patience and being still are aptitudes every person can benefit from learning. Waiting for a meal is the perfect time for engaging children in conversation, playing interactive word games, or coloring a picture together rather than all sitting together but apart on electronic devices, distracted and disconnected. Does this parent desire to connect with, understand, and enjoy her child? Or does she want her child addicted to electronic devices? **Daily choices reinforce and reflect the priorities of parents.**

Do you think you could begin to see each day with your children as full of opportunity to invest in them? It is easy to fall into the habits of arranging life so that you can escape your children or not face the responsibility of parenting them. But the final destination of that kind of parenting is not where you want to go. Children long to be valued, seen, and understood. Even as you long for others to spend time with you and affirm your value, children long to be more than just in the way. When other things are more important than concentrated time with your children, and you are constantly substituting another diversion to occupy them rather than investing your own time with them, your children may begin to see themselves as a nuisance instead of a treasure. Yes, time with friends is important, work and household chores demand your time, and uninterrupted time with your husband is a priority. But if you have spent time training, loving, and attending to your children, then they will not feel cast aside when you need time elsewhere. That is not escaping responsibility; that is balanced time management. "Children don't expect that parents give up all of their activities and fun times just so that they are always available for them. But they must see that these other activities are not as valuable as they are to their parents" (Smalley, 1992, p. 66).

The Purpose of Parenting Is Equipping, not Enabling

Have you ever set out to accomplish something only to realize you were ill-equipped for the job? How about when you were a child? Do you remember facing some task that was overwhelming for you because you did not feel prepared for it? When my husband, Kelly, was a boy, he was working for his water life-saving merit badge in Boy Scouts. There were four elements to earning the badge: 1. reach; 2. throw; 3. row; and 4. go. Kelly passed the first three and had only to do the last part, go. This required rescuing a person in the water who was in danger of drowning. Well, as a scrawny ten-year-old, you would think he would be assigned to rescue another boy about his age. But no, the instructor—a grown man—jumped in the pool and acted like he was drowning. As soon as Kelly swam to him, the instructor grabbed him and pushed him under the water. Kelly was completely outmatched in size and strength and had no idea how to get himself out of the situation. Terrified he was going to drown, he struggled and struggled until finally, when he was about to pass out, the man let him up. Without any empathy, the instructor told Kelly, "Don't ever try to rescue someone in the water, or you will drown." I have known my husband for 36 years, and even though he is a good swimmer, he has always had a fear of drowning. He was thrown into a situation as a small child he was not equipped for and could not have been no matter what. Instead of being taught he needed to get older and bigger before attempting to rescue a grown man in the water, he was bullied and punished for his size by an adult.

Just like that situation, children often face circumstances for which they are not equipped. We may assume what they are facing is no big deal, but we have to recognize what is new, difficult, or overwhelming for them. Some children are curious, talkative types who ask lots of questions. But many children don't have the words to convey their fears and anxieties, and we need to look out for them. When your children face something new, stop and talk with them about what to expect. Ask them if they want you to come along for support. Find out if they are nervous or overwhelmed, and help build their confidence beforehand. If they say anything that leads you to question whether or not it is safe, well-supervised, or appropriate for them, step up and make sure this activity is not dangerous or questionable.

If your children are caught up in something they enjoy that is not good for them, they are probably not mature enough or adequately equipped to say no or limit their own time in that activity. This is usually the case with technology. If parents are not careful to enforce boundaries, children can be absorbed in their games for hours. A growing body of evidence shows that too much time on screens is significantly detrimental to brain development and negatively impacts focus, the ability to regulate emotions, creativity, motivation, sleep, communication skills, and impulse control. Screen obsessed children run the risk of developing learning disabilities, increased aggression, as well as obesity, anxiety, and frustration (Lathbury, 2010). These are major issues, and for parents to reduce risk, they should limit screen time, reduce access to devices as much as possible in the home, and encourage activities that promote physical exercise, social interaction, the development of fine and large motor skills, and solving problems. Make a family plan for screen use, and set an example to your children by being active and creative, not turning to your device at every still moment.

In addition, it is good to remember that some things will never be good for our children, no matter how much we try to equip them. Pornography, for example, is beyond devastating to every child and should be off limits for every adult. Please recognize that with the onslaught of electronic access to pornography, younger and younger children are being hypersexualized and robbed of the innocence they need for a healthy and balanced view of themselves and the world around them. Parents constantly have to monitor and control what their children are viewing online for their safety. An ounce of prevention is worth a pound of cure. The younger the age of exposure to porn, the more devastating it is to our children's souls. Be proactive about the content of their activity online, and do not assume that a website or game is innocent just because it is geared for children. The emotional, mental, and spiritual destruction within a person addicted to porn is impossible to spell out here, yet it is currently a widespread issue. Do not even give it a chance to take hold of your children's minds (Proverbs 2:10-22).

So how do we equip our children? Well, we can prepare them for the common issues in life every person must face by teaching them God's Word, giving them boundaries and consequences, teaching them how to obey, training them in character development, and helping them understand how to treat others. Parents also need to talk about new situations, helping prepare their children for them and letting them ask questions and express their feelings. Beyond that, it is also necessary to teach children how to defend themselves, to walk (or run) away from a bad situation or unfamiliar person, and how to say no if anything makes them uncomfortable.

Boundaries help equip children to stop what they are doing and switch to doing something else. If they cannot stop an activity without pitching a fit, they have become too engrossed and need for it to be removed completely until they are more mature and capable of calm obedience. All of this requires constant engagement with your children to draw them out, discuss what is happening in their lives, and give boundaries while supporting, loving, and encouraging them.

So in light of what we know about equipping, what does it mean to enable? Well, in a positive context, it is empowering people by giving them the tools they need to develop and grow. But we most often use the word "enabling" in our culture in the negative context, as in supporting or encouraging unhealthy choices by not allowing people to experience the full consequences of their behavior (Kala, 2016). Parents do this when they make excuses for their children, blame someone else for their children's behavior, laugh at the behavior, prevent correction of the behavior, or create an environment that allows the behavior to continue.

Look at this example of the difference between equipping and enabling. Melanie has a second-grade daughter, Hannah, who makes a new friend, Emmy. At school, Hannah is beginning to learn all kinds of unhealthy behaviors from Emmy and is getting in trouble with the teacher. If Melanie wants to equip Hannah for this situation, she will instruct her to be kind and friendly to all the children in her class while also reminding her that she is expected to obey the teacher, follow the classroom rules, and be a good example to the other children. Melanie will hold Hannah responsible for her own behavior regardless of what Emmy does. She will also tell the teacher to please give Hannah full consequences for poor behavior in the classroom, even if she is imitating Emmy. As a mom who is determined to equip and build character, Melanie will not blame Emmy for Hannah's behavior or allow Hannah to blame Emmy either. At home, she will remind Hannah that no matter how other people act or whether or not they get away with it, she will not allow her to be disruptive or disrespectful.

In contrast, if Melanie is an enabling parent, she will not concern herself with the negative influence Emmy is having on Hannah. She will not give consequences when Hannah gets in trouble at school. She will blame Emmy as the reason for Hannah's actions and will expect the teacher to excuse Hannah simply because Emmy is a bad influence. This kind of mom expects Hannah to imitate Emmy and does not hold her responsible for her own choices. Even after Hannah has moved on to third grade and is no longer around Emmy, the habits she developed due to Emmy's influence will still be excused as someone else's fault.

When Melanie equipped her daughter, Hannah learned through the consequences of her behavior and her mother's boundaries that if she chose a friend that did not follow directions, it did not mean she was exempt from doing what was right. Hannah learned to obey the teacher even with peer pressure to do otherwise. She also understood that whom she chooses as a close friend is important because friends can influence her choices. In contrast, when Melanie enabled her daughter, Hannah developed bad habits, was in trouble all the time at school, and thought her poor behavior was acceptable because her friend was acting that way. Hannah heard her mother blame Emmy, and so she came to believe she could not help how she acted because she was bound to imitate whomever was around. Hannah headed into the next school year without any idea how to choose friends wisely and carried the bad habits with her, believing she had become a troublemaker.

This is just one example of how equipping children works to build character and prepare them for future struggles. **Enabling children leaves them at the mercy of their own impulses and reinforces the belief that they do not have a choice in the way they behave. If their parent does not expect that they do better, they will not be motivated in any way to change and make smarter choices for themselves.**

What are some ways you may have been enabling your children instead of equipping them? Have you made excuses for them? Have you blamed others for their behavior? Learning Christlike traits such as kindness, respect, obedience, patience, diligence, and self-control take focused effort, and children will not simply grow into individuals who display these attributes without your intentional help.

Chapter 2 Study Questions

What Is the Purpose of Parenting?

Day One

1. Read Matthew 28:16-20. Write out verses 19 and 20, but in place of "them," write your children's names: ____________

   ____
   ____
   ____
   ____

2. What does it mean to "disciple" someone? ____________

   ____
   ____

3. Read Luke 14:25-33. Are you a disciple of Jesus Christ? ____ How do you know?____________________

   ____
   ____

4. Has anyone ever "discipled" you? __________ How has that impacted your life?____________________

   ____
   ____

5. Oftentimes, even in the church environment we receive more praise and attention for doing good deeds outside the home, and our work of faithfully parenting our children during the everyday stuff of life goes unseen and unrewarded.

   a. Who sees your obedience as a parent when no one else does, according to Matthew 6:1-21? ____________________

   ____

   b. Who will reward you for your obedience as a mom when no one else notices?______________________________________

   ____

When you are restless and bored, when you feel alone, when the sacrifice doesn't seem worth it, or you are tempted to believe there must be something more interesting to do than invest your life in your children, hold on to an eternal perspective, and trust the Lord will reward you for your obedience to Him as a mom. He will. God will reward you in ways you could never comprehend and for generations to come!

Day Two

1. Define obedience: ________________________________

   ____

   ____

2. Read Ephesians 6:1. When you were a child, were you expected to obey? ______________________________________

   ____

3. Were the boundaries clear? Or were you always struggling to figure out what obedience meant day to day?______________

____

____

4. In God's Word, the meaning of obedience is clear. We may not like God's commands. We may disagree with them and even want to change them. But they are there. God's expectation that His children obey His commands is also clear. Look up the following verses, and write down what they say about obedience:

   Deuteronomy 27:10_______________________________

   ____

   Jeremiah 7:23-24 _______________________________

   ____

   John 3:36 _____________________________________

   ____

   John 14:21 ____________________________________

   ____

   Hebrews 13:17 _________________________________

   ____

5. In light of these Scriptures, is obedience important in the Christian life? Why or why not? ____________________________

____

____

6. If you are discipling your children to be followers of Christ, why does their obedience to you matter? ____________________

____

____

7. How do you think you are doing in teaching your children to obey?

____

____

8. In what ways could you do better? ______________________

____

____

Day Three

1. In today's culture, we all struggle to focus. It doesn't matter if we have a diagnosis of Attention Deficit Disorder or not. All of us have to work to keep our minds on the task at hand. We carry around in our pockets infinite amounts of information and the ability to connect with people 24/7, not to mention the plethora of media outlets and games available to entertain us.

   a. Read Hebrews 12:1-2, and list anything in your life that is an encumbrance or an entangling sin, i.e., anything that gets in the way of your walk with God: ______________________

____

____

b. Not all good things are best, and those things that are less than the best are not necessarily evil. However, adults who live their lives jumping from one distraction to another are more likely to parent by distracting their children. How much are you on a screen? _________________________

____

____

c. Most people are addicted to their phone. It is easy to say, "Not me!" But try challenging yourself: How many hours can you go without it? How often do you typically check it? How hard is it to put it down and walk away from it? ____

____

____

____

d. It may sound impossible, but truthfully not every email, text, or phone call has to be dealt with immediately. Your children are more important than all the people/Facebook posts/Instagrams/Tweets/messages/calls that clamor for your attention. What do you think your children are learning about screens in general if every time they look at you, you are looking at your phone? _________________________

____

____

e. Eye contact is an essential part of human connection, healthy attachment, and normal relationships. We are increasingly in a world where people no longer know how to look another person in the eye. Your quick response to your children's needs, with eye contact, is enormously important in their development of trust. How well and how often do you make eye contact with your children?______________

____

____

f. Pray for discipline in regard to your phone. My suggestion is to set aside times to deal with calls, texts, and emails when your children do not require your time and attention (naptime, after bedtime, during school, etc.). Write out some guidelines for limiting your phone use: ___________

____

____

2. How often do you distract your children as a parenting method?

____

a. What are some ways you can engage with your children instead of distracting them? ________________________

____

____

b. It is so often easier to distract than to expect obedience or engage in relationship. In what areas do your children need to learn obedience, develop character, and engage in communication rather than to depend on distractions?

____

____

c. What character qualities are needed in order to obey what the Scripture asks of us in the following verses?

Psalm 46:10 ________________________________

Psalm 27:14 ________________________________

Ephesians 4:1-3 ____________________________

Isaiah 26:3 ________________________________

Ask the Lord to develop these qualities in yourself and in your children, and ask for the Lord to help you as you teach and train.

Day Four

1. Define the word "equip": ____________________

____

____

2. Look up the following verses, and record what they say about being equipped to do what God has called us to do:

   a. 2 Timothy 3:16-17 ________________________

   ____

b. Hebrews 13:20-21 ______________________________

____

c. 2 Peter 1:2-4 ________________________________

____

d. Ephesians 2:10 ______________________________

____

3. In your own words, describe how God equips His children to accomplish all that He asks of us: ________________

____

____

4. What do you need to do in order for God to be able to equip you? ______________________________________

____

____

5. In what ways did your parents either equip you to handle life's situations or fail to equip you for the things you have faced?

____

____

Day Five

1. To enable people can be a wonderful thing if it is in the context of helping them to accomplish something good. But in the negative context, enabling allows an unhealthy behavior to continue when we could do something to discourage it. Can you think of any ways your parents enabled you in bad habits

or unhealthy behaviors? What do you think they should have done instead? ______________________________

____

____

2. Think of the areas in which your children need to grow right now. How are you encouraging appropriate, correct responses and discouraging the wrong ones? ______________________________

____

____

Is it possible you might be enabling, encouraging, or reinforcing the wrong thing either by ignoring it, excusing it, or rewarding it?

____

____

3. As the perfect Father, what does God do when we are not obeying Him? What are we called to do when those we are responsible for are not living in a way that pleases the Lord? Look up the following Scriptures, and record what you observe:

a. Proverbs 3:12 ______________________________

____

b. 2 Timothy 4:1-2 ______________________________

____

c. Titus 2:11-15 ______________________________

____

4. How does the culture enable negative, unhealthy, sinful behaviors? (See Philippians 3:18-19; Isaiah 5:20.) ______________

____

____

5. Are you willing to live counterculturally and do what God asks you to do as a parent even if it means your children will not be popular with those who are ruled by today's trends?________

____

____

Ask the Lord to give you the courage to equip your children to be faithful Christ-followers rather than easily led crowd-pleasers.

Chapter 3

What Is the Role of Parenting?

Has anything in your life ever gotten upside down? How about the day when you found yourself caring for your parents instead being cared for by them? Or when you were suddenly handed the responsibilities of your boss but none of the reward? Or that day your child grew taller than you, and you looked up instead of down? Other examples of when life feels upside down are when the leader becomes the follower or the teacher becomes the student. In this chapter, we will discuss one role of a parent that has been completely upended by our culture; that is, in the relationship between parent and child, who is supposed to be in charge?

The Role of Parenting Is as the Authority, not as the Buddy

Authority is defined as "the power to determine, adjudicate, or otherwise settle issues or disputes; the right to control, command, or determine" ("Authority," 2012). **The concept of authority implies power, and many of us are uncomfortable with the idea of power.** The thought of another person being in a position to control or punish us may cause us to recoil. If we have experienced any kind of inappropriate or abusive authority, we tend to think of authority negatively. At the writing of this manuscript, there is a great deal of unrest in the United States over the inappropriate and criminal use of force by some police officers. Their abuse of authority resulted in the deaths of citizens. Fear spreads when the people who are charged with maintaining law and order break the very laws they were given to uphold. Victims abound when authorities of any kind abuse their power.

The concept of authority also implies control. In our culture, if you refer to someone as controlling, it is a negative description. The idea that a person, especially in our free society, would want to control another makes us uncomfortable. When you interact with a controlling spouse, friend, or parent, you know it does not feel loving, accepting, or understanding. Authority also involves obedience and submission. Whenever these terms are mentioned as biblical concepts, there is usually resistance. In a culture that says we should be free to do, say, think, and live however we want, we are not interested in being submissive, obedient subjects.

All that being said, if the word "authority" has gotten your back up and your toes curled, it is completely understandable. We live in a fallen world that is a poor representative of the truth God wants us to experience and understand. The reality is, however, that without some obedience and submission, without someone calling the shots, without some form of headship, all of society falls apart. No culture has lasted with chaos and anarchy as the ruling forms of government. So if you are willing to agree that some kinds of authority are actually good, healthy, and loving, then the kind of authority God calls parents to demonstrate over their children is understandable and valued.

The biblical concept of authority is rooted in God Himself. He is the ultimate authority over all humankind and the example of what authority is intended to be. God created the world and everything in it (Revelation 4:11), and He created it to work a certain way. We learn the way God intended it to work by looking at the truth as found in His Word. For example, God created humankind to live according to His moral Law as outlined in the Ten Commandments in Exodus 20:1-17. He also implemented systems of consequences and rewards directly related to obedience of His Law (Deuteronomy 11:26-28). Then, because he is a loving God, He sent His Son to redeem us from the consequences of our sin, or the breaking of His Law. He gave us the Gospel (Romans 3:10, 23; 5:8, 12; 6:23; 10:9-10, 13, 17) to save us from our sin, to give us eternal life, and to call us His children. This Gospel message is freely given and available to us because He is a loving Father. He forgives our sin when we confess it, and He cleans us from unrighteousness (1 John 1:9).

Everything God does is out of love for us. In Micah 7:18-19, we discover God delights in mercy and has compassion for us. In Zephaniah 3:17, we learn He rejoices over us, and in John 3:16 we hear God gave His only Son because He loved us so much. 1 John 4:7-10 says that love is from God, and it is only through Him we can truly understand love.

Hebrews 12:6, however, offers another perspective about God's love. It says because God loves us, He disciplines us. If it is hard for you to understand how consequences or discipline can be loving, then you have bought into the world's definition of love, not God's. The world says love is whatever makes us feel good, happy, or what we want in the moment. **The truth is not everything that makes us feel good is good for us, and not everything that makes us happy is in God's perfect plan for our life. Many things that appeal to us are sinful and therefore unhealthful for us. As a matter of fact, those things could even be destructive, ruining our life in the long run (Galatians 6:7-9).**

As a loving Father, God convicts and corrects us when we are sinful so that we will return to and trust in Him. This is a good and loving thing because He knows what is best for us. Correction and discipline are the responsibilities of parents as well. A toddler who has just learned to walk is delighted in his newfound freedom. Walking and running make him happy. He doesn't know that running into the street is dangerous; it is what he wants to do. A loving parent, however, will firmly correct and prevent that activity for the child's safety, regardless of whether the child understands or likes the reason or not. Not to discipline that behavior would be very unloving indeed, with a natural consequence that is too horrible to imagine. In the same way, outbursts of anger, selfishness, greed, deceit, complaining, and disobedience are not good for our children's souls (Galatians 5:16-26) and need to be corrected.

In addition to being loving, God is trustworthy and faithful (1 Corinthians 1:9; 1 Thessalonians 5:24). His character does not change (Hebrews 13:8). He is all powerful (Psalm 66:3-4; Daniel 2:20), yet He exercises great mercy, kindness, and patience (Psalm 86:15; Hebrews 8:12; Ephesians 2:4-7). He is worthy of imitating (Ephesians 5:1), and He sets the example for us of how authority can be unselfish, loving, and good even while it disciplines disobedience. **God's authority is not abusive, nor is it intended to harm. It does not manipulate or take advantage, and it is never destructive. God's intentions are for good, never for evil. And if God says "no," it is because He knows it will lead to ultimate blessing and positive growth in our lives.**

This is the kind of authority God has called parents to have in their children's lives in Colossians 3:20 and Ephesians 6:1. God does not ask children to obey those who have no authority. The very fact He requires children to obey their parents indicates the position of authority that parents should hold. With God as our example, we can imitate Him and parent our children faithfully with love, patience, understanding, and encouragement. Christian parents should not abuse this authority as a power to be wielded but instead use it as a motivator to help their children become more like Christ for their own benefit. This kind of parent maintains the last word, expects obedience, and stays steadfast regardless of emotional manipulation. These parents follow through with consequences, are reliable and consistent, and do not allow the children to run the show. The children are not the authority of the home. Their wishes do not run the decision-making, and their happiness is not the ultimate goal. Everything the parents do is for the development of their children's hearts and characters so that they will respond to the call of God on their lives.

The opposite of parents who are loving authorities are parents whose primary goal is to be their children's best buddies. While authority figures can be friendly and demonstrate the characteristics of a good friend, their primary goal is not to be a pal. Rather, those in authority seek to be positive role models. If the parents are in charge of the home, not the children, there is discipline, teaching and training, rewards and consequences, as well as high expectations. When parents are preoccupied with being a pal, the children inevitably end up in charge. The parents are so concerned with being liked they forget they are supposed to be steering the ship. They are also so absorbed with wanting their children to be happy they let the children dictate how life will go. Instead of making decisions to run their family life smoothly, honor God, and do what is best for the children, they inadvertently hand the household reins to the children who then expect to take charge of running the show. Could you imagine the outcome if police officers stopped speeding cars then let the drivers write their own tickets, or if teachers allowed their students to grade their own tests, or if a coach let his players decide the rules of the game, or if bosses let their employees work on whatever they wanted and get paid whatever they like. Any of those scenarios ultimately would not work out well. Citizens would not obey traffic laws, students would not learn, athletes would not know how to play their sport, and work would not get done.

Consider these additional comparisons to help you understand the difference between being your children's parental authority and being your children's buddy:

- Authorities give instructions; buddies make suggestions.
- Authorities expect obedience; buddies expect eventual cooperation.
- Authorities give consequences; buddies just act disappointed.
- Authorities expect improvement; buddies do not expect change.
- Authorities teach and train through clear boundaries and guidelines; buddies cajole and try to reason, focusing on words rather than action.

A long-term view is helpful when considering the idea of authority. The goal is to be your *adult* child's best friend. If you fail to gain your children's respect when they are small by putting them in charge and not giving them what they really need, they will not be as inclined to stay close to you when they are older. **Children are actually happier in a home with expectations, boundaries, and consistent consequences. They thrive in this environment because they are secure, and they do not feel the burden of being in control. They also feel loved because this is how God intended the relationship to be.**

It is not loving but actually stressful to put your child in the position of the boss. According to Paul David Tripp, "It is a crushing burden for your children to have to get up every morning and carry the heavy load of your identity and meaning and purpose and all the expectations and demands that flow from it" (Tripp, 2016, p. 77). So take the time to establish boundaries. Choose consequences you will follow through with consistently, and consider how you want to encourage them. Pray and ask the Lord to give you wisdom.

The Role of Parenting Is as a Corrector, not as a Controller

How does a person get labeled as "controlling"? Isn't that the point of discipline, to get children under control? Shouldn't our home be in control and not out of control? These are good questions to ask concerning this idea of control. Sometimes it is assumed that strict parents are controlling. However, you can be a strict parent without being controlling, and controlling parents are not necessarily strict. In the broad sense, yes, parents do need to help their children live their lives with self-control, but this is done through teaching, training, discipling, and correcting. Even then, the ultimate goal for Christian parents is not outcomes in behavior, but rather that their children are saved by Jesus Christ. The truth is "no matter how successfully you control their choices and behavior, your control cannot and will not free them from this deeper need" (Tripp, 2016, p. 170).

In this context, when I refer to being "controlling," I am speaking of a need to control others from a heart of fear, anger, selfishness, or insecurity. Interestingly enough, a mother who is doing her part can relax and trust God with the outcomes in her children's lives. The mother who tries to control outcomes often gets the cart before the horse. Instead of focusing on her responsibility, the mother starts forcing behavioral results in her children through anger, manipulation, bribery, or passive aggression. When a mother is faithful but not controlling, she does her part, lets go of what she cannot control, and trusts God to do the work only He can do in her children's hearts.

Scripture shows us some examples of people who used control to manage outcomes. In Genesis 12:10-20, Abram, who later became Abraham, headed to Egypt to escape a famine. His wife Sarai, later

Sarah, was very beautiful, and Abram was afraid the Egyptians would kill him in order to have her. Instead of going to God with his fear and asking for wisdom, Abram told Sarai to say she was his sister. Then because he did not know any better, Pharaoh took Sarai into his house. Abram's need to control the situation to protect his own safety turned into a horrible circumstance for his wife! When the truth came out, Abram looked foolish before Pharaoh and was promptly sent away. When a person makes decisions to manipulate people and circumstances out of fear, this is controlling behavior.

Another example is in 1 Kings 21:1-15. Ahab, the king of Israel, saw a beautiful vineyard and wanted it for himself. He asked to buy it, but the owner refused to sell it to him. So King Ahab pouted, throwing a royal pity party. When Ahab's wife Jezebel found her husband depressed, she decided to take things into her own hands. She used threats and manipulation, abusing her position of authority to have the vineyard owner murdered. Ahab was then able to get the vineyard, but God did not let it go at that. Ahab and Jezebel were both cursed, and the Lord brought evil on their house. When a person makes decisions to manipulate outcomes because they want their own way, this is controlling behavior.

As you see from these examples, controlling behavior can show up in any relationship, whether it be parent-child, husband-wife, or any authority over any subordinate. But in the context of the parent-child relationship, recognize there is a difference between teaching your children how to cooperate, obey, and help as opposed to forcing them to be what you want them to be through coercion, bribery, manipulation, or inappropriate punishment. There is a difference between managing, guiding, correcting, and training versus controlling. **Controlling parents often have personal preferences that are not imperative according to God's Word. When they use their position of authority to make their children comply with behaviors that**

are unnecessary or inappropriate, they have become controlling parents.

Let's look at an example of how control might play out in a parent-child relationship. Caroline only eats an organic vegan diet and has a strict policy about foods in her home. She is preoccupied with the healthy way to shop, cook, and eat. She does not let "bad" foods in her house and does not want her children to eat such foods. When her children go to friends' houses to play, she tells them they are not allowed to eat any meat, processed food, or junk food. If Caroline's children disobey and eat any of the foods designated as bad—and this is not referring to foods they may be allergic to!—they won't be allowed to play there again.

Food is not meant to be an idol. God does not want us to be so focused on eating that we make food choices the most important thing. Food is not good or bad, it is just food. There are choices that are healthier than others, and those should be included in a balanced diet. However, God does not give food a moral value. In this example, at times there may be nothing else for Caroline's children to eat but junk food at their friends' homes. When it is time to eat, they must choose between going hungry so as not to lose the privilege of playing at their friends' homes again, or eating forbidden foods and lying about it. They will either feel guilty because they ate the food and lied about it or angry because they had to go hungry in order to obey. The consequence will be that negative emotions and unnecessary conflict is now associated with food. If children eat when they are hungry, they are not sinning. Because this is not a heart issue, the children will feel confused, stressed, and like a victim in a completely normal situation. It is a lie for parents to think they can guarantee their children's health if they control their every food choice.

What is the balance? Well, it is fine to eat organic foods and as an adult to choose to be a vegan. It is also fine to make healthy choices in your own home, cook according to your likes and dislikes, have guidelines in regard to food, and teach your children healthy habits. But the parent who is not controlling will not get hung up on food being good or bad. She will let go of what her children eat away from home. She will allow them to be exposed to other types of foods and won't be afraid if they try new things. She trusts God that her children are learning good habits at home and will more than likely grow up to make wise food choices as adults.

Parents need to correct their children rather than to control them. Let's look at a similar example in a different way; this time with the parent as a corrector. Consider Natalie, who feeds her children a balanced diet from all the food groups. She keeps healthful foods in her home, but is relaxed about food in general. On the day before her son Charlie's birthday party Natalie makes a cake. She works for hours to decorate it and tells all her children it is off-limits until the party. Later, Charlie's sister Christi sneaks into the kitchen and eats a fistful of that cake. When Natalie discovers that Christi has ruined the cake, she disciplines her. Is this because she is overly paranoid about sugar? No, this is because Christi directly disobeyed Mom's request, disrespected her wishes, and did not honor Charlie's birthday. Correction is needed in order to deal with the hurtful actions and attitudes in this situation so that they will not be repeated.

Another way control can show up in parent-child relationships is through the use of rewards. While I believe children need lots of encouragement, I prefer to teach moms to use *reinforcement* rather than rewards. Using rewards as bribery always backfires in the end. Trust me, if your children behave a certain way to receive some type of reward, typically the behavior is not linked to a change in their heart. More than likely, they will return to their previous behavior as soon as the reward is off the table. "Change is about learning what is right, acknowledging that it is right, confessing that you have been wrong, committing to a new way of living, and seeking the help you need to do it" (Tripp, 2016, p. 66). To encourage this kind of change, reinforcement is a better strategy. This can take a lot of different forms, but it always comes after the parent sees a true change of heart, not before.

For example, if a child has been struggling to share, and his mother says, "If you share with your brother for the next week, I will take you out for ice cream," she will have no idea if the sharing behavior is for the ice cream or because her son is learning to be unselfish. However, if Mom observes this son sharing with others of his own accord on several occasions, without having to be reminded, she can say, "Son, I am so proud of you for sharing. I see that your heart is changing, and you are learning how to be unselfish and kind. That warms my heart! Thank you for listening and doing what God wants you to do. Let's go out together and get some ice cream to celebrate your caring heart!" Now Mom has spontaneously chosen to do something special because of what she has already seen in her child's heart. This kind of encouragement reinforces that her son is learning something important, and that it matters. He will want to continue in his new habit of sharing.

The issues God calls parents to correct are ones of attitude, action, thought, and word that are not glorifying to God. These include disobedience, disrespect, rudeness, greed, selfishness, pride, carelessness, lack of control, laziness, impatience, destructive behaviors, lying, complaining, anger, gossip, and rebellion, to name just a few. When these problems are acted out, children need to be corrected, disciplined, reminded, taught, and encouraged to choose a Christlike response instead. The goal is for children to adopt the characteristics that glorify God. What are they? There are many, but they include the following: obedience (Ephesians 6:1), respect (1 Peter 3:16), kindness (Ephesians 4:32), unselfishness (Philippians 2:3), humility (1 Peter

5:6), thoughtfulness (Philippians 2:4), self-control (2 Peter 1:5-7), diligence (Proverbs 21:5), patience (Ephesians 4:1-2), cooperation (Ephesians 4:3), honesty (Psalm 15:2), gratitude (Colossians 2:6-7), forgiveness (Colossians 3:12-13), love (John 13:34), and faithfulness (Luke 16:10). These are areas that Christian parents pray God will also keep developing in their own lives. Will your children immediately develop Christlike character the first time they are corrected? No, as we all know, becoming like Christ takes time, repetition, and growth. What if your children don't seem to get the point of the lesson at all? Don't worry, and keep doing what God has called you to do: correcting, teaching, and reteaching as many times as needed.

All the parenting jobs we have covered so far—teaching, training, discipling, equipping, and correcting—require repetition. It can be frustrating for parents to have to repeat themselves again, and again, and again. Teaching the same lessons repetitively can drive parents crazy *if* they start out thinking they only need to do it once. Consider brushing your teeth. You do it every day, usually twice a day. You expect to keep doing it for the rest of your life. Do you have conversations with your friends like this: "I can't believe I have to brush my teeth *again*! *Every day!* It is insane. Over and over I do this, day after day"? No, of course not. Why? Because you were taught as a child that brushing teeth is something that has to be done daily. You have always known this is a daily job and always anticipated it would be repeated because your expectation was set from the beginning. **So let me help you with your expectations as a parent: You will have to repeat the lessons you teach your children over and over again.** They will not get them right away. They may struggle with them all through childhood, even if they are corrected and disciplined every time. If you think otherwise, you will be exasperated. Just like brushing teeth daily, you will have to say "be kind" many times. You will have to reteach "share with your sister," "be gentle," "don't talk back to Mommy," "obey the teacher," again and again. If repetition is your expectation, you will be able to do so much more calmly.

When I became a mother, I thought being angry when my kids messed up was the appropriate response. I learned the hard way that my children's disobedience required action, but not necessarily negative emotion. It was not imperative for me to be angry and loud to be effective. Consequences can be given with a calm and gentle, but firm, demeanor and are just as powerful. The purpose of discipline is not to withhold love and acceptance or manipulate with negative emotion but to correct and train in love and acceptance. We want our children to understand the need to obey but not carry the burden to make us happy.

What is your emotional response when your children defy you? Do you feel angry? Why do you think that is? Maybe you are embarrassed because you think they are making you look bad. If that is the case, their behavior is about you, not about them. Are you surprised? Don't be. It is normal for children to act like children and need to be corrected. Are you tired? That may mean you need to take a break before you can be calm enough to correct and teach effectively. Ultimately, we don't want our children obeying us because they are afraid of our anger; we want our children's obedience because their hearts have changed.

When your children defy you, do you feel intimidated? If so, do you fear and avoid confrontation in general? Is following through with correction hard for you because you'd rather not deal with it? If so, you will put your strong-willed children in control and teach them that if they push back, they will get their way. Remember that regardless of your personality, God has instructed you to teach and train. You are the adult who must decide to act not on your emotions but on God's Word.

When your children defy you, do you feel rejected? If you fear your children will not love you, you may back off from doing what your children really need. God's command to your children is not to love you but to obey you. Love and respect will come as you train your children to obey. Do not put the responsibility on your children to make you feel loved and accepted. It will destroy the relationship because it is a burden children are not meant to bear. Just love your children God's way, and don't worry about how they feel about you. Feelings are fleeting things, and children are still learning what love is all about.

Finally, when your children defy you, do you feel indifferent? Some parents think that if they try, they will surely fail, so they'd rather not try at all. But ignoring children in their time of need can be an even greater rejection than an overreaction of negative emotion. They will feel neglected and may look elsewhere for instruction. Step up and do. Don't just try, *do*. Teach, instruct, train, correct, and disciple with full trust that God is going to multiply your efforts every single day. Following through imperfectly is better than doing nothing! Generations will thank you for being faithful, bold, determined, and intentional as a Christian mother.

Chapter 3 Study Questions

What Is the Role of Parenting?

Day One

1. Define the following terms:

   a. Authority ____________________

   ____

   ____

   b. Obedience ____________________

   ____

   ____

   c. Respect ____________________

   ____

   ____

   d. Honor ____________________

   ____

   ____

2. List the people who were authorities in your life when you were a child.

   ____

   ____

   a. Did you recognize and respect their authority? __________

   b. Did you obey and submit to their authority? __________

c. What is your general attitude toward authority?________

____

d. Do you or have you considered God as the ultimate authority? _________ Why or why not? ____________________

____

____

3. Look up the following verses and write down your observations. What do they say about God as an authority?

Isaiah 30:30________________________________

____

Matthew 28:18 ______________________________

____

Luke 12:4-5 _________________________________

____

John 5:26-27 ________________________________

____

Colossians 1:15-18 ___________________________

____

1 Timothy 1:17 ______________________________

____

Revelation 1:8 ______________________________

____

Revelation 19:11-16 ______________________________

____

4. Who are you in authority over? ______________________________

   a. Is your authority over them recognized and respected?

      ____

   b. What are you doing to teach your children to respect authority? ______________________________

      ____

      ____

   c. Do your children respect and honor God as an authority?

      ____

      If not, how do you think that you can teach them to do so?

      ____

      ____

Day Two

1. God is the ultimate authority over all things, yet He is also full of grace. When we are placed in a position of authority, we are called to imitate God. Look up the following Scriptures and write down the attributes of God that give balance to His power and authority.

2 Peter 3:9 ______________________________

____

Ephesians 2:4-7 ______________________________

____

Colossians 1:13-14 ______________________________

____

1 John 4:10 ______________________________

____

2. Obedience can be hard, and surrender and submission to the Lord goes against our fleshly nature. But it is so worth it! Look up the following Scriptures and write down the benefits of obeying the Lord.

   Acts 5:32 ______________________________

   ____

   Philippians 2:12-13 ______________________________

   ____

   Hebrews 5:9 ______________________________

   ____

   1 Peter 1:2 ______________________________

   ____

John 14:21 ____

____

3. When you were a child, were you expected to obey? _______

   If so, was it hard to obey? _______ Do you remember how you felt when you did what was right, even if you didn't want to?

   _______ What were the rewards for obeying?____________

   ____

4. Now list all the benefits to your family when your children choose to be obedient: ______________________________

   ____

   ____

5. Are there areas of your life where you are struggling right now to obey the Lord? _______ If so, what are they? __________

   ____

   Write a prayer of confession and surrender, asking the Lord to help you be obedient in these challenging areas:__________

   ____

   ____

6. Do you believe that, since you often struggle to display Christ-like character, you shouldn't correct your children when they do the same thing? _______ If so, your children will never learn because you will not be perfect until you get to Heaven. However, you can still teach your children the truth even if you are working on the same issues yourself because that is how they will learn, and it is what God wants you to do.

7. Do you struggle to be respectful toward your husband? ________ If so, be aware that disrespect carries over and is easily imitated. Your children will not respect your husband if you don't, and you will undermine his authority in their lives if you do not build him up. If you slip in this area, bring it up to both your husband and your children. Apologize, and ask them for forgiveness. Make it clear to your children that your words or actions of disrespect were wrong. Remind them they need to treat their dad with respect.

Day Three

1. There are people who are known as controlling due to their personality and demeanor. However, the truth is all of us want control in some form. It is the nature of the flesh! Our children are no different. Can you list some areas you seek to be in control? Or another way to say it, in what areas do you struggle with trusting God? ______________________________________

   ____

   ____

2. The overwhelming need for control is often born out of fear. We all have fears. What scares you as a mom? ________________

   ____

   ____

3. We will look at our parenting fears in depth later in this study. But right now, read Matthew 6:25-34, and write down what is applicable to parenting. What speaks to you in this passage?

____

____

____

Day Four

1. As you think about being a correcting parent as opposed to a controlling parent, what struggles with your children come to mind? ____

____

____

2. Read the following parables and make notes as to whether the authority in the passage was controlling or correcting and why.

    a. Luke 14:16-24 ________________________________

    ____

    b. Luke 15:11-32 ________________________________

    ____

    ____

3. When your children misbehave, are you responding to your children as a correcting authority or reacting to them out of fear? ___________________________________ When you correct your children, are you able to do so with patience and

love, or does fear cause you to be panicked, angry, and explosive? ____________________

____

Ask the Lord to help you discover any source of fear that drives you to control your children with negative emotions.________

____

____

(Reacting in fear is not always a bad thing. If your child runs out in front of a car, fear will give you the adrenaline you need to snatch her to safety and teach her a lesson she hopefully won't soon forget. But reacting out of fear to daily, childish things that require training is unnecessary. Examine your heart for the difference.)

Day Five

1. Who is ultimately in control of all things? ____________
   Look up the following verses, and record what God is actually in control of:

   a. Luke 8:24-25 ____________________

   ____

   b. Daniel 2:20-22 ____________________

   ____

   c. Romans 13:1 ____________________

   ____

d. Psalm 74:12-17 ______________________

____

e. Isaiah 40:21-26 ______________________

____

2. Did you feel controlled as a child? In other words, did you feel like your parents had an agenda for you that was not biblical but rather their preferences? Did your parents try to coerce you, manipulate you, or use their position to make you comply? If so, how did that make you feel? What was the result of that behavior in your life? ______________________

____

____

3. God is not manipulative. He does not use backhanded means to form people's character. God uses His Spirit, who is love, to convict and draw His children near to Himself. We are not forced against our will to be like Christ. We are called, and if we are willing, He gently teaches, corrects, and helps us understand how to walk in His truth (John 16:7-14). Yes, there are consequences in our lives if we disobey God, but He is there to forgive us, pick us up, and give us the courage to obey. If you have misunderstood God and who He is as an authority, fearing He would be controlling and manipulative, talk to Him about that by journaling here, and praise Him for who He really is.

____

____

____

____

Chapter 4

What Is the Responsibility of Parenting?

Most moms want to be fun and desire for their children to be happy and have a good time. However, the culture offers so much entertainment for children that a mom can easily get pulled in a hundred directions. Instead of focusing on the most important things her children need, moms can end up dragging whiny, argumentative, weary children from one activity to the next. I can't tell you how many times I have observed the happiest children in quiet, simple homes where special outings are few and far between. If busy, entertainment-driven mothers stop and think about it, the frenzied pace isn't fun for them either. They are often irritated the whole time they are pursuing the title of "Fun Mom," barking at the kids, angry they aren't enjoying themselves, and upset at the money spent in the pursuit of happiness only to receive grumbling in return.

The Responsibility of a Parent Is to Be a Provider, not an Entertainer

Provision is often viewed in the context of basic needs, such as food, clothing, shelter, and education. Most parents do a great job of providing these things and understand they are essentials in caring for their children. But God asks parents to provide more than the basics, and these important things trump entertainment every time. Let's look at what some of these key items might be.

1. **Parents are responsible to provide opportunities for their children to grow, develop character, learn the truth of God's Word, and be challenged.** Luke 2:52 says Jesus Himself grew in "wisdom and stature, and in favor with God and men." Each one of these is important. Of course, Jesus' growth in stature happened because His earthly parents fed Him well. But wisdom comes from knowing the truth, and favor with God and men comes from the truth being demonstrated in choices, actions, attitudes, and words. If your son is struggling with a complaining attitude, it will not be fixed by taking him to the zoo. If your daughter is being rude and disrespectful, it will not magically disappear by going to a movie. Your job is not to distract with entertainment but to deal with your children's heart issues and teach them how to live in a way that pleases God.

2. **Parents are responsible to provide an environment of peace, safety, and love where growth can take place.** Psalm 4:8 says, "In peace I will both lie down and sleep. For You alone, O Lord, make me to dwell in safety." God is a perfect Father and sets the example for us to follow. In this verse, David expresses that God is providing what he needs to sleep well and to feel safe. Obviously, children who are physically, emotionally, or verbally abused do not feel safe, but there are other things that can remove a child's peace and cause a fearful heart. When the television is always on, it is a huge distraction for little ones. Additionally, if the TV programming is characterized by violence or rude language, it adds an unsettling, negative undercurrent to the home. Loud music with inappropriate lyrics can have the same effect. Pornography streaming in and easily accessed on computer screens, phones, or tablets destroys the harmony of family life. Not

only porn, but screen time in general can be unhealthy and unsafe for both adults and children if not carefully monitored and managed. A frantic schedule, overworked and exhausted parents, irritability, loud marital disagreements, and a complete lack of routine can all be enemies of a peaceful, safe home.

We also need to provide an environment of love. Love should be spoken often and reinforced in multiple ways. Tell your children you love them, and be loving in your attitude, tone of voice, and demeanor toward them. Children need affection, lots of hugs and kisses and gentle touches throughout each and every day. Reinforce your love to them even when they have disobeyed or misbehaved. Discipline and rejection are not the same thing. Discipline can and should be done in love because the reason we correct our children in the first place is because we love them! Give your children encouragement by building them up with kind, loving words and times of closeness, tenderness, and care.

3. **Parents are responsible to provide discipline and correction when necessary and praise when appropriate.** Hebrews 12:11 says, "All discipline for the moment seems not to be joyful, but sorrowful; yet to those who have been trained by it, afterwards it yields the peaceful fruit of righteousness." It is actually unkind to fail to discipline your children. If they can act however they like at home without any consequences, they might be shocked when they go out into the world and are shunned because they are selfish, rude, lazy, unkind, disrespectful, angry, or impatient. Failing to discipline your children may cause them to have a difficult time making friends, thriving in school, getting a job, or being responsible. Undisciplined children may not even understand why they are struggling because their parents, by neglecting discipline, have taught them nothing is their fault. If everything is everyone else's fault, and children are incapable of

taking responsibility for their own behavior, then generalized helplessness, entitlement, self-pity, and misery often take hold.

4. **Parents are responsible to provide social experiences that will strengthen their children's ability to work well with others.** Proverbs 27:17 says, "Iron sharpens iron, so one man sharpens another." It is important for children to have siblings or playmates who allow them to learn the skills of cooperating, encouraging, sharing, and kindness. When children are little, parents should be close by to observe, correct, coach, and help them understand how to be good friends. Parents should make suggestions and mediate when they squabble and teach them good habits in getting along well with others.

5. **Parents are responsible to provide children with chores requiring obedience and diligence, offering the intrinsic reward of a job well done.** In Colossians 3:23-24, it says, "Do your work heartily, as for the Lord rather than for men." We can start early with training our children to do age-appropriate tasks (see Appendix C) and to take care of and manage their own things. Children should be contributing, cooperating members of the family who do their part to help the household run smoothly. Just like adults feel accomplished when they complete tasks, children learn that work is a normal part of life, and there are rewards in finishing well (Psalm 90:17). We tend to think only certain entertainment activities can be fun, but the truth is, children can learn to enjoy working hard. Some of the best family times are when everyone is working toward a common goal, like getting the leaves raked or the playroom organized.

6. **Parents are responsible to provide educational experiences (Proverbs 1:5).** You may immediately think, "That is the school's job!" But children who are taught at home as well as at school do much better overall. In the first chapter, I talked about how a parent's job is to teach, and I focused on teaching them God's Word. But

teaching life skills involves everything and happens all the time. We teach our babies to make eye contact. We teach our toddlers to walk and talk. We teach our preschoolers to eat their vegetables. Every moment of parenting is an opportunity to teach. Pointing out the wonders of nature, teaching them how to work with their hands, introducing them to new sights and sounds, and helping them get ready to read are all jobs involved in parenting. Later, grade-schoolers need help navigating friendships, middle-schoolers need to be taught how to manage emotional and physical changes, and teenagers need to learn how to handle their first job. God's Word can and will constantly support and fortify all these lessons! While these are just a few examples, remember the best time to teach is when a child is eager to learn, so don't miss out on the primary teachable moments that spring up when your child is ready.

7. **Parents are responsible to provide quiet time for children (Psalm 131:2).** There is no long-term reward for overstimulation. When children's lives are constantly bombarded with activity, noise, screens, and frantic schedules, they miss out on significant parts of their growth and development. A calm, quiet, peaceful home life is of profound benefit to a child's mind and soul. It is where creativity blossoms and imagination soars, and these are the seeds of early intelligence. Quiet is where children can focus best, think their own thoughts, ask questions, and develop trust. Isaiah 30:15 says, "In repentance and rest you will be saved, in quietness and trust is your strength." Peace and quiet is strengthening! Your children can be encouraged to talk to God in the quiet (Psalm 46:10) and to listen to Him as well. With limited screens, they can become interested in quality books, which will facilitate their reading skills.

In addition to quiet, one of the most unusually valuable gifts you can offer your children is boredom. My children came up with their most creative games when there was nothing to do. They entered worlds of their own design, learned to cooperate with one another, role-played, problem-solved, and figured how to implement their ideas. By not planning every moment of their day, I gave them time to be imaginative children. They knew if they complained with "I'm bored," my response would always be, "I have toilets that need cleaning!" Children who are constantly entertained are incredibly disappointed as adults to find so many ordinary, boring days. To train children that an ordinary day is a blessing, and to be grateful for the little things, prepares them to enjoy a simple life.

So how should a parent handle entertainment? It should be rare and special, and more often active rather than passive. While seeing a movie, watching television, or playing on an iPad may be considered fun, those activities are passive and not the best for the use of time. Physically active or mentally engaging activities, such as going to parks or museums, are better. When parents limit or eliminate screens as much as possible, children are more likely to choose reading, building, drawing, running, climbing, exploring, gardening, cooking, creating, crafting, or playing hard.

As mentioned before, researchers are starting to see alarming consequences of screen use in children and teens (Cross, 2017). Sadly, our youngest generations are so immersed in technology that the real world holds no wonder for them. Electronic gadgets are essentially programming their minds to be uninspired by anything else. This is a tragedy, as childhood is meant to be a time of wonder and discovery! Screen saturation also affects intellectual development, and these children are more prone to symptoms of ADHD in a classroom environment because they have a shortened attention span and need constant stimulation (Rosenblatt, 2019). The opportunity to learn through hands-on experiences and direct instruction gets short-circuited because their brains are hungry for the dopamine hit they receive when gaming. In addition, there are relational consequences as these youngsters fail to learn vital skills such as eye contact, listening, conversational skills, patience, and respect.

As you consider these things you as a mom are responsible to provide, do you feel overwhelmed? If you are a mother who has been depending on technology, outings, and entertainment to fill the time, you may be struggling with the concept that fun isn't always the best parenting strategy. However, instead of thinking you are giving up fun times with your children, try to think of the blessing you are giving your children when an ordinary day is full of joy because they have learned to be content. Maybe part of the struggle is that you as a mom do not know how to be content. Are you always avoiding boredom? Do you constantly require entertainment in order be OK? Are you always engaging with screens and social media? What about plain, ordinary days? Do you grumble when things are not stimulating or exciting? Do you get restless? **Because if you can't be at peace in the still and quiet, then your children won't be able to discover the blessing of an ordinary day.**

Even though I am emphasizing your most important job is not as family entertainment coordinator, I still think planning your family's activities is important. However, instead of completely filling the calendar with programmed pursuits, purposefully plan quiet days, chore days, together time, friendship time, and times to teach and train, all with flexibility for the guaranteed interruptions that will come. Spend time with the Lord as you plan, submitting to Him, and drop the guilt. Trying to keep up with the neighbors is not what God has called you to do. Though your mom friends may choose to enroll their children in every lesson and activity in your community, you need to be balanced. Consider the elements of your family dynamic, your budget, and your objective of honoring the Lord to keep your priorities straight when deciding on your children's activities.

Development of your children's character and heart for God happens in the ordinary days when you as a mom are paying close attention and dealing with the issues at hand. You do not have to pay professionals in every stage of your children's lives for them to develop normally. Anyone can direct planned activities, but only you can parent your children.

The Responsibility of a Parent Is to Be a Protector, not a Bystander

The world is so absorbed in consuming images, it has completely forgotten what innocence looks like. There was a day when the innocence of children was an assumed reality, and it was recognized as valuable and worth protecting. But today our culture is so entranced by pornography it has become commonplace and mainstream. As desensitization continues, the horror of pedophilia has also become less shocking. I hope all of you had the privilege of an innocent childhood, but if you had that ripped away from you, you are not alone. In this sex-crazed world, you may feel there is no way to give your children the precious, priceless gift of innocence. Please remember that in Christ, there is always hope (Hebrews 6:17-20). Not only can your past be redeemed by Him (Lamentations 3:57-59), but you can also experience peace, comfort, and new life in Him (2 Corinthians 5:17; 2 Thessalonians 2:16-17). God can equip you to protect your children (Hebrews 13:20).

In Acts 20:28-35, Paul exhorts the believers in Ephesus to be on guard and to shepherd the church of God. He speaks of men who will come and speak "perverse things," drawing away the disciples after them. While we as parents are not necessarily overseers of a church, we are the shepherds of our children. They are our flock, and it is our job to be on alert on their behalf. We are the ones who are given the responsibility to watch over and protect their souls (Hebrews 13:17). **If we do not fight for their innocence, who will?**

Protect your children! Protect their eyes, their ears, and their precious little minds. I know it is getting harder to do this, but it is your job! **The sweetness of childhood can thrive when children are free from wrestling with adult issues, dark realities, and painful broken things.** Innocence doesn't just include sexual purity. It also involves being unscarred from fearful burdens such as violence, horror, war, and crime. Children's minds are not wired to absorb or process most of the movies, television, and video games that adults view today. Nor should children have to deal with their parents' extreme fits of temper or ugly, destructive language. Developmentally, they do not have categories or context for these sights and sounds, so they can quickly become confused and frightened. They could also form a fearful worldview as their ability to trust erodes.

When you do lose your temper or say things you wish you hadn't, or if you find your children viewing something they shouldn't have, deal with it right away. Don't let time pass. Apologize, ask their forgiveness, and let them express how they feel about what they saw or heard. Cover them with prayer and ask the Lord to forgive you in their presence. His grace is sufficient to cover our worst days (2 Corinthians 12:9), thank goodness, so cry out to Him and seek His help in the moments you sense you didn't protect them as you know you should have.

In addition, when sensitive issues arise, you can protect your children by communicating the general idea while leaving out specifics. For example, if a beloved family member is in rehab for an addiction, your children may need to know they won't be able to see that person for a while, but they do not need to know all the circumstances. Be aware of other adults in your children's lives that may give too much information or overburden your children with details. Limit the time they spend with those adults. If your children keep pushing for information, set firm boundaries and get them back to focusing on healthy, childish, and appropriate things for their little minds. Remind them they do not need to worry or try to fix anything and teach them how to pray for the person they are concerned about.

As you protect your children, pray they will value their own innocence. Pray they will be bothered and uncomfortable with inappropriate things. Pray they will have a soft heart and their conscience will be active and strong when they encounter things outside the boundaries you have set for them. Stay close and be observant. If your children act like something is bothering them, draw them out. Ask if they heard, saw, or experienced something that upset them. Encourage your children to share with you when they feel badly about something and not to be afraid. Our children have an adversary who wants them for himself (1 Peter 5:8), and he is not still. By training our children and staying connected, we are protecting them from his schemes. Evil loses its power when it is exposed to the Light (1 John 1:5-10; Ephesians 5:6-17). As long as evil remains in the dark, it will fester and grow into something much more devastating—giving birth to evil ideas, drowning children in shame, creating unhealthy desires, or fostering anger. Fight evil by praying warfare prayers over your children every day (2 Corinthians 10:3-6; Ephesians 6:10-17).

Don't believe the lies that say there is nothing you can do, that children are who they are, and things will be what they will be. Don't settle for simply being a bystander in your children's lives, observing from a distance what they are going through while you stay absorbed in making your own life happen. **Children are not meant to raise themselves. They are not equipped to navigate the adult world or to know what is good, trustworthy, right, or healthy automatically. They are also not developmentally able to handle the black hole of the Internet and social media, where there is no control.** Facebook and its counterparts, like YouTube, Twitter, TikTok, and Snapchat, are purposefully wired to keep the user looking at and searching for the next unlimited thing. (I recommend parents view *The Social Dilemma*, a 2020 documentary that details the psychological manipulation built in to social networks.) Many adults are addicted to these sites, so children certainly cannot be expected to manage their powerful pull. Stand in the gap for them, and say no. Your children are so worth it! Don't abandon your God-given responsibility to protect your children because you fear being overprotective. Honestly, it is far better to overprotect than not to protect enough in this current culture, as long as your protection is not borne out of fear and anxiety. (We will explore more about that in chapter 5.)

For some of you, this teaching about protection may be upsetting. You may not have been protected as a child, and you may be concerned you won't be able to protect your children enough. You may also be afraid that no matter how hard you try, you will miss some things that will hurt them deeply. I understand your fear. I have walked that road, and it is a painful one. Even though I understood the necessity of protecting my children, I missed some critical moments with one of my teenagers. I remember being utterly brokenhearted in the counselor's office as I wept, saying, "How could I have missed this?" Her response was full of compassion as she handed me tissues, sighed, and said, "Oh, Becky, the things we miss." So while my exhortation to you to protect your children is sincere, I also recognize our limitations as mothers. We are not omniscient, nor are we omnipresent. We do not always catch the things right under our nose, much less the sneaky or deceitful things, even when we are fully engaged in parenting the best we can before the Lord. But that is no reason to give up. Being diligent to pray, protect, and pay close attention is vital.

Please understand in the midst of your slip-ups, frustrations, and fears, God is with you. He will not leave you or forsake you (Deuteronomy 31:8)! He can heal (Psalm 30:2), restore (Psalm 80:3), build up what has been torn down (Acts 20:32), forgive (Psalm 86:5), and make even the most broken things right again (Psalm 147:3). Our hope is in Him (Psalm 62:5), not in our own ability to parent well. As you implement these principles and follow through in the best ways you know how, God is there to undergird you with His supernatural power and abundant grace. Keep praying, walking with Him, and obeying with your whole heart. God will catch the things you miss.

Chapter 4 Study Questions

What Is the Responsibility of Parenting?

Day One

1. You, as a parent, are expected to provide for your children. There are the basics, of course: food, shelter, clean water, clothing, education. But what else? Read the following Scriptures. Write down what other things you need to provide for your children as implied in these verses:

   a. Psalm 4:8 ______________________________

   ____

   b. Hebrews 12:11 ______________________________

   ____

   c. Proverbs 27:17 ______________________________

   ____

   d. Colossians 3:23-24 ______________________________

   ____

   e. Proverbs 1:5 ______________________________

   ____

   f. Psalm 131:2 ______________________________

   ____

   g. Isaiah 30:15; 32:17 ______________________________

   ____

h. Psalm 90:17 ______________________________

____

2. God is our perfect Father. Oftentimes, He provides things for us we don't necessarily like or appreciate. For example, God provides trials to teach us to trust Him. He provides times of waiting to teach us patience and perseverance. He provides challenging people in our lives to teach us how to forgive. He provides unexpected difficulties for us to grow in faith. As you provide what your children need, as opposed to what they want, you won't always be adored for it, and your decisions won't necessarily be popular. But when you are doing what is best for your children, the fruit of character will eventually grow. That will be far more valuable than being liked for a moment. Look up these verses, and write down how they encourage you to endure in providing what is right and best for your children, as opposed to what is easy and popular:

   a. Galatians 6:9-10 ______________________________

   ____

   b. Romans 5:1-5 ______________________________

   ____

   c. Hebrews 10:35-36 ______________________________

   ____

   d. James 1:1-5 ______________________________

   ____

Day Two

1. Entertaining activities are not necessarily wrong. However, our current culture teaches us to fill our lives with constant activity to the point of having no quiet, no time for reflective thought, and no time to enjoy the simple things. With the advent of the smartphone, we now have constant stimulation available, and we are in great danger of passing this type of restless living on to our children. Our children do not have the developmental capacity to separate what is important from what is meaningless, fragmented activity. There is an enormous amount of growth and potential, as well as mental and emotional health, lost by children constantly interacting with screens.

    a. You are called to be more than an entertainer or activity coordinator for your children. You are called to be the best parent you can be, even if that means going against the cultural norms to do what is best for your children. What are some boundaries you have set for yourself and your family regarding entertainment, screens, and activities? (If you haven't made any, now would be a good time!) __________

    ____

    ____

    ____

    ____

    b. Write out Ephesians 5:15-17. ______________________

    ____

    ____

    ____

c. Paul said the days are evil, and we must be diligent to fight evil and keep it out of our homes. But when it comes to choosing activities for our kids, sometimes only avoiding evil isn't enough. Sometimes we can make a mistake of choosing the good or mediocre over the best. Your children may have good games on their iPad and watch only appropriate TV shows, but it may be even better for them to be outside, doing a constructive activity, or doing chores! List some non-screen activities your children can participate in to develop in the following ways:

1) Problem-solving______________________________

____

____

2) Hand and eye coordination______________________

____

____

3) Fine motor skills ______________________________

____

____

4) Concentration_________________________________

____

____

5) Language development _________________________

____

____

6) Physical strength, coordination ____________________

____

____

7) Social and communication skills ____________________

____

____

8) Creativity ____________________________________

____

____

2. Plan and implement! Give your children as much opportunity to learn the above things as you can, and embrace your responsibility to train, provide, and plan! Read the following verses, and apply them to your job as a parent:

   a. Matthew 5:16 ________________________________

   ____

   b. 1 Corinthians 15:58 ___________________________

   ____

   c. Ephesians 2:10 _______________________________

   ____

   d. 2 Thessalonians 2:16-17 _______________________

   ____

Day Three

1. Look up the following verses, and write down how God protects:

   a. Psalm 61:1-4 ______________________________

   ____

   b. 2 Thessalonians 3:3 ______________________________

   ____

   c. 1 Peter 1:3-5 ______________________________

   ____

2. As a small child, did you feel protected? ________ If not, what were you exposed to that was upsetting? __________________

   ____

   Were you ever able to speak to your parents about it? Was it ever resolved? Or do you still feel the pain of that time? _____

   ____

   ____

   ____

   Talk to the Lord about that now, and speak to a wiser, older sister in Christ who can help you with those memories that may be frightening, overwhelming, or raw. Let the Lord heal you in the deep places.

3. God has blessed us as moms with a strong drive to protect our children. Sometimes that need to protect can be so overwhelming we feel like sheltering them from everything.

Unfortunately, that isn't possible. The truth is, we need to do our best to protect and then trust God is also invested in protecting our children. We do not need to allow our natural desire to shelter our children to consume us with fear. Read the following verses, and explain how they encourage you to trust God with your children:

a. Psalm 9:9-10 ______________________________

____

b. Psalm 28:6-9 ______________________________

____

c. Psalm 37:3-6 ______________________________

____

d. Psalm 56:3-4 ______________________________

____

e. Proverbs 3:5-6______________________________

____

f. Proverbs 29:2 ______________________________

____

g. Isaiah 26:3-4 ______________________________

____

Day Four

1. What should we protect our children from? Refer to the chapter, and look up Ephesians 5:3-5, Galatians 5:19-21, and Colossians 3:5-10 to help you answer this question. ____________

   ____

   ____

   ____

   ____

   ____

2. List some practical things you have implemented—or would like to implement—in your home and family life that protect your children from being exposed to evil:

   ____

   ____

   ____

3. Since our children will often be away from us, we cannot always protect them. Look up the following verses. How can you implement these truths in your family life so that your children learn to take an active part in protecting themselves?

   a. 1 John 5:21 ______________________________

      ____

   b. 2 Peter 3:17-18 ______________________________

      ____

c. 1 Timothy 6:20-21 ________________________________

____

d. Philippians 4:6-9 ________________________________

____

e. 2 Timothy 2:22-26 ________________________________

____

f. 1 Corinthians 6:18 ________________________________

____

4. As you think about your children's lives and all they are involved in and exposed to, what are your biggest concerns right now about protecting them? ____________________________

____

____

What practical steps can you take as a parent to help make sure they are protected even with these concerns? __________

____

____

____

Day Five

1. Sometimes there is confusion about what we need to protect our children from. Parents with good intentions may be protecting when they need to be training. For example, we should not necessarily be protecting our children from the following:

a. Getting their feelings hurt—When your children get their feelings hurt, what can you teach them? How is it a character-building opportunity (Matthew 5:38-45)? ___________

____

____

____

b. Being told they are wrong—When your children are told they are wrong, by either you or another adult, what is the biblical lesson for them? How do you encourage them to handle this? What do you need them to understand (1 Peter 5:5; 2 Timothy 2:24-26)? ___________________________

____

____

____

c. Being treated unfairly—It's frustrating, but it happens. Unfairness is a reality in this world. How do you teach, train, and encourage when this happens to your children? What do you want them to learn (Romans 12:14-21)? ________

____

____

____

d. Losing in a contest—(Hint: More character building can happen from losing than from winning.) How do you coach, encourage, and train your children when they don't win? What lessons can they learn through this disappointment (1 Corinthians 9:24-27; 1 John 5:4-5)? ________________

____

____

____

e. Failing—It is hard to fail personally and even more difficult to watch your children fail. But failing is part of growing up and necessary to building character. How a person handles failure is a testimony to others. What do you say during these teachable moments? How do you encourage your children (1 Corinthians 13:8a; Proverbs 15:22; 1 Kings 2:3)? ______________________________

____

____

____

f. Making mistakes—If you do your children's homework for them or take over every time something is too hard, what are you teaching your children? ____________________

____

____

What do you want your children to learn from their mistakes (James 1:12; 1 Corinthians 15:58; Philippians 3:15)?

____

____

____

2. A balanced parent recognizes the difference between biblical, wise protection and overprotection. For example, while you may expect your children to get their feelings hurt sometimes, you can also choose to limit the time they spend with those who always act hurtful toward them. What are some other

examples you can think of that require balance in the area of protection? ____

____

____

Were your parents balanced? ________ If not, would you call them overprotective or careless?________________________

____

What was the result of that imbalance in your life, especially regarding the development of your character? ____________

____

____

____

Be willing to trust the Lord with your childhood. Ask Him to help you forgive your parents if they were too extreme one way or the other. Seek Him for ways to be more balanced in the way you protect your own children today.

Chapter 5

What Is the Proper Perspective on Parenting?

Anyone who is a student of the Bible has learned that courage is a common theme. I have often tried to imagine what it must have been like when David faced Goliath (1 Samuel 17); Daniel entered the lion's den (Daniel 6); Shadrach, Meshach, and Abednego confronted the fiery furnace (Daniel 3); and Paul and Silas encountered the prison cell (Acts 16). When we face great difficulties, our heroes of the faith stand out as wonderful examples of courage who were dependent on God during the most fearful and desperate of times, willing to go the distance for their beliefs. I revere and remain in awe of such overcoming faith.

The Biblical Perspective on Parenting Is Courageous, not Cultural

When I consider what it means to be courageous as a mom, I remember my own mother and her willingness to stand for us without backing down, no matter the adversary. I never doubted I was loved, as her constant presence and protection was guaranteed in difficult situations. I wondered throughout my growing up years if I would have the same kind of courage when I became a mother. I have found courage is given to me by God as a protective instinct that came into my life the moment my children were born.

My children didn't always appreciate it when I said no to certain movies and television shows, when I limited video games, when I refused to let them spend the night away from home at times, when I removed them from certain schools, discouraged certain friendships, or didn't let them have a phone until high school. I confronted teachers about certain reading material, always met the parents of their friends, kept them in church activities, and monitored all influences that entered their lives. My neighbors mocked me for quite a few of these choices, but I didn't mind. All I really cared about was my children's safety—and their knowledge and love for Jesus with all their heart, soul, mind, and strength. My children had great childhoods! They did all kinds of fun things, had adventures, enjoyed great friendships, played sports and instruments, got great educations, and loved life. But the people outside my family were never the ones that dictated how our time was spent and our hearts were focused. Joshua 1:9 says, "Have I not commanded you? Be strong and courageous! Do not tremble or be dismayed, for the Lord your God is with you wherever you go." While it may be challenging at times to make choices for your children that go against the culture, it is also empowering to know that obeying God is best and produces lasting character in the long run.

Picture a large river covered with rafts full of people who are slowly drifting along with the current. On the shore, there are occasional signs posted: "Warning: 500-foot waterfall ahead, DANGER." But the people in the rafts respond to the signs saying, "Well, I never heard of anyone falling over that waterfall," or "Those signs are really old and don't apply anymore," or "I'm sure that's an exaggeration," or "I heard someone built a dam," or "There will be plenty of time to get out of the raft if it is true." Then others standing on the riverbank are holding a sign, yelling about the danger, weeping, and saying their whole family died going over the waterfall! A mom chooses to believe those people, gets into the water with her children, and starts swimming against the current, in between all those rafts, going in the opposite direction. When people in the rafts ask what she is doing, the mother says, "I am choosing to save my child!" "Hey," they say, "get back in my raft! It's comfortable! It's fun! It's so much easier than swimming! Why would anyone want to do such a thing?" But this one courageous mom, determined not to go over the falls, keeps swimming, taking her children in the opposite direction with very few people choosing to do likewise.

This culture is eating young people alive. The suicide rates have increased 57% for people ages ten to 24 since 2007 (Brueck, 2020). Our children are heading over the falls in droves. Like Dory in *Finding Nemo*, I say to you mothers, "Just keep swimming." **When you are doing what is right by your children, there is rest and reward ahead. It is impossible to calculate the immense impact you are having as a parent when you choose to be a courageous Christ-follower.** Obeying God's Word is not necessarily going to be popular, or applauded, so just accept this fact ahead of time. Parenting according to the Bible will be odd, antiquated, extreme, or even foolish to many of the people in your life. Set your heart on Jesus, and He will help you to see the eternal reasons why. Then you will be just fine. You may even bring some other moms along with you!

Children need courageous parents who can stand on God's truth against a hostile world. This requires putting on the armor of God daily for the battle against evil (Ephesians 6:10-18). God is with you and will fight for you as you depend on Him for wisdom and pour into your children. Remember, "God has not given us a spirit of timidity, but of power and love and discipline" (2 Timothy 1:7).

Consider Daniel, who was raised in Judah during a time when the majority of his people were worshipping idols, drowning in sexual sin, rebelling against God, and mocking His prophets. When the nation was overthrown by Babylon and the people taken captive, Daniel was also seized. But unlike those around him, Daniel's life was characterized by an unwavering commitment to God and a determination to obey Him (Daniel 1:8-9, 19-20). How did he become such a man of conviction? I imagine he had faithful, courageous parents who raised him according to God's Word even when no one else was doing so. They taught him God's precepts, and Daniel clung to them as a teenager in the court of a corrupt king. God blessed Daniel and used him mightily for decades in the kingdom of Babylon. He grew up to be a prophet that was respected and revered. When you obey the Lord in your responsibilities as mother, you have no idea what challenges your children may face that you are preparing them for. Yes, it takes courage, sacrifice, and time. But it is so worth it!

My oldest daughter graduated from her public high school with honors. She had been an excellent student, and her teachers and school counselors expected her to apply to ivy league colleges and universities. She chose a small private Christian college instead. They did not understand and tried to persuade her differently. As graduation approached, I was praying for direction because my husband was between jobs and we did not have the money for her to go to college, even though she had been accepted and had received a scholarship. As I prayed, the Lord impressed upon me that I was to call the missions pastor at our church. I asked that pastor if he knew of any missions opportunities for our daughter. He shared that he had just received a request from a missionary for a nanny. Our daughter already had a heart for missions, and through this God called her to another country to care for this child instead of heading off to college like all her peers. Her teachers and school counselors were even more confused by that decision, and communicated we were wrong in encouraging her choice. Though it was challenging, God used that time to grow her and teach her important things about herself and His plan for her life. It was an odd choice to many, even one that was mocked, but it was the right choice, and she had the courage to obey the Lord and trust His plan.

So do what is right and best for your child without flinching. Take your instruction from the Lord, not from the culture, without fear (Psalm 56:11). Stand up to the lies and deception of the enemy and communicate without timidity who God calls you to be (Romans 1:16-17). Be willing to humble yourself and take responsibility for your own wrongdoings. Be willing to demonstrate in front of your children your own need for God (1 Peter 5:6-9). All of this takes courage, and God will give it to you in your time of need!

The current cultural agenda for your children undermines the biblical definition of family, marriage, gender, sexuality, and morality. It redefines freedom as "free to do whatever I want without consequence." It does not encourage taking responsibility for one's own behavior, vilifies the Bible, and rejects it as a reliable source for instruction for life. It denies the existence and power of the God of the Bible. It believes that fulfillment is found in wealth, status, talent, experiences, and feelings. It worships media and entertainment in all its forms, encourages exposing children to unhealthy and immoral messages and images, and discourages innocence. While the culture in general feigns a mock disgust and disapproval of the growing worldwide industry of sex slavery, it does nothing to stand firm against pornography, which is the very root of its existence.

So how are we supposed to swim against such a powerful current? Pray, pray, then pray some more (1 Thessalonians 5:17). Know God's Word by studying it for yourself (2 Timothy 2:15) then teaching it to your children all the time. Arrange your life to be present with your children as much as possible so that you are the primary influence in their lives. Be intentional, monitoring all influences and information from media, friends, technology, teachers, babysitters, and reading materials. Take a stand on truth; don't compromise (Colossians 1:21-23)! Keep your heart clean (Proverbs 4:23). Stand firm and follow through (Ephesians 6:13). Put your children's welfare above your own popularity and comfort. Resist overcommitting yourself and getting too busy. Check the temptation to disengage, check out, unplug, or escape from parenting. Eighteen years seems like a long time when you are standing at the beginning, holding an infant in your arms. But you will have a different perspective when you look back at the end of those days of primary influence. That season doesn't seem long at all. While the days may seem long, the years are short. Seize the day!

The Biblical Perspective on Parenting Is Trusting, not Anxious

After reading about all the ways the culture is pushing against the Christian parent while pulling at kids to walk on the wider road of destruction, you may feel anxious. As a matter of fact, thinking about all that is required to teach, train, disciple, protect, provide, correct, and courageously stand in the gap may have you curled up right now in the fetal position wishing you had never picked up this study. You may already be struggling with anxiety over so many things that the principles presented here tip the scales, creating an overwhelming sense of inadequacy. If so, please stop and take a deep breath.

While this all is a lot to absorb, it is not up to you alone. There is a wonderful verse tucked in 1 Thessalonians 5:24 that says, "Faithful is He who calls you, and He also will bring it to pass." Your God is all-powerful (Psalm 62:11)! He can teach you (Psalm 32:8), guide you (John 16:13), give you help (Isaiah 41:10), and provide understanding (2 Timothy 2:7). God speaks to your heart (John 14:26), offers wisdom (Proverb 2:6), and encourages you (Romans 15:5-6) every day on this journey. He has not left you alone to manage motherhood. He is vitally interested in and concerned about the growth and wellbeing of your children—even more than you are! He wants them to be His children more than anything! **All this happens one day at a time, as you do life as a mom, keeping your eyes and ears open, spending time in the Word and in prayer, and dealing with your own sin.** Because even though knowing what your job is as a parent is critically important, knowing how you will do it is remarkably simple—not necessarily easy, but simple: Depend on the Lord, know His Word, ask for His help, and rejoice that He is "… able to do far more abundantly beyond all that we ask or think, according to the power that works within us" (Ephesians 3:20)!

I am tremendously proud of my children. They have grown into remarkable adults, and I am in awe of their wisdom, love for the Lord, and persevering character. But I want you to know it is only by God's incredible grace they are who they are. There were years when I had no idea if they were going to walk with God, and the choices they were making broke my heart. I spent hours weeping on my knees, interceding for them, as they ran hard from Jesus as teens. If you are a hurting mom right now, I know the way you feel. My family walked a very broken road, and I will never forget the despair of not knowing when or if they were going to choose to come back to Jesus.

I do not write this parenting study because I think I did the parenting thing so well. Far from it! I know many godly women who were far better at mothering than I was. Oh friend, I lost my temper. I said things I wish I had never said and did things I wish I could take back. I have plenty of regrets. I got tired, overwhelmed, and stressed, so often reacting instead of responding in patience and kindness. I was human, imperfect and flawed in every way. However, I understood these basic principles of parenting, and I loved my children ferociously, apologized often, asked their forgiveness, and leaned hard into Jesus through it all, seeking Him in His Word. Nonetheless, their lives now are not a testament to me. Any one of them could have focused on my mistakes, refused to forgive me, and chosen to let their resentment overrule Christ's grace in their lives. No, their love for God now is a testament to the miraculous power of the saving Gospel of Jesus Christ. The fact my adult children walk with God is because He has done amazing things in their hearts, opened their eyes to His truth, and answered prayer. The reason I write to you mothers is because I know how much you can trust the King of Kings and Lord of Lords! He is so faithful, and He hears every prayer! **He is always—*always*—at work in your children, even if you do not see it. God has a plan for them that is beautiful in spite of the many times we stumble and fall as moms. And the things we miss? He sees them, and His plan is sufficient to rescue them and bring them back to Himself.**

If we put our eyes on ourselves or on the broken world around us, we will be controlled by fear. But the truth is our God can do amazing things. Even if you feel lost, inadequate, or like a complete failure, you can trust God! You can trust Him in the good times and bad. You can trust Him when the worst thing you could ever imagine happens to your children. You can trust Him when they defy you, turn their back on truth, lie to you, or carry on in secret sin. As you set your heart on Jesus, obeying and following Him, trust God hears your prayers (Psalm 34:4); trust He is doing a mighty work you cannot see in the depths of your children's hearts (Psalm 72:18); trust He can convict and change the hardest of hearts (John 16:8); trust He will shepherd you and show you what to do when you seek His face and walk in obedience.

There are many things my husband and I did as parents because God directed us clearly when we were praying for wisdom and guidance. Some of those things didn't make any sense to family and friends, but the direction was so clear from the Lord, we had to obey. That obedience showed us without a doubt God's will is best. God showed us the way to go so that our children were also kept on His desired path for them. God loves your children! He wants them to love Him and follow Him. His will for them may take them down a rocky, uncertain road, but hold on: "Trust in the Lord with all your heart And do not lean on your own understanding. In all your ways acknowledge Him, And He will make your paths straight" (Proverbs 3:5-6). God can see what you cannot, and you can trust Him to be the God He promises to be: faithful (Psalm 91:4), loving (Psalm 25:10), merciful (Psalm 86:15), redeeming (Psalm 34:22), victorious (Psalm 45:3-4), restoring (Malachi 4:6), healing (Acts 10:38), patient (2 Peter 3:9), and full of grace (1 Peter 5:10). Your faith and trust in the Lord Jesus will not be in vain! You may have to wait until you see a child turn back to Him. My own father turned to Jesus at age 91! So you can certainly believe nothing is impossible with God (Luke 18:27).

Familiar verses in Philippians 4:6-7 tell us: "Be anxious for nothing, but in everything by prayer and supplication with thanksgiving let your requests be made known to God. And the peace of God, which surpasses all comprehension, will guard your hearts and your minds in Christ Jesus." God does not want us to be anxious. He wants to replace every anxious thought and feeling with His supernatural peace. There is a reason for that. Anxiety can be destructive to relationships.

Fear and anxiety are complex struggles. The mom who is afraid and worried usually does not recognize these emotions as unhealthy for her children. This is in contrast to other emotions. For example, mothers oftentimes understand the hurtful and destructive nature of their anger; therefore, far more moms visit a counselor's office for help managing their anger than reach out for help overcoming their fear. Yes, anger is destructive, but fear is equally so. And fear can be the root of anger. Fear is a powerful, overwhelming emotion. Fear is helpful in situations of extreme danger, of course, as it sets off a chain of adrenaline-pumping reactions in our bodies that aid us in fighting or fleeing a problem. But some people get stuck in a cycle of overreacting out of chronic fear and anxiety to normal life circumstances, wearing themselves out with an adrenaline-induced panic that does not help or change anything. Eventually the brain gets exhausted, and depression may follow.

My mother was a very anxious person, and so many of my memories are of her on the edge of panic. I had an angry alcoholic father who made life difficult for her. In light of my mother's challenging marriage, she was a remarkably strong, godly, loving mom. Honestly, I am in awe of all she did so well, and I am grateful I was raised by her. But the truth is, looking back, her anxiety affected me just as negatively as my dad's anger. Mom tended to always anticipate and then believe in negative results, making decisions based on the fear of what might happen instead of recognizing the good things around her. Her constant habit of imagining the worst outcomes caused her to be uptight even when I was making good choices. It was confusing as a youngster to be doing everything I possibly could to please my mom and still only receive a fearful, untrusting, or negative response in return. This baffled me because while I knew she loved the Lord, I didn't see her trusting Him. Peace was simply an unknown entity in my home growing up.

Fast forward to my own parenting journey. In 2005 my husband and I felt called to adopt a child. After traveling to the other side of the world, we picked up a complete stranger and brought him home. We had prayed for over a year about this decision, and God had clearly directed us. But from the moment I became his mom, I was hit with the most overwhelming fear I had ever experienced. This six-year-old child had been severely neglected and abused. He had no understanding of family, and no concept of attachment. He had only experienced surviving by his wits. While he had significant developmental delays, he was also incredibly clever. His street smarts were very useful for surviving starvation, extreme cold, abuse, and loneliness. However, his learning experiences were not at all applicable to a loving, safe home. In other words, this boy's hard-earned skills, worldview, and ways of coping simply didn't translate into his new life as our son. I wasn't raising a child who saw me as a loving provider of help and happiness, but rather a threat to be avoided and an obstacle to outmaneuver. He wanted nothing to do with me. God used this little boy to break me of my fear and teach me trust.

Learning how to raise this complicated stranger was the first time I found myself completely out of my element as a mother. I literally had no idea what to do, and it scared me to death. I was sure this new son was going to ruin our family. I tried everything, and nothing that had worked with my other three children worked for him. His hostility was palpable and constant. I spun myself into an exhausted frenzy trying to deal with his bizarre actions and reactions and to keep him from following his impulses, which were unhealthy to say the least and downright scary to say the most. It took me several years of reading every book, going to every counselor, and praying my heart out to realize the only thing left to do was let go of my fear and anxiety. Humbling myself, I had to admit many of my son's complex issues were beyond my skills to help. If I didn't let God have him, the stress was going to kill me, literally. During this anxious period I developed high blood pressure, sleep issues, chronic pain, and clinical depression.

All that time, God wanted me to understand He was in control, and He had a perfect plan. But because of my lack of trust, I wasn't able to listen. In complete surrender, choosing to place my hurting son completely in God's hands, my heart began to change. I began to see both him and myself differently. I became more teachable about what needed to be done and how God's plan might be completely different than mine. I decided to trust God with all the possible outcomes, and I stopped letting this needy and broken little boy have the power over my day, my attitude, and my actions. I realized I could be completely fulfilled in Jesus even if my son never changed, and the freedom of that truth was remarkable. In the face of his anger, I learned to calm down, to trust God, and to let His Holy Spirit do the necessary work in both of us. Even so, this child's behavior didn't improve. In fact, it got worse. But my heart was able to trust God would love him, lead him, and save him. And He did, showing me exactly what steps to take because I was finally listening. **Fear is our enemy. It doesn't make things better but rather twists our perspective, blocks our peace, and keeps us from hearing God's voice. God is bigger than our fears, and His plans can be trusted.**

When a mother parents out of anxiety, there are different possible outcomes. The compliant child, desperate to make Mom happy and calm her down, will do absolutely anything she says without argument or complaint. If the anxious parent is also a controlling parent, which usually goes hand in hand, the pleasing child might bend to her will in every detail of life, not learning to think or make decisions for herself. This can result in a young adult going out into the world not having any idea who she is, not having developed her own faith, handicapped by her inability to trust her own mind.

When that anxious parent is in charge of the strong-willed child, a different kind of damage occurs. Not appreciating the constant feeling of projected fear, this child might tend to push back to prove to Mom there is nothing to be afraid of, desperately trying to find his own way and think for himself without being controlled by her anxious perspective. The harder the worried parent tries to enforce controls on the willful child out of fear, the harder that child will rebel and question the validity of the parent's claims of faith. This child will think: If what you say is true, why are you so scared?

In Christ, we do not need to fear. God's Word repeats the command "fear not" over one hundred times because God's intention is for us to be free from fear. If God is God and His Word is true, we can stand on that truth unwavering and calm. With our eyes on Him, we can be firm and confident, giving consequences or boundaries, yet still full of peace and love. **Our children need to know we believe the best about them, we trust God to do a mighty work in them, and we trust the power of the principles we try to teach them every day.** Do we really believe, "the truth will set you free" (John 8:32)? Are we confident "[God] is able also to save forever those who come to God through Him" (Hebrews 7:25)? Are we sure the "word of God is living and active" (Hebrews 4:12)? Do we understand God's Word does not return to Him empty, but always accomplishes what He desires (Isaiah 55:11)? If we do, then we do not need to put our faith in worst possible outcomes! We can instead set our hearts and minds on the amazing things we are trusting God to do to reach and save our children. God only gives grace for today. We do not have grace for the imagined possible disasters of tomorrow. Trust God for the difficulties of today and walk through those with Him while leaving the unknown up to Him as well (Psalm 9:10; 37:5-9; 56:3-4).

To review, parenting out of fear creates an environment of stress for your children. It causes you as a mom to react instead of respond, instigating drama and a heightened emotional environment in the home. Parenting out of fear is the opposite of trust. Trust will create an atmosphere of rest and peace in which children can grow healthy and strong. The fearful parent projects the worst possible outcome, which sets children up for negative expectations. Fear is often communicated in anger, creating either an insecure child who is a slave of approval or a defiant child who sets out to prove there is nothing to fear. When decisions are made out of fear rather than out of wisdom, grace, and truth, they will not be the best decisions. Oddly enough, fear teaches God cannot be trusted and often ends up creating the very thing the parent feared the most.

Fear has its own presence, just like anger does. It is loud and clear, palpable, and changes the atmosphere of the home. People who are ruled by anxiety tend to be uptight, tense, defensive, and reactive. Fear is also a great distractor, causing us to focus on what we are afraid of rather than obedience, relationships, opportunities, gratitude, peace, and joy. **A walk with God should be characterized by a restful spirit, and this speaks to our family and the world around us of God's work in our lives almost more than anything else (Isaiah 30:15).** If you struggle with fear, God can deliver you from it! It is not a disease without a cure. With each step you take to focus your mind on the Lord, His truth, His love, and His saving Gospel, you move away from the thoughts that spin you up into the wilderness of fear. Choosing to trust God instead of your feelings will lead you out of those scary places and into a place of peace where you can offer your children safety, balance, and a healthy worldview. Renewing your mind to the wonderful plans God has for you will help you see the praiseworthy and beautiful things ahead.

While living free from fear is the desire of our hearts, it doesn't mean experiencing fear is unusual or should be condemned. Don't believe the lie that God is not with you if you are afraid. We all experience the raw, uncomfortable, and overwhelming emotion of fear. Cry out to the Lord in those moments. Kneel before Him, and remember the Psalmist's words, "When I am afraid, I will put my trust in You. In God, whose word I praise, in God I have put my trust; I shall not be afraid. What can mere mortals do to me?" (Psalm 56:3-4). God can deliver you, and by seeking Him, you will go deeper into a sweet relationship with Him that lifts you above the anxiety crashing over you. God will hear your cries for help; He is not deaf to your needs (Psalm 40:1-3). He understands why you are afraid and has compassion on your mother's heart. Take it to Jesus. He can bear it (Matthew 11:28-30), and He can deliver you to a new place, where there is comfort, hope, and peace for your trembling soul.

Chapter 5 Study Questions

What Is the Proper Perspective on Parenting?

Day One

1. Read Joshua 1:9.
2. Define the following:
   a. Strong ______________________________
   ____
   b. Courageous ______________________________
   ____
   c. Dismayed ______________________________
   ____
3. Realistically speaking, Joshua had a lot to be dismayed about. He was taking one million nomadic men, women, and children into a land inhabited by well-armed giants in fortified cities. He was going to take over this land because God said so. At that time God also said to Joshua, "Do not tremble"! Why would God say that to Joshua? Doesn't he have the right to be terrified?

____
____
____

4. As a Christian parent, what kinds of things make you tremble?____

   ____

5. Joshua's courage was proven through his obedience to God. He succeeded in leading the people of Israel into the promise land, and they were established there and conquered their enemies. Joshua did what he was told, and God did what He promised He would do if his people obeyed. Even if there are things that seem overwhelming about parenting and you can't understand how it will all work out, how can you be courageous every day? ______________________________

   ____

   ____

   ____

6. Do you have to do God's part? _______ Is it a relief to know you are simply called to do your part, and He will take care of the rest? ____

   Will you trust Him then to do His part, even if you can't see the how, what, when, or where of His plan? _________________

   ____

   ____

Day Two

It seems like the culture is against us as Christians. The truth is, there have always been and will always be cultural battles. They rage on in every part of the world between ethnicities, religions, political parties, and economic classes. It is easy to get distracted and think these cultural battles are the same as spiritual warfare. Let's look at what spiritual warfare is so that we don't get focused on the wrong enemy.

1. Who is our adversary? (1 Peter 5:8) ____________________

   ____

2. What is he like? (John 8:44; 10:10; Acts 13:10; Ephesians 2:1-3)

   ____

   ____

3. What is his dominion like? (Acts 26:18; Jude 1:6-7; Colossians 1:13; Psalm 11:5-6; Revelation 21:8) ____________________

   ____

   ____

4. How are we supposed to battle effectively against him? (2 Corinthians 10:3-6; Ephesians 6:10-17; Zechariah 4:6) ________

   ____

5. Who is driving the culture we live in, and why is there so much hostility toward the Word of God and His truth? __________

   ____

   ____

6. If we try to picture ourselves battling the world or the culture, our enemy becomes vague and awfully overwhelming, doesn't it? But if we understand we battle an enemy who is a liar, then we know we can be effective in our fight against him by knowing and walking in the truth. Knowing this, we can recognize the enemy when he shows up. We can know how to keep his lies out of our hearts, minds, and homes, and we can encourage our children to walk in truth. Write out 1 John 1:5-10:

Day Three

1. Read Isaiah 41:10. Do you really believe God is *with* you? (Don't just put down the "right" answer. Stop and think about what you really believe as reflected by your thoughts, feelings, and actions.)

2. When you find yourself living anxiously, can you recognize you are acting like God is not with you? ________ Just as your children do not need to be anxious, looking about for help and comfort when you are present, you do not need to be anxious while in God's presence, which because of Christ's blood is all the time.

3. God says He will strengthen you and help you. When do you feel like you need the most strength and help as a mom? ___

___

___

___

4. What do you think it means for God to "uphold you" with His "righteous right hand," and when do you think you would be wise to ask Him to do so? ___

___

___

___

5. Write Isaiah 41:10 and memorize it. Believe God's Word and begin to ask Him for strength and help. Request for Him to uphold you when you need it. He is faithful. He will hear you, and He will be with you. You are not alone, and He is not asking you to obey Him without His presence and help.

___

___

___

Day Four

1. Read Isaiah 30:15.

2. Define the following:

   a. Rest ____

   ____

   b. Quietness ____

   ____

   c. Trust ____

   ____

3. We often associate salvation with repentance, but we don't necessarily link salvation with rest. But God says, "In repentance and rest you will be saved." What do you think this means?

   ____

   ____

   ____

4. Do you ever remain anxious about your sin after repenting? ________ Your anxiety is a sign of unbelief—you do not trust God has forgiven you and cleansed you from your sin (1 John 1:9). Receiving God's forgiveness brings rest and peace to your soul. There can be no benefit from His forgiveness if you refuse to forgive yourself. By not accepting God's forgiveness, you give Satan an open door to assault you with shame and condemnation. Repent, receive God's forgiveness as a gift, and rest.

5. How do you think we can find strength in quietness and trust? ____

____

____

6. Think about a child's trust in her father as she jumps off a diving board into his arms, even though she cannot swim. Her trust allows her to have fun, even though without her daddy she would be in peril. In her father's presence there is joy and laughter where without him there would be panic and danger. Her heart is calm because she has no doubt her dad will catch her. Where in your life are you lacking quietness in your spirit and trust in your Savior, resulting in fear? Ask the Lord to help you recognize fear in your own heart so that you can turn from it and choose to trust Him instead. Write down what He brings to your attention and ask Him to remove those fears from your heart and replace them with His peace. ____________________

____

____

____

____

Day Five

1. Read Proverbs 3:5-8.

   a. Are you trusting in the Lord with *all* your heart? ________ Ask Him to show what areas of your heart are not fully trusting Him right now. What are they? ________________

   ____

Ask God to help you trust in those things.

b. In what areas might you be leaning on your own opinions or experiences or understanding rather than the truth of God's Word? ____

____

Ask God to help you let go of your right to understand before you fully trust. As you fully trust, He will give you His perspective, and you will continue to grow into more and more understanding. (Remember the child on the diving board? She doesn't necessarily understand how her dad is strong enough to catch her, or how he is able to swim, or why she can trust him to keep her safe. She just trusts—and experiences joy.)

2. Read Matthew 6:25-34.

   a. Does worry add to your life or take away from it?________

   ____

   b. Are you more valuable to God than birds or lilies? _______

   ____

   c. While you may not spend a lot of time worried about your next meal or having something to wear, there are plenty of things you may worry about that eat up emotional and mental energy. God wants us to use our strength for other things.

d. What is outside your control or responsibility that you find yourself worrying about? ______________________________

____

Let go of what is outside your control and responsibility.

e. What is within your control or responsibility that you find yourself worrying about? ______________________________

Ask for wisdom from the Lord, search His Word, and seek counsel for the things that concern you that are your responsibilities, and then actively pray and obey *instead of* worrying.

3. Answer these questions:

a. What kind of person do you enjoy spending time with?

- A chronically anxious, uptight worrier? ______________
- A peaceful, loving, trusting soul____________________

b. What kind of person was Jesus?______________________

c. Which kind of person do you think your children will enjoy spending time with? ______________________________

____

d. Look at chapter 5 and its study guide for the biblical references regarding fear and trust. Which of these Scriptures encourage you the most as you battle anxiety?__________

____

____

Choose one, and write it out here, committing it to memory this week. ______________________________________

____

____

____

Chapter 6

What Is the Heart of Parenting?

In the first five chapters of this study, I have used the word "grace" many times. There are many Christian books about "grace-based parenting," and they are excellent resources. However, there is confusion on this topic. Even though grace-based parenting is biblical parenting, the concept of grace itself is often misunderstood and even abused. This is hardly a new area for confusion. Paul addressed the Romans about their abuse of grace many times in his letter to them: "What shall we say then? Are we to continue in sin so that grace may increase? Far from it! How shall we who died to sin still live in it?" (Romans 6:1-2). Let's dive into the true meaning of being a grace-filled parent and explore how grace should apply to all we do as believers.

The Heart of Parenting Is Grace-Filled, not Law-Filled

Grace is not permissiveness. Grace is not, "Sure! You can do whatever you want because God gives grace!" That is not biblical. What is the grace of God exactly? It is the full forgiveness and acceptance of God which came to us at a very high price. We walk and live in grace every day as saved believers because Jesus paid the ultimate price for our sin (Romans 5:8-9). Our sin cost Him everything, causing His blood to flow to the point of death. If Jesus had not paid that price, the payment for our sin would be our own eternal death (Romans 6:23).

We cannot appreciate the seriousness of our sin and our complete inadequacy to save ourselves without the Law revealing to us our lack. All of us have tried to overcome a besetting sin in our lives in our own power. We have given our best efforts not to gossip, to be unselfish, or to control our temper and still found ourselves incapable of change. Standing in the light of the truth, God calls us to see our helplessness to reach His holy standard apart from Jesus' sacrifice on our behalf. When we come to Jesus, we receive salvation by grace through faith (Ephesians 2:8-9) because we finally realize we are unable to keep the Law perfectly in our own strength. Therefore, we have accepted we truly are lost apart from Christ (Romans 7:21-25). We must understand we are imperfect and experience conviction over our sin in order to seek Christ in the first place and turn to Him for salvation. Salvation means to be saved. If we do not need to be saved from anything because we have it all under control, then we do not need Jesus. We must not have anything to repent of, and there is nothing to which grace can be applied. Asking Christ Jesus to save us includes a recognition that only by His amazing grace can we become His children and have access to His Holy Spirit, who then gives us the power to walk in truth and overcome sin (Ephesians 2:1-10).

As parents, if we do not teach or train our children what is wrong and how to do right, they will never understand they are not able to save themselves. We will not be preparing them to receive the Gospel of Jesus Christ in their hearts because they will not realize they are sinners or learn what it means to repent of sin. We are in a serious predicament: We all fail to meet the perfect mark (Romans 3:23)! We cannot, in our own strength, be holy as God requires (1 Peter 1:15-16). If children never learn this basic lesson, they will never understand the meaning of grace. As parents, giving grace means we love our children enough to help them realize their need for Jesus, just as we went through the process of realizing our own need for Jesus and crying out to Him to be saved from our sin.

In summary, grace does not mean we deny, overlook, or excuse sin. Grace means we deal with sin and correct it without condemnation, leading our children to forgiveness and restoration, just as Jesus did for us. We do not need to berate our children for being sinners. We are sinners, too! We do not need to be angry in our discipline or shocked our children do wrong things. But we must discipline them because they are at the beginning of life, learning what is right and wrong, and our heavenly Father disciplines us (Hebrews 12:6). Grace in parenting involves presenting a solution to sin. So we must always be praying and leading our children to the cross of Christ, where they can receive eternal forgiveness that they do not deserve and complete restoration to God they did not earn.

A lack of grace in parenting, or a law-filled attitude of the heart, means holding our children to a standard of righteousness with an attitude of condemnation for their failure to comply. Having a law-filled heart means we hold ourselves to a list of "laws" we keep well and look down upon those who do not keep them. Parents can be legalistic in almost any area. When my children were small, a clean and organized home was very important to me. I was legalistic about things being in their right place and tended to get frustrated if my children didn't keep things orderly the way I liked them. It was fine to want to be clean, and organization is a gift. But I was wrong to be angry. I lacked grace toward their childish messiness. Instead of getting upset, I needed to teach my children to clean up and give calm, logical consequences to motivate them when needed, understanding they would not be able to meet the expectations of my adult standard at all times.

Some parents are legalistic about their children getting straight As, eating a certain way, being athletic, being quiet, being neat, or having a certain type of appearance. When the laws get broken, negative emotions reign. Rather than talking to their children calmly about the problem, these parents act like their children are offensive to them, like they are disgusting, failures, or disappointments. This isn't training. This is parental egos out of control. The fact these parents' children are not tidy, athletic, attractive, or academically profound is offensive to the parents and embarrasses them. Their goals for their children have been upset, and their purpose in parenting has been disrupted by their children's failure to perform. A legalistic household is sometimes about God's Law, but more often it is about an arbitrary list the parents have chosen. It completely bypasses the heart and attitude of the children by basically saying, "If you do this, you will be acceptable to me. But if you don't, I will reject you until you step up and do it." When the focus is only on the certain laws that are important to the parents, the children can become invisible. Their own personality, likes and dislikes, interests, and struggles become irrelevant next to the parents' need to have their children perform well in particular areas. And these things are often what make the parents feel good about themselves when they should be more concerned about the hearts and characters of their children.

Consider an example of what a grace-filled response versus a law-driven response might look like regarding the biblical principles of kindness and self-control: Little three-year-old Gracie has a new friend, Sara, over to play. Sara is the pastor's daughter, and Gracie's mom wants to make a good impression on the pastor's wife. Gracie and Sara go upstairs to play while the moms have coffee and chat downstairs. Suddenly they hear Gracie screaming and run upstairs to see her in the middle of a major temper tantrum. Gracie's mom is embarrassed, grabs her daughter, and shakes her, yelling, "Stop it right now! How dare you treat your new friend like this! What is the *matter* with you?" The mother puts Gracie in her room and slams the door. Then she turns to Sara's mom and says, "I am so sorry my daughter acted like that. She knows better!" With Gracie shut in her room sobbing, Sara and her mom decide to leave to get away from the whole situation. Gracie's mom is so angry with her daughter she can hardly see straight because she ruined her time with someone she hoped would be a new friend. She leaves Gracie in her room for a long time, staying frustrated and disappointed.

Now, let's look at how Gracie's mom could have showed a grace-filled response. Gracie suddenly screams. Her mom is surprised because that is not how she typically acts with friends. Mother runs upstairs and sees her daughter having a full-blown temper tantrum. She is baffled but stops and observes for a minute, taking in the room and looking for clues. Then the mother sees it: Gracie's favorite doll—the doll she sleeps with and carries everywhere, the doll given to her by her favorite grandmother who passed away last year—has its head torn off and is lying in the corner. Sara is holding the doll's head behind her back.

Mom takes a deep breath. This is an expected three-year-old response to something precious being destroyed. She runs to Gracie and scoops her up. "Oh Honey, I see. I understand. That is hard and hurtful." She holds her and turns to little Sara, asking, "What happened to the doll, Sara?" Now Sara's mom sees the doll's head in her daughter's hand and begins to realize what happened. Both moms calmly address the children, find out what happened, and talk about solutions. Gracie's mom promises to fix the doll good as new, and Sara says she is sorry. Sara's mom promises to deal with Sara's behavior once they get home. Gracie calms down and feels loved and cared for. The girls start playing again, this time with Gracie's most precious possessions out of the playroom.

After the friends have left, Gracie's mom spends time teaching Gracie how to ask for help the next time someone hurts her feelings. She reminds her that instead of screaming and pitching a fit, she can run find Mommy and talk about what happened. Until Gracie learns how to ask for help instead of losing control, her mom stays close by whenever friends come to play so she can observe and be available to teach, train, and help if there is a problem.

So, as you can see, grace in parenting is not ignoring bad behavior or failing to teach or train. It is reflected in the way the parent chooses to handle situations. Degrading, condemning, or embarrassing children only teaches them they are bad. This kind of response may change their behavior temporarily, but it will also create a deep resentment and an insecurity about their relationship with you. If you can approach your children with love and acceptance no matter what, help them understand what the problem is, and give them a consequence that is appropriate to the action, then there is no need for anger. The consequence itself will make the necessary impact.

Earlier, I emphasized the need to teach children to obey. Obedience is an important part of the Christian life. When we give our lives to Jesus, He gives us the desire to love Him with all our heart, mind, soul, and strength. Jesus said if we love Him, we will obey Him (John 14:22-24). God gives us the grace to teach our children to obey us and in turn will give them the grace to follow through as they learn to depend on Him. But when we teach obedience, we should ask ourselves if what we ask them to obey is even possible. Do we ask our children to make straight As? Or do we ask them to do their best, complete their daily homework, and pay attention in class? One is vague and might not be possible; the other is completely attainable. Do we ask our children to be a good team player, treat their coaches with respect, and work hard on the field? Or do we ask them to win the tournament? Some things cannot be obeyed because the expectation is not associated with a measurable action. Do we demand our children love their siblings? Or do we ask our children to use kind words, share during play, and not hurt one another? We should be clear, supporting what we expect with actions they can understand. When children are expected to obey vague directions, this can create anxicty for thc plcasing child and apathy for thc willful child.

When I was in middle school, my mother suddenly became obsessed with my weight. Throughout my childhood, she had talked about healthy eating and calories a lot, but I was just a kid. Besides, Mom was the one who fed me, so I didn't give it much thought. I did not have a weight problem and was very active. I liked healthful foods, and I felt very loved. But suddenly one day, Mom's attitude toward me changed. She was determined that I weigh a specific—and very low—number on the scale. Starting around age 12, my mother used passive-aggressive behaviors and constant comments to drill into me my need to be extremely thin to be pretty, to please any guy who might be interested in me, and in essence, to be a valuable person. She also made weight a spiritual issue, criticizing anyone overweight and reminding me constantly that those who really loved God should be thin. She was obsessed with her own weight, and her anorexia became twisted into a need to control my size as well.

I felt like I disappeared, and my outward appearance was suddenly all that mattered. Mom started setting my goal weight lower and lower. Even when I was underweight, I could never please her. As you can imagine, in trying to deal with her impossible standard, I figured out how to meet my mother's demands with a full-blown eating disorder. I felt unloved and rejected because suddenly my appearance was all she seemed to care about. I was in a great deal of pain, trying to figure out why my mother didn't accept me anymore and why the only thing that mattered to her was my size. I made straight As, loved God, was a leader in my church youth group, and made good choices as a teenager. But Mom didn't seem to see anything but a number on the scale she never liked. Her unhealthy way of viewing size could have destroyed me, and almost did. But for the grace of God, I would have never healed. Eventually, I was able to move past the way she saw me and the pain of her rejection through wise counsel and a loving husband. However, sadly, my mother continued to view her own body with a harmful perspective and never was able to change her own unhealthy views about image.

I have shared earlier in this study that my mom did an incredible job as a parent, and she did! In so many ways, she was an amazing, godly, and faithful mother. But she was in a difficult marriage, and my dad's criticism and anger greatly affected her. However, I am mentally and emotionally healthy today because she taught me to value God's Word and seek the Lord, which is exactly what I did when she became imbalanced. She had areas of blindness, fear, and insecurity that deeply affected me. But God rescued me from those in the same way He has rescued my children from my failures and inadequacies.

Therefore, the point of the story is we all have hang-ups, and we can pass them on to our children. So be careful you do not create a biblical law out of an idea or personal preference or even a common standard. Loving our children is not demanding they fit our ideal mold. God's moral Law makes sense, and obedience to His ways is rewarded throughout all of life. But **your children will quickly figure out if your expectations are based on God's truth or on your own broken perspective of a certain subject.** We destroy relationships with the laws we create out of our own inadequacies, pain, and imbalanced priorities. Be sure that while teaching and training your children, you are seeking God's will for them, not your own. Then, when teaching what God says is right and wrong, we can do so with full awareness that we also need the grace of God to obey, and we are leaning on Him for the strength to keep growing and pursuing who He has called us to be.

When we have faced our own sinful heart and received the overwhelming and beautiful grace of God, we are humbled and wholly grateful for the undeserved and unconditional love of our Savior. If we understand we don't deserve what God has given us, we will have patience and understanding in the face of our children's sins. While correcting them, we will know they are also on a journey of learning who God is and who they are. We can give the consequences and the discipline our children need, but we don't have to let their sin destroy our relationship by responding in anger. Instead, we can love them through it, giving them the hope of the Gospel and the truth of the cross so they can find ultimate forgiveness and have the Holy Spirit help them overcome today and forever.

At this point you might be saying, "But Becky, I'm not going to always be grace-filled. I'm only human. I get frustrated, upset, and angry. I get stressed and tired. I overreact and have days when I just don't do this right." I say, of course. You will have bad days. You will say and do things you wish you hadn't. But you aren't alone. The goal is to respond with grace instead of react with anger. However, when you don't, you have Jesus. When you mess up, you can run to Him, ask Him for forgiveness and help, and ask for your children's forgiveness as well. You can let your children see your need for Jesus and how He forgives, restores, and strengthens you. Then the most important lesson of the Gospel is still taught. **Nothing is wasted when viewed through God's lens. He can be glorified even on the worst days if our hearts turn to Him!** Just be sure when you ask your children for forgiveness for your angry response, you still follow through with the consequences they need. Though you may have gone about it the wrong way, it wasn't wrong to discipline. That is your job as a parent. That is how you teach and train.

The Heart of Parenting Is Faithful, not Perfect

Perfectionism is a deceitful trap. It either pumps up our ego toward self-righteousness or leaves us feeling like a complete failure. The idea we can always achieve our very best in every area all the time is an empty, fruitless pursuit that will never give peace or satisfaction. Don't misunderstand: Goals are fine and helpful for the accomplishment of any number of things. However, while goals set a general direction and help us organize our priorities, our goals are not who we are. God loves us, every bit of us, right now, completely and unconditionally. His love and acceptance does not go up and down according to how well we meet our goals on any certain day. We don't have to obey the Lord to earn His love, but rather we obey because we love Him and we already know He loves us (John 14:21-24)! In the joy and security of His love, we can become more like Him every day.

If you as a mother base your worth on your performance, then you will tend to base your children's worth on their performance. You may want to love your children unconditionally, but if you reject them when they mess up, you are telling them your love is conditional on their behavior. Yes, I know it is hard to show love to children when they are being ornery and difficult. It takes a supernatural understanding of God's love and His help to love them through their challenging seasons of life. But this is why disciplining in love is so effective. When you do this, your children know they are loved and fully accepted, but at the same time they are being taught the areas of their life they need to change. Parenting from perfectionism doesn't do this. The parent seeking perfection will often fail to teach because she finds it is easier to do things herself. She may put her need for things to be a certain way above her children's need to learn. The perfectionist can also be too easily satisfied with a checklist and miss the deeper issues of the heart. And if she tends to condemn or reject her children's imperfections, she is failing to remember she also has been saved by grace alone. She may have different imperfections, but she is imperfect, nonetheless.

Let's consider how a mother might love a child through a lesson, and how, in contrast, she might respond as a perfectionist to a problem. Michael is ten years old, and he loves baseball. He loves to play, and every year he is disappointed when the season ends. He watches baseball, collects statistics, has favorite players, and practices all the time. Lately, Michael has been skipping his chores and not doing a good job on his homework. He has baseball practice on Thursday evenings. Mom tells him at the beginning of the week he must finish his chores and get his homework finished if he wants to go to baseball practice. It is his choice. She reminds him every day. Thursday evening comes, and Michael is downstairs at 6:30 dressed for practice and ready to go. Mom checks on his chores and sees they are not finished. Then she checks his homework and sees it is only halfway done—and even that was not done well.

Michael calls out, "Mom! Come on! It's time for practice! We got to go, or we'll be late!"

Mom calmly asks, "Michael, is there something you were supposed to do before practice this week?"

"Oh yeah, that," Michael says. "Well, I thought I'd just do chores after practice."

"What about your homework?"

"I did it!"

Mom calmly responds, "Michael, I am not taking you to practice. You have been neglecting your chores for weeks, and your homework is not finished, nor has it been done correctly. I gave you a choice. If you wanted to go to practice, you needed to do these things first. You may take off your baseball uniform and do what I have asked."

Even though Michael probably won't be happy about this, there is a clear lesson with this consequence. Without his mother raising her voice or getting upset, she has taught him he needs to listen and obey because she will do what she says she will do. She is intent on teaching him responsibility, and she is more interested in his character than his perfect attendance at baseball. He will probably pay closer attention next time and make better choices so that he doesn't miss practice.

How might Mom react if she were a perfectionist? Let's say Michael's mom loves that he is into baseball. She played softball growing up, and she loves the game, too. Mom enjoys taking Michael to practices, having camaraderie with the other parents, and playing catch with him at home. She likes that he is good at it, too, taking pride in him every time he rounds the bases for another home run. But Michael hasn't been doing his chores or his homework. Mom is frustrated because she feels her success as a mother also depends on teaching Michael responsibility. She decides he needs a consequence, so she tells him he won't be able to go to practice if he doesn't do his chores or his homework beforehand.

On Thursday, Michael comes home from school and immediately goes outside to play. His mom realizes he probably isn't going to do his chores, and she doesn't want him to miss practice because that would disappoint the coach. So she does his chores for him, telling herself she can do a better job anyway. Then she calls Michael to come inside, sits him at the table, and does his homework with him, correcting his errors, and making sure it is all done the right way. Now he can go to practice because technically the requirements have been met. But what has Michael learned? Has he become more responsible? No, he has learned he really doesn't have to obey or follow through because

Mom will eventually do his work for him. She cares more about her clean house, his correctly finished homework, and his perfect attendance at baseball than she does teaching him responsibility. If Michael fails to be responsible, Mom will be responsible for him to keep life running smoothly. In the long run, Michael may never learn he is the one who must listen to instructions and be responsible in following through to accomplish anything in life. When his mom is no longer there to do things for him, he may not be able to step up with the maturity and character required.

As you can see, perfectionism expects for there to be a straight, predictable line of growth in parenting. It cannot accept the messy, sometimes uncomfortable process that must be allowed for a child to develop into a mature adult. **Perfectionism hates interruptions, wants everything just so, and needs control in order to be comfortable.** For the perfectionist, who is continually trying to attain a certain standard in order to feel OK about herself, little things can be a disaster. A dirty dish in a sink, an unmade bed, or disorganized toys can send a perfectionist into skyrocketing fits. But there is a balance. You can have a neat, clean home run by organized systems without being a perfectionist, as long as you have the correct focus. Don't let your checklists become idols in your heart. Hold your schedules, to-dos, and goals with an open hand, recognizing your children's heart and character—which are not quick fixes—are the priority.

(I want to emphasize here to those of you who are not perfectionists that I am not saying it is fine to ignore things like cleanliness and organization. We all need to be good stewards of our possessions, and children function best within an orderly environment. Children also need to learn how to care for their own things, and age-appropriate chores are a healthy part of growing up. If you tend to struggle to stay on top of your household responsibilities, ask an organized friend for some advice on how to create systems that will help you keep life under control and avoid chaos in your home. See Appendix C.)

So with understanding what perfectionism is, it becomes clear that perfect parenting is not the goal. Thank the Lord our goal is more attainable: to be faithful. You cannot be perfect, but in Christ you can be faithful. You can be faithful to love your children, pray for them, teach and train them, lead them to Christ, and stay closely connected to them. You can be faithful to protect them, provide for them, lead them, and be available to them. You can be faithful to run to Jesus when life is hard and to apologize and ask forgiveness when you have handled things badly. You can be faithful to stay in God's Word, teach it to your children, and take your children to church, where they will have more opportunities to learn the Gospel and participate in worship. In your relationship with the Lord, you can faithfully depend on Him and ask Him to show you your heart, help you make wise decisions, and grow you into a more faithful parent every day.

Over time, faithfulness adds up. When looking back on their growing up years, your children will not say, "My mom was perfect." But what a wonderful thing it will be to hear them say, "My mom was so faithful." There is a lot to be said for faithfulness. It implies never quitting on the relationship, being available, and being committed to be the best mom you can be in Christ. It says you didn't run away when things got tough, your love was unwavering, your prayer life was consistent, and your heart was intentionally pursuing your children's hearts all their days. It also says on their worst days, you wanted the best for them, and on your own worst days, you could humbly apologize.

I would love for every mom who does this study to avoid the mistakes I made. I wish I could relive my perfectionistic days when I focused on the wrong things or my angry days when I didn't extend my children grace. I wish I could undo my selfish days when I didn't pay enough attention to their needs or my exhausted days when I didn't feel like I could handle another thing. But the amazing thing is, no matter what your mistakes are, Jesus wants to redeem all of it. My children have forgiven me, and I find that to be a remarkable thing. They have also told me that my investment in their lives, my walk with God, and my best efforts mattered so much. So don't give up on yourself. Keep being faithful. Forgive yourself and move on, growing up in Christ, and seeking Him for help and wisdom. Commit yourself to Him, and He will show you the way to walk. The rewards may be a long time coming, but I promise you, they are coming. Keep telling yourself the Gospel every day and repeat it consistently to your children. God knows your heart, He hears your prayers, and He sees your efforts as a mother. All of it, every minute of it, matters to Him.

Chapter 6 Study Questions

What Is the Heart of Parenting?

Day One

"Amazing grace, how sweet the sound,

That saved a wretch like me.

I once was lost, but now am found,

Was blind but now I see." (John Newton, 1772)

Our hymnals are filled with references to God's grace. On Sunday mornings we sing with praise and gratitude in our hearts for what our Savior did to purchase such priceless grace for us. Somehow, though, grace seems to get devalued when we use it in everyday language. Look up the following verses, and answer the questions:

1. John 1:14-18

   a. Who is the Word who became flesh?____________________

   ____

   b. What was He full of? ______________________________

   ____

   c. How do you think grace and truth might be related in the person of Christ?__________________________________

   ____

2. Romans 1:1-6

   a. How is Jesus, the Son, described in these Scriptures? ____

   ____

b. What had Paul received from Jesus in verse 5? ________

____

c. What was it supposed to bring about in verse 5? ________

____

3. Romans 5:18–6:7

a. What came as a result of Christ's one act of righteousness in 5:18-19? ____

____

b. What came in so that the offense would increase (5:20)? _

____

c. Where sin increased, what abounded in 5:20? __________

____

d. How does grace reign (5:21)? ______________________

____

e. Why shouldn't we just sin, then, so that grace can increase (6:1-2)? _______________________________________

____

f. What happens to us and to our sin when we trust Jesus as our Savior (6:3-4)? ______________________________

____

____

g. What kind of life are we then able to walk (6:4) ________

____

h. What is the relationship between grace and obedience?

____

____

Day Two

1. What do you think the following means: "Give grace to others as God has given it to you"? ____________________________

____

____

2. Look up the following verses, and write down ways we can give grace to others:

a. Luke 17:3 ____________________________________

____

b. Ephesians 4:32________________________________

____

c. Psalm 86:15 __________________________________

____

d. Colossians 3:12-13 ____________________________

____

e. 1 Peter 3:8-9 ______________________________

____

3. Since biblical grace doesn't ignore, excuse, or embrace sin, what does the Bible say a grace-filled response to sin looks like?

   a. Read the story of the woman caught in adultery in John 8:1-11. How did Jesus handle her shame and her sin? ______

   ____

   ____

   b. Read the story of Peter's denial of Jesus in Matthew 26:31-35; 69-75. Then read Jesus' response to Peter in John 21. How did Peter respond to his own sin? What do you see in the attitude of Jesus toward Peter? ______________

   ____

   ____

   c. Now read Matthew 18:21-35. How does this parable compare with the two stories you have already read? What is different? What is the same? How do you think it might apply to your life and to parenting? (Hint: It's all about the heart!) ______________________________

   ____

   ____

Day Three

1. The Bible outlines God's moral Law for us in the Old Testament, and it is restated many times in the New Testament. God's morality is not the notion of "whatever feels good is right for you," as is the moral code of our culture today. There is nothing in the Bible that says it is OK to disobey God and to live in sin. What does Jesus say about the Law in Matthew 5:17-20? ___

___

___

___

2. Is anyone capable of keeping the Law perfectly? Refer to Romans 3:10-12, 23 for the answer.___

___

3. So what is the problem with legalism? Doesn't God want us to keep the Law, do the right things, and not do the wrong things? Aren't we supposed to choose not to sin? Read Romans 3:21-31, and write down your observations: ___

___

___

4. Legalists tend to be proud of the way they do what is right. Since no one can do all things right, this kind of pride is the result of an individual keeping a few laws well. (Sometimes they aren't even God's laws; they are just a person's good habits.) The legalistic kind of life is independent of the grace of God. Legalists forget that apart from the blood of Christ, they would not be capable of saving themselves. Though they may do some things well, they are actually completely dependent

on the blood of Christ to be right with God. Legalism is when we believe our salvation comes through our own performance, doing right according to our own priorities, or checking a list. Read the following Scriptures and write down why and how we as believers obey the Law. Do we obey in order to be saved by Jesus or because He has saved us already?

a. Romans 6:15-18 ______________________________

____

b. Colossians 1:9-12 ______________________________

____

c. 1 Thessalonians 1:5 ______________________________

____

d. 2 Timothy 1: ______________________________

____

e. 1 Peter 1:2 ______________________________

____

f. 1 Peter 1:22-23 ______________________________

____

g. 2 Peter 1:3 ______________________________

____

5. Not one of us is good enough to save ourselves, and not one of us is able to continue to bear eternal fruit through our own

efforts. This includes our children. So as we train our children to do what is right, they begin to realize they are not able to do it all right all the time. If we have given them the Gospel, they know the solution to their inadequacy to please God perfectly is Jesus Himself. Look up the following verses, and write down your insights about the wonderful, amazing, priceless saving grace of Christ.

a. Romans 3:24 ______________________________

____

b. Romans 5:1-5______________________________

____

____

c. Romans 6:14 ______________________________

____

d. Romans 11:6 ______________________________

____

e. 2 Corinthians 4:13-15 ______________________________

____

f. 2 Corinthians 9:8-9 ______________________________

____

____

g. 2 Corinthians 12:9-10 ______________________________

____

h. Ephesians 1:7________________________________

____

i. Ephesians 2:8-9 ______________________________

____

j. 2 Timothy 1:9-10 _____________________________

____

k. Titus 3:4-7 __________________________________

____

Day Four

Some of us, due to our personality or upbringing, are driven by performing well and accomplishing goals and tasks. Others of us are more motivated by relationships and social activity. But any of us can be a perfectionist. Depending on the areas in which we pursue perfection, those tendencies may be more obvious in some than in others. But if it is there, it is like an internal hamster on a wheel, always pursuing something but never actually arriving. The problem is most of the time perfectionists receive a lot of praise and affirmation from others in their area of pursuit. It can be hard for perfectionists to relax their standards when their high level of execution is the very thing that brings them the most accolades. But parenting and perfection don't mix well. Usually, if our children are going to receive the time and attention they need, perfectionistic parents must let go of some of their relentless goals in order for that to happen.

1. Are you a perfectionist? ______ If so, in what ways? _______

   ____

   Since becoming a mother, have you let go of any of those things? ____________________________________

   ____

   Does letting go of some things or relaxing standards make you feel anxious? ______________________________

   If so, what is the worst thing you think could happen? ______

   ____

2. Rarely do I meet people who are pursuing perfection in the things God really cares about. I can't remember the last time I heard someone say she never wants to gossip again, or covet, or be selfish. Usually the things I hear people pursuing are certain ways of eating, certain goals for exercise, keeping a clean house, or meeting goals at work. Having goals in these areas of life isn't bad, but consider the kind of world we would live in if people's highest priorities were issues of the heart. What does God want us to pursue? Are you currently reaching for those things?

   a. Luke 10:27 ______________________________

      ____

b. James 1:27 ______________________________

____

c. Galatians 2:10 ______________________________

____

d. Galatians 5:13 ______________________________

____

e. Galatians 5:22-23 ______________________________

____

f. Colossians 3:12-13 ______________________________

____

3. Christlike character is not necessarily achieved by setting goals or by charting a disciplined course of action. Becoming more like Jesus is accomplished by His Spirit as we spend time with Him, lean on Him, and depend on Him moment by moment to do His supernatural work in our hearts. Look up the following verses, and jot down how they encourage you to walk with Christ:

a. 1 John 1:5-10 ______________________________

____

b. Colossians 3:17 ______________________________

____

c. Colossians 2:6-7 ________________________________

____

d. Ephesians 5:15-17 ______________________________

____

e. Galatians 5:16 _________________________________

____

Day Five

1. Define faithfulness ______________________________

____

2. Who has been faithful to you? ____________________

____

What did their faithfulness look like? ______________

____

How did their faithfulness impact you and make a difference in your life? ________________________________

____

3. When you think about being a faithful parent, as opposed to a perfect parent, do you think it just might be possible? ______ If not, why not? ____________________________

____

4. If you had a parent or parents who left you, you may feel you can't be faithful because you do not have a good example in your life of faithfulness. But God says in Him you can be committed and faithful because that is who He wants to be in and through you! Read the following, and write down how these Scriptures encourage you:

   a. Psalm 91:4 ____

   ____

   b. Psalm 94:18-19 ____

   ____

   c. Psalm 100:5 ____

   ____

   d. Psalm 136 ____

   ____

   e. 1 Corinthians 1:9 ____

   ____

   f. 1 Thessalonians 5:24 ____

   ____

   g. 2 Thessalonians 3:3 ____

   ____

   h. 2 Timothy 2:13 ____

   ____

i. Hebrews 10:23 ______________________________

____

5. What are some areas of your life in which you desire to be more faithful? Talk to the Lord about these and ask Him to help you seek Him and do His will. ______________________

____

____

____

Chapter 7

What Is the Goal of Parenting?

We all pursue success: hope for it, dream of it, and even sacrifice for it every day one way or another. Success is a word that transcends economic status, geography, family background, age, political persuasion, and religious association. Everyone understands the meaning of the word, whether it is the elementary school janitor in a small town or the CEO of the largest corporation on Wall Street. There is a measure of success for the toddler as well as for the elderly widow. Each person has an idea of what it means to be successful for herself and measures her life against that standard in some way. The homeless man may consider himself successful if he finds the best spot in the park to spend the night. The executive may consider himself successful if he lands the latest million-dollar deal. The drug dealer may consider himself successful if he makes good money without getting caught. And a mom may think herself successful if her child eats his vegetables three nights in a row.

But what is success, really? If there are so many definitions, and each person has a different measuring stick, how can we know if we have succeeded? Is that even the right question? Are we even supposed to pursue success? What does God think about success? What if I am successful at my job but lose my marriage? What if I meet my lifetime goals, but my kids hate me? Or what if I have wonderful relationships but can't keep a job? Who is successful in the end? Or who is a failure?

As parents, we can have as many definitions of success for our children as we do for ourselves. Some parents would be perfectly content for their children to do mediocre in school as long as they are happy and kind. Other parents aren't even aware of their children's attitudes; they just expect them to perform academically with excellence in order to get into the best college so they can get the best job. And then there are parents who demand their children succeed in athletics or talent or appearance. Some parents are so busy pursuing success for themselves, they have no expectations of their children in any area. In any case, children figure out quickly what a parent's expectations are and will either embrace or reject them. Did your parents have an idea of success for you that wasn't at all what you dreamed for yourself? Do you have a need for your children to be successful according to your definition or God's?

Focusing on the development of godly character in your children will benefit them in whatever path of success they choose to pursue. After all, if their goal is high academic achievement, children can cheat to get there, or they can persevere and study hard to do well. One is a shortcut; the other is the application of character that is formed through a thousand little life lessons along the way. A high school senior doesn't wake up one morning with a persevering attitude. He learned it as a toddler when he had to put his blocks away before getting a snack. He learned it as a five-year-old when he had to help rake leaves before he could play. He learned it as a seven-year-old when he had to swim laps every day to compete in the swim meet. And he learned it as a ten-year-old when he got his first job walking the neighbor's dog every morning before school. Children who are taught that perseverance is rewarding and who develop that habit early in life have a strong chance of becoming persevering adults. This characteristic will carry them through challenging times. The same goes for other character traits, such as kindness, gratitude, helpfulness, unselfishness, cooperation, and patience. But is pursuing a life of character enough?

In the big picture, what is the reason for character? If building good character is just to enable your children to have a good life, what is the end goal of that good life? Is it simply so they will be happy and have what they need? Do they need character to get through school with good grades so they can go to college and get a good job … so they can have a certain standard of living? Do they need to be kind so others will be kind to them and they won't get their feelings hurt? Why should they be patient? So they won't be annoying to others? Or do our children need a deeper reason to pursue the development of character? Do we want this for them so they can get along with others and manage their lives well? Yet even with good character, our lives still sometimes fall apart, don't they? And even when people have good habits and make choices with relatively strong character, applying good principles, there is still an end to everything. Death is 100% guaranteed. So what is the ultimate reason for the pursuit of strong character? What is a goal that holds all the way through until the end and beyond?

The Goal of Parenting Is Salvation, not Success

The pursuit of excellence for personal gain eventually dries up. **In light of life's challenges, disappointments, and unexpected pitfalls, it becomes much easier to ditch good character traits and find the quickest, most self-serving shortcuts to get one's needs met.** As much as we wish the world always rewarded character and punished deceitful pathways to success, it is not so. Unfortunately, many are rewarded for being devious, and some are punished for standing for what is right.

So how do we teach our children to have the character God calls them to have for a reason that reaches beyond their own self-interest and into eternity? We give them Jesus. Every single lesson in character is to draw them closer to Jesus, to glorify Him, and to make Him known. If our children understand the goal in all of life is to "love the Lord your God with all your heart, and with all your soul, and with all your strength, and with all your mind" (Luke 10:27), then they have context for doing what is right that is completely beyond themselves. If they embrace what it means to have a personal relationship with Jesus, then they will want to please Him, follow Him, and know Him (1 John 4:15-19). Their choices will eventually not be driven by a need only to please their parents or their bosses or to make their own life work, but by the great desire to glorify God with their life and make an eternal impact on the world around them (Psalm 86:12; Matthew 5:16; Romans 15:5-6). Therein lies the greatest purpose any person can have for absolutely everything she does: "Man's chief end is to glorify God, and to enjoy Him forever" (Psalm 86, Isaiah 60:21, Romans 11:36, 1 Corinthians 6:20, 31, Revelation 4:11, Psalm 16:5-11) (Westminster Shorter Catechism, 1648). Because God Himself is the only one who can infuse every moment, whether profound or mundane, with eternal meaning.

So how do we, while teaching and training our children, help them understand this bigger, profound reason for persisting with godly character? How do we teach them in such a way they will want to stand firm for what is right even when what is wrong is easier? Manipulation, deceit, lying, and selfish motivations are often applauded in this world (Psalm 73:3). What will help our children understand the bigger purpose for which they live? Make everything, absolutely everything, about Jesus. Eat, drink, breathe, read, talk, sing, listen to, and adore the Gospel of Jesus Christ. Remind yourselves and your children He is the one that makes life worth living, character worth pursuing, and relationships worth mending. His sacrifice reminds us all how we should also live our lives for others, not just for ourselves. **His abounding love is the ultimate reason to get up in the morning and live with purpose, joy, and hope in every blessed, bleak, glorious, ordinary, private, public, easy, hard, and precious moment.** Our children are His creations, entrusted to us to lead to Him so that they too can know His purpose for their lives.

Jesus is everything. When your children grasp His love and understand His grace, they will come to the place you have been leading them: the place of wanting Jesus to be in charge of their hearts, lives, and success. When they fall in love with Jesus, He will be faithful to lead them, grow them, and make them more like Himself for the rest of their days. When my oldest son was 21, he surrendered his whole heart to the Lord Jesus. Lock, stock, and barrel, he laid his life down at Jesus' feet and said, "I'm Yours." It was a profoundly beautiful moment because I had spent the last ten years of his life praying for him to stop running so fast and far from God. He took many a winding road his dad and I would not have chosen for him, and he was determined to prove he could handle his life better than his Creator ever could. When he finally chose Christ over all other things, he said to me, "Mom, I finally realized when I am in control of my life, I make a mess of things." Humility. Reality. Living for self has a broken, empty end. **It takes some people longer than others to realize it, but the joy of letting go, the beauty of a redeemed life, and the honesty of a surrendered heart are the stuff miracles are made of.** When your child cries out, "King Jesus, take my heart, take my life, and be in charge," your mother's heart will soar to heights you never even knew existed before that day.

So don't put your ideas of temporal success ahead of Jesus. Don't make grades or popularity or talent more valuable than the salvation of your children's hearts. Give them Jesus above every other thing. Let every lesson be ultimately all about Him, so they might know the joy of worshipping Him with their lives and honoring Him with their whole hearts. Jesus is the faithful one you know they need more than all the things the world may dangle in front of them as "The Answer." Until they bow their knees before Him, they will only find emptiness at the end of every glittering rainbow. Until they let Him have their whole hearts, they will know only disappointment in all the broken promises of this world and the inadequacies of its people. Jesus is the only one who fulfills completely (Psalm 20:4-5), the only one who never leaves or forsakes (Isaiah 41:10), and the only reason that withstands the test of time (Isaiah 43:10-13). He knows their hearts better than you do, and He has a glorious, beautiful plan for them you can trust is good (Romans 8:28-30). Lead them to Him, and don't stop. Even when they are tired of hearing it and are looking elsewhere, keep giving them Jesus. Keep praying with your whole heart for God to keep doing His everlasting, glorious redemptive work in their lives. It is a prayer He dearly loves to answer!

Chapter 7 Study Questions

What Is the Goal of Parenting?

Day One

In 1 Timothy 1:5, Paul tells Timothy, "The goal of our instruction is love from a pure heart and a good conscience and a sincere faith." This study was written to instruct you in God's Word so that you come to a deeper understanding of the power of the Gospel of Jesus Christ in your parenting journey. Your children need you to instruct them in love from a pure heart, a good conscience, and a sincere faith.

1. Look up the following verses and write down what you learn about "love from a pure heart."

    a. Psalm 119:140 ______________________________

    ____

    b. Philippians 4:8 ______________________________

    ____

    c. 2 Timothy 2:20-23 ______________________________

    ____

    d. What can you do to grow more in this love? ______________

    ____

    ____

2. Look up the following verses and write down what you learn about "love from a good conscience."

   a. Romans 13:8-10 ______________________________

   ____

   b. Titus 1:15-16 ______________________________

   ____

   c. Matthew 5:23-24 ______________________________

   ____

   d. What can you do to grow more in this love? ____________

   ____

   ____

2. Look up the following verses and write down what you learn about "love from a sincere faith."

   a. Hebrews 10:19-25 ______________________________

   ____

   b. 1 Timothy 6:10-11 ______________________________

   ____

   c. Ephesians 3:14-19 ______________________________

   ____

d. What can you do to grow more in this love? ____________

____

____

Day Two

1. Has the Gospel of Jesus Christ changed your life?__________
2. Do you remember a time when you cried out to the Lord, repented of your sin, chose to believe in Jesus, and surrendered your life to Him? ______________________________
3. If you do not remember a specific time, go to Appendix B, and review the truths of the Good News of Jesus Christ. Spend time looking up the Scriptures and asking God to show you what He wants you to see and understand. If you are unsure of your salvation, pray and ask God to come into your life and forgive you, becoming your Savior and your Lord, and tell someone of your newfound faith! If you are sure of your salvation, write out your testimony—your personal story of how you came to know Jesus—below:

____

____

____

____

____

____

____

Day Three

It is never too early or too late to share the Gospel with your children.

1. If your children are still small, decide about ways you will introduce them to Christ.

    a. Purchase age-appropriate Bibles for you to read to them or for them to read for themselves.

    b. Find age-appropriate devotionals that will allow grade-schoolers, middle-schoolers, and teens to begin to study the Bible on their own, having quiet times with Jesus when He can speak to their heart through His Word.

    c. Play Christian music in your home, and let it be the backdrop of the environment you create. Play children's praise songs and Scripture songs in the car so they are constantly hearing truth.

    d. Pray to the Lord as a regular habit—before meals, before bed, and all the times in between. Pray! Don't stop praying for and with your children!

    e. Memorize the Gospel so you are ready at any moment to share it freely and with conviction to your family. Let Jesus be woven throughout every day.

    f. Take your children to a Bible-believing church where they can hear from pastors and Sunday school teachers about God's beautiful plan for their lives, reinforcing what you are teaching them at home.

2. Even if your children are grown, you can share with them the beautiful truth of the Gospel. Tell them what God has done for you, and pray they will be able to understand it, receiving forgiveness and eternal life as they enter a relationship with Him.

Days Four and Five

We have come to the end of *Learning Trust, Finding Treasure: Helping You Solve the Puzzle of Parenting.* You have finished seven chapters and the homework, all packed with Scripture. Take the next two days to go back and review what you have learned. Use these questions to help guide you:

- Which chapter or concept was the newest to you? What did you learn? How has it affected the way you see yourself or your children? What have you changed as a result?
- Which chapter or concept was the most difficult for you? Do you need to study it again? Maybe you need to discuss it with someone and ask questions about the things you didn't understand.
- Did you skip some of the homework? Go back and see if you can finish it. Look up the Scriptures and devote time to allowing the Lord to speak to you through His Word.
- As you read the chapters, did you look up the embedded Scriptures? Go back and do so for those chapters you may have skimmed.
- What have you learned about yourself? Your parenting style? The way you were parented? Has your perspective changed? How? Share it with someone!

- Have you implemented strategies to teach, train, disciple, equip, correct, provide, protect, trust, persevere, and share the Gospel? How's it going? How are you? How are your children? What is God doing in your family life as a result? Knowledge without application won't bring change!

If this study has encouraged you, influenced your parenting, impacted your family life, or strengthened your relationship with Christ in any way, please share it with another mom!

Appendix A

Suggested Bible Verses for Teaching your Children

Argumentative	2 Timothy 2:24
Angry	Colossians 3:8
Lying	Colossians 3:9
Jealous	James 3:16
Selfish	Philippians 2:3-4
Use of words	Ephesians 4:29; 5:4
Unkind	Ephesians 4:32
Greedy	Ephesians 5:3
Ungrateful	Colossians 3:15
Anxious	Philippians 4:6-7
Disobedient	Ephesians 6:1-3
Disrespectful	Romans 12:17
Whining	Philippians 2:14
Impatient	1 Thessalonians 5:14
Demanding	Luke 6:30

Appendix B

The Gospel of Jesus Christ

1. **We are all sinners, and our sin separates us from God.**
    a. Romans 3:23 "For everyone has sinned; we all fall short of God's glorious standard."
    b. Romans 6:23 "For the wages of sin is death"
2. **Our good works cannot save us.**
    a. Romans 3:28 "For we are made right with God through faith and not by obeying the Law"
    b. Ephesians 2:9 "Salvation is not a reward for the good things we have done, so none of us can boast about it."
3. **Jesus Christ is the Son of God. He died on the cross as the only payment for our sin.**
    a. Romans 5:8 "But God showed His great love for us by sending Christ to die for us while we were still sinners."
    b. John 14:6 "Jesus told him, 'I am the Way, the Truth, and the Life. No one can come to the Father except through Me.'"
4. **Jesus Christ rose from the dead, conquered death, and lives as our Savior**
    a. John 11:25 "Jesus told her, 'I am the resurrection and the life. Anyone who believes in Me will live, even after dying. Everyone who lives in Me and believes in Me will never ever die.'"

b. Romans 1:4 "and He (Jesus) was shown to be the Son of God when He was raised from the dead by the power of the Holy Spirit. He is Jesus Christ our Lord."

5. **Confess your sin to God, accept His forgiveness and the free gift of eternal life.**

   a. 1 John 1:9 "But if we confess our sins to Him, He is faithful and just to forgive us our sins and to cleanse us from all wickedness."

   b. Romans 10:9 "If you openly declare that Jesus is Lord and believe in your heart that God raised Him from the dead, you will be saved."

   c. Romans 10:13 "Everyone who calls on the name of the Lord will be saved."

   d. John 5:24 "I (Jesus) tell you the truth, those who listen to My message and believe in God who sent Me have eternal life. They will never be condemned for their sins, but they have already passed from death in to life."

   e. Romans 3:23 "The free gift of God is eternal life through Christ Jesus our Lord."

6. **Grow closer to God every day**

   a. 1 John 5:1 "Everyone who believes that Jesus is the Christ has become a child of God.

   b. Romans 8:1-2 "So now there is no condemnation for those who belong to Christ Jesus.

   c. Romans 8:38 "Nothing can ever separate us from God's love."

d. 1 Thessalonians 5:17 "Pray without ceasing."

e. John 14:15 "If you love Me (Jesus), obey my commandments."

f. Hebrews 10:23-25 "Let us hold tightly without wavering to the hope we affirm, for God can be trusted to keep His promise. Let us think of ways to motivate one another to acts of love and good works. And let us not neglect our meeting together, as some people do, but encourage one another, especially now that the day of His return is drawing near."

Appendix C

Suggestions for Age-appropriate Chores for Children

Ages 2-3

Pick up blankets

Put toys away

Throw away trash

Put books on a bookshelf

Pick up the pillows on the floor

Put dirty clothes in the hamper

Get the diapers, wipes

Ages 4-5

Make the bed

Clean out under the bed

Feed the pets

Pick up toys

Water the plants

Dust the furniture, baseboards

Set the table

Clear and clean table

Get dry laundry out of dryer

Fold washcloths

Make easy snacks

Ages 6-7

Sweep the floors

Empty the dishwasher

Collect household trash

Rake leaves

Help spread mulch

Fold clothes and match socks

Make a simple salad

Peel carrots and potatoes

Keep bedroom organized and tidy

Hang up bathroom towels

Get the mail

Ages 8-9

Do the laundry

Fold and put away clean clothes

Walk the dog

Clean kitty litter

Sweep the front porch and walkway

Put away groceries

Make scrambled eggs

Bake cookies

Change a light bulb

Clean bathroom sink and vanity

Wipe down kitchen counters

Tend a garden

Ages 10-11

Clean the toilets, tub, shower

Vacuum

Clean mirrors and windows

Make a simple meal

Clean the refrigerator

Mop the floors

Bring garbage cans up from the driveway

Help younger siblings with homework

Ages 12+

Clean the garage

Clean cars inside and out

Mow the lawn

Iron clothes

Babysit younger siblings

Cook a complete meal

Help with simple home repairs

Help grocery shop

Manage a budget

References

Authority. (2012). In *Collins English Dictionary Complete and Unabridged Digital Edition*. Retrieved from https://www.dictionary.com/browse/authority?s=t

Brueck, H. & Gal, S. (2020). Suicide rates are climbing in young people. *Insider*. Retrieved from https://www.insider.com/cdc-suicide-rate-in-young-people-10-24-continues-climb-2020-9

Cross, J. (2017). What does too much screen time do to children's brains? *New-York-Presbyterian, Health Matters.* Retrieved from https://healthmatters.nyp.org/what-does-too-much-screen-time-do-to-childrens-brains/#:~:text=Excessive%20screen%20time%20may%20inhibit,be%20detrimental%20to%20overall%20development.

Kala, E. (2016). What is enabling? *Hazelden Betty Ford Foundation*. Retrieved from https://www.hazeldenbettyford.org/articles/kala/enabling-fact-sheet

Lathbury, P. (2010). Is viewing the same as doing? What parents need to know about how screen time is affecting the growing brains of their children. *The Center for Parenting Education.* Retrieved from https://centerforparentingeducation.org/library-of-articles/kids-and-technology/is-viewing-the-same-as-doing-what-parents-need-to-know-about-how-screen-time-is-affecting-the-growing-brains-of-their-children/

Mohler, J. W. (2007). Proverbs 22:6: A promise to parents? *Biola Magazine.* Retrieved from http://magazine.biola.edu/issue/07-spring

Parnell, J. (2014). What is a disciple? *Desiring God*. Retrieved from https://www.desiring god.org/articles/what-is-a-disciple

Rosenblatt, J. (2019). More screen time linked to higher risk of ADHD in preschool-aged children: Study. *ABC News* Retrieved from https://abcnews.go.com/Health/screen-time-linked-higher-risk-adhd-preschool-aged/story?id=62429157

Smalley, G. (1992). *The Key to Your Child's Heart.* Dallas, Texas: Word Publishing.

Tripp, P. D. (2016). *Parenting.* Wheaton, IL: Crossway.

The Westminster Standard. (1647). *Shorter Catechism Text and Scripture Proofs.* Retrieved from https://thewestminsterstandard.org/westminster-shorter-catechism/